# ETHICS
*in the world religions*

THE LIBRARY OF GLOBAL ETHICS AND RELIGION

*General Editors: Joseph Runzo and Nancy M. Martin*

Volume I, *The Meaning of Life in the World Religions*, ISBN 1–85168–200–7
Volume II, *Love, Sex, and Gender in the World Religions*, ISBN 1–85168–223–6
Volume III, *Ethics in the World Religions*, ISBN 1–85168–247–3

RELATED TITLES PUBLISHED BY ONEWORLD

*Avatar and Incarnation*, Geoffrey Parrinder, ISBN 1–85168–130–2
*Believing – An Historical Perspective*, Wilfred Cantwell Smith, ISBN 1–85168–166–3
*Concepts of God*, Keith Ward, ISBN 1–85168–064–0
*Faith and Belief: The Difference Between Them*, Wilfred Cantwell Smith,
     ISBN 1–85168–165–5
*The Fifth Dimension*, John Hick, ISBN 1–85168–191–4
*Global Philosophy of Religion*, Joseph Runzo, ISBN 1–85168–235–X
*God and the Universe of Faiths*, John Hick, ISBN 1–85168–071–3
*God, Chance and Necessity*, Keith Ward, ISBN 1–85168–116–7
*God, Faith and the New Millennium*, Keith Ward, ISBN 1–85168–155–8
*In Defence of the Soul*, Keith Ward, ISBN 1–85168–040–3
*Jesus and the Muslim*, Kenneth Cragg, ISBN 1–85168–180–9
*Muhammad and the Christian*, Kenneth Cragg, ISBN 1–85168–179–5
*Muslims and Christians Face to Face*, Kate Zebiri, ISBN 1–85168–133–7
*Patterns of Faith Around the World*, Wilfred Cantwell Smith, ISBN 1–85168–164–7
*The Phenomenon of Religion*, Moojan Momen, ISBN 1–85168–161–2
*Pluralism in the World Religions*, Harold Coward, ISBN 1–85168–243–0
*Religious Truth for our Time*, William Montgomery Watt, ISBN 1–85168–102–7
*Scripture in the World Religions*, Harold Coward, ISBN 1–85168–244–9
*The Sense of God*, John Bowker, ISBN 1–85168–093–4
*Sexual Morality in the World's Religions*, Geoffrey Parrinder, ISBN 1–85168–108–6
*Ultimate Visions*, edited by Martin Forward, ISBN 1–85168–100–0
*The Universe Within*, Anjam Kursheed, ISBN 1–85168–075–6
*A Wider Vision*, Marcus Braybrooke, ISBN 1–85168–119–1

# ETHICS
## *in the world religions*

EDITED BY

*Joseph Runzo and Nancy M. Martin*

Volume III
in
The Library of Global Ethics and Religion
General Editors: Joseph Runzo and Nancy M. Martin

ONEWORLD
OXFORD

ETHICS IN THE WORLD RELIGIONS

Oneworld Publications
(Sales and Editorial)
185 Banbury Road
Oxford OX2 7AR
England
http://www.oneworld-publications.com

Oneworld Publications
(US Office)
237 East 39th Street
New York
NY10016
USA

ISBN 1–85168–247–3

Cover design by Design Deluxe
Typeset by LaserScript, Mitcham, UK
Printed and bound in Great Britain by Creative Print and Design

*This volume is dedicated to*

KEITH WARD AND CHRIS CHAPPLE

*friends whose lives combine sophia and praxis*

[D]esiring to justify himself, [a lawyer] said to Jesus, "And who is my neighbor?"

Jesus replied, "A man was going down from Jerusalem to Jericho, and he fell among robbers, who stripped him and beat him, and departed, leaving him half dead. Now by chance a priest was going down that road; and when he saw him, he passed by on the other side. So likewise a Levite [lay-associate of the priest], when he came to the place and saw him, passed by on the other side. But a Samaritan [a despised outsider], as he journeyed, came to where he was; and when he saw him, he had compassion, and went to him and bound up his wounds, pouring on oil and wine; then he set him on his own beast and brought him to an inn, and took care of him. And the next day he took out two denarii and gave them to the innkeeper, saying, 'Take care of him; and whatever more you spend, I will repay you when I come back.' Which of these three, do you think, proved to be the neighbor to the man who fell among the robbers?"

[The lawyer] said, "The one who showed mercy on him."

And Jesus said to him, "Go and do likewise."

(Luke 10:29–37 RSV)

One should never do that to another which one regards as injurious to one's own self. This, in brief, is the rule of dharma.

(*Mahabharata* XIII:113,8)

# CONTENTS

## Part III ETHICS AND RELIGION IN ASIA

## Part IV ETHICAL ISSUES ACROSS RELIGIOUS TRADITIONS

## Part V GLOBAL VIEWS OF RELIGIOUS ETHICS

# ILLUSTRATIONS

Photographs: Joseph Runzo, Nancy M. Martin, Valerie Reed, and N. Prasad

# CONTRIBUTORS

JOHN H. BERTHRONG is Associate Dean for Academic and Administrative Affairs, Director of the Institute for Dialogue among Religious Traditions, and Assistant Professor of Comparative Religion in the School of Theology at Boston University. Among his most recent books are *The Divine Deli*; *All Under Heaven: Transforming Paradigms in Confucian–Christian Dialogue*; *Transformations of the Confucian Way*; and *A Short Introduction to Confucianism*. He is a founding member of the North American Interfaith Network, a member of the Interfaith Relations Commission of the National Council of Christian Churches, U.S.A., and Vice-President of the Society for Buddhist–Christian Studies.

CHRISTOPHER KEY CHAPPLE is Professor of Theological Studies and Director of Asian Pacific Studies at Loyola Marymount University in Los Angeles. His research interests have focused on the renouncer traditions of India: Yoga, Jainism, and Buddhism. He has published eight books, including *Karma and Creativity*, a co-translation of the Yoga Sutras of Patanjali, and *Nonviolence to Animals, Earth, and Self in Asian Traditions*. Founder of the Southern California Seminar on South Asia, he continues to serve as its director. He is currently editing two volumes for Harvard University's Center for the Study of World Religions: *Hinduism and Ecology* and *Jainism and Ecology*.

VRINDA DALMIYA is Assistant Professor of Philosophy at the University of Hawaii. Her research focuses on epistemology, environmental ethics, and Indian and feminist philosophy. Bringing classical Indian philosophy into conversation with feminist philosophy and ecofeminism, she is currently working to develop a care-based ethic.

ELLIOT N. DORFF is Rector and Professor of Philosophy at the University of Judaism. The leading spokesperson for ethics in conservative Judaism today, he is the author of over one hundred articles and nine books on Jewish theology, Jewish law, and Jewish ethics, including *Contemporary Jewish Ethics and Morality* and *Matters of Life and Death: A Jewish Approach to Modern Medical Ethics*. He has served on the ethics committee of the national healthcare task force and testified before the President's National Bioethics Advisory Committee.

BRIAN HEBBLETHWAITE is Fellow at Queens' College and Senior Lecturer in Divinity at Cambridge University and Canon Theologian of Leicester Cathedral. He is the author of numerous books including *Evil, Suffering and Religion; The Adequacy of Christian Ethics; The Problems of Theology; The Christian Hope; The Incarnation;* and *The Ocean of Truth,* and editor of *Divine Action: Studies Inspired by the Philosophical Theology of Austin Farrar; The Philosophical Frontiers of Christian Theology;* and *Christianity and Other Religions.*

ZAYN KASSAM is Assistant Professor of Religion at Pomona College. She is a historian of religion with expertise in Islam and Hinduism and secondary specializations in Buddhism and Judaism. Her primary areas of research include gender issues, especially related to women in Islam, and comparative philosophy and mysticism. She is currently working on a book on divine–human configurations in Hinduism and Islam.

JAMES KELLENBERGER is Professor of Philosophy at California State University, Northridge. He has published seven books including *The Cognitivity of Religion: Three Perspectives; God-Relationships With and Without God; Inter-religious Models and Criteria;* and most recently *Relationship Morality* and *Kierkegaard and Nietzsche: Faith and Eternal Acceptance.*

WILLIAM R. LaFLEUR is E. Dale Saunders Professor in Japanese Studies and Professor of Religious Studies at the University of Pennsylvania. He has published eight books on Buddhism and Japanese culture including *The Karma of Words: Buddhism and the Literary Arts in Medieval Japan; Liquid Life: Abortion and Buddhism in Japan;* and *Freaks and*

*Philosophers: Minding the Body in Medieval Japan.* He is now completing a book on Japanese attitudes toward organ transplantation.

VASUDHA NARAYANAN is Professor of Religion at the University of Florida. She has published five books on various aspects of devotional Hinduism and has four books forthcoming: *Nammalvar's "Sacred Utterance": A Complete Translation*; *The Hindu Tradition: An Introduction*; *The Hindu Traditions in the United States*; and *The Life of Hinduism*. She has been a Guggenheim Fellow and a National Endowment for the Humanities Fellow and is currently President of the American Academy of Religion.

C. RAM-PRASAD is Lecturer in Religious Studies at Lancaster University, England. A specialist on Hinduism and Jainism, he is the author of some twenty-five articles. He is currently working on Blackwell's *New Introduction to Hinduism*, and his book *Knowledge and the Highest Good: Liberation and Philosophical Inquiry in Classical Indian Thought* is forthcoming in Macmillan's "Library of Philosophy and Religion."

PHILIP ROSSI, S.J. is Professor of Theology at Marquette University and editor of the journal *Philosophy and Theology*. A specialist in philosophy and religion and Christian ethics, his work focuses on the philosophical and theological foundations of moral thought and practice. He has published three books, *Together Toward Hope: A Journey to Moral Theology*; *Kant's Philosophy of Religion Reconsidered*; and *Mass Media and the Moral Imagination*. He is currently working on a book entitled *A World of Human Making: Kant on Evil, Culture, and Moral Progress* and preparing a collection of his essays for publication under the title *Practical Reason and Its Domain: Dimensions of the Kantian Moral World*.

DANIEL L. SMITH-CHRISTOPHER is Professor of Theological Studies (Old Testament) and Director of Peace Studies at Loyola Marymount University. An active member of the Society of Friends (Quakers), he served for two years in volunteer peace research in Israel/Palestine from 1986 to 1988. His books include *The Religion of the Landless*; *Subverting Hatred*; *Text and Experience: Toward a Cultural Exegesis of the Bible*; and a new commentary on the book of Daniel, appearing in *The New Interpreter's Bible*. His commentary on Ezra–Nehemiah will soon appear as part of *The Oxford Bible Commentary*.

NATHAN TIERNEY is Professor of Philosophy and chair of the Department at California Lutheran University. He is the author of numerous articles and the book *Imagination and Ethical Ideals*. He is currently working on a new book entitled *Naturalistic Ethics and the Evolving Self*. He is co-founder of the consulting firm Philosophy in the Real World.

MARY EVELYN TUCKER is Professor of Religion at Bucknell University and Coordinator of the Forum on Religion and Ecology. She is the author of *Moral and Spiritual Cultivation in Japanese Neo-Confucianism*, and the editor of *Worldviews and Ecology*. Along with John Grim, she coordinated a ten-conference series on World Religions and Ecology at Harvard's Center for the Study of World Religions. She is the co-editor of the volumes in the series "Confucianism and Ecology" and "Buddhism and Ecology" and is currently editing a two-volume work on Confucian spirituality with Tu Wei-ming.

KEITH WARD, an eminent philosopher of religion and theologian, is Regius Professor of Divinity at Oxford University and a Canon of Christ Church Cathedral. His numerous books focus on a variety of theological issues, and among his more recent works are *Images of Eternity*; *God, Chance and Necessity*; *Defending the Soul*; and his monumental comparative theology: *Religion and Revelation*; *Religion and Creation*; *Religion and Human Nature*; and *Religion and Community*. He has just completed *A Short Introduction to Christianity*.

DALE S. WRIGHT is Professor of Religious Studies and Chair of the Asian Studies Program at Occidental College and has been a visiting professor at Waseda University, Japan. His research focuses on Buddhist philosophy, particularly those forms which developed in Japan and China – Hua-yen Buddhism and Zen or Ch'an Buddhism. His recent publications include two books, *Philosophical Meditations on Zen Buddhism* and *The Koan*, with Cambridge University Press.

## The Editors

NANCY M. MARTIN received her M.A. from the University of Chicago Divinity School and her Ph.D. from the Graduate Theological Union, Berkeley. An Assistant Professor of Religious Studies at Chapman University, she is a historian of religion with expertise in Asian religions, gender issues, and comparative mysticism. Involved in extensive fieldwork in Rajasthan, her research focuses on devotional Hinduism, women's religious lives, and the religious traditions of low-caste groups in India. She is the recipient of a Graves Award for the Humanities. As the co-editor of the "Library of Global Ethics and Religion," she has published *The Meaning of Life in the World Religions* and *Love, Sex and Gender in the World Religions*, and she has just completed a book manuscript on the sixteenth-century saint Mirabai, entitled *Mirabai Manifest: The Many Faces of a Woman Poet-Saint in India.*

JOSEPH RUNZO received his Ph.D. in philosophy from the University of Michigan and his M.T.S. in theological study from Harvard Divinity School. He is Professor of Philosophy and Religious Studies at Chapman University and Life Fellow at Clare Hall, Cambridge University. He is the recipient of six National Endowment for the Humanities Fellowships and Awards. Working in the fields of philosophy of religion, epistemology, and religious ethics, he has published eight books: *Reason, Relativism, and God*; *Religious Experience and Religious Belief*; *Is God Real?*; *Ethics, Religion and the Good Society*; *World Views and Perceiving God*; and (co-editor with Nancy M. Martin) *The Meaning of Life in the World Religions* and *Love, Sex and Gender in the World Religions*. He has just completed *Global Philosophy of Religion: A Short Introduction.*

# ACKNOWLEDGMENTS

This is the third volume in Oneworld's "Library of Global Ethics and Religion," offering a pluralistic and global perspective on questions of religion and ethics. The editors wish to thank Novin Doostdar and Juliet Mabey of Oneworld for their steadfast support for this project. We also wish to thank our Oneworld editors – Helen Coward, Victoria Warner, and Rebecca Clare – for their superlative work on this series.

The present volume would be meaningless unless the ideals of religious ethics were exemplified, and so the volume is dedicated to our dear friends Keith Ward and Christopher Key Chapple, not only for the importance of their scholarship but also for their example in taking the more difficult narrow way and admirably living out their beliefs.

The groundwork for this volume was begun at a conference held at Chapman University and Loyola Marymount University in spring 2000 which was made possible by the Huntington, Francis, and Griset Lectureship Funds of Chapman, the College of Liberal Arts and Program in Asian and Pacific Studies at Loyola Marymount, the Roman Catholic Diocese of Orange, and the Southern California Seminar on South Asia. We wish to acknowledge all those who participated in those initial conversations, including not only a number of contributors to this volume but also Daniel Campana, Arindam Chakrabarti, Virgilio Elizondo, Charlotte Fonrobert, James Fredericks, Ananda Guruge, Phyllis Herman,

Cynthia Humes, Jerry Irish, Brian Lepard, Rafael Luevano, Lance Nelson, June O'Conner, Joseph Prabhu, Philip Quinn, Arvind Sharma, Muzammil Siddiqi, Ninian Smart, Brian Swimme, and Robin Wang. We also wish to thank Bishop Tod Brown, President James Doti of Chapman, and President Robert Lawton of Loyola Marymount for their support of the initiating conference.

We are grateful to Dr. and Mrs. Robert G. Albertson and Yukihiro Aizawa for helping make possible the photographs for this volume. We would also like to thank a number of our students: Gloria Lam, Charles Deus, Josh Farrar, Michelle Gajewski, Janet Hoelscher, Timothy Johnson, Jennifer Jones, Allison Libeu, Shellagh Marshall, Suzanne Meler, Rema Merhi, Bronwyn Proffit-Higgins, Sarah Quadri, Brandi Saenz, Stephen Yarbrough, and Jim Zvonec for the help with the conference that first brought a number of the contributors together. We owe a special debt of gratitude to Jessie Rose Stevens, whose dedication, organizational skills, and good humor made the conference and the completion of this manuscript especially enjoyable experiences.

Finally, this book benefited from the co-operative efforts of the Global Ethics and Religion Forum, a new society of scholars in Europe, Canada, India, and the United States, dedicated to promoting a wider understanding both of religious pluralism and of ethical issues among the world religions in a global context. We wish to thank our friends in the Forum, many of whom have essays in the present volume, for their steadfast support.

# INTRODUCTION
## Inter-Religious Understanding

*Nancy M. Martin*

The challenge of inter-religious understanding has a new urgency and new dimensions in our day and for our increasingly global world community, but this challenge has been with us for a long time. In some parts of the world, like India, the encounter with people from different religious traditions has been a daily fact of life for centuries. Hindus of many different persuasions – Buddhists, Muslims, Jains, Sikhs, Christians, and even small and very ancient communities of Jews and Parsis – have long lived together in villages across the South Asian subcontinent and have shared each other's holy days and rituals, honored each other's saints, and debated and appreciated each other's religious teachings. Medieval poet-saints like Kabir have called for Hindus and Muslims to realize the sameness of the God they worship, just as there have also sometimes been violent conflicts, particularly when religion, communal identity, and politics have been interwoven.

We can learn much from the Indian case, for the inter-religious encounter there has not been abstract but personal and immediate. Take for example one recent evening when I was in western Rajasthan in north India, not far from the Indian border with southern Pakisthan. Darkness had fallen and a dozen people converged on the courtyard outside a simple, small dwelling. The visitors, dressed in finery for the occasion, were directed to sit outside on string cots covered with brightly colored fabric mats, and a kerosene lamp was brought to offer a soft circle of light.

Everyone's spirits were high, and there was great anticipation of the meal to come. This was a time of celebration. The Muslim hosts were observing one of the five pillars of Islam – fasting between sunrise and sundown everyday for the entire lunar month of Ramadan – and the day's fasting had come to an end. There was much laughter and conversation, and the spicy array of goat meat and vegetables with fresh flat bread called *chapatis* or *rotis* was eaten with relish (though some did not partake of the meat).

Gathered in that courtyard were Muslims but also Jains, Hindus, and Christians. Though this was a distinctly religious occasion and a decidedly Muslim one, it was joyously shared by others of different faiths – a difference that was not merely tolerated but celebrated, enjoyed, relished. Similar gatherings are held throughout the month of Ramadan in many villages and on the occasions of other Hindu and Muslim holy days. In this village world, those belonging to other religions are friends and neighbors, and this mutual appreciation and celebration is much more characteristic of India than the sporadic violence inflamed by religious rhetoric which is the stuff of newspaper articles or television news.

Unlike in India, in many parts of the world it was possible until quite recently to live without truly encountering people with radically different religious beliefs. But it is now becoming increasingly impossible and, indeed, undesirable, to live in religiously homogeneous or isolated communities. And though dialogue might begin with an attempt to explain the teachings of one's own tradition to another (possibly with the intent of conversion) and with the comparison of religious experience, it often very quickly moves into the exploration of how we might be able to live harmoniously with one another, treating each other with dignity and respect, and how we might work together for the betterment of the world.

Perhaps we might never reconcile divergent religious worldviews and truth claims, but dialogue can lead to a firmer basis for mutual action in the world, for standing together to denounce injustice and to promote the welfare of all. If we are going to work together, we will need to understand each other, to find our common ground, and to learn to appreciate and even celebrate our differences. The majority of the world's population is religious, and although some continue to predict the imminent demise of the world religions, these religions are playing an increasing rather than decreasing role on the world stage. So much of our understanding of what is right and wrong and how we think about the way we should act in the world is grounded in our understanding of the nature and meaning of life, an understanding that for the majority of the people in the world is circumscribed by religion.

Potentially the world religions have much to offer. Their potential power is evidenced by the continuing political use of religion. But the challenges before us are great and global in scale – famine in a world of surplus; violent ethnic conflict; the horrific violation of rights and human dignity based on gender, race, sexual orientation, and political affiliation; the exploitation and destruction of the environment. We will need all the resources we can muster, and this includes the powerful ethical motivation that flows from the committed religious life, whether one is a Muslim or a Buddhist or a Confucian or a Christian.

In the global twenty-first century, inter-religious understanding is not an optional or idle intellectual pursuit. This volume and the larger series of which it is a part, "The Library of Global Ethics and Religion," take up the challenge to further mutual understanding among religions, particularly with regard to the basic ethical principles they hold and the resources they might bring to their adherents and to the global community as we face pressing ethical challenges. This focus on ethics is a fundamental characteristic of inter-religious encounter at the beginning of the twenty-first century. But how did we get to this point?

## INTER-RELIGIOUS ENCOUNTER IN THE PAST

Religions have always been in conversation with each other, especially those in geographic proximity and particularly when what will become a new religion is in its formative stages. Clearly early Judaism had to come to terms with the religions of the surrounding people in order to differentiate itself and then maintain that distinctive identity. That this was no easy task is clear from the references to the Canaanites and others in the Hebrew scriptures. And the question of how much to adapt to changing circumstances and cultural contexts and what elements are essential to being a Jew is a recurring theme in the history of Judaism, separating the distinctive branches of reform, conservative, and orthodox Judaism today.

Christianity began within Judaism, and its earliest members, including its leader Jesus, understood themselves to be Jewish. Only with time did the followers of Jesus come to understand themselves as a new and distinct tradition, in part as a response to non-Jewish converts who questioned whether following the laws of Judaism was essential to the central teachings of Jesus. Muhammad grew up among Jews and Christians and saw his revelation as directly in line with that of the Jewish and Christian traditions. It was their resistance to his revelation more than anything else that first drew the line between them.

In South Asia six centuries before the birth of Jesus and twelve hundred years before Muhammad, Buddhism and Jainism grew up along with the Upanishadic traditions of Hinduism, reacting against some aspects of the existing tradition while embracing others. Indeed until only very recently, many Jains identified themselves as being within the inclusive fold of Hinduism (though now because of the politicization of religion in contemporary India and the assigning of special privileges to religious minorities, it has become expedient to assert Jain separateness). Daoism and Confucianism grew up together in China also from the sixth century BCE, and in part defined themselves against each other. In the Daoist philosopher Chuang Tzu's humorous stories, Confucius and his followers often appear as the misguided foil to a Daoist adept. When Buddhism entered China around 0 CE, these traditions were well established, and there was initial resistance to Buddhist monastic leanings as antithetical to the central value placed on family in Confucianism.

New forms of Buddhism arose in China. Two schools, T'ien T'ai and Hua-yen, reflected the Chinese (both Daoist and Confucian) focus on harmony by integrating the various and sometimes seemingly conflicting Buddhist teachings and texts into unified systems, and Ch'an (Zen) emerged out of the confluence of Buddhism and Daoism. Confucianism responded to Buddhism by developing a meditational inner dimension in its Neo-Confucian forms. But these religions also co-exist in the lives of individuals who, in Japan for example, identify themselves as followers of Buddhism, Shinto, and Confucianism, with these different traditions seen not as competitive but as playing different roles and answering different needs in a single life. Indeed one might even be both a Christian and a Buddhist; as Japanese Christian friends explained to me, they are culturally Buddhist, incorporating many Buddhist elements into their lives, and religiously Christian.

## Colonialism, Denigration, and Romanticization

When religions are not in geographic proximity, or when that proximity involves only isolated individuals or is the result of slavery or colonial domination, then inter-religious understanding is often more limited, as we find in early encounters between "Western" Christians and "other" religions such as Hinduism and Buddhism. Though some of the writings of travelers, missionaries, and colonializers showed deep appreciation, most accounts were marked by an emphasis on the "otherness," the utter differentness of those encountered. As European Christendom has often done with Muslims, what they saw was an inverse of themselves – an "other" who was alternately exotic or the embodiment of either all those things they wished they were or all the things they did not want to admit they were or potentially might be.[1] In the latter case, this often meant that the "other" was seen as backward, stupid, childlike, superstitious, weak, cruel, immoral, and, in the colonialist rhetoric of hyper-masculinity, effeminate. An example of today's version of this would be the false images perpetuated in the American media of all Muslims as violent terrorists who oppress women.

Many Christians saw "polytheists" everywhere (a term whose meaning is primarily "not monotheist") and the unsaved who, if not converted, were all destined for eternal damnation. Such a view left little room for an appreciation of the religions of these "others." Further when Protestant Christians looked at Hindu ritual practice, they saw what seemed to be both the idolatry condemned in the Hebrew scriptures and the kind of superstition and blind slavery to priests that they had rejected in the name of Enlightenment rationality and the Reformation. Such an understanding (or lack thereof) bolstered the British justification of their right to rule over India – they were, after all, moral people who could justify ruling over others only if they saw themselves as superior and helping an inferior people.

On the other hand, some European colonial officers and certain early scholars saw in India a mystic and spiritual depth that seemed to have been lost in the industrial revolution and materialistic focus of the West. They romanticized India. But again, what they saw was a reflection of themselves rather than India or Hinduism in itself. (This kind of romanticization is with us still, particularly in the way Buddhism is seen in America today. The strictness of the true Zen Buddhist monastic life in Japan would quickly shatter most American images of Buddhism.) At the same time, some Indians in South Asia, struggling to define themselves and reclaim their own heritage in the face of British colonial domination and technological superiority, also embraced the idea of Hindu spiritual superiority. They accepted the critiques of Hindu ritual practices and located the true Hindu tradition in the distant past and the texts of the Upanishads and interpretations of the Vedas that they claimed were the more ancient and true.

Though there is considerable variation in the nature of interaction through the nineteenth century, inter-religious encounter was marked primarily by a sense of the radical *difference* between world religions.

## The First Parliament of the World's Religions

In 1893, however, a watershed event took place in the history of inter-religious encounter for the West.[2] The Parliament of World Religions was organized at the World's Fair in Chicago, with the intent of bringing together leaders of the world's religions to promote inter-religious understanding (though the organizers were primarily American Protestant Christians).[3] Many of those invited refused to attend – the Archbishop of Canterbury would not come, since he considered only Christianity to be true; the Sultan of Turkey's similar refusal prompted the Arab Islamic nations to do likewise; and Japanese Zen monks tried in vain to persuade their master Soyen Shaku that it would be unseemly for him to go to such an uncivilized country as the United States.[4] The hope of the organizers of the Parliament, however, was to provide a venue where leaders of each tradition could present their traditions to each other without condemnation.

Although the Christian delegates showed an open appreciation of other traditions, they did not see them as the equal of Christianity. Japanese Buddhists openly challenged Christian judgment of their tradition because the Christians knew little about Buddhism, and, encountering signs banning Japanese from some establishments, claimed that they preferred to remain "heathens" if this prejudicial treatment represented Christian ethical behavior. Further they challenged the notion that only one religion could be right or that people must follow only one – in Japan this was not the case.[5]

Swami Vivekananda of India made perhaps the greatest impact. Vivekananda spoke from the *Bhagavad Gita* of the multiple paths of Hinduism and the unity of all.[6] "Hinduism" is itself an inclusivist term, originally coined by outsiders and referring merely to the people on the other side of the Indus (that is, on the whole South Asian subcontinent) and later applied to the wide range of religious orientations found in this geographic region. But the fundamental affirmation of the oneness of Ultimate Reality in Hindu traditions also supports an inclusiveness that is widespread, even among unsophisticated and formally uneducated Hindus. When I was riding on a bus through rural Rajasthan, a poor farmer asked me who my *ishtadev* was (in what form did I worship God?). Seeking to show understanding, I spoke of God being one. The man said rather impatiently, well of course God is one, but who is your *ishtadev*? On a grander scale, Vivekananda's teacher Ramakrishna had visionary encounters with Muhammad and with Christ which affirmed the ultimate unity of religious paths.[7] Although many delegates at the Parliament were not yet ready to accept this Hindu inclusivity, they were deeply impressed with Vivekananda's philosophical and theological presentation of Hinduism, which offered them an appealing glimpse of a tradition radically different from their previous understandings.

There was a general call toward universality and common ground at the Parliament and an affirmation that revelation was not confined to any one tradition and that all had perceptions of truth and the real. Ethical considerations were raised, both challenging the religious institutions themselves and also calling for religious people to work together and to strive to live up to their own high ideals. Critical voices, such as Elizabeth Cady Stanton, who was in the process of writing *The Woman's Bible* at the time, spoke out against racism and sexism across traditions and called for attention to the plight of the poor.[8] Notably, however, there was a complete silence with regard to Native American traditions – it was as if Americans were as completely blind to these "other" religions as they had been to practitioners of various African indigenous religious traditions and African Muslims among the slave populations. Forced conversion to Christianity marked much of the encounter with Native traditions, with European Americans seemingly unable to recognize these other traditions as religions, and the massacre at Wounded Knee had happened only three years before.[9]

## Commonality and Difference

After the first Parliament true inter-religious dialogue began in earnest. The intensive translation work that was initiated in the nineteenth century continued and increased, making a vast array of new material available to the wider world, and there was a shift away from the radical "othering" of different traditions toward a search for the commonality between traditions.

Religious experience and particularly mystical experience seemed to be a point where the traditions might meet, for the descriptions of those experiences sounded similar and often seemed to transcend the particulars of doctrine and practice. William James published *The Varieties of Religious Experience* in 1902, mapping out the characteristics of a mystical experience that is seemingly common to all religions and beyond the distinctive content of particular religious beliefs.[10] The German scholar Rudolph Otto explored this issue further in *The Idea of the Holy* (1923) and *Mysticism East and West* (1932), offering his now famous notion of the encounter with the Divine as the numinous – *mysterium tremendom* and *fascinans*, invoking in the human being a sense of awe and humility, passion and yearning, and the experience of the "wholly other."[11] In so doing, he was reclaiming for religion the suprarational experience of this reality, a consciousness of which must be awakened in us rather than taught (and arguing against the "masters of suspicion" – Feuerbach,[12] Freud,[13] and Marx – who had radically challenged the validity of all religion).

Even as he found this universal, however, Otto's language remained thoroughly Christian – the commonality he saw was a "like us" kind of commonality – a reflection of his own Christian context. As he developed his comparison between East and West, he showed a deep appreciation for Shankara, the eighth-century formulator of Advaita Vedanta, but in the end it was clear that he made his comparison in order to judge traditions. In the final analysis his judgment was a resounding affirmation of Christianity which he saw as the culmination of the evolution of the spiritual consciousness of humanity, even as Christian delegates attending the Parliament in 1893 had. And much of the comparative study in the first half of the twentieth century shared this same orientation (although James managed largely to avoid this pitfall).

The openness in the West to the possibility that religions other than Christianity might contain truth began to encompass wider and wider circles. In the radical reforms of the most recent council of the Roman Catholic Church, Vatican II, in the early 1960s, the Dogmatic Constitution regarding Catholic attitudes toward the other religions of the world is inclusivist, affirming that there may be truth in other religions, calling for respect for their practices and teachings, and encouraging dialogue and the acknowledgment and support of "the spiritual and moral goods found among these [people], as well as the values of their society and culture."[14] Although still asserting the final and ultimate truth of Christianity, the roots of this inclusivist vision are traced back in the document to the writings of the early church fathers.

We must keep in mind that what we recognize as common we too often assume is just like us, imposing our meanings and experiences on those of others. Indeed some academics reacted against such claims of religious commonality and sameness for this reason, asserting that religions are in fact so radically different that they cannot be compared. The emphasis shifted to preserving and exploring difference as the pendulum swung back to the need to recognize that other religious traditions were not simply variants of "us." A positive result of this swing was that scholars became much more careful about speaking in generalities about other traditions (and their own) and much more attentive to their assumptions and positioning within a given tradition. But not everyone accepted such a radical return to seeing other religions as completely different from one's own.

During the latter decades of the twentieth century, dialogue between religious leaders to enhance understanding began in earnest. Following the model of the early Parliament, this was first and foremost an explanation and defense of one's own tradition to another. But progressing beyond this, the dialogue included using the other's tradition to then explain one's own tradition in their terms by comparison and contrast. A fine example of this can be found in the work of the Kyoto School Zen philosophers who worked to explain Buddhism through a comparison with Western philosophy and Christianity.[15] The aim was not to convert one's dialogue partners but to deepen understanding. Key is a recognition and mutual appreciation, across the boundaries of religious traditions, of a common spiritual depth coming out of disciplined religious practice, though there might not be agreement on metaphysical and theological issues. The Catholic Church in particular has sponsored formal dialogues between Catholics and leaders and practitioners of Judaism, Islam, Hinduism, Buddhism, and other branches and denominations within the Christian fold.

In addition to promoting mutual understanding, these encounters often led to the rediscovery of forgotten elements and untapped potential within the participants' own traditions. The Archbishop of Canterbury and the Sultan of Turkey had seen no reason for dialogue in 1893, but Buddhists and Christians gained much from their encounters in the next century. In the case of Christianity, the encounter with Buddhism (and forms of Hinduism) led to a re-examination of the meditative prayer traditions within medieval Christianity as religious leaders asked why young people raised within their fold might be turning to other traditions – what was missing from the Christianity they were being taught? Some Roman Catholics also began to practice Zen-style meditation in a Catholic context, even in monasteries. Buddhists like Thich Nhat Hanh in turn encountered Christian charity in practice and recognized these practicing Christians as embodying the Buddhist ideal of the *bodhisattva* in a way that most Buddhists were not encouraged to do. Out of this realization came the movements for socially engaged Buddhism drawing Buddhist compassion into the realm of social action. Christians did not become Buddhists or Buddhists Christians, but the practice of each was enhanced in the encounter.

Two more Parliaments of the World Religions were also convened in 1993 and 1999, the first in Chicago and the second in Cape Town. These gatherings again provided a forum for religious leaders to present their traditions to receptive audiences seeking deeper understanding and appreciation and were marked by celebrations of the abundant richness of human religiosity. But they also had a central focus on ethical action. At the 1993 gathering, under the leadership of Hans Küng, delegates issued an "Initial Declaration for a Global Ethic." It was clear to all concerned that religions had both a power and an obligation to provide leadership in the ethical realm. The aim of this project was to find a common ground – a shared floor to begin building ethical consensus – one marked by a commitment to "nonviolence and respect for life," "solidarity and a just economic order," "tolerance and a life of truthfulness," and "equal rights and the partnership of men and women." Given the history of earlier "universalizing," any such attempts must be approached with great caution, but members of the world's religions and organizers of the Parliament felt very strongly that the world religions had an ethical role to play, and this was one way to begin the discussion.

At the third meeting of the Parliament in Cape Town this focus on ethics continued with a call to the guiding social, political, economic, and religious institutions of the world to act for a more just and peaceful world. When the Dalai Lama addressed the Parliament in the final days, he took this commitment one step further, calling delegates and religious leaders to join together to engage in concrete action – to go to Bosnia, for example – to make a real difference in the world. And parliamentary debate of the call to guiding institutions resulted in many participants finding specific ways to bring about change in the institutions in which they participated in their home countries. This represents an immense shift from a century before, when the focus was primarily on listening and coming to understand each other.

Let me offer one concrete example of the kind of inter-religious action the Dalai Lama was advocating, again from India. In early 2000, a Christian missionary and his two children were burned alive in their hut. Ostensibly this was because they were converting people, and Hindus had to defend their faith against such incursions. But such violent anti-Christian sentiment is not the norm in India, and further investigation showed the killings to be politically motivated. Leaders of all the religions of India and beyond – Christians, Jains, Sikhs, Hindus, Parsis, Jews, and Buddhists – came to that place to honor this man who had served lepers for years as a physician and to denounce this kind of violence couched in religious terms. Such solidarity across religious lines offered a powerful and very public challenge to the individuals and institutions who would perpetuate such acts even as it diffused retaliatory violence.

## ETHICS IN THE WORLD RELIGIONS FOR THE TWENTY-FIRST CENTURY

As we move into the twenty-first century, there is a need to affirm *both* commonality *and* difference in religious perspectives on ethical issues. Religious differences need not be a "problem" to be eliminated but may rather be a source of expansion and creative interchange, as important as biodiversity for our mutual flourishing. Christian liberation theologies, engaged Buddhism, and the nonviolence of Gandhi all prefigure what must be a part of religion's increasing role in this new millennium, as an active force for social change.

In the first volume of this series, entitled *The Meaning of Life in the World Religions*, John Hick suggests that religions offer a source of "cosmic optimism" – a deep source of hope in the face of the world's struggles. And Huston Smith echoes this, suggesting that, by addressing life's most fundamental problems and most profound suffering and by offering the greatest possible hope, religion provides the greatest possible motivation to solve these problems and also posits the unequaled support of divine grace. Keith Ward further suggests that those of us who are religious will do well both to recognize that we all travel toward similar transformations of our individual selves into people marked by "wisdom, compassion, and bliss" who act in care for others rather than for self alone, and to agree to travel together encouraging our hopes and supporting shared ethical action grounded in our different but not necessarily conflicting senses of ultimate purpose and meaning. Though religion may not be an absolutely necessary ingredient for a meaningful life, these scholars affirm the unparalleled power of a religious perspective to give greater meaning, hope, and motivation – all deeply needed in our world today.

The essays in this volume take up the challenge of inter-religious understanding and examine the ethical resources offered by the world religions. The volume begins with an exploration of the fundamental connection between ethics and religion and the possibilities and difficulties of understanding and finding agreement across traditions. Joseph Runzo sets the framework for the discussion by analyzing the nature of ethics and the relation of the moral life to the religious life. He argues that "metaphysics drives ethics," and explores the manner in which people from different religious traditions and thus with different metaphysics might reach ethical agreement. To that end, he defines the moral point of view and addresses what place religion might have in a global ethic. Keith Ward then explores the possible basis for such a global ethic, identifying benevolence, truthfulness, liberty, and justice as basic shared moral values, though they may be interpreted differently across religious traditions. The most important contribution of religions to the search for a universal ethic, he argues, is in terms of both the emphasis within religious traditions on the need to overcome ego-centeredness and the affirmation that these highest values are not only arrived at by human reflection but are truly grounded in reality itself.

James Kellenberger then explores the nature of moral diversity, setting forth a notion of moral pluralism that parallels John Hick's religious pluralism and arguing for the pre-eminent importance of relationships as the ground for moral decision making, a theme that will be picked up in other chapters as well. According to him, a fundamental affirmation of basic human relationships lies at the heart of the religious perspective and the religious motivation for ethical action. This theme of relationality is developed in subsequent chapters with respect to the ethics of individual traditions and in relation to issues such as the ethics of transplants and the need for an ecological ethic. And indeed an increasing focus on relationality will undoubtedly also be a dominant theme in inter-religious encounter in the twenty-first century.

The wider questions of religion and ethics having been delineated, the next section of the volume focuses on specific religious traditions in both the West and the East. Elliot Dorff offers a comprehensive look at ethics and morality in Judaism, exploring the Jewish version of Divine Command theory and the values that shape individual Jews, the Jewish community, and Jewish ethical decision making – the integrated and positive understanding of the body which ultimately belongs to God, the meaning of all people being created in the image of God, and the importance of family, education, and community. Zayn Kassam then turns to the Islamic tradition, exploring the resources for ethical decision making within Islam, particularly with regard to matters not addressed directly in the Qur'an. She then takes up two issues that specifically harm women within some Islamic cultures and which are often justified as "Islamic" – female genital mutilation and honor killings – and shows both how culture and religion become entangled and how, using fundamentally Islamic strategies of ethical decision making as well as the Qur'an, these practices might be challenged.

The latter two essays in this section address Christianity. Nathan Tierney explores traditional understandings of the soul in the face of the challenges of modern science, advocating a non-reductionist evolutionary notion of the self in a move to heal the split between the spiritual and the material, the body and the soul, and to affirm the interrelationality of the human – a fundamental shift in worldview which would have serious and important implications for Christian ethical practice. Philip Rossi analyzes the redefinition and relativizing of life's meaning in contemporary society, leaving little room for other-directed action and little motivation for ethical living in a culture of unconcern. He then suggests that Christianity and other religious traditions must offer a voice of challenge in the midst of this crisis of indifference through a re-imagining and reawakening of an awareness of the spiritual dimension (and higher callings) of human beings and of a Transcendent Reality beyond the human.

Having examined aspects of ethics and religion in the West, we then turn to the East. Vasudha Narayanan details the concept of *dharma* as it relates to ethics in Hinduism and examines how the laws recorded in *dharma shastra* texts play out in real life situations, specifically in the context of renunciation and reproduction. Dale Wright turns to Buddhism and the cultivation of the six perfections (generosity, morality, patience, energy, meditation, and wisdom) that characterize the ideal Buddhist and are epitomized by the lay *bodhisattva* Vimalakirti. He demonstrates in a powerful way how Buddhist understandings of dependent co-origination shape notions of ethical responsibility through the words of Thich Nhat Hanh, who claimed a responsibility for the beating of Rodney King by police in Los Angeles in 1991. Christopher Key Chapple then introduces us to Jain purification practices and vows, undergirded by a deep commitment to nonviolence. Ethical concerns for other beings drive these Jain ascetic practices, and their nonviolence extends also to a nonviolent approach to those holding other religious views, as the example of Haribhadra makes clear, and to a commitment to fight violence on a global scale. In the final chapter in this section, John Berthrong gives us a window onto the current conversations within Confucianism as adherents ask themselves what shape their tradition will take in the coming century. A fundamental call for the active development of "concern-consciousness" in addition to "civility" emerges from recent gatherings in China.

Having explored these separate traditions, we then turn to the ways in which different religious traditions might challenge and assist each other in the face of pressing ethical concerns. Daniel Smith-Christopher examines the strategies used by Jews, Christians, and Muslims as they look to their own scriptures for support for nonviolence, suggesting that the Christian strategy of developmental evolution from violence to nonviolence within the tradition may not be the best – sawing off the branch on which one is sitting so to speak – and that the uncovering of elements of nonviolence throughout the history of the tradition, including the early Hebrew scriptures (as he finds in Jewish and Muslim commentaries), appears a more promising strategy.

William LaFleur explores the issue of organ transplantation in medical ethics, showing how Christians and Jews in American readily and almost unquestioningly embraced this practice in the 1960s (in spite of earlier understandings of a connection between the bodily integrity of a corpse and resurrection and considerable differences between the two traditions with regard to attitudes toward the body, as Elliot Dorff makes clear in chapter 4). LaFleur clearly demonstrates that the issue is not so cut and dried, by contrasting it with Japanese Buddhist/Confucian opposition toward cadaveric transplantation, fundamentally in terms of the violation of relationships, and through careful examination of the actual arguments given for it, particularly by Joseph Fletcher, identifying organ donation as the epitome of *agapé* or unconditional love in the Christian case.

Vrinda Dalmiya takes the opposite tack, addressing a problem within feminist care ethics of "caring" action potentially contributing to the self-sacrifice and oppression of the care-giver. She draws on classical Indian traditions to enrich the understanding of care, through a retelling of several episodes from the classic Hindu epic of the *Mahabharata* and a detailed examination of a parallel term to Western notions of care – *anukrosha*. In so doing, she offers an alternative vision of autonomous and uncoerced action that strengthens rather than denigrates the individual and radically alters the way moral imperatives play out, again with an emphasis on the fundamental importance of relationships in ethical considerations.

In the final section of the volume, Brian Hebblethwaite, Mary Evelyn Tucker, and C. Ram-Prasad explore the global implications of particular traditions. Hebblethwaite begins by offering a comprehensive account of the discussions within Christianity over whether there is a genuine Christian social ethic at all and then what might be unique about it and where common ground might be found with other religious ethics and with secular ethics. He concludes with an exploration of the place of religion generally and Christian ethics specifically in the context of global ethical consensus and action. Mary Evelyn Tucker addresses the environmental crisis and explores how the fundamental understandings of the nature of the world in terms of the holistic *qi* (matter-energy or vital force) and the structuring principles of *li* found in Confucianism might provide useful insight for the restructuring of human attitudes toward the non-human world which is essential to creating a global environmental ethic. The volume concludes with C. Ram-Prasad's explication of the Jaina doctrine of *anekantavada* or "multiplism" as a possible way to approach inter-religious understanding and moral pluralism with an ethic of toleration and nonviolence.

In their exploration of the confluence of religion and ethics, the essays in this volume contribute significantly toward advancing these newest directions in inter-religious understanding – the generation of ethical insight when issues are viewed from alternative religious worldviews, the deepening perception of the fundamental relationality of humans and the world embedded in and affirmed by the teachings of diverse religions, and the exploration of the specific and vital contribution that the world's religions might and indeed must make in the realm of ethical action in our increasingly global world.

## NOTES

1. Edward Said's *Orientalism* was a ground-breaking work in this type of analysis, and a broad array of postcolonial criticism followed.
2. I am drawing here on the insightful description of the Parliament given by Diana Eck in her essay "Frontiers of Encounter," in *The Ways of Religion: An Introduction to the Major Traditions*, 3rd edn, ed. Roger Eastman (New York: Oxford University Press, 1999), especially pp. 5–11. For further details, see John Henry Barrows, ed., *The World's Parliament of Religions* (Chicago: Parliament Publishing Company, 1893); Richard Seager, ed., *The Dawn of Religious Pluralism* (Chicago: Open Court Press, 1992); and Richard Seager, *The World's Parliament of Religions: The East/West Encounter, Chicago, 1893* (Bloomington: Indiana University Press, 1995).
3. See Brian Hebblethwaite's discussion of the Parliament in the context of Christian social ethics in chapter 15.
4. Eck, "Frontiers of Encounter," p. 6.
5. Ibid., p. 7.
6. Swami Vivekananda, *Chicago Addresses* (Calcutta: Advaita Ashrama, 1968).
7. Swami Nikhilananda, trans., *The Gospel of Sri Ramakrishna* (New York: Ramakrishna-Vivekananda Center, 1984).
8. Eck, p. 10. Elizabeth Cady Stanton, *The Woman's Bible* (Amherst, NY: Prometheus, 1999).
9. Eck, p. 11
10. William James, *The Varieties of Religious Experience* (New York: Triumph, 1991 [1902]).
11. Rudolph Otto, *The Idea of the Holy* (1923) and *Mysticism East and West* (1932).
12. Ludwig Feuerbach, *The Essence of Christianity*, trans. George Elliot (New York: Harper, 1957).
13. Sigmund Freud, *The Future of an Illusion*, trans. James Strachey (New York: Norton, 1975).
14. Walter M. Abbott, S.J. and Joseph Gallagher, eds, "Declaration on the Relationship of the Church to Non-Christian Religions," in *The Documents of Vatican II* (American Press, 1966).
15. See, for example, Masao Abe, *Zen and Western Thought*, ed. William LaFleur (Honolulu: University of Hawaii Press, 1985); Keiji Nishitani, *Religion and Nothingness*, trans. Jan Van Bragt (Berkeley: University of California Press, 1982).

*Part I*

# RELIGION AND ETHICS

*Plate 1* Memorial to Mahatma Gandhi (1869–1948) in Delhi. The inscription on the side reads "Oh God" (*Hai Ram*), Gandhi's last words as he was assassinated. Gandhi brought the Jain religious ideal of *ahimsa* (nonviolence) to international attention during the birth of the modern nation of India. Photo: *Nancy M. Martin*

# 1

# BEING RELIGIOUS *and* DOING ETHICS *in* A GLOBAL WORLD

*Joseph Runzo*

The world in which we find ourselves in the twenty-first century is a global world. Iconoclastic religious outlooks and provincial ethical ideals are challenged by a global economy, global communications, the global movement of peoples and, above all, by a new way of seeing ourselves as members of global humanity. How can the traditional ways of being religious and the old ways of doing ethics apply to this global world?

A religion or a religious tradition consists of a complex set of social elements – symbols and rituals, myths and stories, concepts and truth-claims – which a community believes gives ultimate meaning to life by connecting the religious adherent to a transcendent: Allah or Brahman or Nirvana or the Dao or God or Akal Purakh, and so on. A religious way of life thus rests on specific claims about the nature of reality, about how meaning and value are to be achieved, and about what is the desired end for humankind. Moral meaning is an inextricable part of any religious meaning of life, and moral structures are a critical part of religious conceptions of the structure of reality. Hence, part of what it means to follow the religious life is to follow the moral life. So before we can determine how the religious life could fit into a global world, we must first ask how the moral life fits into such a world.

## MORALITY AND ETHICS[1]

Morality is a set of interrelated principles and imperatives about right and wrong, good and bad, which a society holds as true and normative of the relations between members of that society. We can approach moral systems in one of three ways (or a combination of these three). First, there is the sort of descriptive investigation historians, sociologists, anthropologists, and psychologists do when they ask such questions as "what have Hindus historically thought?" or "what do Japanese Buddhists today think?" or "do Christians in non-Western cultures think differently from those in Western European cultures?" or "what do subjugated religious women think?" about various moral issues. In the scientific approaches of history, sociology, anthropology, and psychology, we are concerned with accurate description, not with evaluative judgment; we are not concerned with whether the people being studied are right or wrong to think about morality as they once did or now do. In contrast, the other two ways to discuss or assess morality, "normative ethics" and "meta-ethics," are not purely descriptive, for they are concerned with the correct way to think about moral issues. Ethics is *reasoning* about morality. Ethics is an attempt to determine what *is* right and wrong, good and bad. As such, ethics involves giving systematic reasons, or developing fundamental principles, as to *why* one should give the answers one does to moral questions.

The first, foundational level of ethics is "normative ethics," a system of reasoning about morality with the double intent of explaining why things are right and wrong and good and bad, and, on the basis of that, of providing a systematic way for deciding moral issues when confronting moral choices. Moral issues arise in the context of choice and conflict, usually conflict between competing ethical ideals or between self-interest and morality. Often moral conflicts take the explicit form of cross-cultural conflicts over moral stands. But in any event, it is conflicts over questions of morality which typically initiate the reasoning about morality which is ethics. And since normative ethical systems are intended to give answers in times of moral choice in order to deal with moral conflicts, normative ethical systems do not merely give an answer to what is moral but attempt to provide a principled justification for why it is moral.

The second, even deeper level of ethics is meta-ethics. Meta-ethical questions are questions about or across normative ethical systems. Thus one might ask: "how are morality and ethics different from other action guides like the legal system?" or "how does a religious normative ethics differ from a purely secular normative ethics?" Now, one hopes to produce or adhere to a normative ethical system that holds universally. Meta-ethical investigations can help us determine to what extent the normative ethical system that we do follow is or can be universal. For example, any particular ethical principle within a normative system must conform to the principle of universalizability. Universalizability is the formal idea that if an action is morally right for you, then it is morally right or permissible for anyone else who finds himself or herself in circumstances similar to those you are confronting. The principle of universalizability mitigates against thinking of ourselves as always being the exception to the rule. The principle of universalizability mitigates against egoism, the enemy of morality.

But the acceptance of the basic formal principle of universalizability does not mean that ethical agreement is easy, even among rational and well-intentioned people. Perhaps more than any other major religious tradition, Jainism has recognized the difficulty of applying moral duties to our real life situations and reaching moral agreement. In Jain ethics, to be moral is to follow the *dharma* – the universal law of nature – out of a sense of duty, especially the duty of *ahimsa* (nonviolence). But what does this mean in real life situations? For instance, is the laboratory testing of pharmaceuticals on animals acceptable in order to alleviate great human suffering (say, from cancer)? Is there only one right answer to this question on a Jain perspective? After all, as Christopher Chapple points out in his discussion of this issue, some modern Jains figure prominently in the Indian pharmaceutical industry.[2] Rather than a cut-and-dried approach to ethical issues, Jainism has developed the notion of *anekantavada*, an explicit recognition that knowledge is always from a particular perspective and that no single person has a perspective that is the whole truth. It is worth bearing in mind that the likelihood that any normative ethics could be universal is undoubtedly increased with the acceptance of something like this flexible *anekantavada* approach, which C. Ram-Prasad has termed "multiplism."[3]

The potential for a universal ethic, and so a universal religious ethic, will also increase if humans share a common human nature. A paradigmatic exposition of the idea of a common human nature was developed by the third-century BCE Confucian philosopher Mencius:

A man without the feeling of commiseration is not a man; a man without a feeling of shame and dislike is not a man; a man without the feeling of deference and compliance is not a man; and a man without the feeling of right and wrong is not a man. The feeling of commiseration is the beginning of humanity; the feeling of shame and dislike is the beginning of righteousness; the feeling of deference and compliance is the beginning of propriety; and the feeling of right and wrong is the beginning of wisdom. Men have these Four Beginnings just as they have their four limbs. Having these Four Beginnings, but saying that they cannot develop them is to destroy themselves.[4]

But many would argue against this, as Lao-Tzu did in early Chinese thought and European existentialists and Western postmodernists have more recently argued. Perhaps there is no common human nature. But even so, there might still be a common moral point of view, that is, a perspective shared by all systems that we would call moral systems. For even though there are substantive differences among moral systems, especially moral systems considered cross-culturally, that very difference and our ability to compare and contrast those diverse moral systems imply an underlying commonality.

## THE MORAL POINT OF VIEW

As we have already noted, one feature of taking the moral point of view, that is, one formal feature that is to be applied to particular principles of all normative ethical systems, is universalizability. Another cornerstone of the moral point of view, the idea of being just or impartial, is found in these words of the early Chinese philosopher Mo Tzu:

When we set out to classify and describe those men who hate and injure others, shall we say that their actions are motivated by universality [impartiality] or partiality? Surely we must answer, by partiality, and it is this partiality in their dealings with one another that gives rise to all the great harms in the world. Therefore we know that partiality is wrong ...

Whoever criticizes others must have some alternative to offer them. To criticize and yet offer no alternative is like trying to stop flood with flood or put out fire with fire. It will surely have no effect. Therefore ... Partiality should be replaced by universality [impartiality].[5]

In addition to universalizability and impartiality, we can add, as a third minimal feature of taking the moral point of view, benevolence (to wish well to other persons). The principle of benevolence tells us that we ought to take the intents of others into account. Any putative moral theory that takes account only of self-interest – such as so-called "ethical egoism," which holds that the standard of moral right and wrong is what will produce one's own greatest good – is not really a theory about morality but merely a theory about prudence.

This means that at least four characteristics of taking the moral point of view and being committed to the moral life are: (1) taking others into account in one's actions because one respects them in themselves as persons (benevolence); (2) the willingness to take into account how one's actions affect others by taking into account the good of everyone equally (justice or impartiality); (3) abiding by the principle of universalizability – that is, the willingness to treat one's own actions as morally laudable or permissible only if similar acts of others in comparable circumstances would be equally laudable or permissible, and to treat the actions of others as morally impermissible only if similar acts of one's own would be equally morally culpable; and (4) the willingness to be committed to some consistent set of normative moral principles.[6]

Taking these in reverse order, different communities, including different religious traditions, will specify the normative principles in (4) differently. But all moralities share the formal feature of universalizability (3). The willingness to take others into account (2), that is, the willingness to be just, is a psychological trait or feature of the moral life, and it too is enjoined by all moral systems. This brings us to the crux of taking the moral point of view, (1): being benevolent or *taking others into account in one's actions because one respects them as persons*. Notice that (1) can extend beyond non-human forms of life. Thus, since in Jain metaphysics animals too have *jiva* (self), for Jains the normative principle of *ahimsa* applies to animals as well as to humans.

## METAPHYSICS AND ETHICS

As the Jain application of *ahimsa* to all living beings or *jivas* indicates, metaphysics drives ethics. One's conception of the self and of the good and whether and how one conceives of an afterlife and of a Transcendent frames, structures, and delimits one's ethics. Religious answers to these sorts of metaphysical issues result in different directions within ethics than do secular responses to these issues.

To give another example, Hinduism has the metaphysical notion of *karma* – the character that one develops as a result of one's habitual actions – and has consequently developed a religious deontological (duty-based) ethics around the notion of *karma-yoga*. Eliot Deutsch explicates the devotional *bhakti* Hindu treatment of *karma-yoga* in the *Bhagavad Gita* as a

> redirecting of one's being away from an involvement with the fruit of one's action to an eternal Spirit which is at one in and beyond the phenomenal world. *Yajna* [sacrifice] means the turning away from our lower self (of desires, attachments) for the sake of our higher spiritual self.
>
> ... one must fill one's consciousness with the power of loving devotion. Implicit in the whole teaching scheme of the *Gita* is the belief that there is no other way to establish non-attachment than through a new attachment to that which is greater, in quality and power, than that to which one was previously attached. One overcomes the narrow clinging to results, the passionate involvement with the consequences of one's own action, only when that passion is replaced by one directed to the Divine. *Bhakti* or devotion is thus in no way excluded from *karma yoga*, but it, on the contrary, is a necessary condition for it.
>
> ... *Yajna*, as applied to all actions, means then a self-surrender to the Divine, not in simple resignation or quietistic withdrawal, but rather in an active state of *nishkama karma*, action without desire for the fruits.[7]

*Nishkama karma* is moral action out of a sense of duty which is motivated by love of God. Only through devotion to God (*bhakti*) can one successfully align oneself with the *dharma* or underlying order. Paradigmatic of the manner in which the metaphysics of one's worldview drives the ethics of one's worldview, this particular *bhakti* understanding of the *karma-yoga* ideal postulates an inextricable connection between the religious life and the moral life, between devotion to God and right action.

This brings us to the meta-ethical question of the relationship between morality and religion. Are morality and religion necessarily connected? Just as the Hindu *bhakti* deontological ethics of *nishkama karma* in the *Bhagavad Gita* holds that the divine makes true morality possible, the divine command theory of Western monotheism suggests another possible connection between religious metaphysics and ethics. The divine command theory of ethics holds that what is right and wrong, good and bad, is what God actively and intentionally commands. Here, not just devotion to God in Godself but a conscious obedience to God's commands leads to right action.

In assessing this latter view, William Frankena argues that

> when one accepts a definition of any term that can be called ethical, one has already in effect accepted an ethical standard. For example, when one agrees to take "right" to mean "commanded by God," and at the same time to use it as a key term in one's speech, thought, and action, this is tantamount to accepting the moral principle "We ought to do what God commands" as a guide in life.
>
> ... when a theological definition is offered us, we may always ask why we should adopt this definition, and to answer us the theologian in question must provide us with a justification of the corresponding moral principle. And the point is that he cannot claim that either it or the definition follows logically from any religious or theological belief (which is not itself a disguised ethical judgment).[8]

To put this point more broadly, once one accepts a religious definition of morality, one has already accepted the correspondent religious form of life. Thus, a religious ethics only works internally to a religious worldview as a justification for moral actions; the implicit religious considerations for morality will not be convicting to those not already committed to the religious life in question. The divine command theory works only internally to Western monotheistic worldviews. Likewise, the *bhakti* view of *nishkama karma* works only internally to *bhakti* Hinduism, for unless one is already committed to a *bhakti* religious metaphysics, one will not accept the notion that only devotion to God makes following one's moral duty fully possible. Each religious ethics offers specifically religious explications of and religious exhortations to morality which will not convince those outside the religious worldview of the suggested connection between morality and religion.

## ETHICAL COMMONALITY AMONG THE WORLD RELIGIONS

If religious considerations will not convince the unreligious, are there universal religious considerations that all sincerely religious people – at least in the world religions – could accept? On this score, although "the devil is in the details," the ethics of the world religions do in fact have a great deal in common despite their differences. In the first place, the world religions have a largely shared morality: murder, lying, stealing, sexual impropriety, and so on are universally prohibited. Moreover, important general ethical principles are shared among the world religions.

In the *Analects*, Confucius says, "Do not impose on others what you yourself do not desire."[9] The monumental classic Hindu epic the *Mahabharata* expresses a similar idea:

> One should never do that to another which one regards as injurious to one's own self. This, in brief, is the rule of dharma. Yielding to desire and acting differently, one becomes guilty of adharma.[10]

A close parallel is found in the best-known collection of Buddhist aphorisms:

> He who for the sake of happiness hurts others who also want happiness, shall not hereafter find happiness.
> He who for the sake of happiness does not hurt others who also want happiness, shall hereafter find happiness.[11]

In the West, Jesus says in the Gospel of Mark (13:33) that one should "Love your neighbor as yourself." And the *hadith* records Muhammad as saying, "No man is a true believer unless he desires for his brother that which he desires for himself."

Now, even though the Christian notion of love[12] is not identical to the Confucian emphasis on *ren* (human-heartedness), say, or the Buddhist focus on compassion, what the world religions do share is the rejection of self-aggrandizing behavior and the promotion of other-regarding behavior, even if they ground this religious point of view in divergent metaphysics. This both aligns the world religions with each other and serves as a ground for mutuality with secular ethics. Obviously it is not the features of their normative ethics which are based on religious metaphysics which the world religions can share with secular ethics. Rather it is the essential orientation of the world religions toward the moral life and their insistence on the importance of promoting the moral point of view which they share with secular ethical perspectives. As Keith Ward puts it, the "religions ally themselves with those who seek to decrease egoism, and in that way they support the most basic moral motivation, the pursuit of what is right, whether or not it is conducive to one's own good in this world."[13]

## THE ETHICAL DANGER OF RELIGIOUS EGOISM

The shared religious ideal that potentially provides a basis for a universal ethic is to be other regarding. But of course the institutions of religion not only can be but too often are twisted into just another vehicle for promotion of self, becoming the enemy of secular as well as religious ethics. There is all the difference between rightness or righteousness, on the one hand, and the self-righteousness of what I shall call "religious egoism" on the other. Just as ethical egoism is self-interest cloaked in the appearance of morality, religious egoism is self-interest masquerading as religious idealism. Religious egoism stems from the *hubris* of thinking that only one's own worldview has ideological purity, and from the common human failing of thinking that moral purity flows from one's ideological purity.

A salient example of the sort of ethical disaster that can be wrought by religious egoism can be found in the quasi-religious foundations of apartheid in South Africa. After their break with the original Cape Colony and the Great Trek, Dutch-speaking people in South Africa formed a new colony in which their society was

> not a complete society. It was the dominant part of a society that included servants of African, Asian, and mixed descent. Those they assumed to be of a separate species. Indeed, they often referred to them as *skepsels* (creatures) rather than *mense* (people). That was what custom prescribed, self-interest demanded, and (for those who were religious) what God ordained. That was how it had always been and always must be in South Africa.[14]

Here, benevolence and justice are supplanted by self-interest and racism, and the test of universalizability is not met – unless of course one subscribes to apartheid. For the metaphysics that drove this "ethics" held that humans were created unequally. Combined with the institutions of religion, this became religious racism. Slavery had just been abolished by the British, and the memoirs of Anna Steenkamp, the niece of Piet Retief, one of the key leaders of the Great Trek, show that the intent of the new society was to avoid the appearance of slavery while keeping the fact of a slavery founded in the twisted logic of religious racism. Referring to the emancipation of the slaves, she wrote

> It is not so much their freedom that drove us to such lengths, as their being placed on an equal footing with Christians, contrary to the laws

of God and the natural distinction of race and religion, so that it was intolerable for any decent Christian to bow down beneath such a yoke; wherefore we rather withdrew in order thus to preserve our doctrines in purity.[15]

This racist religious outlook reached its despicable apogee when it was subsequently conjoined with the idea in the Hebrew Bible of God's "chosen people." At the end of the nineteenth century, S.J. du Toit, a Dutch Reformed minister, created an ethnic mythology for Afrikaners through a newspaper, *Die Afrikaanse Patriot*, and in his book *Die geskiendenis van ons land in die taal van ons volk* (The history of our country in the language of our people). On du Toit's view, Afrikaners "were a distinct people, occupying a distinct fatherland and endowed by God with the destiny to rule South Africa and civilize its heathen inhabitants."[16] And by the 1940s this quasi-religious idea of God's chosen people had reached a logical conclusion in the idea that the different races had different spiritual bases as well as different biological bases. Thus, G. Eloff described distinct white, black, and yellow races in his book *Rasse en Rasvermenging* (Races and race mixing) and concluded that

> The preservation of the pure race tradition of the *Boerevolk* must be protected at all costs in all possible ways as a holy pledge entrusted to us by our ancestors as part of God's plan with our People. Any movement, school, or individual who sins against this must be dealt with as a racial criminal by the effective authorities.[17]

However, the very religious ideals that were corrupted by the religious egoism and racism that served as underlying causes of apartheid can also be a powerful force on the side of morality. As we know, the Christian churches of South Africa came to oppose apartheid:

> Soon after the election of 1948, leaders of all the white South African churches except the Dutch Reformed churches issued statements criticizing apartheid. In following years, many clergy came into conflict with the government. In 1968, the South African Council of Churches labeled apartheid a pseudo-gospel in conflict with Christian principles.[18]

Importantly, a great deal of the opposition to apartheid was secular. But when the secular opponents of apartheid like Nelson Mandela were imprisoned or exiled, often it was the clergy, such as Desmond Tutu, Anglican archbishop of Cape Town; Allan Boesak, moderator of the Dutch Reformed Mission church and president of the World Alliance of

Reformed Churches; and Beyers Naude, general secretary of the South African Council of Churches, who came to the forefront in the struggle against the evils of apartheid.[19] Moreover, the religious fortitude of these religious leaders enabled them to exert moral leadership in the face of the resistance of powerful secular leaders like the British prime minister, Margaret Thatcher, and the American president, Ronald Reagan, who naively and grotesquely said in 1985, during apartheid's final period of vicious repression, that South Africa "has eliminated the segregation we once had in our country."[20]

## CAN THERE BE A UNIVERSAL RELIGIOUS POINT OF VIEW?

If the religious dimension of the other-regarding ethics of the world religions is to be efficacious in the global arena of secular ethics, religious ethics needs to have a global outlook, and possibly even needs to be universal. Now, no religious ethics could be universal unless in some sense religion can be universal.

Despite the historically and geographically limited locus of each of the world religions, the adherents of each of the great religious traditions believe that their own religious worldview is correct. Yet until rather recently, the vast majority of the world's population was either Hindu or Buddhist or Confucian or belonged to an African tribal tradition. The first step in the present global pattern of religion with Christianity and Islam as the largest world religions was produced by the rapid spread of Islam under the great Umayyad Dynasty centered in Damascus (until 750 BCE), which extended Islam up the Iberian Peninsula into France, displacing Christian influences, and into central Asia and western India. More recently, the Christian population has surged past the huge Islamic, Hindu, and Buddhist populations, primarily through colonialism with its trinity of "gold, God, and glory." But although colonialism spread Christianity to the Americas in the west, central and southern Africa to the south, and to the Philippines, Australia, and New Zealand in the east, it was largely unable to penetrate the established geographic home of Islam, Hinduism, Buddhism, or Confucianism/Daoism.

Given this geographic and historical pattern of change, the question that confronts religious adherents in our global world is whether only one system of religious truth claims is correct, or whether more than one system can be correct. Religion is a human construct (or institution) that fundamentally involves beliefs at two levels: (I) at one level religion involves the meta-belief that the religious life can effectively orient one away from self aggrandizement and toward the transcendent, and (II) at a level below that it involves specific beliefs – including vital core beliefs – about the nature of the Transcendent and/or the way in which the Transcendent gives meaning to life. The first level of meta-belief (I) is shared by the world religions. The second level of beliefs (II) is the point of conflict of truth claims among the world religions.

Four possible religious responses to the problem of conflicting religious truth claims are the following:

1. *Exclusivism.* Only one world religion is correct (one's own), and all others are mistaken.
2. *Pluralism.* Ultimately all world religions are correct, each offering a different path and partial perspective *vis-à-vis* the one Ultimate Reality.
3. *Inclusivism.* Only one world religion is fully correct, but other world religions participate in or partially reveal some of the truth of the one correct religion.
4. *Henofideism.* One has a faith commitment that one's own world religion is correct, while acknowledging that other world religions may be correct.

It is largely a matter of history and geography whether one grows up as a Hindu or Buddhist or Christian or Muslim, etc. Even the extent to which one understands the parameters of one's *own* tradition is largely determined by family circumstances. Consequently, religious exclusivism makes a religious elite of those who have privileged knowledge, or who are intellectually astute, or who are socially fortunate, while penalizing those who either have no access to the putatively correct religious views or who are incapable of advanced understanding. Exclusivism would seem to underestimate the degree to which all religious truth-claims are human constructs, subject to the limitations and fallibility of the human mind.

A very different and powerfully pluralistic view is religious pluralism. John Hick offers a concise description of pluralism as the view that "There is not merely one way but a plurality of ways of salvation or liberation ... taking place in different ways within the contexts of all the great religious traditions."[21] John Hick's own religious pluralism holds that there is only one Ultimate Reality, but the world religions offer different enculturated "images" of that one Ultimate Reality.[22]

A difficulty faced by Hick's position is this. The idea of a *personal* God is a vital core belief of Jewish, Christian, Muslim, Zoroastrian, Hindu *bhakti*, Sikh, Baha'i, and, in a certain way, even Pure Land Buddhist worldviews. Atheistic Hindu Advaita Vedantists, Confucians, Daoists, and Theravada and Zen Buddhists hold an opposing vital core belief that the Transcendent is not personal. Hick attempts to account for this by suggesting that among the world's religions the "Ultimately Real" is only experienced as *either* personal or non-personal. Yet this contradicts the understanding of the first group of religious traditions that a personal God *correctly* reveals, indeed is the proper form of, the immanence of the Transcendent. Although a personal reality might have non-personal aspects, it could not be identical to something that is non-personal. Hence, Hick's pluralist account would entail that the monotheist's and henotheist's experiences of a personal divine reality ultimately fail to correctly represent the Transcendent.

Another alternative to exclusivism is inclusivism, which has become the official view within Roman Catholicism since Vatican II.[23] It might be argued, however, that of all the world religions, Hinduism is the most inherently inclusivist. Fundamentally, inclusivism supposes that a specific sort of religious experience and understanding of the Transcendent is elemental to all religion (indeed, is elemental for all humans). However, even in the broadest terms, the notion of an elemental apprehension of the Transcendent is understood in *personal* terms in monotheistic and henotheistic traditions, whereas it is *non-personal* in Confucian, Advaita Vedanta Hindu, and Theravada and Zen Buddhist traditions. Moreover, each world religion has a different idea of this elemental apprehension, and tends to see *itself* as the culmination of the elemental apprehension of the Transcendent,[24] as for example when the Roman Catholic theologian Karl Rahner says that the Christian has, "other things being equal, a still greater chance of salvation than someone who is merely an anonymous Christian."[25]

A fourth alternative is to embrace a stronger form of religious tolerance and acceptance by according level II doctrines that adherents of different world religions devoutly profess and follow the claimed status of being *essential* to the adherents' religious life, while still retaining the specific level II claims of one's own religious life. I shall call this view "henofideism," from the Greek *heno* (one) and the Latin *fide* (faith).[26] A henofideist is one who both has fidelity to a single religious worldview and, aware of other cultures and their religious perspectives, acknowledges that other religious worldviews might be correct. A henofideist might be a henotheist, but a henofideist might just as well be a monotheist. "Monotheism" and "henotheism" refer to one's religious metaphysics. "Henofideism" refers to one's faith commitment. The parallel expressed in a Hindu context might be between *ishtadevata* ("the god of one's choice") and *ishtavishvas* ("one's chosen faith"). The henofideist is an *ishtavishvasi* (or one inspired by a chosen faith), and may or may not hold to the *ishtadevata* of henotheism.

Of the four alternative ways to respond religiously to the conflicting truth-claims of the world religions, religious exclusivism would be actively opposed to attempts to achieve a concurrence among diverse religious ethics. Inclusivism, pluralism, and henofideism are more conducive to the possibility of a universal religious ethic. Henofideism would be the most conducive of these three views, though many religious adherents may view henofideism as an unacceptable attenuation of their faith. But in any case, once one has moved beyond exclusivism, agreement about the status of the vital core beliefs of each tradition is not as important as a shared religious point of view. And I would suggest that there is indeed a religious point of view, which serves as the point of commonality and the manifestation of universality in religion, even though the adherents of the world religions have quite different specific religious worldviews.

Since religion supervenes on morality, the religious point of view supervenes on the moral point of view. In *Relationship Morality* James Kellenberger explains the moral point of view by arguing that "the ultimate grounding of obligation, and finally of all morality, is a single but universal relationship between each and all," suggesting that it is a realization of this "person/person relationship" to others which creates "a sense of duty grounded in a recognition of the intrinsic worth of persons."[27] To be genuinely religious is to realize the person–person relationship Kellenberger identifies, but with the added or supervening dimension of the realization of a single universal relationship both among all persons as spirits and with the Transcendent. I call this universal religious relationship a "spirit–spirit" relationship.

Although this universal religious relationship will be particularized in different ways for different people, in general to take the religious point of view is to direct one's life through prayer and meditation, text and ritual toward a felt Transcendent – whether Allah or Krishna or Akal Purakh or the Dao or the Dharmakaya or God – and by so doing to treat other persons as spiritual beings. By this I mean that one treats others as having the same spiritual value as oneself, as being on the same spiritual quest as oneself and with the same potential for salvation or liberation. This is precisely what the quasi-religious foundation of apartheid lacked with its racial hierarchy of the spiritually inferior and the spiritually superior. To the extent that a religious worldview, and so the religious ethic of that worldview, incorporates the religious point of view, it will be open to the prospect of a global religious ethic.

## THE PLACE OF RELIGION IN A GLOBAL ETHIC

The religious point of view together with a non-exclusivist view of conflicting religious truth claims and an *anekantavada*-like flexibility would provide three key elements for a universal religious ethic. But even if there could be a global religious ethic, how would such an ethic figure in a global ethic that was neither religious, *per se*, nor anti-religious? This is an important question because, apart from the collective points of view of the world religions, any purely secular attempts at a universal ethics, such as the 1948 U.N. Declaration on Human Rights, will ultimately be hollow reeds, easily broken by the internationally corrosive forces of self-interest: military imperialism, cultural imperialism, colonialism, tribalism, gender oppression, and racism and its evil twin of ethnic purity. Against these divisive forces, the religious point of view and a genuine religious ethics celebrate the unique personhood of each and the spirituality of all.

To see the means by which a religious ethics could be incorporated into a global ethics, consider the structure of any social ethic. Everyone in a society does not follow the ethic of the society in the same way. Moreover the structures of a social ethic can be structures of good or structures of evil, and often involve both. So we might say that a particular Buddhist society has an ethic and that the Nazi state had an ethic. The former would primarily involve structures of good and the latter more predominantly structures of evil. Yet any religious society will have some structures of evil (such as xenophobia and authoritarianism) just as a secular totalitarian state will have some structures of good (such as loyalty and truthtelling).

Now, the members of a community with a social ethic can be divided into six different non-exclusive categories in terms of their adherence to that ethic:

1. the theoreticians
2. the administrators
3. the devout
4. the acquiescent
5. the apathetic
6. the opposition.

Theoreticians are those who actually develop and extend the ethical reasoning for the society. Theoreticians are usually devout *vis-à-vis* the social ethic, and in a religious society these would be the philosophers and theologians of the tradition. The administrators are those who are charged with special authority to carry out the ethical norms of a society. In a religious society these are the religious leaders but may include secular leaders as well. The administrators are often devout, but probably less often devout than theoreticians. Then there are the devout, the majority or the empowered minority, who are fully committed to the social ethic.

However, although many people will follow the ethic of the society, they are not necessarily devout. These are the acquiescent. The acquiescent are often people who are loyal to the social ethic, but their loyalty stems from considerations of prudence, not morality. Another category of those who are not opposed to the social ethic are the apathetic. This is the group of people in a society who neither resist the accepted ethic nor support it, finding it irrelevant to their daily lives. Finally there is the opposition, those directly opposed on moral or prudential grounds to the reigning ethic of the society. Within a religious ethic the opposition can include the most significant religious figures. In this regard Jesus was part of the opposition within the context of the dominant pharisaic ethos of first-century Judaism, and Shakyamuni Buddha was part of the opposition in the Brahmanical Hinduism of his day; Mahatma Gandhi was part of the opposition to traditional uses of force to defend religious ideals, and Martin Luther King, Jr. was part of the opposition to the complacent racism of twentieth-century Christian America.

Now let us apply this to the secular U.N. Declaration on Human Rights, which sets out a potential social ethic. The leadership in various bodies within the U.N. constitute the administrators of this ethic. The theoreticians are in some cases influenced by religious traditions, but this is not an overt part of their role. And of course there are the devout. But setting aside the opposed, many are at best acquiescent, if not apathetic. This is in part because the majority of humanity is religious, and it is, at best, a difficult task to convince a primarily religious global population that secular theoreticians are comparable to religious theoreticians. Thus, the devout with respect to any such human rights declaration are limited and the opposition is expanded against the secular foundation of U.N. proposals, an opposition based not on the moral quality of the proposals but on the final authority of the proposals.

To reduce this opposition and increase the numbers of devout, any universal ethic like the U.N. Declaration must take account of religious commitments and religious theoreticians.[28] This would not entail a subservience of secular to religious theory but rather the participation of religious theory in the construction of a social ethic that takes account of both the secular and the religious. The trick is to expand the ethically devout to include both those with a religious and those with a secular metaphysics. Hopefully the secular and the religious will be partners in this enterprise: the secular can provide a constructive voice against the dangers of religious egoism and the religious can add a powerful voice to the call to other-regarding action which lies at the heart of both the religious life and the moral life.

## NOTES

1. This section and the next section are drawn from chapter 11 of my *Global Philosophy of Religion* (Oxford: Oneworld, 2001).
2. See Christopher Key Chapple, *Nonviolence to Animals, Earth, and Self in Asian Traditions* (New York: State University of New York Press, 1993), p. 44.
3. See C. Ram-Prasad's essay "Multiplism: A Jaina Ethics of Toleration for a Complex World," which appears in the last part of this book.
4. Mencius, *The Book of Mencius,* Part 2a:6, in *A Source Book in Chinese Philosophy,* ed. and trans. Wing-Tsit Chan (Princeton, Princeton University Press, 1963), p. 65.
5. Mo Tzu, *Mozi,* in *Basic Writing of Mo Tzu,* Hsun Tzu, and Han Fei Tzu, ed. and trans. Burton Watson (New York: Columbia University Press, 1967), reprinted in *A Sourcebook in Asian Philosophy,* ed. John M. and Patricia Koller (New Jersey: Prentice Hall, 1991).

6. Cf. Joseph Runzo, "Ethics and the Challenge of Theological Non-Realism," in *Ethics, Religion, and the Good Society*, ed. Runzo (Louisville: Westminster/ John Knox, 1992), p. 90, n. 45.
7. Eliot Deutsch, trans. and ed., *The Bhagavad Gita* (New York: University Press of America, 1968), pp. 162–164.
8. William K. Frankena, "Is Morality Logically Dependent on Religion?" in Gene Outka and John P. Reeder, ed., *Religion and Morality* (Garden City, NY: Anchor/Doubleday, 1973), pp. 303–304.
9. Confucius, *The Analects* (London: Penguin, 1979), p. 135.
10. Chapple, *Nonviolence to Animals, Earth, and Self in Asian Traditions*, p. 16.
11. Juan Mascaro, trans., *The Dhammapada* (London: Penguin, 1973), p. 54.
12. Julius Lipner argues for strong parallels between Hindu *bhakti* and Christian notions of love in "The God of Love and the Love of God in Christian and Hindu Traditions," in *Love, Sex and Gender in the World Religions*, ed. Joseph Runzo and Nancy M. Martin (Oxford: Oneworld, 2000), pp. 51–88.
13. Keith Ward, "Religion and the Possibility of a Global Ethic," in this volume.
14. Leonard Thompson, *A History of South Africa* (New Haven and London: Yale University Press, 1995), p. 92. Thompson's sources here are A.J. du Plessis, "Die Republiek Natalia," in *Archives Year Book for South African History* (1942), vol. 1, and Eric A. Walker, *Great Trek*, 2nd edn (London: A.C. Black, 1938), pp. 206–233.
15. John Bird, *The Annals of Natal: 1495 to 1845* (Pietermaritzburg, 1888), vol. 1, p. 459.
16. Thompson, *A History of South Africa*, p. 135.
17. G. Eloff, *Rasse en Rasvermenging* (Bloemfontein, 1941), p. 104 in Thompson, *A History of South Africa*, p. 184.
18. John de Gruchy, *The Church Struggle in South Africa* (Grand Rapids: Eerdmans, 1979) in Thompson, *A History of South Africa*, p. 204.
19. *The Times*, 1 July 1988. See also F. Chikane, *The Church's Prophetic Witness against the Apartheid System in South Africa* (Johannesburg: South African Council of Churches, 1988); de Gruchy, *The Church Struggle in South Africa*; and C. Villa-Vicenicio, ed., *Theology and Violence: The South African Debate* (Johannesburg, 1987). Thompson, *A History of South Africa*, p. 239.
20. Thompson, *A History of South Africa*, p. 234.
21. John Hick, *Problems of Religious Pluralism* (New York: St Martin's Press, 1985), p. 34.
22. John Hick, *God Has Many Names* (Philadelphia: Westminster Press, 1982), p. 96. For a detailed defense of religious pluralism, see Hick's *An Interpretation of Religion* (London: Macmillan, 1989).
23. See the dogmatic constitution *Nostra Aetate* from Vatican II.

24. Frank Whaling, *Christian Theology and World Religions: A Global Approach* (Basingstoke: Marshall Pickering, 1986), p. 87. "Other religions can have their own fulfillment theology. Sri Aurobindo sees the world religious process converging on Mother India rather than the Cosmic Christ, and Sir Muhammad Iqbal sees it converging upon a kind of ideal Islam."
25. Karl Rahner, *Theological Investigations*, vol. 5 (London: Darton, Longman & Todd), p. 132.
26. For a more detailed exposition, see chapter 2 of Joseph Runzo, *Global Philosophy of Religion* (Oxford: Oneworld, 2001).
27. James Kellenberger, *Relationship Morality* (University Park, PA: Pennsylvania State University Press, 1995), pp. 42, 53.
28. For an attempt to frame a religious Declaration of Human Rights, see Arvind Sharma, "Universal Declaration of Human Rights by the World's Religions," *Religious Ethics*, 27, 1999, pp. 539–549.

*Plate 2* A pledge for action endorsed by religious leaders at the 1999 Parliament of the World Religions in Cape Town to combat the scourge of HIV/AIDS. The international symbol for solidarity with the victims of HIV/AIDS is on the front of the podium. Photo: *Nancy M. Martin*

# 2

# RELIGION AND THE POSSIBILITY
# *of* A GLOBAL ETHICS

*Keith Ward*

Is there such a thing as a global ethics, a universal system of ethics or a set of moral principles which all humans could agree to live by? For many years, especially at the beginning of the twentieth century, some anthropologists argued that human moral systems were so diverse that there was no point in speaking of any universally accepted moral principles. Inuit were alleged to eat their grandparents, South Sea Islanders to have sex with anybody, and National Socialists to think that genocide was morally right. In such a world, searching for moral agreements on even the most basic issues seemed a hopeless quest. In less spectacular ways, there seems no way of resolving moral disagreements on such matters as capital punishment, abortion, and the treatment of animals. Human moral views were said just to be fundamentally diverse. There is no point in seeking anything like a global ethics.

On the other hand, it is clear that human beings all have certain things in common. They all have forty-six chromosomes. They all belong to a species that is, on earth, uniquely capable of abstract intellectual thought and responsible moral action. They all have basic biological needs like eating, reproducing, and obtaining shelter from the elements. Is there not a possibility that some moral principles, however general and vague, may be based on these common qualities, and thus be universal among humans?

## MORAL PRINCIPLES AND BASIC HUMAN NEEDS

Such a thought underlies an approach to ethics which has been well established in Christian tradition for centuries, an approach that seeks to found basic moral principles on the basic needs and inclinations of human beings. Humans may claim to have many different needs and inclinations, but a basic need is one that is necessary to surviving as a human being, and to obtaining any of the diverse things that humans might desire. In some countries owning a television set might be classified as a need, but it is clearly not necessary to surviving as a human being. Although it might be necessary to obtaining many specific desires, like watching quiz programs, it is not necessary as a condition of obtaining the satisfaction of human desires in general, of obtaining anything at all that humans might find desirable.

An example of a basic need is the need for food and drink. If these are not forthcoming, humans cannot survive, and in that sense food and drink are necessary to obtaining anything at all that humans might call desirable. As basic needs, food and drink are basically desirable. All humans (indeed, all animals) have good reason to desire them. Something that all humans have good reason to desire is a basic good, on the simple supposition that what is desirable is as such good, as long as it carries no overwhelming harm in its train. Thus in a very simple way one can see that there is at least one basic and universal human good, the good of having food and drink. Whatever the Inuit or the Trobriand Islanders are alleged to do, they have in common the belief that nourishment is a basic human good. It is good, not just for me or my family, but for all humans.

That may not seem like very much, but it does mean that every thinking person really knows that the provision of food to the hungry is a basic human good, and that withholding food when it could be provided and when it is needed is a basic evil. We do know some simple truths about good and evil, without any need of revelation and without being inclined at all to think that it is just a matter of personal preference. There are at least some universal moral truths.

The provision of food is a basic good for all animals, not just for humans. It is also very largely an instrumental good. Eating and drinking are not primarily good for their own sake, but because they are necessary to health and to survival. They in turn are necessary conditions of doing anything that one believes to be worthwhile. Of course, they may also produce pleasure, and one may well think that the pursuit of pleasure and the avoidance of pain are not only instrumental but intrinsic goods. They can be considered worthwhile objects of the pursuit of a rational being simply in themselves.

## THE PRINCIPLE OF BENEVOLENCE

Bentham and Mill were surely right in thinking that every rational sentient being has a good reason to wish to avoid pain and to experience pleasure. When this personal desire is generalized by the application of the simple logical rule that what is a good reason for one sentient being is, other things being equal, a good reason for any being of the same general sort, one obtains the moral rule that it is bad to cause pain to any sentient being – or, in the positive version, that it is good to sustain or increase the pleasure of any sentient being. Thus, from these simple considerations, one obtains a basic and universal moral principle which could be called the principle of "benevolence" or "compassion." It is morally good to decrease the pain of all beings and to increase their pleasure.

Of course, there are many different ways of understanding what pleasure is. Someone who thinks that eating, drinking, and sensual pleasures are the greatest pleasures thinks very differently from someone who thinks that the love of music or the worship of God is the greatest pleasure. John Stuart Mill, in particular, agonized about this problem of distinguishing different sorts of pleasure. It does not seem unreasonable to say that all pleasure is, as such, good. But many sorts of pleasure may carry with them other consequences that are evil – as the pleasure of sex with another person's partner will be far outweighed by the harm done to the personal relationships involved. Pleasures may be outweighed by other goods, and many pleasures are quite low-level goods. In saying that pleasure is a good, one is not committed to saying that it is the only good, or that all pleasures are alike.

Yet one must not overlook the fact that some of the very highest goods of religion, like the attainment of human liberation or the beatific vision of God, involve supreme pleasure. *Nirvana* is spoken of as a state of bliss, and the beatific vision is obviously one of supreme happiness. Some may think that "pleasure" is a very inadequate term for such states, and so it is. Yet they lie on the same continuum as the pleasures of eating and drinking, even if at the opposite end of it. Some religious views recommend self-denial and the setting aside of sensual pleasure. But that is for the sake of a deeper and longer-lasting happiness, untainted with suffering, if not for oneself then for other beings. The most self-denying Christians consider it right to work for the happiness of others, and the most selfless Buddhists work for the liberation of all beings from suffering. It is true, then, that there are a number of different conceptions of what true pleasure is, ranging from the view that anything goes ("pushpin is as good as poetry," as Jeremy Bentham said) to the view that only a life free of sensual desire can achieve freedom from suffering and supreme bliss (as the Buddha taught). In this respect, as in others, religious views typically recommend the subordination of sensual pleasures to intellectual and spiritual goods. They recommend the subordination of personal pleasure to the good of others. All those goods, however, involve pleasure, and it would be absurd to say that it is not good to take pleasure in loving God or in attaining final freedom from suffering.

So although one can arrive at the principle of benevolence simply by reflection on basic human desires and the respects in which human beings resemble one another, there are different views of what exactly benevolence implies, and religious faiths give distinctive interpretations of benevolence. I will consider only two main traditions of religious thought, rather broadly conceived as the Indian and the Semitic. Indian traditions, at least in their non-theistic forms, often tend to concentrate on the fact that existence inevitably involves suffering, from which liberation is to be sought as the main spiritual goal. They tend to see happiness in an overcoming of the distinctive sort of individuality a person possesses in this lifetime, aiming at the overcoming of a sense of distinct individual personality. For instance, the Jain principle of *ahimsa* enjoins that no harm must be done to any sentient being. The goal of liberation is the attainment of pure consciousness, free of all trappings of this-worldly identity. There is an extreme of renunciation among Jain saints, and it may seem that sensual pleasure is completely denied. Nevertheless, lay people and householders are usually counseled to enjoy life without attachment, and to take pleasure in simple things, acknowledging their transience. Even the Jain saint will seek to attain supreme pleasure in being free from desires and in possessing unlimited knowledge.

In the Semitic traditions happiness is usually found in some sort of conscious relationship to God, and it is usually seen as a fulfillment of the individual personality. Judaism and Islam have divinely revealed laws that outline the will of God and which cannot be overturned. Pleasure is certainly not denied, and paradise is seen as a place of enduring pleasure. But it must conform to divine law. In these traditions and in Christianity, as well as in Indian theistic traditions, however, there exists a more personalist view which would see all earthly pleasures as good, as long as they can be set in the context of a loving relationship with God. So the rule of benevolence is interpreted primarily as doing good to other human beings. It is not considered wrong to seek pleasure for oneself. Indeed, one rabbinic saying states that all humans will be judged on the good things they might have enjoyed, but did not. One should certainly cause minimal harm, and seek the happiness of others and oneself. This happiness will come primarily from loving and obeying God, so it springs from a certain sort of personal relationship. One cares for created things because God creates them, and they are to be treated as God commands. Happiness lies in accepting the relationship of love that God offers to created persons, not in some state of liberation from all earthly desires.

That seems very different from the Jain view. Both the extent of compassion for other beings and the nature of the goal that brings true happiness differ. Nevertheless, no observant theist would deny that one should have compassion for God's creatures wherever they suffer, and no pious Jain would deny that the worship of a divine being involves the renunciation of purely selfish desires and an insistence that the sensual must be always ordered to higher spiritual goods of worship and love. No religious view permits the pursuit of personal or sensual pleasure where it is not subordinated to the pursuit of a supreme spiritual good for its own sake. Jains and Buddhists think that the nature of the supreme good (the liberation of the soul from the material realm) rules out sensual pleasure and requires the avoidance of all harm to living beings. Jews, Muslims, and Christians think that the nature of the supreme good (knowing and loving God fully) allows or even enjoins the enjoyment of many sensual pleasures, though it subordinates them to more distinctively human pleasures. And they think that benevolence is more a matter of helping other persons to enjoy life than of avoiding any harm whatsoever. The differences in ethical assessment are due to differences in the conception of the supreme good and the conditions of its attainability by human beings. The basic moral principle is the same, for them and for non-religious views too. But how it is interpreted depends upon whether one believes there is one supreme good, what its nature is, and how humans can attain it.

## THE PRINCIPLE OF LIBERTY

Religious faiths are most unlikely to think that pleasure is the only or even the main goal of human activity. The mixture of so many pleasures with so many evils and the nature of the human condition, in which pleasure is only one factor in human endeavor and self-knowledge, make pleasure a very improbable candidate to be a supreme human good, even though without pleasure there would perhaps be no supreme human good. It is partly for that reason that religious believers feel wary of the utilitarian philosophy of seeking the greatest happiness of the greatest number. The greatest number, believers are likely to say, do not fully realize what true happiness is or how to attain it. And there are more distinctively human goods that are more important, and which are required to make human striving after greater self-understanding and self-control intelligible.

What are these distinctively human goods? They are again to be found in a consideration of what any rational sentient being has good reason to desire, if they desire anything at all. Humans are distinguished from the vast majority of other animals by possessing the ability to think conceptually and intelligently, to understand truth and to appreciate beauty, and also by having the capacity to act responsibly and freely. These two capacities, of rational thought and responsible freedom, are distinctive to humans, on this planet at least. They have a good claim to be the essential capacities that constitute a truly personal life, and in human beings the exercise of these capacities becomes a condition of achieving most of the things that humans might want. If a person wants anything, it is good, and often necessary, that they should have knowledge and understanding of what it is and of how to get it. And it is necessary that they should be free to get it, without being prevented by conditions beyond their control. Two basic moral principles follow from these facts, and I will consider each in turn.

The first is based on the fact that every rational responsible agent has a good reason to wish to avoid restriction and constraint, and to extend the range of free action as much as possible. By the principle of generalization, it can be seen that it is bad to constrict the freedom of any responsible agent, or, more positively, it is good to preserve or extend the range of free actions of any responsible agent. This gives rise to a principle that could be called the principle of liberty, the principle that it is wrong to infringe the freedom of others without good reason, and that it is right to extend the freedom of others as long as all have roughly equal possibilities of freedom of action.

The formulation of this principle already contains the possibility of a tension between alternative interpretations. Some would stress the negative interpretation of not interfering with the freedom of others, even to bring about greater equality. Others would stress that freedom should be extended only by not allowing vast inequalities which will inevitably limit the freedom of some in comparison to that of others. So commitment to the moral principle of liberty is not going to prevent moral disagreements about whether adherence to the principle of liberty lies in the preservation of absolute personal freedom or in the provision of more or less equal freedom for all. Commitment to a basic moral principle does not bring reflective thinking to a stop. It provides the firm basis from which reflective thinking can begin. So to say that liberty is a basic moral principle is not to say that all will agree on what liberty is. It is to say, however, that freedom is a good for each and every responsible agent and that the moral good lies in seeking the best way to ensure that this good is preserved and extended. Any view that entails that one need not care about the freedom of all, or that one should impede freedom even when it is not harming others, is ruled out.

Religious traditions are concerned about freedom, even though they may sometimes seem to be indifferent to considerations of political freedom and they often oppose unrestricted liberty. Even a human in a prison cell, it may be said, can be spiritually free, and one main monastic virtue in Christianity is obedience, which is a voluntary restriction of freedom. So it may seem at first as though freedom is not a major religious virtue. On closer inspection, however, it is clear that believers are very concerned about "true" freedom. In the Indian traditions, the concern is with freedom from attachment, and most of those traditions describe the liberated state as one in which there is complete freedom and power over all the states of one's own being. In the Semitic traditions, one seeks freedom from sin, and God is of course a being of supreme power and creative freedom, with whom one seeks relationship. There is a supreme state of freedom which the believer can hope to achieve, and which is rather different in kind from the sorts of freedom most people may desire. Once again the consideration of typical Jain and Semitic views of the matter may give a good idea of the range of interpretations that can be taken.

For a Jain, true freedom lies in not being bound to matter and the suffering that matter entails. Each liberated soul is free in being self-determining, content in its own state of supreme knowledge, in need of nothing and desiring nothing. This idea has something in common with the secular notion that freedom consists in being able to do whatever one wants. The liberated soul wants nothing, for it sees the vanity of all sensual desires. So Jains have little interest in extending the sort of freedom that will result in bondage to desire. Such a renouncing tradition in its full severity is for the few. Most householders will have an interest in the freedom to practice their faith, and thus in the construction of a society in which freedom of conscience is secured. There is a social dimension to freedom even in the most extreme renouncing traditions, for renouncers cannot exist without householders to support their practice. Nevertheless in general the ideal of freedom is determined by the ideal of the supreme good as one of freedom from suffering.

For a theist in the Semitic tradition, by contrast, true freedom lies in the ability to enjoy the good things of life without being oppressed and enslaved. Freedom has a political or social dimension, and to be free is to be creative in making and enjoying the many good and beautiful things God gives. Some would stress the primacy of divine law, which lays down the limits of permissible human freedom. But such law typically has many possible interpretations, and it is believed to be given by God for human good. So a law-based religion need not be as inflexible as it sometimes is, and there may well be an inner impetus in such traditions to see the law as a living tradition of divine teaching (which is what "Torah" properly means), rather than as an immutable set of literal rules. Other theists prefer to emphasize the creative freedom of growing into the sort of self-expressive agent that truly mirrors the creative agency of God. In either case, the idea of freedom is again determined by the ideal of the supreme good as God, a being of supreme creative power who creates the universe for the sake of its goodness.

The interpretation of freedom thus presupposes a certain sort of insight into the way the world is, into its deepest possibilities and the proper goal of human beings within it. Yet that insight is itself highly evaluative. Renouncing traditions see the sensory world as filled with suffering. Theistic traditions see it as essentially the product of a good creator. Is such evaluative insight itself a moral matter? One may hesitate to call it moral, on the grounds that morality is concerned with the principles that guide human relationships. But it is not neutrally descriptive and unaffected by the perspective of the perceiver. It is a mixture of what one finds worthwhile and of how one describes the world one experiences. To know what is really worthwhile requires both experience and insight, and such knowledge claims to be of what is objectively the case (whether or not particular individuals think it is the case). It is knowledge that is possessed in differing degrees, and those who are accepted as great religious teachers are said to possess it pre-eminently. The *tirthankaras* of the Jains discern the vanity of sensual desires in their own experience, and see that the true description of the universe involves knowledge of higher realms than the material. The prophets of Judaism see the corruption of the human heart by egoism and discern the existence of God as the real ground of all existence.

There is a sort of knowledge here, not accessible to all, which is closely bound up with an appropriate evaluation of the elements of human experience. Knowledge and evaluation are here bound inextricably together. The sage sees what is truly of intrinsic and supreme worth, which may be known only by few, and the sage sees how that supreme value is instantiated in a realm beyond the material. Perhaps that is the foundational claim of religion, that there is a supreme value, known by few, and that it exists and is realizable or knowable by human beings. It is because it is known by few that such a claim is a matter of revelation or of authoritative teaching. It would seem that it must therefore far transcend any common knowledge of universal moral principles. In the prophetic or enlightened experience, perception of a supreme spiritual reality and insight into what the highest values are go together.

Renouncers, servants of divine law, and personalist theists all accept the basic value of liberty. None will interpret liberty as freedom to pursue any way of life one likes, and in that respect they all stand distinct from many secular views. Such liberty would be, in their view, bondage to desire or to human self-will. True liberty is liberation from such bondage, and on that all are agreed. For the renouncer, true liberty is freedom from all attachment, whereas for the theist, liberty lies in realizing the creative possibilities God has given, in a society in which such possibilities can be fruitfully expanded by co-operative action. These are different ideals of liberty, but for each the idea is supremely instantiated in one supreme case, either the liberated soul or the being of God, and it is the experience of that existent ideal which governs the interpretation of human freedom.

How is this relevant to the question of global ethics? It means that all are agreed that liberty is a basic moral value, and that it is, other things being equal, good to preserve liberty and bad to impede it. This is the "natural" or non-revealed basis of ethics in this respect. Its implementation in particular principles and social codes requires much discussion and reflection, but at least it should be clear what one is trying to implement. For religious believers, there is also a "revealed" aspect of ethics. It gives to concepts such as liberty an interpretation that may be surprising to many, but which follows from the alleged perception of an existent ideal that instantiates liberty in a supreme degree (the liberated soul or the being of God). Even if it is surprising, the religious view does not undermine or contradict the natural basis of morality. It seems clear that a global ethics cannot be based on some religious view, if only because religions are many and diverse and based on different revelatory experiences and traditions. Perhaps in some sense religious beliefs need to be shaped by natural moral perceptions, if they are not to be harmful and destructive. From a moral point of view, for example, religions ought not to impede liberty of conscience by refusing to allow people conscientiously to adopt or leave a particular faith. The fact that such a statement is highly contentious in some parts of the world shows that religions could yet profitably reflect on the natural basis of a global ethic. Yet religious views certainly modify natural moral perceptions in distinctive ways. That modification may turn out to have very important implications for the implementation of a global ethic, which I shall seek to spell out a little later.

## THE PRINCIPLE OF TRUTHFULNESS

For the moment, however, I will turn to the other distinctive human value that grounds a universal moral principle, the value of conceptual thought, reasoning, knowledge, and understanding. There is always good reason to have knowledge of what is possible and of how to make it actual. So at the most instrumental level, knowledge is a universal human good, the lack of which decreases possibilities of free action and enjoyment. Every conscious and intelligent being has good reason to avoid ignorance, misinformation, and deceit and to be able to accumulate knowledge or understanding, which is both useful to the success of one's endeavors in general and also of intrinsic value and interest. By the generalization principle, it is bad to restrict or frustrate the cognitive capacities and achievements of any intelligent agent. Positively, it is good to encourage and extend the knowledge and understanding of any intelligent agent. This might be called the moral principle of truthfulness, ranging from the minimal condemnation of lying to the idealistic injunction to seek complete understanding and appreciation of the world.

Human cognitive capacities include both the ability to formulate and understand general principles in science and philosophy, and the ability to appreciate the intrinsic beauty of works of art. To understand the nature of things and to appreciate the beauty of particulars are values of intrinsic worth which engage the most distinctive conceptual powers of the human mind. Religions are concerned with an understanding of the ultimate nature of things, the truth that underlies all other truths. Theistic faiths often describe God as absolute truth and beauty. The glory of the divine being is its beauty and magnificence, and the ultimate disclosure of the divine being is the truth that sets one free from all illusions and partial perceptions.

Non-theistic religions do not find final truth in the beauty of a personal Lord. But they are concerned with the discovery of the ultimate truth of things – perhaps the truth of conditioned co-origination, as in Buddhism, or of the ultimate unreality of dual consciousness, as in Advaita Vedanta. They often characterize the liberated state as one of omniscience, or of discernment of the real character of being. Truth is thus a fundamental value for religious thought, though typically knowledge of the truth requires great wisdom and is hidden from many.

Religions sometimes ignore the sorts of truth that are discovered in the sciences and the sorts of beauty that are expressed in the arts, finding them irrelevant to the spiritual quest or even distractions in the search for ultimate truth. The war depicted in Plato's *Dialogues* between the philosophers and the poets is legendary, and many religious believers have turned aside from works of art and drama and from the investigation of the natural world. Such attitudes spring from a feeling that the material world is itself a realm of illusion or deceit, which needs to be escaped to find ultimate truth. There is no despising of the value of truth in such views. But there is a belief that spiritual truth is very different from the truths known through sense experience.

There can be no doubt that some religious traditions present within every world faith are in this sense world-denying. They turn aside from engagement with the material world, in all its manifestations, in order to explore a spiritual reality that is above and beyond it, or which is its negation in many ways. It cannot be said that religion as such enjoins such attitudes, however. For most theists, the fact that God has created this world for the sake of its goodness implies that the good things of the material world are to be understood and appreciated as fully as possible. For most religious non-theists, too, insight into the transience of all things does not deprive them of value, but rather intensifies one's experience of the present moment, to be enjoyed without clinging or attachment.

There is a tension, however, between religious attitudes that think of the material world as illusory or corrupted, and secular attitudes that seek truth only in the material world if only because there is nowhere else to find it. This reflects a more general tension between valuing the things of the material world as intrinsically good and finding them to be corrupted to such an extent that one must seek true intrinsic values beyond that world, either in complete renunciation or in obedience to God's will alone.

The variety of religious attitudes means that there is no simple relationship between the basic value of truth and the principles of truth seeking which religions recommend. It is precisely in this area that great disputes between secular and religious attitudes arise, some secularists arguing that truth can be found only by scientific methods of observation and experiment and some believers holding that truth comes only from revelation, which must be obeyed unquestioningly. Both, however, need not try to prevent the others from seeking truth in the way they desire. Recollection that truthseeking is a basic value should remind religious believers that such a search should be respected, whatever form it takes, as long as it does no harm. And for some believers, at least, the search for scientific truth is part of respect for the world that God has created.

What I have attempted so far is to bring out some basic principles that are rooted in human nature and to show how they form the basis for universal or global ethical principles. It is apparent that elucidating such a basis does not eliminate moral disagreement, though it helps to locate the points at which such disagreement arises, and the reasons for which it exists among morally serious people. Religious views take these global principles as fundamental parts of the objective moral ideal that they uphold, but again interpretations of them vary, as revelatory insights into that ideal vary from one tradition to another and as ideas of liberation, of divine law, or of devotional theism predominate.

## THE PRINCIPLE OF JUSTICE

There is one other basic value, implicit in the generalization of benevolence, liberty, and truth, that it is worth making explicit. It is based on the fact that humans are social animals and can realize their potentialities only by co-operation with others in society. So there is always good reason for humans to desire co-operation with others. It is bad to destroy the basis of such co-operation and good to build on it. This may be called the principle of justice, interpreted in a positive way to include the virtues of friendship and family. There are many particular principles of justice, but they all focus on sustaining a society where people shall be encouraged to do co-operative and useful actions and dissuaded from harming social institutions, where all can see that things are ordered fairly and where friendship and family are supported by social sanctions, both positive and negative (rewards and punishments).

Religions are social phenomena, and they usually have authoritative rules of justice by which their societies are ordered. Some religions, notably Judaism and Islam, believe that the revealed laws of justice operate over the whole of society, so that all activities can be ordered according to the love and fear of God. They hold that God is above all a God of justice, who rules justly and commands justice for the good of creatures. So justice is given an objective instantiation to a maximal degree by being associated with the one and only creator God.

Divine laws need to be interpreted and applied, and there exist various traditions of interpretation. At the limit of such interpretations lies the reading of the law in terms of a few basic principles of justice and mercy, such as "love God, and your neighbor as yourself" in Christianity. Here personal relationship largely replaces law, but considerations of justice are not overlooked. In Christianity, divine forgiveness and healing are stressed to an overwhelming extent, but God is still the judge of all the earth and requires just dealing of the human race.

In the Indian traditions the idea of divine law and judgment is not primarily stressed. The constant background to Indian reflection on these matters is the law of *karma*, by which the deeds one does, good and bad, all determine one's future destiny. In Hinduism, this belief has been associated with the caste system, but it can easily be dissociated from that system, as it often is in the renouncing traditions. In any case, laws of caste do not excuse social injustice, since there is a cosmic law of justice, if an impersonal one, which inexorably repays all injustice with suffering. It may seem that monks and nuns do not contribute much to social justice, since they renounce all activity in society. However, there exist many movements of socially engaged Buddhism and Vedanta in the modern world, which maintain that the principles of compassion and selflessness that inform the monastic community should be applied appropriately in the world of householders, who can and should exercise active service of others.

Religious traditions do have a primary concern with justice as a basic value, and they do objectify justice either in the person of a just creator and judge or in the cosmic law of *karma*. Nevertheless, there is often conflict between secular ideas of democratic justice and religious views. This seems most obvious today in conflicts over the imposition of the religious law of *shari'ah*, and in the question of whether either Islam or the Roman Catholic Church can or should ever be truly democratic. What religious traditions object to in the idea of democracy is what Plato called the "rule of the mob," the idea that a simple majority (or even a dominant minority in most democracies) can make moral and social decisions of great importance. Religions may have an authoritative teaching or a revealed law of what makes for true human good, and they may hold that a democratic vote can never have power to countermand it.

The ideas of social equality and the democratic participation of all the people only truly saw the light of day with the French and American Revolutions of the eighteenth century. Before that, social hierarchy was regarded as natural and was usually supported by religious authorities. Religious institutions have not usually been in the forefront of movements to extend democratic participation, even though there have been notable individuals motivated by their faith to espouse causes thought revolutionary in their day, like Lord Wilberforce in the case of slavery, and there have always been radical religious movements in favor of democratic ideas. However, there is a natural tendency in religious groups to form hierarchies protective of the revelatory tradition and to regard spiritual insight as more important than democratic agreement. Religious societies also tend to require obedience and self-negation of their adherents and to limit their lives in various ways for their own ultimate good. It may be thought, then, that religion is not by nature democratic.

This does not mean that religions tend to be unjust. It means that their idea of justice is liable to conflict with an egalitarian and fully democratic idea. It will tend to favor proper order in society, the rule of the wise (or of those committed to safeguarding revelation), and sometimes the suppression of those whose acts or words undermine the faith. It must be appreciated that the revolutionary doctrines of equality and democracy arose in large part as a protest against the perceived oppressiveness of social and religious authorities in Europe, resulting either in the deposition of the old regime or in the establishment of a new country in America. Proper order had become social oppression. The rule of the wise had become the rule of the hereditarily stupid. The suppression of heresy had become the extermination of all dissent. The European Enlightenment was a protest against the corruptions of religiously backed views of justice.

It cannot have gone unnoticed that the Enlightenment has had its corruptions too. The "inalienable right to the pursuit of happiness," in Jefferson's memorable phrase, all too easily becomes a license for unmoderated self-indulgence. Liberty becomes the freedom of the rich to leave the poor in some unnoticed backwater of the world. Critical inquiry turns easily into skepticism about reason itself. And the defense of democracy, as Plato feared, turns into populist appeals to the mob to be able to give them a better time than one's political opponents. There is some point in religious criticisms of secular humanism, even though that humanism was a revolt against religiously sanctioned oppression.

There is not, it is clear, just one vision of justice. There are many, and all are corruptible. The religious visions – which include the ones I have described, of justice as the cosmic law of retribution, of justice as the divinely given commands of God, and of justice as the means to the universal flourishing of created persons – stand in tension with the vision of the secular Enlightenment. Yet this tension is not necessarily opposition. Although religious traditions can deny many secular values, they can also accept them, while subordinating them to religious considerations, or they can even positively affirm them, seeking only to transform their character by relation to ultimate religious values. These three attitudes of denial, subordination, and transformation can and do exist in each of the three religious traditions here outlined.

## THREE RELIGIOUS ATTITUDES TO BASIC HUMAN VALUES

The renouncing tradition may seem most obviously to deny the values of the material world. Yet the religious elite are concerned with the life of the vast majority, who are not monks and nuns but householders with families and social responsibilities. They may attempt to imbue the ordinary social virtues with a temperament of compassion for all beings and non-possessiveness and to encourage social action for justice and benevolence. In a paradoxical way, they may come to embrace the material world as an object of delight, when seen with right mindfulness. Thus what one may think of as the Enlightenment values of the search for individual happiness, of realizing the creative potential of the individual, of free critical inquiry, and of social democracy can find their proper place within the renouncing traditions of religion.

The divine law tradition may seem most likely to subordinate secular social issues to the revealed law, and the rhetoric of the ultra-orthodox in those traditions is sometimes strident in its demand that the law alone must govern society. This attitude is very unrealistic, since the orthodox do not even agree with one another about how the law should be implemented and a vast number of issues in modern government are not covered by the law without a great deal of supplementary interpretation. So, while one can find those who proclaim that only the *shari'ah* or Torah should govern society, it is more usual to find the religious authorities requiring only that secular laws should conform to *shari'ah* where that is a relevant consideration, not that *shari'ah* should actually be the source of all such laws. Moreover, there are strong movements in Islam, for instance, to claim that democracy is implicit in *shari'ah* and that respect for other traditions and for freedom of conscience and inquiry is an integral part of the qur'anic faith. Since the divine law is, after all, given to promote true human well-being, it is quite consistent with a divine law tradition to insist on freedom and democracy, as long as the divine law is not violated. Though exponents of divine law traditions are often insistent that secular foundations for social morality are dangerous and unstable, they may nevertheless appropriate the insights of Enlightenment humanism so as to interpret the divine law in ways that fully respect individual rights to freedom and participation, while appealing to revealed law to guard against the libertarian corruptions of humanism.

Devotional traditions can be rather introverted and self-satisfied, not seeking to deny or subordinate secular concerns but simply being indifferent to them. What, after all, they may ask, has Jerusalem, the holy city, to do with Athens, the capital of humanistic thought? The answer to that question, historically speaking, is that Athens has mediated the faith of Jerusalem to the gentile world and, in the course of doing so, has sanctified that world as a place in which God can be experienced as present and active. So art and music become sacraments of a transcendent presence and value. As God became incarnate in matter, Christians would say, so he made the material a vehicle of the divine. Still, this attitude can be rather restrictive about the sorts of material existence which can properly express the divine. The religious may still seek to control the artistic and scientific spirit, and confine it within bounds that impede free inquiry into beauty and truth. It took the revolutionary impact of the Enlightenment to allow the devotional tradition to break out of its self-imposed limits on propriety and find in the secular worlds of art and science a true celebration of finite forms of goodness which reflect in their own way the creativity and sensitivity of the creator.

What general conclusions might one draw from this discussion? The first would be that there are indeed basic global values and among the most important and obvious are the values of benevolence, liberty, truthfulness, and justice. The second would be that there is not a simple relationship between religious belief and these values. There is a range of religious traditions, and I have discussed three major sorts of attitude which are found to varying degrees within most traditions: renunciation, obedience to divine law, and devotional theism. The third is that even then one cannot simply relate these traditions to the global values in a direct way. All religious traditions have a distinctive interpretation of basic human values, which is determined by some revelatory experience of a reality of supreme value, which sets the goal of spiritual striving. But how that religious vision relates to basic human values depends on many other factors and can range from denial through subordination to mutual transformation. The fourth is that, despite the existence of universal moral principles, moral disagreement seems set to be a permanent feature of the human condition, which no appeal to religion or revelation will resolve. Even among Christians, some find artificial methods of contraception to be morally forbidden whereas others find them to be obligatory in certain circumstances. And seemingly irresolvable disputes about pacifism and justified violence, socialism and capitalism, and the right to take innocent lives in some circumstances are not alleviated by appeals to revelation.

This need not, and I think should not, be taken as an acceptance of some form of moral relativism – that different moral principles are acceptable by different social groups, without any further reason being called for. But it might be taken as an indication of the great difficulty of coming to know the truth in matters of morality, even among serious and morally concerned people. Religions will not alleviate this situation, for however much they may claim certainty for their beliefs, other faiths will claim equal certainty for different and often conflicting beliefs. It may seem, then, that religions only make a complex situation of moral diversity even worse. Despite the existence of a global basis for ethics, which does enable moral conversations to take place, there will never be universal agreement on all moral principles. Religions often seem to intensify moral disagreements by opposing ordinary secular moral views and adopting positions based on revelation that others find hard to accept.

## RELIGION AND SUPREME OBJECTIVE VALUE

Religions, however, can have a much more positive role than this. It is extremely difficult to find a general characterization of religion which will prove acceptable to most scholars. But I think there is one thing that can be said about most religions in the contemporary world, even if one hesitates thereby to claim to have successfully defined what religion is. What most religions do is to promulgate ways of overcoming egoism and attachment and achieving knowledge of, or union with, a being or state that embodies the highest possible degree of reality and value. This seems to be true of the major traditions of both Semitic and Indian origin. There is no religion in those traditions which holds that it is right to be selfish and to pursue material prosperity as the ultimate goal in life. The overcoming of egoism, whether phrased in terms of losing a sense of self, of realizing one's unity with one all-embracing self, or of obeying or loving a higher self, is basic to religious practice. So religions ally themselves with those who seek to decrease egoism, and in that way they support the most basic moral motivation, the pursuit of what is right, whether or not it is conducive to one's own good in this world.

However, religions are not merely societies for overcoming egoism. Their more important function is to relate human moral striving toward a goal that is considered to be of supreme intrinsic value. Theists aim at knowledge and love of a God who is supremely blissful, compassionate, creatively free, faithful, and just. The goal is knowledge of a being who embodies to a maximal degree those values that are basic to all personal life. Such knowledge will bring an appropriate sharing in those values, but the being of God itself defines what those values are in a distinctive way and gives them objective reality.

Non-theistic traditions aim at the attainment of *nirvana* or release. In that state, which may be conceived of as the liberation of the eternal soul, the cessation of duality, or simply the attainment of enlightenment, there is a supreme realization of bliss, compassion, freedom from suffering, knowledge of truth, and complete impartiality. These are the same basic values as in the theistic case but given an interpretation in terms of a realizable human state instead of in terms of relation to a supreme deity.

In both these major religious traditions, the basic values become not just values that humans may decide to adopt or that are somehow "right" in a rather obscurely self-evident way. They are embodied objectively in reality and to a maximal extent either in an existent God to whom humans can relate or in an existent state beyond direct description into which humans can enter.

What difference does this make? A religious view may make a difference to the way in which one interprets the basic human values. The ideas of freedom and truthfulness will be given a distinctive interpretation if one sees them as supremely embodied in God or in a state of the liberated soul. They will certainly not be interpreted merely as freedom from political oppression, as freedom to do whatever one wants, or as the duty to avoid telling lies or breaking promises. They will be seen much more positively in terms of creative power to do what is worthwhile, and complete knowledge of all that is possible and actual.

Insofar as one wishes to imitate God or to achieve the liberated state, one will strive for such positive values, both for oneself and for others so far as that is possible. Morality will not be merely a limit or constraint on desire. It will define the supreme objects of well-ordered desire. The most satisfying object of desire, for a theist, is God and the relationship to God which obedience makes possible. For a religious non-theist, the most desirable state is the state of freedom from suffering which only liberation can completely give. The religious believer has a reason that the unbeliever cannot have for striving to realize moral values. This is because the unbeliever has little reason to suppose that the supreme values are actually realized anywhere at all and little reason to suppose that they can be realized by human effort, whereas the believer thinks that supreme values are realized and can thus be an object of desire and striving for their own sake. Moreover, such values can be realized in one's own life, not by sheer effort perhaps but by divine or supernatural help.

So one difference religious belief can make to natural morality is that it makes moral values objects of desire and striving, as existent states to which one can be consciously related. The morally motivated secularist cannot do this but must simply aim at acting out of respect for moral principles for their own sake, simply because it is right to do so. That is wholly commendable. But to do something simply because it is right is very different from revering a supreme value as part of an existent reality that is the highest object of rightly ordered human desire. To that extent a religious morality is rather different in character from a secular morality – not necessarily better or worse but decidedly different. The moral life, for the religious person, is primarily a matter of responding to the lure of an objectively existing supreme value, of seeking to understand it more fully and to desire it more undividedly. A life of response to a perceived supreme value (whether in God or in the example of liberated souls) is very different in character from a life of heroic obedience to self-legislated moral principles.

## NATURALISTIC AND RELIGIOUS MORALITY

This means that religious morality will have a motivating power that non-religious moralities lack. Both may possess the motivation of doing right for its own sake. And it may be held that this is the only motivation that matters. Yet it may come to seem rather odd if one gives, for example, a wholly naturalistic account, from evolutionary psychology perhaps, of morality as a set of genetically embedded beliefs that have been implanted because they had survival value at some earlier stage of evolution. Once one recognizes that the sense of obligation is a possibly obsolete survival mechanism, it may come to seem reasonable to weaken or obliterate it if one can think of more effective ways of surviving and flourishing. For example, one may choose to eliminate the genetically "defective" in order to increase the health of the species, subduing one's moral urges to keep them alive as outmoded survival mechanisms that are no longer efficient.

The point I am making here is not that naturalistic moralists will tend to do immoral things or to be morally worse than religious moralists. It is rather that naturalistic moralists will have no particular reason to prefer a traditional sense of obligation to new and rationally formulated policies of action. If those policies are oriented to the survival of the species, as they think the traditional obligations once were, then accepted moral beliefs may be overturned with impunity, if it is possible to do so. Thus the sheer sense that one ought to do certain things will not be enough to form a moral obligation that should not be overridden. Rationality can take over from the sense of "ought," and it will rightly pursue whatever goals and purposes humans decide to adopt. Such goals may or may not be in line with those of religious moral ideals. But there is no particular reason why they should be. Indeed, to the extent that all religious views are regarded as false by naturalistic thinkers, there is some reason why they should not be. The policies of the religious and of the non-religious may therefore well diverge.

But what of the universal ethical principles that I have defended? Will ethical naturalists not be bound to adopt them? My argument has been that they are rationally bound to agree that happiness, freedom, truth, and justice are basic goods for all humans whatsoever. But on this account to say that something is a good is just to say that it is rationally desirable by all responsible agents. The question is, why should I do what is rationally desirable by all? Why should I even care what all such agents think? Logic compels me to say that what is good for me is equally good for any being who is just like me. But logic cannot compel me to aim equally at the good of all. It may be as good for you to have a new car as it is for me to have a new car. But I will still buy the car for myself, not for you, because it is my good I care about.

If moral principles state that I should aim impartially at the good of all, or at least of a group of beings, why should I adopt them? For the naturalist, my sense of obligation, my sense that it is simply right to do so, is genetically programmed and may be reprogrammed with the right technology or even willpower. I need another reason for acting on moral principles. But what could that be? Of course the naturalist can think of some reasons – other people will like you better, and perhaps morality pays in the long run. But these are rather pragmatic considerations, which may well be overridden in particular cases. The naturalist has reasons of a pragmatic and defeasible sort for acting in accordance with moral principles. And herein precisely lies the difference from religious morality.

The religious believer has non-pragmatic reasons for acting morally. The theist will do what is right because it is commanded by a God who has the good of the whole universe at heart and who is supremely perfect. The theist who cares to know anything of God will do what is right out of love of the supremely perfect God, and love is a non-pragmatic reason. Similarly, the renouncer will do what is right because it is the only means to the ending of suffering for all beings. It must be noted that this attitude expresses universal compassion, compassion for all beings and not simply desire to escape suffering oneself. That would be a selfish motivation and would be self-defeating according to the renouncer's viewpoint. Compassion is the appropriate attitude because there is a way of liberation from suffering for all, not because I can escape suffering myself.

So religious morality can appeal to different sorts of motives than non-religious morality. This is not always, one may think, a commendable thing. Some religious believers may appeal to God in defense of the extermination of their enemies in a holy war. They may set aside basic moral rules in the belief that God has commanded them to do so, whereas secularists may be appalled at the suffering such strange beliefs seem to cause. On the other hand, religious believers may also appeal to their love of God, and God's love for them, in defense of their policy of self-sacrificial service. And secularists may decide that there is good reason to abandon the commonly agreed rules of morality if they can get away with it, and if it accomplishes non-morally justifiable ends they decide to follow, like those of racial purity or ethnic superiority. Moral ends, they may say, are not so important after all.

So there is no simple equation of religion with superior moral observance. Nevertheless, there is little doubt that the sort of religious belief that asserts the objective existence of a supreme value offers a sort of motivation for moral obedience that naturalistic thinkers would find it very hard to match.

I have stressed that this motivation is not prudential. It is not a matter of saying that it will pay if I am moral and that is why I am moral. Such a motivation would, I have suggested, be self-defeating. Yet there is another element of religious morality that does hold out the hope of a sort of success that naturalism cannot guarantee, or even render very likely. The purposes of God will eventually be realized. *Nirvana* can be attained. So even if present moral effort seems to be futile, to produce no discernible results, the believer may believe that there will be results of a very definite sort. Things will be objectively better in future because of my moral striving.

Although this is not a prudential consideration, since I am not primarily concerned about my own future good, it is a consideration about the objectively good consequences of moral endeavor. The believer has a hope, grounded in belief in a moral order in the universe, that can sustain effort even in the face of apparent futility. That is an element that a totally secular view might find hard to sustain, since there is no power, for the secularist, that can ensure future moral success and so there may be no attainable goal of human moral striving. This is no doubt one of the factors Immanuel Kant had in mind when he argued that moral commitment requires one to believe that a moral goal – of happiness in accordance with morality – will be achieved. Although this argument has not generally found favor with subsequent critics, it does seem to be true that belief in the realizability of the moral goal provides a very strong additional reason for moral commitment.

Finally, for many religious believers God, or a compassionate *bodhisattva*, will help moral endeavor by empowering one's life in a positive way. Morality will be empowered by an objective being of supreme compassion and wisdom and so is a co-operative enterprise rather than a matter of heroic self-determination.

In all these ways religious belief makes a great difference to one's conception of morality and to the way in which one lives a good life. Although all may agree on basic universal goods, whatever their worldviews, religious believers will have a distinctive attitude to such goods and a distinctive way of interpreting them. This may have good or bad consequences, depending on one's point of view. But it is something that must be taken into account in any attempt to formulate a global ethics.

## MORAL PRINCIPLES AND THE RELIGIOUS IDEAL

My conclusion is that the real driving motivation of morality will not come from some sort of agreed global ethic, the foundations for which can seem rather abstract and hypothetical. Religion needs the proper autonomy of humanist ethics, the recourse to thinking about the foundations of ethics in natural human desires, to prevent it from interpreting religious rules in ways that are dismissive of those who differ from oneself or repressive of basic human goods. But humanist ethics needs religion to give its moral principles a strongly motivating moral goal and a real hope of its realization. People's hearts will not be moved by considerations of a rather abstract universal rationality alone. They will be moved by a vision of goodness which is empowering and realizable.

This is what that great humanist Immanuel Kant wanted to provide, in adding his postulates of God and immortality to his analysis of the moral life, though he never found a satisfactory way of putting it. This is largely, I think, because he missed what is for most believers the most important part of religion, the experience of God (or of liberation) as a life-transforming encounter. It is such experience which grounds the claim that morality is encountered as an inexorable moral command or as a way to a supremely desirable goal, which provides a ground for hope that such a goal can be realized, even if only by divine help.

In the Semitic traditions, it is very clear that the prophets encounter God as a morally demanding power, who wills justice and mercy and who promises that a society of justice and peace can be realized, whether in this world or in the world to come. In the Indian traditions, the emphasis is rather on the renunciation of desire for the sake of realizing one's true nature. There may not be a moral command here, but there is a sense of the true self beyond desire or of a liberated state that is beyond change and suffering. It is out of the sense that such a realization or liberation has been experienced and is open in principle to all that the motivation comes to pursue liberation as the greatest goal. The vision of liberation attracts by transforming one's vision of sensory and desire-led experience and by promising the eventual attainment of a goal of complete freedom and peace.

If the sense of axiological transcendence found in these religious traditions is combined with the focus on human flourishing which autonomous ethical reflection stimulates, then forms of religious faith could develop which might help to shape a convergent global vision of the sort of human life which is truly worth living. In the enormously diverse cultural pattern of the contemporary world, that may only be one vision among others. But it is one that has been shaped in the light of the new global vision of one fragile earth for the whole human race, and which perhaps holds out our best hope for a continuing and truly human future.

*Plate 3* A depiction of Adam and Eve on the ceiling of the nave of Ely Cathedral, England (begun in 1083 CE), which was painted in the mid nineteenth century. The story of Adam and Eve tempted by the snake and eating of the fruit of the Tree of Knowledge is foundational in the ethical understanding of the three great Western monotheisms: Judaism, Christianity, and Islam. Photo: *Joseph Runzo*

# 3

# RELIGIOUS MORAL DIVERSITY
*and* RELATIONSHIPS

*James Kellenberger*

## CULTURAL DIVERSITY

In this chapter I want to discuss moral diversity, in particular religious moral diversity. My effort will be to offer an explanation of religious moral diversity, and of religious moral commonality, which respects both the integrity of morality and the integrity of religion. Let me begin with a comment on cultural diversity and moral diversity. More than twenty years ago Claude Lévi-Strauss said in *Tristes Tropiques*, "Mankind has opted for monoculture, it is in the process of creating a mass civilization, as beetroot is grown in the mass." His concern was the loss of "the primeval innocence of the American or Melanesian forests" in the "smother[ing] concrete" of "Western civilization," with the concurrent loss of primeval social ways of life.[1] Lévi-Strauss had an anthropological concern with the loss of cultural diversity, in particular the loss of primeval societies that were untouched by the influences of modernization. He saw these ways of life as being threatened by an encroaching "monoculture," as he calls it.

More recently the political scientist Samuel Huntington has reflected that cultures do not become "Westernized" in any significant sense either by adopting and using the popular-culture trappings of so-called Western civilization or by becoming less traditional and more modern. Drinking

Coca-Cola, wearing blue jeans, and being entertained by Hollywood movies, he argues, does not "Westernize" non-Westerners any more than Americans in the United States become like the Japanese or "Japanized" by buying Japanese cars and televisions. Similarly, he argues, traditional societies can become modernized through increased "levels of literacy, education, wealth, and social mobilization, and more complex and diversified occupational structures," without adopting the culture of the "West." Thus, he observes, that "in addition to Japan, Singapore, Taiwan, Saudi Arabia, and, to a lesser degree, Iran have become modern societies without becoming Western."[2] There is nothing in the culture of Islam, for instance, that forbids modernization, understood as an increase in literacy and education and so on. The *shari'ah* can be followed in a modern society.

Although a more modern world with fewer traditional societies may be emerging, it is not a monocultural world. It is a multicultural world in which different cultures co-exist. When geographically apart they are put in proximity by electronic communication. But, moreover, often cultures co-exist in their diversity in the same physical place.

As a matter of descriptive fact there is cultural diversity about us in the world and, depending upon where we live, to a greater or lesser extent in our immediate surroundings, *within* our larger culture. In Singapore or London or Los Angeles cultural diversity is and has been familiar, and in other cities and towns not known as multicultural crossroads, a new cultural diversity is manifesting itself. In various contemporary settings we find about us diversity in dress (ranging from the Sikh turban to the Iranian *chador* to blue jeans), diversity in food (ranging from *garam masala* to *gefiltefish* to "fast food"), diversity in grooming (ranging from uncut hair to a shaved head), and diversity in language (ranging from Farsi to Tagalog to the various versions of English).

We are all aware of this kind of diversity; however, we may not have that level of familiarity with it that allows us to be comfortable with all the expressions of cultural diversity we encounter. We all often and regularly seek the quiet harbor of the familiar with which we feel comfortable. Although we may enjoy adventure if it is adequately controlled, finally we return to what is familiar. Our friends tend to be like us, sharing our profession or our interests or our neighborhood. Americans abroad seek out other Americans. Nationals of various countries who live in a foreign country form expatriate communities. It is, after all, easier to communicate with those who share our idiom, recognize our common references, and do not think our gestures odd. For whatever reason, we often seek the culturally familiar.

This is not to say that we cannot negotiate and enjoy the new and culturally unfamiliar, as on a vacation to another country. However, we would like the new and culturally unfamiliar not to be threatening or inimical. Sometimes when we live among others who are culturally different from ourselves and who seem comfortable with ways that are not familiar to us, we come to feel perplexed, and other times we may come to feel anxious.

This reaction to the culturally unfamiliar to which I refer is quite ancient, of course. An instance is provided by Amartya Sen. Sen cites the eleventh-century writer Alberuni (al-Bīrūnī), an Iranian Muslim, who, in India, observes that the Hindus

> differ from us to such a degree as to frighten their children with us, with our dress, and our ways and customs, and as to declare us to be devil's breed, and our doings as the very opposite of all that is good and proper.

Alberuni continues, however, that

> we must confess, in order to be just, that a similar depreciation of foreigners not only prevails among us and the Hindus, but is common to all nations toward each other.[3]

It appears to be as Herodotus said, "Custom is the king o'er all."[4]

## MORAL DIVERSITY

But there is another kind of diversity. It is often associated with cultural diversity, and is often influenced by cultural diversity, but this diversity is in fact distinguishable from cultural diversity. It is moral diversity: a diversity in what is or is not regarded as right or wrong, obligatory or permissible, virtuous or not. As a matter of descriptive fact, there are differences that we can observe in different cultures about what people morally value as a virtue and what they regard as obligatory. At an easily accessible descriptive level we can observe differences in what different people, and different peoples, count as, for instance, obligatory respect for parents, as proper expressions of friendship, and much more.

Here is an example of moral diversity that many have reflected on. Peter Freuchen, who lived among the Inuit for years, reported that in traditional

Inuit societies husbands offer to male guests the sexual favors of their wives, and this is approved by custom.[5] Here, it seems, we find a graphic example of moral diversity when we set this Inuit practice over against the practice in the dominant society say, of North and South America and of Europe. In fact we seem to have an instance of an action that is counted as morally allowable in Inuit societies and is *not* regarded as morally allowable in that other society. This initial impression, I shall go on to argue, is not quite right, but for the present let me leave this example hanging.

As one ethnic group comes into contact with the unfamiliar ways of another group, a tension may develop; and this can happen particularly when the diversity is in the moral sphere. If we are prepared to treat those who are culturally different from ourselves as "devil's breed" (to use Alberuni's words), how much more so are we tempted to do so when the difference is a moral difference as well as a cultural one?

## CULTURAL DIVERSITY VERSUS MORAL DIVERSITY

In the case of Inuit marital practice just cited, cultural differences clearly influence marital expectations and hence the different moral practice in Inuit marital relations. However, cultural diversity itself is not quite identical with moral diversity. For one thing, *ceteris paribus*, some cultural differences in themselves – certain small particulars of dress – may correlate with no moral differences. For another thing, there can be moral diversity *within* a culture. Within the dominant culture of the United States we may find a range of marital relationships with quite different moral requirements. In one marital relationship each spouse may expect the other to talk about the work day, each bringing the other up to date on the developments in his or her respective work projects, problems they have encountered at work, and so on. In another marital relationship, within the same culture, the expectation of the relationship may be that no technical shop talk is allowed in the home: talk about work is left at the door. Here there is moral diversity in that what is morally expected in the one relationship would violate the other relationship. Both marital relationships, with their different and opposite expectations, are allowed by the culture in which they occur.

We should note, then, that cultural diversity can influence moral diversity, but they are not precisely the same thing. But there is a more important claim about moral diversity that I want to make. It is this: beyond what different people and peoples *regard* as right and obligatory, there are actual different moralities. There is, to be sure, a diversity of moral claims about what is right or obligatory across and within cultures – there is, that is to say, a diversity in what people *regard* as right or obligatory. But, moreover, there are in fact diverse moralities in which what *is* right is different.

## RELIGIOUS MORAL DIVERSITY

Shortly I shall offer an explanation of this moral diversity of actual moralities – and an explanation of a moral commonality. Before I do that, I need to bring into the picture *religious* moral diversity. The different religious traditions – such as Judaism, Christianity, Islam, Hinduism, and Buddhism – of course exhibit a diversity of rites, rituals, and doctrine. However, I want to distinguish a diversity among these elements from moral diversity, as I distinguished cultural diversity from moral diversity. Of course, rites, rituals, and doctrine may often impact on religious duty, and so religious diversity involving these elements may connect to and influence religious moral diversity. But religious moral diversity itself is, without putting too fine a point on it, diversity involving the way what is right, obligatory, and virtuous is understood.

Religious moral diversity comes into view with, for instance, the observation that for Islam it is permissible, not wrong, for a man to have more than one wife, under certain circumstances, whereas in the Judaic and Christian traditions no circumstances make a man's having more than one wife morally permissible. This is an instance of *inter*-religious moral diversity. There can also be *intra*-religious moral diversity, as within Judaism over the necessity of strictly observing the dietary laws and within Christianity over the propriety of divorce.

Again, as with moral diversity *simpliciter*, we can distinguish between a diversity about what is *regarded* as morally right and a diversity of actual moralities in which different actions *are* morally right. At this point let me expand my earlier claim to include religious morality, so that it is the claim that there is a moral diversity in the sense of a diversity of actual moralities, including religious moralities.

## RELIGIOUS PLURALISM AND MORAL PLURALISM

The moral diversity, including religious moral diversity, to which I have drawn attention, is parallel to the religious diversity observed by John

Hick: the diversity or plurality of world religious traditions. Initially, at the phenomenological level, both religious plurality and moral diversity are an undeniable part of our experience. Hick offered his well-known "pluralism" as an account of the plurality of religious traditions. He regarded his pluralism as a "hypothesis," because, strictly, it could not be proven but he regarded it as the hypothesis that best accounted for the phenomena of religious plurality. Hick elaborated his pluralism in several books and gave it a definitive statement in *An Interpretation of Religion.* Although it is not possible here to give a full statement of Hick's pluralistic hypothesis, we can observe that at its center is the idea that the same real in itself is experienced differently in different religious traditions, and the different religious traditions are different ways of responding to the same transcendent reality. However, our purpose is not to evaluate, or even to present in detail, Hick's pluralism, which over the past several years has received much attention. Rather, I mention Hick's religious pluralism in order to be able to point out that there is in moral reflection an analogous approach, and it is called "moral pluralism."

Moral pluralism may take several forms, but it starts with the phenomenon of moral diversity. Moral pluralists are struck by moral diversity, to which they react sympathetically, although how they regard that diversity can vary. Some, for instance, have characterized moral diversity as a plurality of equally valid *moral outlooks* or *perspectives.* Elizabeth Wolgast considers moral pluralism not so much as an ethical view relating to competing ethical theories as a view relating to the current state of human affairs in which we are all confronted by a "pluralism of perspectives" and challenged "to imaginatively see inside another's moral universe, as we determine which moral differences are tolerable and which not."[6] For her, moral pluralism is a *perspectival* pluralism. For Donald Crosby, moral pluralism involves not only the acknowledgment of a plurality of different moral *perspectives,* but also the recognition of a plurality of useful moral *theories* and a plurality of sometimes irreconcilably conflicting *goods.*[7] Another form of moral pluralism, developed by John Kekes, is stated in terms of a diversity of "values." For Kekes, there is a plurality of values, and there is "a plurality of equally reasonable conceptions of a good life" with its different values. For his pluralism, values can be ranked, but rankings are only reasonable in relation to a particular conception of a good life. Accordingly, there can be a plurality of equally reasonable rankings of values.[8]

Although there are significant differences between John Hick's religious pluralism and moral pluralism in its various forms, moral pluralism is analogous to Hick's religious pluralism in several respects. As Hick's religious pluralism addresses and seeks to accommodate the religious plurality of the world, so moral pluralism addresses and seeks to accommodate the moral plurality of the world. As Hick's religious pluralism allows that various religious traditions are equally valid, so moral pluralism allows that various moral stances are equally valid. And as Hick's pluralism allows that not all forms of religion are equally worthy,[9] so moral pluralism does not countenance all possible moral stances as equally worthy. Both oppose that form of extreme moral relativism that asserts that all forms of moral belief or practice are equally valid.

## MORAL DIVERSITY AMONG RELIGIONS

To what extent is there moral diversity among religions? I have already mentioned the instance of the difference between Islam, on the one hand, and Judaism and Christianity, on the other hand, regarding the requirements of marriage and the number of wives a man may have – one of the examples to which I shall return. In addition to this inter-religious example and the intra-religious examples I introduced earlier, there are easily identified differences between Hindus and those in other religions regarding vegetarianism and between some traditional forms of Islam and contemporary forms of Christianity regarding the role of women in society. There are subtler, or less well-known and less visible, differences as well. Such differences can be inter-religious or intra-religious and may escape broad reflection on religions; yet they may be very significant morally. For instance, among Muslims in Bosnia it is believed that crying over the dead is deeply wrong. The belief that tears are detrimental to the dead is common among Muslims in the Balkans, and for this reason women are not encouraged to attend funerals.[10] In Bosnian Muslim culture there is the concern that crying, or thoughts of closeness from the spouse of the deceased, can "pollute the soul" of the deceased. By contrast, Orthodox Christian Serbs in the same area emotionally lament their dead.[11] And of course Muslims in other cultural settings, too, express their grief in an open way.

Furthermore, there may be religious moral diversity beneath the surface of apparent moral agreement. Take the prohibition against murder.

Though everyone may agree that murder, as wrongful killing, is wrong by definition, there may be a vast disagreement about what counts as murder. Is killing in war murder? Is the killing of noncombatants in war murder? Is abortion murder? If religions answer these questions differently, then, even if they share a prohibition against murder, to an extent they arguably do not share a common moral value prohibiting murder.[12]

A difference between religious groups regarding what appears to be a shared value against murder can come out in an examination of what those groups are and are not prepared to allow as a justification for killing. We can borrow from the thinking of Thomas Kasulis to illustrate this point. Kasulis has argued that in trying to discern the differences between two religious traditions, it is more useful to compare the forms of hypocrisy in those traditions than to compare exemplars or saints in those traditions. "Buddhist hypocrites," Kasulis observes, "are simply not like Christian hypocrites. In the name of strengthening Christianity, Christian hypocrites have sometimes killed for Christ, for example. Buddhists – even hypocritical Buddhists – do not kill for the Buddha."[13] As Christians, those who have "killed for Christ" accept the Christian prohibition against killing, and, as there is a Buddhist prohibition against killing, it would seem that they and Buddhists share a moral value. But, Kasulis argues, such Christian hypocrites get around this prohibition and the Christian teachings that we should love our enemies and avoid violence by saying that they are "not killing their enemies, but the enemies of the Church." And they urge that they are in fact practicing Christian charity in inquisitorial torture, the military conquest of non-Christian populations, and the forcing of baptism; for, they argue, these extreme measures are necessary to save souls for eternity.[14] These Christian hypocrites, Kasulis wants us to appreciate, are not arguing that their killing is excusable; they are arguing that Christian charity requires it. They kill for Christ, as no Buddhist kills for the Buddha.

Thus what counts as justified killing in some strains of the Christian tradition does not have a counterpart in the Buddhist tradition. To be sure, for Kasulis these Christians are hypocrites. Without denying this point, we should observe that Kasulis' own examples of such hypocrites include very many who were Christians in good standing in their time (the inquisitorial persecutors of heretics and witches, the military supporters of Christian missionary efforts in the Americas). To the extent that the justifications for killing proffered by these Christians shed light on the content of their understanding of the prohibition against murder, it would appear that the content of the value prohibiting killing that they embraced is different from the Buddhist value prohibiting killing.

## MORAL COMMONALITY AMONG RELIGIONS

To what extent is there moral commonality among religions? The idea that God has established common moral values for all human beings through his commands is an idea at home in the Western theistic traditions, but the general religious idea that there are universal moral values holding for all persons in all cultures is not limited to the Western theistic traditions.

In the Buddhist tradition, where the final goal is *nirvana* (or *nibbana*), much importance is given to such states as *metta* (loving kindness) and *karuna* (compassion), and there is a recognition of the importance of such virtues as self-restraint and justice, as well as a recognition of the moral significance of such internal actions as willing to slander or using hurtful language prior to any overt action.[15] But, moreover, in Buddhism there is a large number of scriptural precepts. Many of these relate to the life of the *bhikku* or monk, but there are Five Precepts of Buddhism that are binding on all Buddhists. They are (1) "to abstain from the taking of life," – the prohibition against killing or murder that we have just discussed, (2) to abstain from taking "that which is not given," (3) "to abstain from misconduct in sensual actions," that is, sexual misconduct, (4) "to abstain from false speech," and (5) "to abstain from liquor that causes intoxication and indolence."[16] The Five Precepts remain, within Buddhist thought, as universally binding on Buddhists. But for some commentators the scope of these prohibitions is wider than the Buddhist community. Referring to the first four of the Five Precepts – "those forbidding murder, stealing, lying, and sexual misconduct" – Damien Keown observes that "there is little doubt the Buddha intended these four basic precepts, at least, to be absolutely and universally respected," where by "universal" he means "applying to all rational beings," not Buddhists only, and by "absolute" he means "applicable in all circumstances."[17] Another commentator, Bhikku Chao Chu, a Buddhist monk, observes, "Most societies that base their morals and ethics on revealed traditions share basic prohibitions against such acts as killing, stealing, and lying," and these same prohibitions tend to survive in "a secular society that no longer believes in revelation." Although Bhikku Chao Chu does not say so, these three prohibitions correspond to three of the Five Precepts. As he sees it from a Buddhist perspective, there is reflected in these various societies a "[k]nowledge of moral values," and "[t]he reason why different people, whose respective revelations disagree in various ways, tend to agree about prohibitions against such actions as killing, stealing, and lying is because they all perceive, however dimly, the same universal laws inherent in the world itself."[18]

A central moral teaching of Christianity is the Golden Rule, which in a familiar phrasing is: "Do unto others as you would have them do unto you" (after Matthew 7:12). Most Christians would understand actions based on such concern for others to be what ought to be done, not by Christians alone, but universally. However, as John Hick has argued, it is not Christians alone who have this understanding of the universal applicability of the Golden Rule; rather its principle in some formulation, positive or negative, is found in all the major religions. Thus, to cite one or two of Hick's examples, in Confucianism we find "Do not do to others what you would not like yourself," and in the *hadith* of Islam there are Muhammad's words, "No man is a true believer unless he desires for his brother what he desires for himself."[19]

In the Hindu tradition, Bimal Krishna Matilal points out, there are, on the one hand, "group-relative *dharmas*," or duties, and, on the other hand, a "culture-neutral side of morality," *sadharana dharma*, with its duties.[20] Duties that one has by virtue of one's caste or station are associated with the first kind of *dharma*. In the second category, observes Cromwell Crawford, are "generic duties ... independent of caste and station in life ... binding upon man as man."[21] "To articulate [the] culture-neutral side of morality is not an easy task," suggests Matilal, and he continues, "these values or value-experiences may not be totally immutable across cultures or over time."[22] Crawford suggests that importantly embodied in *sadharana dharma*, in Hindu thinking, are a sense of life's sacredness and gratitude for life.[23] Whatever difficulties there may be in an articulation of the exact moral requirements of *sadharana dharma*, for Hinduism there is this universal aspect of morality.

Writing on Islamic ethics, Isma'il R. al Faruqi observes, "Islām has always been universalist ... The religion, as represented by its supreme authority, the divine word or the Qur'an, speaks with utmost emphasis and clarity. 'O mankind, We have created you of one pair, male and female, and constituted you in tribes and peoples that you may complement one

another. Nobler among you is only the more righteous.' [Qur'ān, 49:13]."
He continues, "The ethical principles constitutive of Islāmic humanism are
not denied of any human being even though he may belong to another
faith; to another culture, civilization or age."[24] Muzammil H. Siddiqi says
this: "There are two interesting ethical terms of Islam that frequently occur
in the *Qur'ān*: *Ma'rūf* (good, virtue, etc.) and *Munkar* (bad, evil). *Ma'rūf*
... means an action that is generally recognized and known to people as
acceptable, good, and hence virtuous. *Munkar* on the other hand ... is an
action that is generally unacceptable to people and hence bad and evil.
Thus the *Qur'ān* seems to have recognized a general and common
standard of virtue and evil."[25] "The *sharī'ah*, or law of Islām," says Faruqi,
"is a complete system of desiderata, principles, rules, and laws regarding
human activity... The life that is worthy of man is one totally dedicated to
the pursuit of the divine will in all its detail. Observance of the laws of
traffic is as religious as that of the laws affecting property, life, worship, or
war and peace. The sanctity of life is inseparable from its unity, and its
unity, inseparable from the will of the Creator of all life."[26]

It seems, then, that in more than one religious tradition there is the
abiding sense that there are at least some universally shared moral values.
In fact it is arguable that what appear to be appeals to different moral
authorities in different religious traditions may at bottom be an appeal to
broadly shared moral values that are not different after all – just as it
seems, in accord with my observation about the depth of religious moral
diversity, that the content of apparently similar values in different religious
traditions, such as the prohibition against killing, may be different. There
is not merely diversity and commonality in the moralities of religions, but
as well both diversity-beneath-apparent-commonality and commonality-
beneath-apparent-diversity in religious morality. I shall return to this
point.

## UNDERSTANDING MORAL DIVERSITY
## AND COMMONALITY

How shall we explain moral diversity, and moral commonality, and, in
particular, religious moral diversity and religious moral commonality?
And can we do so in a way that maintains the integrity of religions? I do
not think that moral pluralism will do the job. Moral pluralism accepts
that there is a plurality of moral perspectives or a plurality of hierarchies of

values informing a plurality of good lives – in short, a diversity of moralities – and that many of them, though not all, are equally valid. But moral pluralism has no foundational explanation for the existence of this moral diversity in the first place – let alone a foundational explanation of moral commonality.

However, such an explanation is available, I submit. It resides in an appeal to the category of *relationships between persons*, which is not a purely or quintessential moral category (like *obligation* or *virtue*), although relationships, if I am correct, have foundational moral significance. Moreover they explain both moral diversity *and* commonality.

Let us now return to the earlier Inuit example of marital practice, and let me supply some background. In Inuit societies husbands offer to male guests the sexual favors of their wives, and this is approved by custom. Here, it seems, we find an instance of an action that is counted as morally allowable in Inuit societies and is not regarded as morally allowable in the society of North and South America or of Europe. But this is not quite right, or at least not the whole story. Here is the background. In traditional Inuit societies married couples form an economic unit: the man hunts; the woman dries her husband's clothes, mends his boots, and sews any tears in his clothing (life-and-death matters in the polar region); she also prepares the skins and dries the meat of any animals that he kills, thus giving him more time to hunt. Sometimes, if a man's wife is sick or has a baby to care for and he is going on a hunting trip on which a woman is needed to warm the igloo that is built, to dry his clothes, scrape skins, and so on, he will take another woman, with her husband's permission and her understanding. And on these occasions it is understood that there will be sexual relations.

How do relationships help us to understand this moral diversity? Perhaps the first thing to note is that different *types* of relationships create different *types* of obligations. What violates one type may not violate the other. True, many types of relationships may require honesty and even loyalty of a kind. But the kind of deep and personal commitment that the marital relationship requires one spouse to give to the other is not required of an employee toward his or her employer in the employment relationship. Again, although one's employer may be one's friend, the relationship between employee and employer is different from that between friend and friend: the loyalty that one owes to one's employer is different in scope and depth from that which one friend owes to another.

In this way we may say that *types* of relationships create different *types* of obligations. It is as Aristotle said, "How man and wife and in general friend and friend ought mutually to behave seems to be the same question as how it is just for them to behave; for a man does not seem to have the same duties to a friend, a stranger, a comrade, and a schoolfellow."[27]

The second thing to note is that we should not think once we see how relationship *types* give rise to obligations that it will always be clear just what meets those obligations. In some cases of relationships between persons, as in many friendships and many marital relationships, what the relationship requires may importantly be determined by the *particular* relationship. In such cases, however, it is again relationships, particular relationships, that clarify the particular *form* that obligations take. We may be clear that our friendship relationship requires loyalty to our friend (and that that loyalty is different in character or *type* from the loyalty we owe to our employer), but there can still be a question about just what our loyalty to our friend requires, its particular *form* – and the particular relationship we have to our friend answers that question. So too for marital relationships.

The next thing to be noticed is that different types of relationships can take different forms in different societies, and hence give different forms to basic obligations. In the example previously cited from traditional Inuit society, when a man's own wife is unavailable to come with him hunting, he may take another woman to warm the igloo, dry his clothes, scrape skins, etc., and it is understood by all concerned that there will be sexual relations. In many societies, such as the main societies of Europe and North and South America, marital devotion assumes an expression that requires sexual exclusivity. In these societies a married couple sharing their sexuality is counter to the devotion required by the marital relationship and violates that relationship. In other societies, like the Inuit, it does not. In each of these societies there are forms of respecting and honoring one's spouse. But the way this is done, or can be done, varies in form from one society to the other by virtue of the specific character of the marital relationship in these different societies.

Does the Inuit marital practice of sexual non-exclusivity mean that the Inuit approve of "wife trading"? I think not. Peter Freuchen, who has reported on this practice among the Inuit, observes that Inuit married people generally remain devoted to each other throughout their lives.[28] The difference between Inuit societies and, say, the predominant society of North and South America and Europe is *not* that a lack of devotion, consideration, and fidelity are considered permissible in one society and not considered permissible in the other, or that "being true" is counted morally right in one society and not in the other. Rather, the difference is over the role of sexual exclusivity in devotion. In some societies devotion assumes an expression that requires sexual exclusivity. In these societies a husband's sharing his wife's sexual favors hits at the devotion required by the marital relationship. In other societies, like the Inuit, it does not. In each of these societies it may be that the *same thing* is counted right, namely, respecting and honoring one's spouse, in accord with the *type* of marital relationship. But the way this is done, or can be done – the *form* of the obligation in the particular marital relationship – may vary from one society to the other, depending on cultural beliefs, perhaps unspoken beliefs, about the significance of sexual exclusivity.

In the same way relationships explain moral diversity *within* a culture, specifically regarding different marital relationships. The examples I used earlier were of two marriages within the dominant culture of the United States: in one marital relationship each spouse is expected to tell the other about the work day; in the other, shop talk is forbidden. In each marital relationship devotion and respect are required, but the *form* that such devotion and respect take is different and even opposite.

Relationships between persons explain two elements of moral phenomena across societies. First, relationships explain why the same *types* of values/obligations (such as, loyalty, family commitment, and marital duties) recur in different societies and cultures. Second, relationships explain why such values/obligations take different *forms* in different societies and cultures.

The same types of values/obligations recur in societies because the same *types* of relationships recur across societies. The marriage relationship is found in virtually all societies. In many if not all societies there are friendship relationships, as well as family relationships. In all or many societies, then, marital fidelity will be a moral value and an obligation, arising from the marriage relationship. Similarly the loyalty of friendship is a value in various societies, and in these societies not being loyal to a friend counts as a moral failure by virtue of violating the friendship relationship. A parallel comment can be made about family relationships giving rise to a loyalty-to-family obligation. Many other relationships are to be found across virtually all societies, such as the parent–child relationship and the relationship between the individual and the social group. Other kinds of relationships, such as that between an employee and his or her employer, will be found only in societies with the requisite economic arrangement, but still within a wide range of societies. All of these relationships create types of obligations determined by the type of relationship.

However, although the same *types* of relationships – friendship, the marital relationship, and more – are found in many, if not virtually all, societies, the *forms* of these relationships, and consequently the particular requirements of the relationship – the *form* of the loyalty of friendship and of marital fidelity – can vary greatly from one society to another and from one particular relationship to another within a society. What in one relationship is an offspring's duty toward his or her parents will not be an offspring's duty in another child–parent relationship in another culture *or* within a single culture, and so too for other types of relationships. The *forms* of these relationships can vary *inter*culturally or *intra*culturally. Intraculturally, how a child honors a parent, or a parent nurtures a child, or a friend is loyal to a friend, or one spouse respects the other, may vary from particular relationship to particular relationship. In this way relationships explain at once moral diversity across cultures and within cultures, and as well moral commonality across and within cultures.

## UNDERSTANDING RELIGIOUS MORAL DIVERSITY AND COMMONALITY

So far I have not addressed *religious* moral diversity directly. Let me do so now, using what we have just seen and applying it to an example of moral diversity between religious traditions which I have cited already. In Judaic and Christian morality the marital relationship must be monogamous. In Islamic morality the marital relationship need not be monogamous for men (though it must be for women): a husband may have up to four wives, when certain conditions are met. Here, then, is moral diversity. But also there is moral commonality. There is commonality in that in both religious moralities – the Judaic/Christian and the Muslim – the *type* of relationship, the marital relationship, carries with it the commitment of devotion and fidelity. However, there is also diversity in that the *form* of marital fidelity varies from the monogamous relationship to the polygamous relationship in the Islamic tradition. The specific character of these different marriage relationships, in particular their different requirements regarding sexual exclusivity, differently shape the form of the required fidelity.

Relationships also explain the universality of the Golden Rule. One relationship in particular helps us to understand why the principle of the Golden Rule in some form is widely, even universally, accepted as a universal rule of morality. The relationship to which I refer is the relationship that persons have to persons by virtue of being persons. So far I have drawn mostly on familiar relationships that we have no trouble identifying as "personal" relationships, such as marriage and friendship relationships. Such relationships are close, personal relationships in which the persons involved are well acquainted. However, many relationships between persons are not of this close personal character, such as our relationship to others in our larger urban community (if we live in a city), in our nation, and in our ethnic group. We may not think about these relationships very often, but that does not mean they do not obtain. The relationship to which I now allude is perhaps like those just mentioned in the respect that we do not think about it much. Yet it can be identified: it is the relationship we have to all persons – not by virtue of marriage, parenthood, friendship, citizenship, or ethnic identity – but simply by virtue of being persons. It may be called the "person–person relationship."

As a relationship involving all persons, and that each person has to each person, by virtue of nothing more than being a person, this relationship extends to persons unseen by us and whom we will never meet. Relationships between persons, like the marital relationship and relationships of friendship, can be lived up to or violated. In the case of the familiar relationships that I have used for illustrations, their requirements present themselves as recognizable obligations; thus the requirement of marital fidelity is recognizable as a marital duty. The person–person relationship can also be violated when its requirements are not met. It also gives rise to obligations. The central requirement of the person–person relationship is that we treat persons as persons. We violate this relationship, as it exists between us and some other persons, when we fail to treat them with the kind of respect that persons deserve as persons. Thus the person–person relationship requires one to treat all persons as one oneself, as a person, would be treated. Although it may be too much to say that the various religious traditions would appeal to the person–person relationship as the grounding for their form of the Golden Rule, it is not too much to say that it is open to them to do so, and that, in any case, this relationship accounts for the principle of the Golden Rule and its universal application.

I believe that relationships can be appealed to as well to explain that quirk of religious morality that we encountered earlier when we observed the paradox that in religious moralities there is both diversity-beneath-apparent-commonality and commonality-beneath-apparent-diversity. Relationships explain at least some of the examples that create the paradox.

Consider, first, diversity-beneath-apparent-commonality. And let us return to a case we had before ourselves earlier. Buddhists and Christians apparently share a common moral value in that they both prohibit killing. But when we look at what justifies exceptions for Buddhists and Christians, we find a difference in the ways they understand this moral prohibition. The apparent commonality here is the common *principle* prohibiting killing. The deeper diversity comes out in seeing that what justifies exceptions in the Christian case would not justify exceptions in the Buddhist case. Christians have in the past urged that they are practicing Christian charity in, for instance, inquisitorial torture, even when the death of the one tortured was brought about. "If someone's action," Kasulis says, "can be seen as not only self-damning but also as endangering the eternal salvation of others, extreme measures, including killing that person, can be justified" and seen as "an act of Christian charity."[29] Kasulis is not endorsing such a justification, but he is drawing it to our attention that it was offered. Such a justification requires the background beliefs that heretical belief will deny the heretical believer eternal salvation and that a person's holding such a belief will tempt others and so endanger their eternal salvation. What we should note is that *to the extent* torture is done for the good of the one tortured, and the good of others, it may be seen as an effort to treat persons as persons and to be an implicit endeavor to be in accord with the requirements of the person–person relationship.

My point is not that this thinking really excuses or justifies, or that it was unalloyed with other unworthy motives; however, to the extent that inquisitorial torturers acted for what they understood to be the greatest good of those tortured and of others, to that extent the explanation for the difference between the Buddhist and Christian ways of understanding the prohibition against killing in this instance is to be found in the different conceptions of what the person–person relationship requires. The diversity is in the *form* that respecting persons or acting for their good and the good of others (or respecting the person–person relationship, in my language) will take, or rather in what medieval Christians, as opposed to Buddhists, understood to be such a form, given certain background beliefs.

The obverse of the paradox in religious morality which we encountered is the phenomenon of moral commonality-beneath-apparent-diversity. Here too relationships help us to understand at least some of the examples that create this side of the paradox. A word or two will suffice. The apparent diversity is the diversity of moral *authority* appealed to by different religious traditions (*shari'ah*, Five Precepts, Christian commandments). The deeper shared value, or one such shared value or commonality, is the prohibition against killing *simpliciter*. What explains this commonality in religious morality is an implicit appreciation that killing persons, *ceteris paribus*, does not treat persons as they deserve to be treated as persons, that is, it violates the person–person relationship.

## RELIGIOUS EXPLANATIONS OF THE MORAL SIGNIFICANCE OF RELATIONSHIPS

So far I have offered a *moral* explanation of moral diversity including religious moral diversity. My explanation appeals to the category of relationships between persons, which, as I said, is not a purely or quintessential moral category (as *obligation* and *virtue* are); yet relationships, I have argued, do have foundational moral significance. In this sense the explanation I have offered to this point is moral, not religious.

Nevertheless, this explanation of moral diversity does not deny the fundamental beliefs of any religion. Furthermore, it allows religious appropriation. Let us ask: *why* do relationships have this moral significance? Any answer to this question will of course have to go beyond relationships themselves. To this question about the source of, or the reason for, the moral significance of relationships, religion can provide the answer. From within the traditions of the Western religions, we may say that God has established relationships, and their forms, and their requirements – those of love, trust, fairness, mutual respect, and justice – and a Christian can continue, echoing Paul (2 Corinthians 2:15), to say that the way the law is written on our hearts is through the understanding of the demands of relationships that God has given us. Going further in theological specificity, in accord with that strand of Christian ethics which looks to "natural law," we may understand the demands of relationships as what are being appealed to as the natural "laws" found in "nature." Buddhism too, in some expressions, cites what are in effect "natural laws." So we may understand Bhikku Chao Chu's claim that various societies that prohibit lying, stealing, and killing dimly appreciate the "same universal laws inherent in the world itself." And we may understand the inherency of these "universal laws" in a Buddhist way.

Alternatively, Buddhism may say that the Buddhist reason that relationships have moral significance is that when one violates relationships one has to others or the relationship one has to oneself, one thereby harms oneself in one's journey toward *nirvana* and harms others in their journey.[30]

## DIFFERENT RELATIONSHIPS TO GOD OR THE REAL AND DIFFERENT MORAL DUTIES

What I have said to this point does not show how a relationship explanation will address every instance of religious moral diversity. Among the examples I mentioned earlier are the intra-religious differences within Judaism over the dietary laws and within Christianity over divorce, and the inter-religious difference between Hinduism and other religions over vegetarianism. Let me now expand the relationship explanation. In doing so, I will not depart from an appeal to relationships, but I will have to go beyond relationships between persons (or at least human persons) including the person–person relationship. I shall need to appeal to God relationships or relationships to the Real or Transcendent (using John Hick's terms, but not his alone of course).

What we should observe is that within religious understanding, in different traditions, there can be different relationships to God or to the Real, with different requirements. Sometimes within a particular religious tradition this point is graphically clear. Within Judaism and Christianity, in the story of Jonah, God calls Jonah to give his message to the people of Nineveh. Jonah, as we recall, decides to take a sea voyage instead. But that is neither here nor there so far as the present point is concerned. The point here is that God can have a relationship to Jonah by virtue of his calling Jonah to do a particular thing, and it is a relationship that he does not establish with others. The point can of course be generalized to apply to others in Jewish and Christian scripture. But I am interested in its application across religions, so that we may understand orthodox Jews as being in one relationship to God, reform Jews in another, Christians and Hindus in other relationships, and Buddhists in other relationships to God or to the Real – the Real being understood, from the standpoint of different traditions, as *Brahman* or as God or as *Dharmakaya* (the Buddha-nature) and so on. The relationship of orthodox Jews to God or the Real carries with it duties regarding dietary observance which are not requirements of the relationship to God of many reform Jews. The relationship to God in which Christians stand may make no food "unclean" in itself, as Paul says (Romans 14:14–15), but require respect for the conscience of others. And so on for the multitude of possible relationships to God or the Real across the religious traditions.

Let me offer an analogy, a kind of parable, that captures in human relationships the understanding I mean to present. Consider a family setting. I have in mind an extended family. The head of this family, we will imagine, is a venerable matriarch. She is loved and revered by the members of her family, even those younger members who hardly ever see her and sometimes chafe against her authority. She does not treat every member exactly the same. She has asked one member to study law in order to watch out for the family's interests. Another she expects to stay with her to oversee the house. Another she has encouraged to develop her artistic talents. Another she has called upon to be her confidant. In short various members of her extended family have different relationships to her, and those relationships carry different duties and expectations. Moreover, the various members of the extended family may honor her in very different ways: one may write a poem in her honor; another may bring her her favorite dish, prepared just as she likes it; another may keep her company. Similarly, and by analogy, those in different religious traditions may have different moral and religious duties to God or the Real and may have different ways of honoring God or the Real. To the extent that this parable reflects our moral and religious lives, our human relationships mirror our religious relationships.

## SUMMATION

I have not argued that anything counted right by a society or a religion is right; what I have defended does not entail such a claim; and it is clearly wrong in the light of some of the atrocities approved of by societies and some of the atrocities committed with religious approval.

Nor have I argued that if some relationship requires something, then what is required ought to be done. It may be that some relationships ought not to be entered in the first place – such as abusive relationships and various power relationships. They ought not to be entered because they violate the underlying person–person relationship.

I have argued that, far from denying moral diversity, we should acknowledge it. We should acknowledge a diversity of actual moralities in which different things are obligatory, and we should specifically acknowledge such a *religious* moral diversity. And, I have argued, we should as well recognize a moral commonality, specifically in religious morality. Both, I have tried to show, are illuminated by relationship.

## NOTES

1. Claude Lévi-Strauss, *Tristes Tropiques,* trans. John and Doreen Weightman (New York: Ateneum, 1974), p. 38.
2. Samuel P. Huntington, *The Clash of Civilizations and the Remaking of World Order* (New York: Simon & Schuster, 1996), pp. 58–59, 68, 77.
3. Amartya Sen, "Human Rights and Asian Values," a revised version of his Morgenthau Memorial Lecture, given at the Carnegie Council on Ethics and International Affairs, 1 May 1997, *New Republic,* 14–21 July 1997, p. 38.
4. Herodotus, *The History of Herodotus,* in *Ethical Relativism,* ed. John Ladd (Belmont, CA: Wadsworth, 1973), p. 12.
5. Peter Freuchen, *Book of the Eskimo* (New York: World Publishing Company, 1961), pp. 79–84. I first presented this example of moral relativism drawn from traditional Inuit culture in "Ethical Relativism," *Journal of Value Enquiry,* 13, 1979, pp. 13–14.
6. Elizabeth Wolgast, "Moral Pluralism," *Journal of Social Philosophy,* 21, 1990, pp. 111, 114.
7. Donald A. Crosby, "Civilization and Its Dissents: Moral Pluralism and Political Order," *Journal of Social Philosophy* 23, 1992, pp. 112–114.
8. John Kekes, *The Morality of Pluralism* (Princeton: Princeton University Press, 1993), pp. 22–23.
9. Nazism, which Hick allows is "within the outskirts of the ... phenomena covered by the concept of religion," does not meet the "ethical criterion." John Hick, *An Interpretation of Religion* (New Haven and London: Yale University Press, 1989), p. 326.
10. Tone Bringa cites a custom among Bosnian Muslims "which forbids women from attending the actual burial ceremony" because, as the accepted explanation has it, "women are generally prone to cry when emotional." Tone Bringa, *Being Muslim the Bosnian Way: Identity and Community in a Central Bosnian Village* (Princeton: Princeton University Press, 1995), p. 186.
11. Ibid., pp. 185, 186.
12. Cf. Max L. Stackhouse, *Creeds, Society, and Human Rights* (Grand Rapids: Eerdmans, 1984), p. 269.

13. Thomas P. Kasulis, "Hypocrisy in the Self-Understanding of Religions," in *Inter-Religious Models and Criteria*, ed. J. Kellenberger (New York: St Martin's Press, 1993), p. 155.
14. Ibid., p. 156.
15. H. Saddhatissa, *Buddhist Ethics* (London: Allen & Unwin, 1970), pp. 90, 182; and S. Tachibana, *The Ethics of Buddhism* (London: Oxford University Press, 1926), pp. 95, 69.
16. Saddhatissa, *Buddhist Ethics*, p. 87; cf. Tachibana, *The Ethics of Buddhism*, p. 59.
17. Damien Keown, *The Nature of Buddhist Ethics* (New York: St Martin's Press, 1992), p. 232.
18. Bhikkhu Chao Chu, "Buddhism and Dialogue among the World Religions: Meeting the Challenge of Materialist Skepticism," in *Ethics, Religion, and the Good Society*, ed. Joseph Runzo (Louisville, Ky: Westminster/John Knox, 1992), pp. 167–168.
19. John Hick, *An Interpretation of Religion* (New Haven and London: Yale University Press, 1989), p. 313.
20. Bimal Krishna Matilal, "Ethical Relativism and the Confrontation of Cultures," in *Relativism: Confrontation and Interpretation*, ed. Michael Krausz (Notre Dame: University of Notre Dame Press, 1989), pp. 352–353.
21. Cromwell Crawford, "Hindu Ethics for Modern Life," in *World Religions and Global Ethics*, ed. C. Crawford (New York: Paragon House, 1989), p. 11.
22. Matilal, "Ethical Relativism and Confrontation of Cultures," p. 353.
23. Crawford, "Hindu Ethics for Modern Life," p. 12.
24. Isma'il R. al Faruqi, "Islamic Ethics," in *World Religions and Global Ethics*, ed. Crawford, p. 224.
25. Muzammil H. Siddiqi, "Global Ethics and Dialogue Among World Religions: An Islamic Viewpoint," in *Ethics, Religion, and the Good Society*, ed. Runzo, p. 181.
26. Faruqi, "Islamic Ethics," pp. 226, 227.
27. Aristotle, *Nicomachean Ethics*, 1162a30, translated by W.D. Ross, in *Introduction to Aristotle*, ed. Richard McKeon (New York: Modern Library, 1947), p. 491.
28. Peter Freuchen, *Book of the Eskimo*, pp. 79–84. Freuchen allows that "wife trading" is approved in traditional Inuit society; however, his use of this term is misleading, for what he is referring to in Inuit society does not violate either the relationship as originally entered and understood by married partners or the cultural understanding of the requirements of the marital relationship, whereas what is referred to by "wife trading" in the predominant society of North and South America and Europe does both.
29. Kasulis, "Hypocrisy in the Self-Understanding of Religions," p. 156.
30. Cf. P.D. Premasiri, "Ethics of the Theravada Buddhist Tradition," in *World Religions and Global Ethics*, ed. Crawford, pp. 51–52.

*Part II*

# ETHICS AND RELIGION IN THE WEST

*Plate 4* Stained-glass window, Exeter Cathedral, England (completed about 1350 CE), portraying Moses descending from Mount Sinai with the Ten Commandments. The Law of Moses, foundational to the Jewish religion, exerted enormous influence on the later Christian and Islamic faiths. Photo: *Joseph Runzo*

# 4

# DOING THE RIGHT *and* THE GOOD: FUNDAMENTAL CONVICTIONS *and* METHODS OF JEWISH ETHICS

*Elliot N. Dorff*

Judaism can educate and guide us morally. That presumption is a major source of Jews' interest in Judaism. Morality is certainly not the sum total of the Jewish tradition, nor its only attraction; but the moral sensitivity and instruction that Jewish religion, law, and history can provide are surely an important part of what the Jewish tradition has meant to Jews historically and what it means for Jews in our day as well. In the contemporary world, where technology and freedom have produced great gifts but also hard moral problems, Jews – including those who are not otherwise religious – look ever more to their heritage for guidance in how to think and act.

## JEWISH ETHICS

Although the terms "ethical" and "moral" are often used interchangeably in common parlance – or even to reinforce each other, as in "He is unquestionably a moral and ethical person" – in philosophy the two terms denote different things. "Morals" refers to the concrete norms of what is good or bad, right or wrong, in a given situation. Thus the extent to which life support mechanisms should be used on dying patients, the degree to which an employee's privacy must be maintained, and the norms that should govern sexual relations among unmarried people are all moral questions.

"Ethics," in contrast, refers to the *theory* of morals. Ethics, in other words, is one level of abstraction higher than moral discussions. That does not mean that ethical questions are more important than moral ones; they just occupy a different level of thought. Thus in a university course in ethics one would examine *questions of meaning, knowledge, justification, and comparison* such as these: How should you *define* the terms "good" and "bad," "right" and "wrong," and why should you define them that way? How are judgments of "good" different from judgments of "right"? Are there universal, absolute standards of moral norms, or do they extend only to given societies (or perhaps only to individuals)? Whatever the scope of moral norms, how do you *know* what is right or wrong, good or bad? (Do you, for example, take a vote, ask an authority figure, decide what pleases you, use your conscience, seek God's will in some way, or do something else?) How do you know that that is the proper method to determine what is moral? To what factors do you appeal in *justifying* your moral judgments? (Some possible answers: the act designated as good provides the most happiness for the greatest number of people; or it fits the requirements of conscience; or it follows from some previously justified principles or decisions; or it obeys an authority figure, whether divine or human; or it is what most people in my community think is right; or it is what the law requires; or it is what pleases you personally; etc.) And how is morality *related* to law? to religion? to custom? to politics? to police or military power? to economics? to art? to education? etc.

Although all of these ethical questions have been addressed from a distinctly Jewish point of view, one particular focus of interest on the part of Jewish ethicists has been the way to define and know what is moral. Classical Judaism defines the moral in terms of God's will as articulated in God's commandments. Some modern theorists, however, have challenged the nexus between God's will and Jewish law, and some humanistic Jews have even denied that we should look to God's will in any form to define the right and the good. Even those who believe that Jewish moral norms are to be defined in terms of God's will and that Jewish law is the proper vehicle for knowing what God wants of us cannot rest with Jewish law alone, for the Talmud itself declares that the law is not fully sufficient to define morality, that there are morals "beyond the letter of the law" (*lifnim m'shurat ha-din*).[1] Beginning, then, with Abraham's challenge to God, "Shall the Judge of all the earth not do justice?" (Genesis 18:25), one ethical question addressed throughout Jewish history has been the relationship between moral norms and God's word.

Another, more modern question, is this: if we assume that God's will defines that which is morally right and good, how shall we discern what God wants us to do now? Reform theories, such as that of Rabbi Eugene Borowitz, maintain that individual Jews should make that decision.[2] They should inform themselves as much as possible about the relevant factors in the case and about the Jewish sources that apply, but ultimately individual Jews, rather than rabbis, should determine what God wants of us on the basis of their knowledge and conscience.

This reform methodology raises major questions about how to identify any Jew's decision as being recognizably Jewish. Indeed, it makes it possible and even likely that there will be multiple, conflicting moral decisions, all claiming to be Jewish, for each and every Jew has the right to articulate what the "Jewish" position on a given issue is. This challenges the coherence and intelligibility of the Jewish moral message. Moreover, Borowitz's methodology depends crucially upon the assumption that individual Jews know enough about the Jewish tradition and about how to apply it to carry out this task, an assumption that regrettably does not correspond to the reality of how much most Jews know about their tradition.

Positively, though, reform methodology empowers individual Jews to wrestle with the Jewish tradition themselves, and it encourages – even demands – that Jews learn more about their tradition in order to carry out this task. By making the decision depend on a specifically *Jewish* self, rather than an isolated, undifferentiated self, Borowitz also goes some way in the direction of explaining how such choices can be identified as specifically Jewish: Jewish choices come from self-identified and self-consciously Jewish people.

At the other end of the spectrum, most orthodox theorists claim that Jewish law as it has come down to us should serve as our authoritative source for knowing God's will, and the more straightforwardly and literally we can read those sources, the more assured we can be that we have discovered God's will. No change is necessary or possible, for God personally has proclaimed these moral norms through the Written Torah (the Five Books of Moses) and the Oral Torah that, orthodox Jews believe, was given to Moses at Mount Sinai simultaneously with the Written Torah.

For those who affirm these beliefs, this methodology imparts a sense of assuredness that one knows how to identify God's will and why one should obey it: God directly demands that of you. On the other hand, though, this methodology rests, first, on the assumption that God's will is literally expressed in the Torah and in later rabbinic literature; that conviction of faith one either affirms or denies. Beyond that, though, to adopt the orthodox approach, one must believe that we have the exact expression of the divine will in hand in the texts that have come down to us. That assertion is largely undermined by the overwhelming evidence that biblical and rabbinic literature – including the Torah itself – are documents that were written at a variety of times and places. Moreover, even if one believes in the literal, divine authority of the Torah and rabbinic literature, one still needs to *interpret* and *apply* those sources, and that leaves plenty of room for human controversy and error. Thus this methodology does not deliver the certainty it promises to inform us about what God demands. Finally, as some left-wing orthodox rabbis have themselves noted,[3] we still have to ask whether the law defines the entirety of our moral duty – and, I would add, whether the law might actually conflict with what morality demands.

Conservative theorists and rabbis (and a few orthodox ones) use Jewish law as much as possible to know God's will (and hence the right and the good), and they pay attention also to Jewish theological convictions and Jewish stories.[4] They combine this broader use of Jewish sources with an historical understanding of them. Thus when it comes time to apply them to contemporary circumstances, conservative theorists look carefully at the ways in which a given contemporary setting is similar to, or different from, the historical one in which a given source was written in order to be able to judge the degree to which it should guide us today. They also look to the sources not so much for specific directions as for the principles that underlie past applications of Jewish law so that we can intelligently apply them to the modern context. For that matter, a historical understanding of the Jewish tradition requires that even past ethical principles themselves be subject to recurrent evaluation. Both past principles and past applications of them, however, are assessed with a bias toward conserving the tradition (hence the name "conservative"), such that the burden of proof rests on the one who wants to change a particular moral or ethical stance rather than the one who wants to maintain what has come down to us.

This conservative approach does not present a neat, clearly identifiable lesson on all moral matters in our day; on the contrary, it invites discussion and controversy. Moreover, it requires judgment; no source may be taken at face value, none is immune to evaluation. This is clearly not a methodology for the anal compulsive.

Unlike the reform approach, though, the conservative methodology requires that such evaluation be done not just by individuals, but by the community, thus preserving a greater degree of coherence and Jewish identity. It makes such decisions primarily through its rabbinic leaders, since they are the ones most likely to know best what the tradition says and how to apply it to modern circumstances. This way of discerning what God wants thus does not depend on knowledge and skills that most Jews lack. In contrast to the orthodox approach, the conservative one has the distinct advantage of historical awareness and authenticity, for it interprets sources in their historical context and, like generations past, combines received Jewish law with an openness to the moral sensitivities and needs of the time. It thus has a greater balance of the traditional with the modern, greater openness to learning from others, and greater flexibility.

Yet a fourth way of discerning God's will is that pioneered by Martin Buber and developed further by Emanuel Levinas and Laurie Zoloth Dorfman.[5] In this approach we discover Jewish moral norms through our encounters with other human beings in one-to-one, direct interactions.

This approach, sometimes called "personalist" or even "feminist," suffers from the same problems that reform individualism has: it is weak on Jewish identity, continuity, coherence, and authority. At the same time, it locates moral decisions where they in fact lie – namely, in the interaction among human beings. Moreover, it invokes the inherent authority another human being has for us simply by virtue of being another human being who faces us directly.

## JEWISH MORALS

Why should Jews use any of these methodologies to determine what is moral? Why, in other words, should we expect that Judaism has anything to teach us about morality?

The reason is inherent in the word "religion." It comes from the Latin root meaning "bonds" or "linkages," the same root from which we get the word "ligament." Religions describe the ties that we have to our families, our community, the rest of humanity, the environment, and the Transcendent. In so doing, religions give us conceptual eyeglasses, as it were, through which we look at the world. Secular philosophies like liberalism, Marxism, or existentialism do that too (although they do not acknowledge a transcendent dimension of the world), but philosophies, *qua* philosophies, are purely intellectual. Religions, on the other hand, by their very nature embody their views of life in myths and rituals and thereby form communities of people connected to each other and to their shared vision of what is and what ought to be. Such religious communities provide comradery, strength, and meaning in the ongoing aspects of life – the life cycle, the seasonal cycle, and, indeed, the progress of each day and week; they furnish moral education in a variety of formats; and they also work together toward realizing their ideals. Religions, then, are related to morality because they provide pictures of the way the world is, visions of what it ought to be, and communities to teach morality and work toward moral goals.

Religions, though, do not all present the same moral view. Some norms, of course, are virtually universal – prohibitions against murder and theft, for example, and demands to help others. Even widespread norms, though, vary in definition; so, for example, for some, pacifist religions, all killing of human beings constitutes murder, whereas for others killing an enemy in war or in self-defense is not only permissible but mandatory. Furthermore, even when a norm is defined in the same way by two religions, each of them may give a different degree of emphasis to it. Finally, some positive duties or prohibitions are affirmed by some religions but not by others.

As a result of these variations, each religion presents a picture of reality and of the ideal which is distinctive in degree or kind. Each religion also inculcates its version of morality in its youth and adults in varying ways. To understand Jewish morality, then, we shall describe some important elements of Judaism's vision of the real and the ideal. Because Jews often think that the entire world thinks as Jews do, it will be helpful along the way to compare the Jewish norm with Christian norms and with Western secular norms as embodied in secular culture.

## THE HUMAN BEING

We begin with several Jewish convictions about the individual.

### The Body Belongs to God

For Judaism, God, as creator of the world, owns everything in it, including our bodies.[6] God loans our bodies to us for the duration of our lives, and we return them to God when we die. Consequently, neither men nor women have the right to govern their bodies as they will; God, as creator and owner, asserts the right to restrict how we use our bodies in ways articulated in Jewish law.

Some of God's rules require us to take reasonable care of our bodies, just as we would be obliged to protect and clean an apartment on loan to us. Rules of good hygiene, sleep, exercise, and diet in Jewish sources are therefore not just words to the wise designed for our comfort and longevity, as they are in American thinking; they are, rather, commanded acts that we owe God. So, for example, Hillel regards bathing as a commandment (*mitzvah*), and Maimonides includes his directives for good health in his code of law, considering them just as obligatory as other positive duties such as caring for the poor.[7]

Just as we are commanded to maintain good health, so we are obligated to avoid danger and injury.[8] Indeed, Jewish law views endangering one's health as worse than violating a ritual prohibition.[9] So, for example, anyone who can survive only by taking charity but refuses to do so out of pride is, according to the tradition, shedding his or her own blood and is thus guilty of a mortal offense.[10] Similarly, conservative, reform, and some orthodox authorities have prohibited smoking as an unacceptable risk to our God-owned bodies.[11]

Judaism also teaches that human beings do not have the right to dispose of their bodies at will (i.e. commit suicide), for to do so would totally obliterate something that belongs not to us but to God.[12] In contrast, the laws of most American states permit suicide (although most prohibit aiding and abetting a suicide).[13]

### Being Created in God's Image Imparts Value to Life, Regardless of the Individual's Level of Capacity or Incapacity

The American way of thinking is thoroughly pragmatic: a person's value is a function of what that person can *do* for others. It is this view, so deeply ingrained in American culture, that prompts Americans to value those who have unusual abilities, who *succeed* – and, conversely, to devalue those who are disabled in some way. In sharp contrast, the Torah declares that God created each of us in the divine image: "God created the human being in His image, in the image of God He created him; male and female God created them."[14] Exactly which feature of the human being reflects this divine image is a matter of debate within the tradition. The Torah itself seems to tie it to humanity's ability to make moral judgments – that is, to distinguish good from bad and right from wrong, to behave accordingly, and to judge one's own actions and those of others on the basis of this moral knowledge.[15] Another human faculty connected by the Torah and by later tradition to divinity is the ability to speak.[16] Maimonides claims that the divine image resides in our capacity to think, especially discursively.[17] Locating the divine image within us may also be the Torah's way of acknowledging that we can love, just as God does,[18] or that we are at least partially spiritual and thus share God's spiritual nature.[19]

Not only does this doctrine *describe* aspects of our nature; it also *prescribes* behavior. Specifically, because human beings are created in God's image, we affront God when we insult another person.[20] On the contrary, we must treat people with respect, recognizing each individual's uniqueness and divine worth because all human beings embody the image of God:

> For this reason Adam was created as a single person, to teach you that anyone who destroys one soul is described in Scripture as if he destroyed an entire world, and anyone who sustains one soul is described in Scripture as if he sustained an entire world ... And to declare the greatness of the Holy One, praised be He, for a person uses a mold to cast a number of coins, and they are all similar to each other, while the Sovereign of all sovereigns, the Holy One, praised be He, cast each person in the mold of the first human being and none of them is similar to any other. Therefore each and every person must say: "For me the world was created."[21]

Consider also the traditional blessing to be recited when seeing someone with a disability: "Praised are you, Lord our God, *meshaneh ha-briyyot*, who makes different creatures," or "who created us with differences." Precisely when we might recoil from a deformed or incapacitated person, or thank God for not making us like that, the tradition instead bids us to embrace the divine image in such people – indeed, to bless God for creating some of us so.[22]

### The Human Being Is an Integrated Whole, Combining All Aspects of Our Being

Western philosophical thought and Christianity have been heavily influenced by the Platonic, Neoplatonic, and Gnostic bifurcation of body and mind (or soul). In these systems of thought, the body is seen as the inferior part of human beings, either because its physical nature lures people to think that the concrete is real rather than the abstract (Plato), or because the body is the seat of our passions and hence our sins (Paul in Romans and Galatians).[23] The Greeks glorified the body in their art and sculpture, but that was only because developing the body was seen as a means to an end, a necessary prerequisite to cultivating the mind (as, for example, in Plato's pedagogic program in *The Republic*). Similarly, Paul regarded the body as "the temple of the Holy Spirit,"[24] but only because it serves to sustain the soul so that it can accept faith in Jesus; the body *per se* "makes me a prisoner of that law of sin which lives inside my body."[25] Augustine, Luther, and Calvin, following the lead of Paul, all maintain that the body's needs are to be suppressed as much as possible; indeed, asceticism and monasticism have been important themes in Christian ideology and history.

Although some Jews were heavily influenced by these doctrines of the people living around them (in particular, Philo and Maimonides), biblical and talmudic literature does not share in this divided understanding of the human being.[26] In the Talmud and Midrash, our soul is, in some senses, separable from our body, but it is not superior to it.[27] Indeed, one rabbinic source speaks of the soul as a guest in the body here on earth: one's host must accordingly be respected and well treated.[28]

Moreover, since the rabbis regarded the human being as an integrated whole, the body and the soul are to be judged as one:

> Antoninus said to Rabbi [Judah, the President, or "Prince," of the Sanhedrin], "The body and soul could exonerate themselves from judgment. How is this so? The body could say, 'The soul sinned, for from the day that it separated from me, lo, I am like a silent stone in the grave!' And the soul could say, 'The body is the sinner, for from the day that I separated from it, lo, I fly like a bird.'"
>
> Rabbi [Judah] answered him, "I will tell you a parable. What is the matter like? It is like a king of flesh and blood who had a beautiful orchard, and there were in it lovely ripe fruit. He placed two guardians over it, one a cripple and the other blind. Said the cripple to the blind man, 'I see beautiful ripe fruit in the orchard. Come and carry me, and we will bring and eat them.' The cripple rode on the back of the blind man, and they brought and ate them. After a while the owner of the orchard came and said to them, 'Where is my lovely fruit?' The cripple answered, 'Do I have legs to go?' The blind man answered, 'Do I have

eyes to see?' What did the owner do? He placed the cripple on the back of the blind man and judged them as one. So also the Holy Blessed One brings the soul and throws it into the body and judges them as one."[29]

Not only is this concept of the human being as fundamentally integrated manifest in God's ultimate, divine judgment of each of us; it is also the rabbis' recipe for life and their method for moral education. Although the rabbis emphasized the importance of studying and following the Torah, even placing it on a par with all the rest of the commandments,[30] they nonetheless believed that the life of the soul or mind by itself is not good, that it can, indeed, be the source of sin:

> An excellent thing is the study of Torah combined with some worldly occupation, for the labor demanded by both of them causes sinful inclinations to be forgotten. All study of Torah without work must, in the end, be futile and become the cause of sin.[31]

Thus, while the rabbis considered it a privilege to be able to study the Torah, they themselves – or at least most of them – earned their livelihood through bodily work, and they also valued the hard labor of the field worker who spends little time in the study of Torah:

> A favorite saying of the rabbis of Yavneh was: I am God's creature, and my fellow [who works in the field and is not a student] is God's creature. My work is in the town, and his work is in the country. I rise early for my work, and he rises early for his work. Just as he does not presume to do my work, so I do not presume to do his work. Will you say, I do much [in the study of Torah] and he does little? We have learned: One may do much or one may do little; it is all one, provided that the person directs his heart to Heaven.[32]

## The Body Is Morally Neutral and Potentially Good

The body is neither bad nor good. Rather, its energies, like those of our mind, will, and emotions, are morally neutral. All our faculties can and should be used for divine purposes as defined by Jewish law and tradition. Within these constraints, the body's pleasures are God given and are not to be shunned, for to do so would be an act of ingratitude toward our creator. The body, in other words, can and should give us pleasure to the extent that such pleasure enables us to live a life of holiness.

Here Judaism differs markedly from both the American secular view of the body on the one hand, and from Christianity on the other. In the

American media, the body is portrayed as a pleasure machine. In contemporary films, commercials, and music, we are encouraged to derive as much pleasure as possible from the body, for that is its primary purpose. The only restriction inherent in this ethic is that I may not deprive you of pleasure in the process of getting it for myself. Yet even this limitation is not absolute. Characters in American popular culture, such as James Bond, are "cool" precisely because they do not care about whether they injure others. In contrast, Judaism teaches that the body's pleasures are indeed to be enjoyed, but only when experienced within the framework of holiness delineated by Jewish law and theology.

At the other end of the spectrum is Christianity, which depicts the body as a negative part of us to be suppressed as much as possible. Thus in Catholic and many Protestant sources, the ideal Christian is the ascetic, who denies himself or herself the pleasures of sex, food, and possessions as much as possible. Of course, not all forms of contemporary Christianity embrace this ascetic way of thinking in its entirety, but Roman Catholicism, by far the most populous Christian faith, still does, and in some degree so do many Protestant denominations.

The closest Judaism comes to this attitude are the rules governing Yom Kippur and historical fast days like Tisha B'Av, on which we are to "afflict our souls" through fasting, sexual abstinence, and other forms of physical self-denial. But in each case such abstinence is restricted to that day alone and is designed to call attention to the spiritual theme of the day; deprivation itself is not expected to effect atonement or historical memory.

The Jewish mode for attaining holiness is thus not to endure pain but rather to use all of our faculties, including our bodily energies, to perform God's commandments. For example, though we eat like all animals do, our eating takes on a divine dimension when we observe Jewish dietary restrictions and surround our meals with the appropriate blessings.

Some bodily pleasures are even commanded. Thus with the exception of Yom Kippur, we may not fast on the sabbath, and we must eat three meals to celebrate it. We should also bathe and wear clean clothes in honor of the day.[33] Furthermore, as we shall see below, the ideal in Judaism is marriage, where sex can bring not only children but joy and companionship.

According to the rabbis, it is actually a sin to deny ourselves the pleasures that God's law allows. Just as the Nazirite was to bring a sin offering after denying himself the permitted delight of wine, so we will be called to account in the world to come for the ingratitude and haughtiness involved in denying ourselves the pleasures that God has provided.[34]

According to Maimonides, bodily pleasures are most appropriately enjoyed when we have the specific intent to enhance our ability to do God's will:

> He who regulates his life in accordance with the laws of medicine with the sole motive of maintaining a sound and vigorous physique and begetting children to do his work and labor for his benefit is not following the right course. A man should aim to maintain physical health and vigor in order that his soul may be upright, in a condition to know God ... Whoever throughout his life follows this course will be continually serving God, even while engaged in business and even during cohabitation, because his purpose in all that he does will be to satisfy his needs so as to have a sound body with which to serve God. Even when he sleeps and seeks repose to calm his mind and rest his body so as not to fall sick and be incapacitated from serving God, his sleep is service of the Almighty.[35]

## THE FAMILY

The family is a critical unit in Jewish ideology and practice, for it serves several purposes.

### Provides for Adult Needs

Ever since the Torah's story about the creation of Eve out of Adam's side, the Jewish tradition has considered it to be God's plan that "a man leaves his father and mother and clings to his wife and they become one flesh" (Genesis 2:24). They do not "become one flesh" in the ontological way of becoming one being, never to be rent asunder through divorce, for divorce, though often sad, is both permissible, as Deuteronomy 24 makes clear, and sometimes the right thing to do. They instead "become one flesh" in several other important ways.

Physically, they become one flesh when they have sexual relations together; marriage and family are designed, in part, to satisfy the sexual needs of both spouses. Most other traditions in both the Occident and the Orient – and in American law as well until recently – assume that men have sexual drives, and women do not, but women acquiesce to the sexual advances of their husbands because they want economic security and children.

Judaism, on the other hand, from its earliest sources, assumes that women have sexual needs just as much as men do. Thus Exodus 21:10 stipulates that even a man who marries a slave "must not withhold from her her food, her clothing, or her conjugal rights," and the rabbis reasoned that that holds even more obviously for a man marrying a free woman. Thus while a husband may never force himself upon his wife, the Mishnah stipulates the number of times each week that he must offer to have sexual relations with her, making that depend upon the frequency that his job enables him to be home. Conversely, he has rights to sex within marriage too, and if his wife consistently refuses to have sex with him, he may gradually reduce the amount of money he would have to pay her in a divorce settlement until he does not have to pay her anything.[36] Both parties may agree to have sexual relations according to a different schedule, but these provisions in Jewish law establish clearly that both partners to a marriage are entitled to have their sexual needs satisfied.

The spouses "become one flesh" psychologically as well. Thus the rabbis declare that "although a man may have many children, he must not remain without a wife," for, as God declares in the Garden of Eden story, "it is not good for a person to live alone."[37] Moreover, the rabbis affirm, "a man without a wife lives without blessing, without life, without joy, without help, and without peace."[38] Conversely, the rabbis denigrate bachelorhood – a far cry from the ideal of asceticism in other cultures.[39] Thus marriage, in the Jewish view, is the optimal context for human development and for all of our adult needs to be met.

Since a major objective of marriage and family is mutual love and support, spousal, parental, or child abuse, aside from being violations of Judaism's laws prohibiting assault and battery, are a total undermining of what family relations should be. They are also desecrations of the divine image inherent in each of us and a failure to respect those so created. Such acts are therefore condemned and punished in Jewish law.

## Creates, Educates, and Supports the Next Generation

Sex within marriage has two distinct purposes: companionship and procreation. Thus, on the one hand, sexual relations are valued as a form of human love even when the couple cannot, or is not planning to, have children. On the other hand, procreation is an important activity, so important, in fact, that it is the very first commandment mentioned in the

Torah: "God blessed them [the first man and woman] and God said to them: 'Be fruitful and multiply'" (Genesis 1:28). The rabbis later define that obligation as the duty to have minimally two children – although, like all obligations, it does not apply to those who cannot comply because of problems of infertility – and the ideal was to have as many children as one could.[40]

Marriage not only provides the venue for having children; it is also, in the Jewish view, the context in which they are educated. Parents have the duty to educate their children in Judaism, including its moral components.[41] Parents may use schools to help them fulfill that duty, but they must periodically check to make sure that their children are in fact learning what they should because ultimately the duty to educate children remains theirs. Moreover, much of the Jewish tradition can be taught only at home, for this is a tradition that is not restricted to the synagogue or school: it intends to influence virtually every detail of life.

## EDUCATION

Education is not only for children; it is a lifelong activity in Judaism. Thus already in the Torah, "Moses summoned all the Israelites and said to them: Hear, O Israel, the laws and rules that I proclaim to you this day! Study them and observe them faithfully!"[42] Moreover, the Torah requires that once every seven years all the Israelites – "men, women, and children" – gather to hear the entire Torah read.[43] Later Jewish tradition would make this instead a weekly reading from the Torah on each sabbath, with smaller sections read on Mondays and Thursdays, the market days, as well. From the very beginning, then, this was not to be an esoteric tradition, kept as a secret by the few privileged to know it; it was rather to be an open, public tradition, studied and interpreted by Jews of both genders and all ages. One striking indication of the depth of this Jewish value is that, though the Bible calls Moses a "prophet" and describes him as a military leader and an intermediary between God and the Israelites, the rabbis call him "Moses, our teacher."[44]

Jews for generations identified this commandment with studying the Jewish tradition, convinced that one should "turn it over, and turn it over again, for everything is included in it."[45] As Jews interacted with other cultures that were making progress in science, medicine, law, and other fields, however, a number of them learned those lessons and integrated their new knowledge into their practice and understanding of Judaism. This trend became considerably more pronounced after the Enlightenment, so much so that even a nineteenth-century orthodox thinker like Samson Raphael Hirsch could affirm that Jews should study other fields, for God's revelation is contained not only in traditional Jewish literature, but also in the world that he created. One's study of the world in fields like science and philosophy must, in his view, be evaluated by what one learns in the Torah, for that was given by God whereas the topics taught in universities were developed by fallible human beings; but one must study the results of human inquiry nevertheless.[46] Not all orthodox Jews then or now agree with this approach, but many do, and certainly the vast majority of Jews, who are not orthodox, take general education seriously. It is not an accident, then, that Jews attend college and graduate school in far higher percentages than the general population, and this is arguably, at least in part, an offshoot of the traditional Jewish commitment to education. In contemporary times, in fact, it is specifically Jewish education that Jews need to acquire more.

## THE COMMUNITY

If the family is the primary unit in Jewish life, the community follows close behind. Communities are necessary, in part, for practical purposes, for only through living in a community can one have what one needs to live life as a Jew – synagogues, schools, kosher food, a person skilled in circumcision, a cemetery, and more. Furthermore, only in a community can all the duties of Judaism be fulfilled, for justice, care for the poor, education, and many other Jewish demands require other people. Thus Jewish life is organized around the community.

The community is not only important for practical purposes, though; it also has theological import. Israel stood at Sinai as a community, and it is as a group that they made the Covenant with God. From then on, each Jew, as the Passover ritual powerfully states, is to see himself or herself "as if he himself left Egypt" and stood at Sinai, thereby sharing in God's work of liberation and God's Covenant with all other Jews in all generations. Judaism, contrary to Enlightenment ideology, does not see us as isolated individuals with rights; it sees us rather as members of a community who have duties to each other and to God.

This sense of community, shared by some sacramental forms of Christianity, by Islam, and by Confucianism, to name a few, is much stronger than the kinds of communities we are used to in modern, post-Enlightenment societies. In the United States, for example, all communities are voluntary: I may choose to join a group or leave it at any time. I may even choose to give up my citizenship as an American. In Jewish law, though, once I am Jewish by either being born to a Jewish woman or being converted to Judaism, I am Jewish for life. If I convert to another religion, I am an apostate, and I lose the privileges of being Jewish (such as being married or buried as a Jew, being counted as part of the prayer quorum, etc.), but I retain all the obligations of being Jewish. This is, then, not a voluntary sense of community but a corporate sense, in which I am literally part of the body of the Jewish community and cannot be severed from it.[47] This thick sense of community in Covenant with God is symbolized by the *minyan,* the prayer quorum consisting of ten Jewish adults. Jews may pray or study individually, but some parts of the liturgy can only be recited, and the official Torah reading can only be accomplished in the presence of ten Jewish adults, the minimum number for a community. Only as such can we bless and sanctify God fully, and only as such can we hear and study God's word adequately.

The following talmudic list of facilities and people that are to be part of any Jewish community fit for a rabbi to reside there reveals the nature of what a community is for the Jewish tradition:

> It has been taught: A scholar should not reside in a city where [any] of the following ten things is missing: (1) a court of justice that can impose flagellation and monetary penalties; (2) a charity fund, collected by two people and distributed by three [to ensure honesty and wise policies of distribution]; (3) a synagogue; (4) public baths; (5) toilet facilities; (6) a circumciser; (7) a doctor; (8) a notary [for writing official documents]; (9) a slaughterer [of kosher meat]; and (10) a schoolmaster. Rabbi Akiba is quoted [as including in the list] also several kinds of fruit because they are beneficial for eyesight.[48]

The community must thus provide the facilities and people necessary for justice (a court and notary), Jewish religious life (a synagogue, a circumciser, and a kosher slaughterer), Jewish education (a rabbi and schoolmaster), charity, and healthcare, including public baths and toilets (remember that this was written before the advent in the past century of indoor plumbing), a doctor, and, according to Rabbi Akiba, even the foods necessary for health.

If the Jewish community of talmudic times had not lived under foreign rule, this list would undoubtedly also include other functions that the rulers supplied – defense, roads and bridges, etc. Still, in many times and places, Jewish communities had semi-autonomy, with the powers of taxation and policing that that implied. The Jewish court would, for example, appoint inspectors of the weights and measures used by merchants to insure honesty in business.[49]

## THE ENVIRONMENT

Long before modern times, the Jewish tradition saw protection of the environment as not only desirable but mandatory. Already in Judaism's foundational text, the Torah (the Five Books of Moses), there is ample evidence of this concern and this demand. Even though the first creation story in the Bible portrays Adam as having dominion over nature, in the second biblical story God placed Adam in the Garden of Eden specifically "to work it *and to preserve it.*"[50] The very first two chapters of Genesis, then, require that we *balance* our use of nature with our preservation of it. This connection between human deeds and environmental flourishing continues in God's Covenant with Israel, where God announces that if the Israelites obey God, there will be rain in its season and crops aplenty, but if they disobey God, then there will be drought and famine.[51] Indeed, the Israelites should obey God so that the land itself "will not spew you out."[52]

The Israelites were commanded to take a number of specific steps to protect the land, the vegetation, and the animals. They were to allow the land to lie fallow one year out of every seven, relying on God's extra bounty in the sixth year to eat during the seventh and eighth. During the fiftieth year, too, the land was to rest, and the Israelites were to eat what grew naturally.[53] A series of biblical laws ensure that human beings will not cause undue pain to animals and will give them a day of rest one day in seven.[54] The Jewish dietary laws restrict consumption of fish, fowl, and animals to approximately four percent of the animal kingdom, and Adam and Eve's vegetarianism remains an ideal.[55] Even when the Israelites were at war, they were to preserve those trees that bore fruit, cutting down for their military needs only those trees that did not.[56] The rabbis later articulate these themes poignantly:

> "Look at the work of God, for who can fix what He has ruined?" (Ecclesiastes 7:13). At the time that the Holy One, blessed be He,

created the first man, he took him and showed him all the trees of the Garden of Eden and said to him: "Look at how beautiful and praiseworthy are my creations. Everything that I created, I created for you. Pay attention not to spoil or destroy My world, for if you spoil it, there is no one to fix it after you."[57]

This last source also describes a piece of Judaism's "deed ecology" which should be noted. Yes, according to these sources God creates the world for human beings, and yes, God gives humanity dominion over it. But that dominion applies only if human beings obey God and take steps to preserve the world. That is, human dominion is only as God's agent, for ultimately God owns the world and all that is in it. Thus God can and does limit our usage, commanding, for example, that we let animals as well as humans rest on the sabbath, and that every seventh year the land lie fallow as a "sabbath to the Lord."[58] These tenets should make us humble and caring in our treatment of the world, for it does not belong to us. Indeed, we can ruin it and be booted out of it if we fail to fulfill our fiduciary responsibility to God to take care of it.

## SOCIAL ACTION AND THE MESSIANIC FUTURE

All of these elements of Jewish life – the individual, the family, education, and the community – are necessary for the ongoing life of Jews, but they are also intended to enable Jews to carry out the Jewish mission. Jews believe that the Messiah has not yet come, that the world is still broken and fragmented by war, disease, poverty, meanness, and the like. Only God can ultimately bring the Messiah; in the *Aleinu*, the prayer that ends every Jewish service, we express our hope that God will "utterly destroy false gods and fix the world through the reign of the Almighty."[59] Nevertheless, we human beings are to help God in that task as his agents and partners in the ongoing repair of the world. This includes research into preventing or curing disease, political steps to avoid war and reinforce peace, political and economic measures to stop hunger, legal methods to assure justice, and educational efforts to teach morality and understanding. Jews have been and continue to be heavily involved in social action; indeed, they overwhelmingly see it as the most important factor in their Jewish identity.[60] This commitment to repair the world stems from the conviction that the world is not now redeemed, that we must act in order to help God bring about the messianic hope for the future.

## EPILOGUE

In the end, it is both Jewish ethics and morality that shape the Jew. Jewish theoretical convictions about the divine source of morality and the ways to discern God's will give Jews a sense of why they should be moral and how, even in the radically changed world of today. Jewish moral beliefs about the nature of the human being, the family, education, the community, and the future define what is important in life and motivate Jews to try to achieve those moral goals. Together they pose a distinct challenge to Jews to know God's will and to do it, just as it was in the time of the Torah:

> Surely, this Instruction which I enjoin upon you this day is not too baffling for you, nor is it beyond reach. It is not in the heavens, that you should say, "Who among us can go up to the heavens and get it for us and impart it to us, that we may observe it?" Neither is it beyond the sea, that you should say, "Who among us can cross to the other side of the sea and get it for us and impart it to us, that we may observe it?" No, the thing is very close to you, in your mouth and in your heart, to observe it.
>
> (Deuteronomy 30:11–14)

*NOTES*

The abbreviations below are used in the following:

    M.   = Mishnah, edited *c.* 200 CE
    J.    = Jerusalem (Palestinian) Talmud, edited *c.* 400 CE
    B.   = Babylonian Talmud, edited *c.* 500 CE
    M.T. = Maimonides' *Mishneh Torah,* completed in 1177.
    S.A. = Karo's *Shulhan Arukh,* completed in 1565.

1. For example, B. *Bava Mezia* 30b. To explore the relationship between Jewish law and morality further, see Elliot N. Dorff, *Matters of Life and Death: A Jewish Approach to Modern Medical Ethics* (Philadelphia: Jewish Publication Society, 1998), pp. 395–417. For other conservative views, see Robert Gordis, *The Dynamics of Judaism: A Study in Jewish Law* (Bloomington: Indiana University Press, 1990), pp. 50–68; and Simon Greenberg, *The Ethical in the Jewish and American Heritage* (New York: Jewish Theological Seminary of America, 1977), pp. 157–218.

    For unusual, but thoughtful, left-wing orthodox approaches to this issue, see David Hartman, *A Living Covenant: The Innovative Spirit in Traditional Judaism* (New York: Free Press, 1985; reprinted, Woodstock, VT: Jewish Lights, 1997), pp. 89–108; and Shubert Spero, *Morality,*

*Halakha, and the Jewish Tradition* (New York: Ktav and Yeshiva University Press, 1983), pp. 166–200.

Since, for reform Judaism, Jewish law is, in Rabbi Solomon Freehof's words, "not directive, but advisory," "our guidance, but not our governance," moral norms, however they are construed, always take precedence over Jewish law, for moral norms are binding, but Jewish law is not. See Solomon Freehof, *Reform Responsa* (Cincinnati: Hebrew Union College Press, 1960), pp. 3–23; the citations are on p. 22. The latest reform platform, *A Centenary Perspective*, issued in 1976, says, "Our founders stressed that the Jewish ethical responsibilities, personal and social, are enjoined by God. The past century has taught us that the claims made upon us may begin with our ethical obligations, but they extend to many other aspects of Jewish living." Reform Jews are therefore "to confront the claims of Jewish tradition, however differently perceived, and to exercise their individual autonomy, choosing and creating on the basis of commitment and knowledge." This represents a wider commitment to Jewish practice, but not a conviction that Jewish law *per se* is binding, and so the relationship between Jewish law and morality does not bother reform thinkers nearly as much as it does those in the conservative and orthodox movements, who hold that Jewish law is binding. See Eugene B. Borowitz, *Reform Judaism Today* (New York: Behrman House, 1983), pp. xxii–xxiii.

2. Eugene Borowitz, *Renewing the Covenant* (Philadelphia: Jewish Publication Society, 1991), especially pp. 284–299.

3. See note 1. above.

4. See the readings by Elliot Dorff and Aaron Mackler on methods to gain moral guidance from the Jewish tradition in *Contemporary Jewish Ethics and Morality: A Reader*, ed. Elliot N. Dorff and Louis E. Newman (New York: Oxford University Press, 1995), pp. 161–193.

5. See the readings by Annette Aronowitz and Laurie Zoloth Dorfman in *Contemporary Jewish Ethics and Morality*, ed. Dorff and Newman, pp. 212–245.

6. See, for example, Exodus 19:5; Deuteronomy 10:14; Psalms 24:1. See also Genesis 14:19, 22 (where the Hebrew word for "creator" [*koneh*] also means "possessor," and where "heaven and earth" is a merism for those and everything in between) and Psalms 104:24, where the same word is used with the same meaning. The following verses have the same theme, although not quite as explicitly or as expansively: Exodus 20:11; Leviticus 25:23, 42, 55; Deuteronomy 4:35, 39; 32:6.

7. Bathing, for example, is a commandment according to Hillel, *Leviticus Rabbah* 34:3. Maimonides summarized and codified the rules requiring proper care of the body in M.T. *Laws of Ethics (De'ot)*, chapters 3–5. He

spells out there in remarkable clarity that the purpose of these positive duties to maintain health is not to feel good and live a long life, but rather to have a healthy body so that one can then serve God.

8. B. *Shabbat* 32a; B. *Bava Kamma* 15b, 80a, 91b; M.T. *Laws of Murder* 11:4–5; S.A. *Yoreh De'ah* 116:5 gloss; S.A. *Hoshen Mishpat* 427:8–10.

9. B. *Hullin* 10a; S.A. *Orah Hayyim* 173:2; S.A. *Yoreh De'ah* 116:5 gloss.

10. S.A. *Yoreh De'ah* 255:2.

11. J. David Bleich, "Smoking," *Tradition* 16(4) 1977, pp. 130–133; Solomon Freehof, *Reform Responsa for Our Time* (Cincinnati: Hebrew Union College Press, 1977), chapter 11; *Proceedings of the Rabbinical Assembly*, 44, 1983, p. 182. All of the above are reprinted in Elliot N. Dorff and Arthur Rosett, *A Living Tree: The Roots and Growth of Jewish Law* (Albany: State University of New York Press, 1988), pp. 337–362.

12. Genesis 9:5; M. *Semahot* 2:2; B. *Bava Kamma* 91b; *Genesis Rabbah* 34:19 states that the ban against suicide includes not only cases where blood was shed, but also self-inflicted death through strangulation and the like; M.T. *Laws of Murder* 2:3; M.T. *Laws of Injury and Damage* 5:1; S.A. *Yoreh De'ah* 345:1–3. This reasoning extends to inanimate property as well: we may use what we need, but we may not destroy any more of God's world than we need to in order to accomplish our purposes in life. This is the prohibition of *ba'al tashhit*, "Do not destroy," based on Deuteronomy 20:19–20 and amplified in the tradition to prohibit any unnecessary destruction: B. *Bava Kamma* 8:6, 7; B. *Bava Kamma* 92a, 93a; M.T. *Laws of Murder* 1:4, where Maimonides specifically invokes this theological basis for the law against suicide; M.T. *Laws of Injury and Damage* 5:5; *Sefer Ha-Hinnukh*, commandment 529; S.A. *Hoshen Mishpat* 420:1, 31.

13. Specifically, forty-four states currently have laws making aiding a person to commit suicide a felony. See David G. Savage, "Supreme Court to Decide Issue of Right to Die," *Los Angeles Times*, 2 October 1996, p. A–16. Oregon is the only state that specifically permits such aid.

14. Genesis 1:27; see also Genesis 5:1.

15. See Genesis 1:26–27; 3:1–7, 22–24.

16. See Genesis 2:18–24; Numbers 12:1–16; Deuteronomy 22:13–19. Note also that *ha-middaber*, "the speaker," is a synonym for the human being (in comparison to animals) in medieval Jewish philosophy.

17. Maimonides, *Guide for the Perplexed*, part I, chapter 1.

18. See Deuteronomy 6:5; Leviticus 19:18, 33–34; and note that the traditional prayer book juxtaposes the paragraph just before the Shema, which speaks of God's love for us, with the first paragraph of the Shema, which commands us to love God.

19. Consider the prayer in the traditional, early morning weekday service, *Elohai neshamah she-natata bi*, "My God, the soul [or life breath] which

you have imparted to me is pure. You created it, You formed it, You breathed it into me; You guard it within me." *Sim Shalom*, ed. Jules Harlow (New York: Rabbinical Assembly and United Synagogue of America, 1985), pp. 8–11. Similarly, the rabbis describe the human being as part divine and part animal, the latter consisting of the material aspects of the human being and the former consisting of that which we share with God; see *Sifre Deuteronomy*, par. 306; 132a. Or consider this rabbinic statement in *Genesis Rabbah* 8:11: "In four respects man resembles the creatures above, and in four respects the creatures below. Like the animals he eats and drinks, propagates his species, relieves himself, and dies. Like the ministering angels he stands erect, speaks, possesses intellect, and sees [in front of him and not on the side like an animal]."

20. *Genesis Rabbah* 24:7. Consider also: "Great is human dignity, for it overrides a negative prohibition of the Torah" (B. *Berakhot* 19b). "The Holy One, blessed be He, has concern for the honor of all His creatures, including non-Jews and even wicked people like Balaam" (*Numbers Rabbah* 20:14). "All the Holy One, blessed be He, created, He created for His own honor" (B. *Yoma* 38a, based on Isaiah 43:7).

21. M. *Sanhedrin* 4:5. Some manuscripts are less universalistic; they read, "anyone who destroys one *Israelite* soul is described in Scripture as if he destroyed an entire world, and anyone who sustains one *Israelite* soul is described in Scripture as if he sustained an entire world." A Hasidic *bon mot* (from Martin Buber, *Tales of the Hasidim* (New York: Schocken, 1948, 1961), vol. 2, pp. 249–250) reminds us that we must balance this recognition of our divine worth with a proper dose of humility:

> Rabbi Bunam said: A person should always have two pieces of paper, one in each pocket. On one should be written, "For me the world was created." On the other should be written, "I am but dust and ashes" (Genesis 18:27).

22. For a thorough discussion of this blessing and concept in the Jewish tradition, see Carl Astor, ... *Who Makes People Different* (New York: United Synagogue of America, 1985). The Torah requires that the body of a person who was executed for a capital crime must be removed from the place of hanging by morning out of respect for the divine image inherent even in such a human being, and the rabbis thus require us to respect the divine image even within a criminal whose past actions we detest and punish. See Deuteronomy 21:22–23; B. *Mo'ed Katan* 16a; J. *Kiddushin* 4:1; J. *Nazir* 7:5

23. Romans 6–8, especially 6:12; 7:14–24; 8:3, 10, 12–13; Galatians 5:16–24; see also 1 Corinthians 7:2, 9, 36–38.

24. 1 Corinthians 6:19.

25. Romans 7:23.

26. The Greek side of Maimonides is most in evidence in his *Guide for the Perplexed*, where he states flatly that

> It is also the object of the perfect Law to make man reject, despise, and reduce his desires as much as is in his power. He should only give way to them when absolutely necessary. It is well known that it is intemperance in eating, drinking, and sexual intercourse that people mostly rave and indulge in; and these very things counteract the ulterior perfection of man, impede at the same time the development of his first perfection [i.e. bodily health], and generally disturb the social order of the country and the economy of the family. For by following entirely the guidance of lust, in the manner of fools, man loses his intellectual energy, injures his body, and perishes before his natural time; sighs and cares multiply; and there is an increase of envy, hatred, and warfare for the purpose of taking what another possesses. The cause of all this is the circumstance that the ignorant considers physical enjoyment as an object to be sought for its own sake. God in His wisdom has therefore given us such commandments as would counteract that object, and prevent us altogether from directing our attention to it... For the chief object of the Law is to [teach man to] diminish his desires. (Part III, chapter 33).

Philo's views can be found, in part, in the selections from his writings in Hans Lewy, Alexander Altmann, and Isaak Heinemann, eds, *Three Jewish Philosophers* (Philadelphia: Jewish Publication Society, 1960), especially pp. 42–51, 54–55, and 71–75. He calls the body a "prison house" on p. 72.

27. For example, when the Torah describes God as breathing life into Adam's body (Genesis 2:7), rabbinic sources understand that to mean not only physical life but consciousness; see B. *Ta'anit* 22b; B. *Niddah* 31a; *Genesis Rabbah* 14:9. As articulated in several early morning prayers said by Jews daily, with roots in *Leviticus Rabbah* 18:1 (toward the end) and *Midrash Shahar Tov,* chapter 25, God repeats that process each day by taking our souls away during sleep and returning them to us again when we awake and regain consciousness. Moreover, at death, the soul leaves the body only to be united with it again at the time of resurrection. Rabbinic sources conflict, however, as to whether the soul can exist apart from the body, and even those who say it can depict the soul in physical terms, capable of performing many of the functions of the body; see B. *Berakhot* 18b–19a; B. *Haggigah* 12b; B. *Ketubbot* 77b.

28. *Leviticus Rabbah* 34:3.

29. B. *Sanhedrin* 91a–91b. See also *Mekhilta,* Beshalah, Shirah, chapter 2 (ed. Horowitz-Rabin, 1960, p. 125); *Leviticus Rabbah* 4:5; *Yalkut Shimoni* on

Leviticus 4:2 (#464); *Tanhuma*, Vayikra 6. The very development of the term *neshamah* from meaning physical breath to one's inner being bespeaks Judaism's view that the physical and the spiritual are integrated.

30. M. *Pe'ah* 1:1; B. *Kiddushin* 40b.

31. M. *Avot* 2:1. See B. *Berakhot* 35b, especially the comment of Abayae there in responding to the earlier theories of Rabbi Ishmael and Rabbi Simeon bar Yohai.

32. B. *Berakhot* 17a; the earlier rabbinic teaching cited at the end as what we have learned appears in B. *Menahot* 110a. Although a few of the classical rabbis belonged to wealthy families, most were menial laborers and studied when they could. Hillel, for example, was so poor that he became the symbol of the poor man who nevertheless found the time and money to study the Torah (B. *Yoma* 35b); Akiba had been a shepherd before he devoted himself to study at age forty, subsisting on the price he received for the bundle of wood he collected each day (*Avot d'Rabbi Natan*, chapter 6); Joshua was a charcoal burner (B. *Berakhot* 28a); Yose bar Halafta worked in leather (B. *Shabbat* 49b); Yohanan was a sandal maker (M. *Avot* 4:14); Judah was a baker (J. *Haggigah* 77b); and Abba Saul kneaded dough (B. *Pesahim* 34a) and had been a grave digger (B. *Niddah* 24b).

33. Cf. M.T. *Laws of the Sabbath*, chapter 30.

34. The law of the Nazirite appears in Numbers 6:11, and cf. the rabbinic derivation from that law – that abstinence is prohibited – appears first in B. *Ta'anit* 11a. Cf. also M.T. *Laws of Ethics (De'ot)* 3:1.

35. M.T. *Laws of Ethics (De'ot)* 3:3.

36. M. *Ketubbot* 5:6–7.

37. Genesis 2:18; B. *Yevamot* 61b.

38. *Genesis Rabbah* 17:2; B. *Yevamot* 62b–63a; *Midrash Psalms* on Psalm 59:2.

39. B. *Kiddushin* 29b–30a.

40. The minimum of two: M. *Yevamot* 6:6 (61b); M.T. *Laws of Marriage* 15:4; S.A. *Even Ha'ezer* 1:5. The ideal of having more: B. *Yevamot* 62b, basing it on Isaiah 45:18 and Ecclesiastes 11:6; M.T. *Laws of Marriage* 15:16.

41. Deuteronomy 6:7, 20–25; 11:19. This was already one of Abraham's duties: Genesis 18:19.

42. Deuteronomy 5:1.

43. Deuteronomy 31:10–13.

44. Moses as a prophet: Deuteronomy 34:10. According to my computer program, the phrase "Moses, our teacher" appears fifty-six times in the Babylonian Talmud. For example, B. *Berakhot* 3b, 12b, 33b, 55a, 55b; B. *Shabbat* 30a, 92a.

45. M. *Avot* 5:24.

46. Samson Raphael Hirsch, *Judaism Eternal*, trans. Isidor Grunfeld (London: Soncino, 1956), vol. 2, pp. 245–250.

47. For more on this, see Elliot N. Dorff, "Training Rabbis in the Land of the Free," in *The Seminary at 100*, ed. Nina Beth Cardin and David Wolf Silverman (New York: Jewish Theological Seminary of America, 1987), pp. 11–28, especially 12–19; and Milton R. Konvitz, *Judaism and the American Idea* (New York: Schocken, 1978), chapter 5.

48. B. *Sanhedrin* 17b.

49. B. *Bava Batra* 89a; M.T. *Laws of Theft* 8:20; S.A. *Hoshen Mishpat* 231:2.

50. Genesis 1:26; 2:15.

51. For example, Leviticus 26:3–4, 14–16, 19; Deuteronomy 11:13–17 (used as part of the second paragraph of the *Shema* prayer, recited twice daily); Deuteronomy 28:1–6, 11–12, 15–18, 23–24, etc.

52. Leviticus 20:22.

53. Leviticus 25:1–7, 11, 20–24.

54. For example, Exodus 20:10; 23:12; Deuteronomy 22:6–7, 10; Deuteronomy 25:4; etc.

55. See Leviticus 11 and Deuteronomy 14 for the Jewish dietary restrictions on animals that may be eaten, and see Genesis 1:29 and 2:16 for Adam's vegetarianism. The estimate of four percent is Jacob Milgrom's ("The Jewish Dietary Laws as an Ethical System," *Interpretation*, 1963, p. xxx).

56. Deuteronomy 20:19–20.

57. *Midrash Kohelet Rabbah* 7:20.

58. Leviticus 25:4. For further reading on Judaism and ecology, see, for example, *Ecology and the Jewish Spirit: Where Nature and the Sacred Meet*, ed. Ellen Bernstein (Woodstock, VT: Jewish Lights, 1998). On this last point, see especially the essay there by Neal Joseph Loevinger, "(Mis)reading Genesis: A Response to Environmentalist Critiques of Judaism," pp. 32–40.

59. This prayer is found in the prayer books of all Jewish denominations, but see, for example, *Siddur Sim Shalom*, ed. Jules Harlow (New York: Rabbinical Assembly and United Synagogue of America, 1985), pp. 162f.

60. Half of American Jews polled across the nation by the *Los Angeles Times* listed a commitment to social equality as the factor most important to their sense of Jewish identity, whereas only seventeen percent cited religious observance and another seventeen percent cited support for Israel. See Robert Scheer, "Jews in U.S. Committed to Equality," *Los Angeles Times*, 13 April 1988, section I, pp. 1, 14–15.

*Plate 5* The great Jama Masjid of Old Delhi, begun in 1644 and completed in 1658, is the largest mosque in India. It represents the final architectural extravagance of the Moghal emperor Shah Jahan, creator of the Taj Mahal, the tomb in Agra which he had built in honor of his wife. Photo: *Nancy M. Martin*

# 5

# ISLAMIC ETHICS *and* GENDER ISSUES

*Zayn Kassam*

Are current Islamic formulations of gender roles, expectations, and social governance amenable to Islamic ethical analysis? This chapter will compare and contrast ethical theory in India with practices pertaining to gender in order to identify whether there are resources internal to the Islamic tradition, in all its diversity, which would provide a constructive framework of analysis with which to approach social and legal customs regarding gender issues in the Islamic world.

## THEORETICAL ETHICAL CONSIDERATIONS

Since in Islamic discourse and praxis the Qur'an occupies a hallowed point of departure from which all subsequent formulations flow, I would like to consider the following questions: what does the Qur'an consider to be "right" or "good" or "just," and how do we know it? George Hourani, whose erudite investigation of the subject is reproduced here, suggests the following framework of analysis.[1] With respect to what the Qur'an considers to be "right," one might take (1) the objectivist approach, which argues that right has an objective meaning that stands whether or not the observer judges something right or wrong, and (2) the subjectivist approach, which means that right is whatever someone or other approves or commands. The subjectivist could mean (a) whatever the Muslim community deems right or wrong, based on the Tradition or *hadith* that states, "Whatever the believers see as good is good with God, and whatever the Muslims see as bad is bad with God."[2] This understanding emphasizes the *'ijma* or consensus of the learned Muslim community and constituted one of the four sources of the classical Islamic legal schools. After about the tenth century, the consensus of the learned was made no longer admissible, since it was thought that all subsequent legal practice had to rely on *taqlīd* or imitation of the laws already on the books. The subjectivist position might also mean (b) whatever is commanded by God is right. This latter understanding is also known as ethical voluntarism and is the prevailing view of all the mainstream Sunni jurists and theologians.

With respect to how one may know what is right, there are two main positions: (1) rationalism and (2) traditionalism. Rationalism says that what is right can be known by independent reason, and this may be further subdivided into (a) absolute rationalism, which holds that what is right can always be known by independent reason, and (b) partial rationalism, which holds that what is right can be known in some cases by reason alone, in others by revelation and derived sources such as the Traditions and consensus and analogy alone, and in others by both in agreement. Partial rationalism was held by theologically-minded rationalists such as the Mu'tazilites, who sought to find a place for both reason and revelation in ethics, but whose influence, though far reaching, did not become part of the majority view. Traditionalism says that we can never know what is right by independent reason but only by revelation and derived sources, and this again was the view of the main Sunni schools of jurisprudence and theology.

Hourani's study of the Qur'an indicates that with respect to objectivism, the Qur'an addresses many ethical sentences to pagans, exhorting them to be kind, charitable, and thoughtful and to reflect and not to be arrogant. This implies that ethical language is something that is common and understood by both the speaker and the audience in a similar manner. That is, humans are capable of intuiting what is right. Regarding the subjective and specifically with respect to human subjectivism, there are verses that decisively discount collective or individual human like or dislike of an action as being appropriate standards of value. Thus, this means that humans may not like what is good for them or may indeed like doing what is not good for them. However, although these verses discount human pleasure as a guide for identifying what is valuable, they cannot be used as a basis for suggesting that humans are therefore unable to hold objective standards of values; humans may see the value in something even as they can be aware that they do not like it despite the fact that it is good for them.

The other kind of subjectivism, known as ethical voluntarism, according to which only God can command or forbid what has ethical value, is a stance that could follow easily from a rejection of human subjectivism. And this is certainly the view that has come to prevail in mainstream Sunni Muslim discourse. However, Hourani argues that a close reading of textual passages in the Qur'an does not readily point to a stance of ethical voluntarism; rather, although there are specific decrees such as dietary prohibitions, with respect to ethical values there are many uses of ethical terms in the Qur'an which do not necessitate a voluntarist interpretation. This leads Hourani to observe "that the Qur'an frequently refers to objective values, which cannot be analyzed completely in terms of commands and obedience."[3] From an ontological point of view, then, the Qur'an neither rejects objectively understood ethical value terms nor promotes an uncompromising ethical voluntarism in which only God can command or forbid what is right and wrong, and it does advance a view that human likes and dislikes (not to be confused with what reflective humans understand) are not a sufficient standard for ethical values.

From an epistemological point of view, with respect to how we know what is right and what is wrong, the Qur'an emphasizes the human "need for divine guidance in ethical matters."[4] The rationalist approach that argues that humans can always know what is right by use of their natural reason, independent of revealed scripture, is not a tenable position in the Qur'an. Rather, the Qur'an continuously stresses the human need for revelation as a source of moral guidance, in verses such as 93:7 ("He found you wandering and guided you") and 40:53–54 ("And formerly We gave guidance to Moses, and bequeathed to the Israelites the Book as guidance and a reminder to men possessed of minds"), and finally 6:71 ("Say: God's guidance is the true guidance, and we are commanded to surrender to the Lord of the worlds").

In these and other verses the meaning of *hudā* or guidance is revealed to be "not so much instruction on particular duties as orientation to man's situation in the world, his belonging to God and awaiting a Judgement from Him."[5] That is not to say that no specifics are ever given, but they are given so very rarely, and that too in such a form as follows: verse 33:36 commands, "It is not for any believer, man or woman, when God and His Messenger have decreed a matter, to have the choice in the affair. Whosoever disobeys God and His Message has gone astray into manifest error." Further verses testify that according to the Qur'an, it is itself the most important source of moral and religious guidance for humans, which, if neglected, leaves humans open to the immoral alternative to follow passions.

However, as noted earlier, the Qur'an is not replete with specific ethical injunctions. Further, although Hourani's classification is by and large useful, it must be borne in mind that the mind or reason need not always be considered to be a source independent of revelation, but rather to be a divinely given facility that enables the better understanding of revelation. (24:61: "Thus Allah makes clear His revelations for you, that haply you may understand"; 24:64: "Lo! verily unto Allah belongs whatsoever is in the heavens and the earth.")

But can humans sometimes, as opposed to always, know what is right by natural reason, independent of scripture? The Qur'an itself refers to its verses as signs for those who understand and often mentions people of understanding or those possessed of minds or people who think. The Qur'an also addresses pre-Islamic Arabs and condemns them for moral evil, tacitly acknowledging their ability to have a moral sense independent of scriptures. Thus, although some specific rights and wrongs are mentioned, such as that it is wrong to kill female children and it is right to free a slave (90:13), by and large the intelligent person is expected to understand what is right and what is wrong. Thus, the Qur'an does allow for independent ethical judgment, and indeed, a good person is one who believes in God and does right. The traditionalist view that humans can only know right through revelation cannot be proven incorrect, but the fact that the Qur'an is not decisively against rationalist views suggests that humans have access to "other paths to ethical knowledge besides [explicit] revelation."[6]

In the spirited theological and legal discourses and debates during the first three centuries of Islam, that is, through to the tenth century CE, ethical voluntarism (also known as theistic subjectivism) was paired with traditionalism in order to become the dominant form of understanding ethics and ethical behavior in the legal schools. This move effectively drew into the shadows the remarkable possibilities for ethical reflection within

Islam. Even though the Qur'an itself does not rule out objectivism with respect to the ontology of ethics, on the one hand, it also does not deny that humans may sometimes, not always, know what is right through natural reason, on the other. Yet these latter considerations were not viewed as useful at the time of the consolidation of the legal schools. According to Hourani, Sunnite jurisprudence "aimed to base all judgements of law and ethics on revealed sources, i.e. on God's approval or disapproval as expressed in the Qur'an and Traditions, and correspondingly to exclude direct human judgments of right and wrong as authorized sources of Islamic law, except in case of unanimous agreement among jurists."[7]

Why the pairing that came to dominate theological and legal discourses did so is a subject requiring further investigation; there certainly were challenges to this kind of formulation of Islamic ethics from the rationalist theologians, the philosophers, and the sectarians. What concerns us here and now, though, is that should the opinion makers in the Islamic world wish it, there is certainly enough scope *vis-à-vis* ethical theory in the Qur'an to enable the Muslim learned to determine how best to organize Muslim society through institutions that would reflect both the fundamental human rights suggested by the Qur'an and ethical frameworks that could guide society, in keeping with the Tradition that states, "My community will not agree upon an error."

## VIOLENCE AGAINST WOMEN

Two issues that are associated with the Islamic world but not restricted to it bear some examination in the context of the need to engage in ethical reflection, both on the part of those engaged in these practices and on the part of those engaged in legal governance and implementation institutions: female genital mutilation and honor killings. It must first be clarified that not all of the six hundred million Muslim women in the world experience these. From a statistical point of view, neither of these two practices amount to the kind of significance that would justify their being identified as Muslim problems; yet from a humanistic point of view, even one killing of a woman on the suspicion of adultery is one killing too many, and if she happens to be Muslim, which is not always the case, then that is secondary to the fact that her life has been taken away from her.

## Female Genital Mutilation

The practice of female genital mutilation – also referred to by the more neutral terms "modification" or "cutting" – did not originate with Islam, based on the evidence that it is practically unknown in the Islamic sourcelands, Arabia and its environs, and there is no sanction or mention of either female or male circumcision in the Qur'an. However, our earliest sources do testify that male circumcision was adopted by Muslims in keeping with the Covenant made with the common progenitor of the Semitic monotheisms, Abraham. It is not surprising, then, that in the Tradition literature Abraham is also made the source of female genital mutilation. Abraham, considered the first monotheist by Muslims, is the husband of Sarah, who cannot bear children; with Sarah's permission he has a child named Ishmael with Sarah's handmaiden Hagar. Ibn Kathīr, a fourteenth-century historian and qur'anic commentator, mentions that Hagar subsequently grew haughty with Sarah, and out of jealousy Sarah vowed to cut "three limbs" off Hagar, whereupon Abraham ordered Hagar to pierce her ears and circumcize herself.[8] In the Tradition literature, which records the deeds and words of Muhammad as an extra-qur'anic record, and which was written down almost two centuries after Muhammad's death, female circumcision is simply identified as having originated with Hagar.

Some Traditions, not found in the most reputable Tradition collections, attest to the Prophet suggesting that only a little of the clitoris be cut in order to allow the woman to experience pleasure. Indeed, in 1994 when activists in Egypt tried to make the practice illegal, one of the chief legal scholars declared that all the Tradition accounts pertaining to female genital mutilation were of unsound provenance and that there was no basis for the practice in Islam. Yet, the view that this was a sound Islamic practice was put forward by the Shaykh Gad al-Ḥaq 'Alī of al-Azḥar, the premier training ground in Egypt for the religiously learned scholars known as the *'ulamā'*, who stated that "female circumcision is a part of the legal body of Islam and is a laudable practice that does honor to the women."[9] Such a statement has the impact of a *fatwā* or legal ruling and was challenged by the Egyptian Organization of Human Rights.

As Marie Assad has observed, "many Islamic jurists believe that 'female circumcision is an Islamic tradition mentioned in the tradition of the Prophet and sanctioned by the Imams (religious leaders) and jurists, in spite of their differences on whether it is a duty of Sunna; they support the practice and sanction it in view of its effect on attenuating the sexual desire of women and directing it to the desirable moderation.'"[10] All this despite the fact that not all Muslims practice this surgical procedure. Indeed it is unknown in Central and South Asia, where large numbers of Muslims live, Muslims who have histories going back to the early centuries; it is very sporadically practiced in the Middle East and Iran. It is a feature primarily of Nilotic peoples and is practiced by communities regardless of faith affiliation in those geographic regions, including some Egyptian Jews, Egyptian Coptic and Sudanese, Somali, and Kenyan Christians and tribal peoples in those regions. It pre-dates the entrance of Islam into Africa by at least a millennium, for it is known from pharaonic times and is in fact referred to as pharaonic in its more extreme forms, such as infibulation, which include not only excising the clitoris and the labia but also vaginal narrowing, which makes both coitus and child-bearing painful and difficult and can cause all manner of health problems well documented by health organizations.

The social and cultural reasons for this practice have also been explored. The importance of honor in patrilineal societies is given as a reason, for it is thought that female genital modification reduces female libido, and the consequent sexual discomfort dissuades women from seeking extramarital partners, thereby ensuring both the paternity of children and simultaneously controlling women's sexual behavior. Despite evidence to show that women's libido is not repressed through the practice, nor is extramarital intercourse prevented, and further, that men report increased sexual gratification with partners who have not been circumcised, and that women experience the many deleterious effects of infibulation, the practice appears to be so culturally ingrained that eradication is a long, slow, and arduous practice. Grassroots organizations utilize the strategies of education to increase awareness of the significant health risks involved and of addressing the larger issues of women's poverty and situatedness in a patriarchal context where the women's identification with the group is signified through control of her body and issues of male honor and shame.

A further complication in the efforts to eradicate this practice, as African women have recognized, is that the Western sensationalist and orientalist portrayal of the practice as confirming the backwardness of Islamic societies is counter-productive to the larger issues of social organization, lack of access to education and the means of production, and poverty which need to be addressed in order to combat the practice. Using female genital mutilation as a rod with which to beat societies for being Muslim causes denial of the practice as being harmful and undermines local efforts to ameliorate economic and educational conditions. The slogan promoted by the campaign in Somalia, for instance, announces that the practice is "not healthy, not clean, not Islamic, and [does] not even guarantee virginity."[11] It might be pertinent to mention that efforts to circumcise female children have been made in Canada and in the United States by immigrant communities from those regions who claim that it is their cultural right, an issue that the medical establishment in both countries must confront.

## Honor Killings

While female genital mutilation is a regional issue extending outward from the Nilotic region and cannot be fought without paying attention to the socio-economic issues of that region, it shares much with other issues of violence toward women in that it is a particularized form in which honor-bound patriarchal societies express control over women. Another form of control over women which is also closely bound to issues of male honor is honor killings, found in the region extending from the Middle East to South Asia. The strategies employed in honor killings in South Asia are the same as those employed in dowry burnings in India: both are represented as "kitchen accidents" in which the victim is severely burnt through the use of kerosene or has acid thrown over her, severely disfiguring her – in both cases often leading to death after much suffering. In the absence of hard data, it is impossible to say how widespread the practice is. A recent documentary on honor killings in Pakistan cites the average number of burnt women brought to just three hospitals as amounting to ten a week, making the total about five hundred a year. An Amnesty International report released in September 1999 suggests that a conservative estimate of such burnings and killings in the Jacobabad district alone totals about fifty a month, amounting to six hundred a year for one small district. It is difficult to collect accurate data that would reflect the scope of the problem, since very few cases are reported, and of those reported even fewer make it to the courts and in even fewer cases is punishment imposed on the perpetrator. Seven to ten thousand women per year is a conservative total estimate offered by some observers.

In Pakistan, a woman may be killed by her in-laws on the merest suspicion of having an illicit relationship that brings shame on the family's honor. According to an Amnesty International report released in September last year, newspaper and journal reportage, and academic findings, in most cases the decision to burn with the intent to disfigure or kill the woman is made by the family, and in some cases by the tribal council or *jirga.* The state in the form of both the law enforcement apparatus and the judiciary has dealt with such cases lightly and in many instances has allowed the perpetrator to go free or with little consequence, both for cultural reasons, according to which the blame is always laid on the woman concerned, and an account of legal loopholes that define such matters as internal family disputes, to be resolved by either the family or the family's tribal council. And, as with genital mutilation, women play a role in the burning and killing of other women.

Whereas dowry burning when associated with Hindu custom in India often occurs because the assets the bride brought with her are not deemed sufficient by the groom, in Pakistan, according to Muslim custom, the groom must pay the bride's father a bride price, allowing in both cases the commodification of women. Further, the woman in Pakistan passes from the guardianship of her father to that of her husband and embodies the honor of the male to whom she belongs. Thus, when a daughter decides to marry someone of her own choice, if such contravenes the wishes of the father – perhaps the bride price is not high enough – then she may be perceived to have shamed his honor and may be accused of adultery while her partner is also accused of having abducted her. Once a man's honor is defiled, he is honor bound to exact payment, and this is the psychology behind the impetus to kill both the female and the male involved.

Although these instances can lead to the murder of both women and men, there are other cases where a woman may be killed for attempting a divorce. In the celebrated case of twenty-nine-year-old Samia Sarwar in April 1999, the young mother of two was shot dead in her lawyer's office by a man hired by her family while her mother stood by and watched. Despite spousal abuse, her family was unwilling to support her plea for a divorce. After Samia's death, her father, the President of the Chamber of Commerce in Peshawar, along with several religious organizations, accused two prominent women lawyers of having abducted and murdered her, and called for their arrest for reasons of "misleading women in Pakistan and contributing to the country's bad image abroad."[12] *Fatwās* were issues against the women and a price was laid on their heads. To date, no one has been arrested for complicity in Samia's murder; the gunman was arrested and shot as he was leaving the office. In Britain during 1999, a South Asian woman and her son were imprisoned for life for having killed a daughter-in-law who was suspected of adultery.

Why? Why do such things happen? The usual suspects have been named: first, the feudal society in which both men and women are subject to the power of feudal lords whose base of power is either land or industry. Second, the devaluation of women in a patriarchal, patrilineal society, in which women are commodified or viewed as chattel that can be owned; are under the authority of a male whether father, husband, or son; do not have the economic resources to be independent, nor the literacy to know and fight for their rights; and, finally, even if they did dare to fight for their rights and dignity, are not supported by the policing and court institutions. Noor Kassamali, in her insightful study of female genital mutilation, observes that women are unwilling to question or compromise group identity even when they carry out practices that hurt them or their daughters or, in the case of honor killings, daughters-in-law. Thus, the situation of women has to be examined within a larger complex of the intersection of economics, culture, access to education and paid labor, and kinship.

And third, although it is clear that there is nothing in the Qur'an or the Tradition literature to support this kind of violence against women, there are, nonetheless, critical junctures at which Muslim social institutions are implicated. For example, in cases where statutory law in Pakistan allows women more equitable access to inheritance, marriage, and divorce, the legal establishment does very little by way of education or intervention to ensure that these are followed rather than customary practices that are much more heavily biased against women. Then, in the name of the Islamization of the law under General Zia ul-Haq, a statute introduced in 1980, called the law of Qisas and Diyat (or retribution and compensation), which relates to manslaughter, murder, and physical injury, "reconceptualized the offences in such a way that they are not directed against the legal order of the state but against the victim," thereby sending out the message "that murders of family members are a family affair and that prosecution and judicial redress are not inevitable but may be renegotiated."[13] Indeed, regarding this law, a Supreme Court judge explained, "In Islam, the individual victim or his heirs retain from the beginning to the end entire control over the matter including the crime and the criminal. They may not report it, they may not prosecute the offender. They may abandon prosecution ... may pardon the criminal ... may accept monetary or other compensation to purge the crime and the criminal ... may compromise ... may accept *qisas* [punishment equal to the offence] from the criminal. The state cannot impede but must do its best to assist them in achieving their object and appropriately exercising their rights."[14]

Another consequence of the law is that if the victim's heir is a direct descendant of the offender, then the maximum allowable penalty for the offender amounts to fourteen years imprisonment. Although the penalty in Pakistan for murder is death, if a man murders his wife with whom he has had a child, then no stiffer penalty than fourteen years imprisonment can be imposed on him. The death penalty could also be averted in the past by taking recourse to Section 300 (1) of the penal code, which allowed that "culpable homicide is not murder if the offender, whilst deprived of the power of self-control by grave and sudden provocation, causes the death of the person who gave the provocation." The charge could then be turned to manslaughter, for which the penalty is again imprisonment.[15] Although the 1980 Qisas and Diyat law did not retain this clause, the courts have continued to accept such mitigation and to place a low threshold on what constitutes provocation.[16]

These remarks relate to only one law. Legal scholars who have worked on other aspects of formal and customary law in Pakistan have remarked that "the interplay of tribal codes, Islamic law, Indo-British judicial traditions and customary traditions ... [have] created an atmosphere of oppression around women, where any advantage or opportunity offered to women by one law is canceled out by one or more of the others."[17] Thus we see that here we have the classic problem of women being considered second-class citizens with rights that are tenable only if they do not encroach upon those of men, who are socially and legally considered to be the primary actors and agents. Maulana Maududi, the founder of the Jamat-e-Islami party, who espoused the view that Pakistan as a society was not sufficiently Muslim and who is committed to creating a revolution within Pakistani society, aided by laws aimed at Islamization, says of the role of women in a good Muslim society, "from the Islamic point of view, the right sort of education for woman is that which prepares her to become a good wife, good mother and good housekeeper," thereby restricting the value of a woman to her connection with the family and setting the stage for the family's legal control over her, especially in relation to violence against her person.[18]

## THE TEXT, THE LAW, AND WOMEN

I now want to examine briefly the Qur'an's position on women and the role of Islamic law in socially instituting gender biases that are present in the Qur'an but nowhere to the same degree or with the same intent. Does the Qur'an make women secondary to men? Leila Ahmed and others have cogently argued that the Qur'an offers both sexes moral and spiritual equality, a perspective that gives members of both sexes much scope with respect to human dignity. However, the Qur'an does in a few instances distinguish between the sexes in the social and legal sphere, predicated on a gendered division of labor. Thus, men are considered a degree above women in a verse that clearly suggests that this is so only because men earn the keep, and recent feminist scholarship such as that of Amina Wadud-Muhsin has argued that the term for "a degree above" means equally to stand up for, to support, and does not entail any ontological supremacy.[19] Women are to inherit half the percentages allotted to men, and half their testimony is counted in the legal sphere.

The central or key issue here surrounds how the Qur'an is to be interpreted. Are these verses binding for all Muslims over all time, or are they to be viewed as speaking to their historical context, as leading thinkers such as the one-time Shaykh of al-Azhar, Muḥammad 'Abduh, have argued? And what of the fact that the Qur'an actually gives us very little by way of legal direction? Much of what is found in the lawbooks emerged as a result of (1) the commentarial tradition on the Qur'an, (2) the Tradition literature that narrates what the eighth-century and ninth-century Muslim community remembered the Prophet having said or done, (3) local custom, (4) the independent reasoning of legal scholars (ijtihād), and (5) the consensus of the learned community – and let us remember that the legal schools were all formulated by the eleventh century.

Two important features need to be mentioned here. First, that although women are not essentialized in the Qur'an, the rapid expansion of Muslims into Byzantine and Persian territories caused an entry into societies that were patriarchal long before the Qur'an was revealed. The research of Barbara Stowasser and Laila Ahmed has shown, for example, that patriarchal interpretations, on the one hand, and patriarchal institutions, on the other, both entered the Islamic intellectual and social arenas with the expansion of the Muslim empire, all of which was occurring during the critical centuries in which the legal schools were developing. A case in point is that in the Qur'an, even though Eve is not created from the rib of Adam nor is she responsible for succumbing to Satan's lure, every Muslim believes to the contrary, and both the Tradition and the commentarial literature testifies to this perception. Yes, Muslims did talk to Jews and Christians in those centuries, read their books, and were more than happy to incorporate what they felt would increase their understanding of their own scripture despite the twentieth-century popular perception that there has always been enmity between these traditions. Muslim legal schools saw fit to elide veiling and seclusion in emulation of the societies in which they found themselves, where both veiling and seclusion were markers of high status. These practices were thus made applicable to all Muslim women, not just Muhammad's wives, as the Qur'an had directed, and along with this, polygamy was put forward as a right of Muslim males without paying close attention to the continuation of the polygamy verse in which God declares doubt as to whether Muslims can treat all their wives equally, which suggests to some interpreters that monogamy is the preferred divine choice.

The second important feature is that Islamic law (that is, *shari'ah*) itself is not as monolithic or as trenchant as it is often made out to be. Apart from the fact that there are differences of interpretation and application across the legal schools, in addition, over the course of the centuries, the state administration under caliphal authority placed significant portions of the law under its control. For example, commercial law, constitutional law, the laws governing foreign relations, and so forth might be named as arenas over which the state established its control.

Under all three Muslim empires – the Persian, the Mughal, and the Ottoman – the state legal system incorporated features of other systems such as the French, the British, and the Roman. What remained under the control of the religiously learned, then, comprised the laws governing ritual obligations, family and inheritance law, and the laws governing religious endowments. During British rule in India, the British imposed a uniform criminal and civil code that did away with prior laws governing Muslims and Hindus but unwittingly promoted the resurrection of religiously coined family laws for all religious traditions in India on the basis that these alone "were of divine origin and therefore should not be touched."[20] On the one hand, this had the effect of bringing family matters under the control of tribal laws connected to ethnic custom (which were understood by their adherents as comprising part of Muslim tradition, whether they were in keeping with Muslim legal codes or not) and, on the other hand, of reviving and revitalizing Islamic family law.

Now, whereas some countries such as Morocco, Tunisia, and Egypt have seen fit to modify their legal codes relating to personal and family law to reflect to a small degree the changing nature of society, including more equitable formulations for women (a move that is in keeping with the spirit of moral and religious egalitarianism found in the Qur'an), other nations have utilized the instrument of Islamization in order to legitimate political authority and have done so within the resistance narrative to which I will return in a moment. The process of Islamization in Pakistan under General Zia ul-Haq has essentially led to the further entrenchment of a patriarchal stance toward women backed by the legal system, all in the name of Islam, entailing a stance that represents Islamic law as fixed and immutable in contradiction to the fact that Islamic law has been a dynamic entity in many other areas of jurisdiction. For example, in 1979 Pakistan's 1973 Constitution was amended to include specialists in Islamic *fiqh* or jurisprudence at the high courts and the Supreme Court, known as the *shari'at* bench. Also in 1979 the Hudood Ordinances declared that a man and woman who were not validly married to each other were guilty of *zina* or adultery when engaging in sexual intercourse, and four male witnesses were required to prove this. Accordingly, rape becomes very difficult to prove, women's testimony is denied legal weight, and the unborn child of a woman so impregnated turns into evidence that the woman did in fact engage in illicit intercourse, thereby turning her rape into a charge of adultery against her, for which the penalty is stoning or death. Urban and upper class women have fought back with the creation of organizations such as the Women's Action Forum, which has sought to challenge the institutionalization of tenth-century Islamic legal codes, and socially through awareness-raising seminars.

As Akbar S. Ahmed has shown in his research among tribal societies in north-west Pakistan, ethnicity or tribal affiliation, religion, and nationality are identities that are concurrently held, and the relationship between these is one that both accommodates and reflects tensions. When these are compounded with issues of literacy, class, and postcolonial discourses, it is no wonder that General Zia's attempt at Islamization is a feature not limited to Pakistan; we have seen similar attempts in Iran after the Iranian revolution under Ayatollah Khomeini, in Afghanistan under the Taliban, and in North Africa, spreading from Egypt south along the Nile and westward to Nigeria and beyond. Young Muslims are joining the call for an Islamically ordered society in various parts of the globe.

In almost every case, the veiling or re-veiling of women is a first step in what Leila Ahmed calls (as reiterated by Stowasser) "the symbol of the validity and dignity of the Muslim tradition as a whole."[21] Akbar S. Ahmed has suggested that "The position of women in Muslim society mirrors the destiny of Islam: when Islam is secure and confident so are its women; when Islam is threatened and under pressure so, too, are they."[22] Leila Ahmed has astutely observed that in the wake of colonization the resistance narrative of Muslims both reversed and ironically accepted the terms set in the first place by the colonizers: "The veil came to symbolize in the resistance narrative, not the inferiority of the culture and the need to cast aside its customs in favor of those of the West, but, on the contrary, the dignity and validity of all native customs, and in particular those customs coming under fiercest colonial attack – the customs relating to women – and the need to tenaciously affirm them as a means of resistance to Western domination."[23] Further, Islamization makes its target the family, and by this it means women who are made the moral guardians of Islamic identity.

## REFLECTIONS OF ISLAMIC ETHICAL GUIDELINES

So, what does any of this have to do with ethics and religion in a global twenty-first century? I see three primary issues intersecting here: how society is organized, regulated and developed economically; how Muslim identity is preserved, perpetuated, and represented; and how states with Muslim governments selectively draw upon and emphasize *shari'ah* law, both to pacify popular calls for an Islamically ordered society and to legitimate themselves as truly Islamic in the face of opposition. Given the preceding discussions, it is clear (1) that women bear the brunt of the patriarchal honor-bound system, (2) that they embody Muslim identity to the outsider looking in and to the insider looking out, and (3) that *shari'ah* law has been acknowledged by Muslims and non-Muslims alike to be punitive toward women. Several modernist Muslims have called for the rehabilitation of juridical reasoning in order to modernize laws, especially those that relate to women, which were formulated almost a millennium ago. Whether such calls will be heeded remains to be seen; certainly much twentieth-century discourse in the Muslim world has sought to include women's participation in the public sphere at the same time as the state has intervened to make education and opportunities for paid employment outside the home more readily available, despite the more conservative calls for a gender-segregated society that encourages women to stay at home and nurture children.

Taking another approach, scholar activists such as Riffat Hassan, in reflecting on why it is that women are victims of honor killings in societies such as Pakistan, have suggested that we need to engage with such issues theologically.[24] This has not been done, in part because most activists want to stay away from Islam and from raising theological issues, for to do so simply draws negative attention and creates further popular resistance to activist effort. Hassan suggests that it is to the ethical framework of Islam that we must turn, in order to examine whether Muslims are in fact creating the morally and socially responsible society that God intended in the Qur'an. Although she is not the first to draw attention to the spirit rather than the letter of Islam, in the twentieth century the spirit was largely ignored by Islamists who believe that the spirit is best expressed in a legalistic and ritual-bound manner that has a political agenda. Hassan argues for the need for profound theological and ethical reflection on the grounds that it is because women are considered to be of lesser value than men, largely because they have been thought to have been created from and for the male, that social attitudes and institutions that discriminate against the female gender in Islamic societies have been able to form and continue, despite the Qur'an's overwhelming assertion that both men and women, who are full moral agents, are accountable to God, implying that women are not a lesser order of being. Hassan's careful examination of the Qur'an reveals the following rights that the Qur'an assures to both men and women:

1. the right to life
2. the right to respect
3. the right to justice
4. the right to freedom

5. the right to privacy
6. the right to protection from slander, backbiting and ridicule
7. the right to acquire knowledge
8. the right to sustenance
9. the right to work
10. the right to develop one's aesthetic responsibilities and enjoy the bounties created by God
11. the right to leave one's homeland under oppressive conditions
12. the right to "the Good Life."[25]

Working with a framework of ethical guidelines punctuated by fundamental rights as opposed to working with a specific list of legal prescriptions that are considered immutable is bound to create tremendous unease and alarm in all societies that fall under the purview of *shari'ah* law.

## CONCLUDING REMARKS

For the Islamic world, the equitable treatment of women in places that have incorporated Islamic law or the *shari'ah* is a pressing issue both among Muslims and within the circles of international human rights groups. For example, are unequal inheritance laws, child marriages, child custody arrangements consequent upon divorce, difficulty of access to divorce, polygamy, the popular conception that men are a degree above women and therefore require obedience from them, the elision of adultery with rape, the unequal weight given to women's testimony in legal settings, and the economic consequences for the woman on the breakdown of a marriage all simply to be identified as Muslim customs, or are there larger issues pertaining to gender equality globally which are at stake?

Moreover, it becomes extremely difficult for the average person to separate Islam from all of these issues because each of them applies to women who are Muslims. This fact leads me to pose two questions. Is it because the women are Muslim that Islam is implicated, or are there other factors at work such that they affect women who happen to be Muslim? In other words, here I am raising the tendentious issue of whether religion can be separated from culture, or whether at the outset we have to acknowledge that culture is an amorphous entity, constantly changing and yet capable of remarkable tenacity, that draws upon whatever ideological currents are at hand in order to justify, legitimate, and perpetuate certain frameworks of reality. Further, cultures work to create and sustain institutions that will represent and facilitate implementations of ideological presuppositions.

Similarly, if one were to make a generalized statement, then I would say that there is very little in the foundational text of Islam, the Qur'an, which is theoretically the highest source of authority for all Muslims, to legitimate the implementation of any of the practices associated with the above-mentioned issues. Yet there is no doubt that in the fourteen hundred years since the revelation of the Qur'an, the interpretation of the Qur'an and its amalgamation with other sources of authority, including pre-existent patriarchal cultural codes and pre-Islamic customs that were seamlessly absorbed into the Islamic cultural ethos have led many Muslims to believe that certain practices that contravene human rights are in fact Islamic. The most obvious of these, of course, are those associated with seclusion, the rights of women to move about freely, domestic violence, in some cases female genital mutilation, and in the case of honor killings the popularly perceived rights of males to exact through death payment for an insult to one's honor. The issue of the relationship between religion and culture is further complicated when Muslim customs, practices, and laws are considered to be laudable because they are thought to emulate the *sunna*, that is, the example of the Prophet, or to be divinely revealed and hence immutable.

The second question is whether theology and/or critical reflection on the religiously authoritative bases of many of the issues mentioned earlier can alone make a difference. Does it matter if a few academic or learned Muslims – and here I might add Christians and Jews – spend rivers of ink showing that the Jewish, Christian, and Muslim God, whom Muslims consider to be one and the same, had nothing to do whatsoever with the prejudiced manner in which these traditions – themselves historically created and socially institutionalized and accepted – have treated women? Feminist theologians, be they male or female, have written many tracts showing that our foundational texts are not entirely discriminatory toward women. Rather, it is our interpretative texts that are patriarchal in their presuppositions, and there is nothing in our "real" religions to justify the ill-treatment of women or the curtailment of their rights and freedoms. This point is well taken both in the academy and among staunch believers who argue that their religion does not discriminate against women even though some interpreters have tried to make their traditions patriarchal.

In contrast to the earlier days of feminism, when many feminists lambasted religious worldviews for their exclusion of the full humanity of women, in recent years we see an increasing discourse created by religious feminists. Within the Islamic world for instance, mirroring the sentiments of their Jewish and Christian counterparts, Islamist feminists, many of whom belong to what the media terms "fundamentalist" Islam, hold the view that it is possible to be Muslim, and proudly so, and uphold with pride and dignity the few requirements imposed on women, arguing that these are essential for a well-ordered society. A good example here is how the veil is in some places regarded by those who don it as a proud symbol of Muslim identity, setting the wearer apart from the religion of its colonizing oppressors of the past, and from the Western cultural hegemonies of the present. How ironic, considering that recent research has shown that the use of the veil in Islamic societies became widespread as a result of increased contact with Jews and Christians and pre-Islamic Persians and not because the Prophet of Islam, Muhammad, required all women to wear it.

All of this preamble is by way of showing that scholarly efforts have already been made to show that there is very little in the Qur'an to suggest that God intended women to be circumcised, sometimes with painful and debilitating consequences, or that God expected men to kill women for reasons of honor, or that God permitted men to beat their wives if they were disobedient, or that God really wanted each male to have four wives, or expected the legal establishment to treat rape and adultery as the same thing. I ask: is it all solely a matter of interpretation? In this regard, a more constructive approach toward attaining gender equity within the Islamic world might lie in re-examining some of the internal ethical resources available to Muslims and undertaking a legal project that would accord with the spirit of Islam.

NOTES

1. The following section relies on George F. Hourani, *Reason and Tradition in Islamic Ethics* (Cambridge: Cambridge University Press, 1985), pp. 15–22.
2. Traditions or *hadith* are narratives preceded by a chain of transmitting relayers which report the Prophet Muhammad's words or deeds, and are considered to be the second most authoritative source of guidance for Muslims after the Qur'an.
3. Hourani, *Reason and Tradition*, p. 37.

4. Ibid.

5. Ibid., p. 39.

6. Ibid., p. 45. The bracketed insertion is mine.

7. Ibid., p. 122.

8. Barbara Freyer Stowasser, *Women in the Qur'an: Traditions and Interpretation* (New York: Oxford University Press, 1994), p. 47.

9. Noor J. Kassamali, "When Modernity Confronts Traditional Practices: Female Genital Cutting in Northeast Africa" in *Women in Muslim Societies: Diversity Within Unity*, ed. Herbert L. Bodman and Nayereh Tohidi (Boulder: Lynne Rienner, 1998), p. 43

10. Ibid., p. 43.

11. Ibid., pp. 52–53.

12. "Pakistan: Honor Killings of Girls and Women," *Amnesty International Report*, ASA 33/18/99, September 1999, p. 7.

13. Ibid., p. 11.

14. Ibid.

15. Ibid.

16. Ibid., p. 12.

17. Ibid., p. 10.

18. Quoted in Sabra Bano, "Women, Class, and Islam in Karachi," in *From Independence Towards Freedom: Indian Women since 1947*, ed. Bharati Ray and Aparna Basu (New Delhi: Oxford University Press, 1999), p. 191.

19. Amina Wadud-Muhsin, *Qur'an and Woman* (Kuala Lumpur: Penerbit Fajar Bakti Sdn. Bhd., 1992), pp. 69–74.

20. Lotika Sarkar, "Reform of Hindu Marriage and Succession Laws: Still the Unequal Sex" in *From Independence Towards Freedom: Indian Women since 1947*, ed. Ray and Basu, p. 100.

21. Stowasser, *Women in the Qur'an*, p. 128.

22. Akbar S. Ahmed, "Women and the Household in Baluchistan" in *Family and Gender in Pakistan: Domestic Organization in a Muslim Society*, ed. Hastings Donnan and Frits Selier (New Delhi: Hindustan Publishing Corporation, 1997), p. 70. He stated this originally in *Discovering Islam: Making Sense of Muslim History and Society* (London: Routledge & Kegan Paul, 1988), p. 184.

23. Leila Ahmed, *Women and Gender in Islam* (New Haven: Yale University Press, 1992), p. 164.

24. Riffat Hassan, lecture given at Pomona College, 9 March 2000.

25. Riffat Hassan, "Women's Rights and Islam: From the ICPD to Beijing." This unpublished work is available from Dr Riffat Hassan, University of Louisville at Kentucky. "ICPD" stands for the United Nations Conference on Population and Development, held in Cairo, 1994.

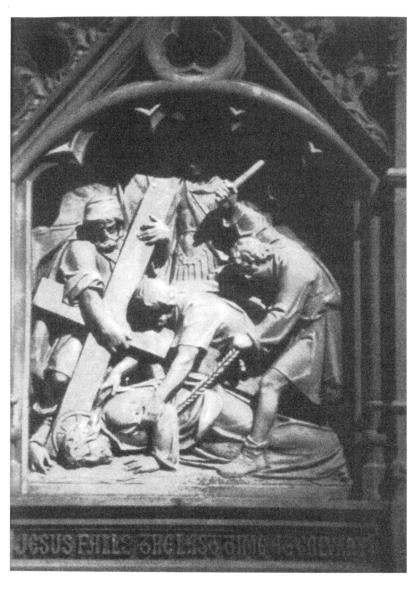

JESUS FHILS 3RC LASG GIR IG

*Plate 6* A sculpture in the side aisle of Our Lady and the English Martyrs Catholic Church (1885–90), Cambridge, England, depicting Jesus being forced to carry the instrument for his death. Christians often use the scenes of the "stations of the cross" as a meditative means for soul-making. Photo: *Joseph Runzo*

# 6

# THE EVOLUTIONARY SELF *in* CHRISTIAN AND PHILOSOPHICAL PERSPECTIVES

*Nathan Tierney*

The peace talks between Christianity and modern science usually hit a snag when it comes to the relationship between the soul and the rest of nature. Most of us believe that we have an interior life and that this interior life is the most important thing about us. When pressed about the metaphysics of this, Christians and other theists typically have recourse to dualism, the view that we are made up, somehow, of two distinct kinds of things, body and soul (or, with slightly different emphasis, "spirit" or "mind" or "self" or "consciousness"). This is a perfectly ordinary and common-sensical way to talk. Given our theological and philosophical history, dualism has become the default metaphysics of the soul. Unfortunately, the path of science and philosophy for the last 150 years has moved slowly but inexorably in the opposite direction of materialism, often of a very reductive sort. There is good reason for this; dualism faces some very difficult philosophical problems – so difficult, in fact, that "soul talk" is almost out of bounds in most philosophy and science departments of Western universities.

Naturalism is a powerful alternative ontological paradigm to dualism and is usually advanced from a scientific perspective. By naturalism I mean the view that (1) nature creates its own systems of order as emerging systems respond both to external conditions and internal dynamics, that is, order is an intrinsic feature of the world; (2) the only order about which we can have objective knowledge is the natural order; and (3) nothing occurs in nature without a physical cause or manifestation. Also, although not definitional of naturalism, contemporary naturalism takes key elements of the scientific picture as core postulates: the atomic theory of matter and the evolutionary theory of biology.[1] Many Christians regard such a position as antithetical to religion. It seems to deny the reality of the soul, the moving power of a transcendent order, and the possibility of religious knowledge. William Dembski, for example, argues that "Either God imparts order to the world or the order in the world is intrinsic to it ... There can be no transcendent God within such a framework ... Naturalism leads inevitably to idolatry."[2]

In my view, this inference is mistaken. Naturalism has achieved its dominance over dualism because it is the better theory. If religion is to sustain its intellectual credibility, it must come to terms with the conceptual successes of science and recent philosophy. Much of the horror that Christians feel toward naturalism stems from its linkage with materialism, which really is inimical to religion. I will try to show that this linkage is far from inevitable and that the problems facing materialism are as great as those facing dualism. I will argue for a view that I call "non-reductive evolutionary naturalism," in which the soul is seen as a superordinate evolutionary structure of the body. Such a view is the natural ground for a peace settlement between science and religion, so that each may draw on the great resources of the other without sacrificing anything of its own essential character. Such an approach will also bring with it, I believe, a more effective and less antagonistic connection between religion and ethics. I will begin with an overview of some of the philosophical problems faced by both dualism and reductive materialism.

## WHAT'S WRONG WITH DUALISM?

The question of the relation between bodies and souls was a major focus of concern in the seventeenth century, when the tension between the competing intellectual and political paradigms of science and religion was brought to a head. Cartesian dualism provided the way through that impasse. Descartes' philosophy had the enormous advantage of carving out a ceasefire in the turbulent struggles between science and religion, giving each a separate methodology and specific object of concern, so that neither need intrude on the legitimate domain of the other.

Although dualism did not begin with Descartes, the formulation that he gave to it in the seventeenth century has become canonical. The basic tenets of Cartesian dualism are that (1) the world is divided into two different kinds of things – physical things that occupy space and mental things that do not – and (2) a thing is a substance possessed of essential properties that define its nature (a metaphysics that Descartes inherited from the Aristotelian tradition). Physical things are extended in space, divisible, determined by physical laws, and perishable. Mental things (minds or souls) have no spatial extension, are indivisible or simple, indestructible, and capable of an immediate, indefeasible inner awareness in the *cogito.*

Throughout the modern period, substance dualism seeped into the background assumptions of Western culture. It fitted much more neatly with the Galilean corpuscular or atomistic theory of matter than the view of medieval hylomorphism that the soul was the form of the body. And despite official Catholic allegiance to the pre-Cartesian doctrine, Christian theologians until fairly recently were for the most part content to leave substance dualism as a background assumption, even while the great majority of professional philosophers were abandoning dualism altogether.

## Philosophical Challenges

The causes of this abandonment are familiar. Three intractable problems have dogged the philosophical fortunes of dualism: the problem of interaction, the problem of freedom, and the problem of knowledge. The first, and in many ways the largest problem, is the problem of interaction, sometimes simply known as *the* mind–body problem. If minds and bodies are completely different kinds of things, how can they interact, especially in a causal way? Our daily experience teaches us that they do interact continuously, but modern physics seems to provide no viable account of this consistent with dualist doctrine; the kinetic energy transfers just don't seem to be there. Descartes, to be sure, was aware of this problem, and tried to answer it by cutting up cadavers from the Paris morgue, eventually arguing that the point of contact was in the pineal gland at the base of the brain, since this was the only organ of the brain that he could find that was not doubled. Few find this kind of approach convincing today.[3]

The second problem, the problem of freedom, is a direct result of placing the two entities in separate kinds of spaces. If the body is in physical space, and is thus determined by a causal past, then even if the soul has complete freedom in mental space, what does this freedom amount to? What difference does it make to what happens between bodies? Free will seems to imply some real causal bridge between the mind and the body, yet dualism rules out this bridge; the mind seems to be a mere epiphenomenon at best, an illusion or fiction at worst.

The third problem, the problem of knowledge, stems from the subjective starting points of the Cartesian meditation. If all that we directly know are our own thought contents, how can we know anything concerning the existence of the external world? Descartes' own solutions – the appeal to an ontological proof of God's existence, and an analogical inference to the existence of other minds – have not worn well. The subjectivist epistemology of dualism leads directly to the radical skepticism that has almost become a background assumption itself today.

There is a fourth problem, which is not so much a philosophical problem, but a spiritual one. This is the problem of our relation to other animals. Dualism typically states that only humans have souls; otherwise heaven would get very crowded, and we would not be able to understand the unique moral dignity of human beings. It does this by tying consciousness fairly tightly to our capacity for language. Apart from the fact that some other animals do seem to have some forms of linguistic capacity, the huge gulf that dualism creates between us and other animals seems scientifically implausible from the point of view of evolutionary theory. And, despite its convenience for Christian theology, the spiritual implications of insisting upon that gulf have caused uneasiness among many who believe that we need to rethink our relationship with the rest of creation.

## Scientific Challenges

Cartesian substance dualism, then, faces serious philosophical problems.[4] In addition, recent science has mounted serious challenges to the intellectual need for dualism. In cosmology, big bang theory has undercut literal interpretations of creation stories.[5] In biology, Darwin's theory of evolution has drawn strong connections between humans and other animals, making the absolute ontological distinction less plausible. Biochemical explanations, especially genetics, have consolidated connectivity between humans and animals, casting doubt on the claim sometimes advanced by some theologians that the soul is a "special ingredient" added at conception. Recently some authors have claimed to be able to account for many high human traits such as morals in biological terms.[6]

Advances in neuroscience, neuroanatomy (brain mapping) and neurophysiology (brain function studies) seem to lend some support to materialism. As we become better able to correlate specific brain abnormalities with behavioral disorders, there appears less need to postulate some invisible causal agent. Cognitive science, computer technology, and artificial intelligence are becoming better at modeling and simulating processes such as decision-making and learning which were previously thought to be acts of the soul. Artificial intelligence, for example, though still in its infancy, has developed machines that can learn and pronounce languages, navigate space, and make a host of discriminations and responses that were previously labeled the province of thinking beings. Recent advances in evolutionary robotics have demonstrated that computers may be able to evolve in ways similar to biological systems, not merely in virtual but also in physical environments.

## Theological Challenges

A number of Christian theologians such as Nancey Murphy and others have been re-examining the supposed centrality of dualism to Christianity.[7] Much of that supposed centrality remains the legacy of the Augustinian attempt to integrate Platonic and Neoplatonic philosophy with Christian religiosity. When Aquinas's Aristotelian alternative later came under attack from nominalistic metaphysics and the rise of empirical science, Descartes' radical revival of dualism became a dominant conceptual tool for later (especially Protestant) interpretations of Christian anthropology and eschatology. But how necessary is it? Joel Green, for example, has argued that the key *imago dei* passage in Genesis 1:26–27 ("Then God said, 'Let us make humanity in our image, after our likeness'") points less to the postulation of an independent substantive soul than to a unique covenantal relationship between God and humans.[8] Ray Anderson and others have argued that scriptural passages in Paul referring to the resurrection of the body need not be interpreted as requiring a detachable soul component in the human person: "The assurance that self-identity will survive death is not based on some nonphysical aspect of the person but on the bond between the risen Jesus Christ and the believer through the Holy Spirit."[9] Nancey Murphy argues that religious experience is best interpreted not by postulating a special faculty of the soul over and above ordinary human emotional and cognitive capacities, but by the unique content and circumstances of those experiences.[10] And Trenton Merricks has argued that a dualistic image of the human person undercuts the moral significance of Christ's victory over death: "if dualism is true, it is hard to see how death is an enemy, and harder still to see how it is overcome in resurrection."[11] Exploration of these issues lies outside the scope of this chapter, but enough perhaps has been said to suggest that substance dualism is not an inevitable metaphysics for Christianity.

## WHAT'S WRONG WITH MATERIALISM?

With the abandonment of dualism by professional philosophers, the choice was between monisms, either nineteenth-century idealism or twentieth-century materialism. Idealism has largely been rejected by Western philosophy. Materialism (or physicalism) is the view that nature consists only of material or physical entities of one sort or another. It consists in the conviction that ultimately all things are explicable in terms of the movement of physical particles. In one sense (a non-reductionistic sense), materialism is obviously true: nothing in nature is done that we know of except through the movement of such physical particles. But materialism has an inevitable push toward reductionism, especially when applied to the mind. Reductive materialism in all its forms plays variations on the theme of "nothing buttery": the mind is nothing but _____ (fill in the blank with one's preferred physical entity).

In the twentieth century, the philosophy of materialism went through four different research projects, all of which eventually foundered on the same rock. In the 1940s and 1950s, logical behaviorism argued that the mind was nothing but a set of dispositions to behave in certain ways. In the 1960s and 1970s the identity theory of mind argued that the mind is nothing but the brain.[12] In the 1970s and 1980s functionalist materialism argued that mind is nothing but a "black box" that can be explained by the causal relations between mental states and their relation to sensory inputs and behavioral outputs. In the 1980s and 1990s, the computational model of the mind argued that the mind is nothing but a piece of software for the brain's hardware and that downward causation from mind to brain is simply implementation of programming.[13]

What was missing from the materialist accounts was what it felt like to be a conscious being, the interior and subjective life of the soul, what philosophers refer to as *qualia*.[14] Semantics could not be gotten from syntax. The selfhood of our consciousness is irreducible to physics. All attempts to account for personal identity over time in terms of bodily continuity alone face major logical problems (concerning clones, brain transfers, split brains, and the like).[15] But they also founder before the tribunal of common sense: if we are not to do away with the concept of personal identity altogether (admittedly an option for some), then it must employ in an essential way the criteria of selfhood arising from our reflective self-understanding. The "hard problem"[16] of consciousness remains: an account of the mind must be found which does justice to practical and scientific reality on the one hand and inner experience on the other.

## NON-REDUCTIVE EVOLUTIONARY NATURALISM

My concern in what follows is to present a philosophically coherent picture of the soul's place in nature which is consistent both with science and with the experience and beliefs of many who hold a religious outlook. I call this picture "non-reductive evolutionary naturalism." My picture will rest on three legs: an expanded concept of evolution, the idea of supervenience, and the idea of interiority.

### Evolutionism without Reductionism

Ever since Darwin published his *Origin of Species* in 1859, the theory of evolution has been at the center of controversy between religion and science. Many saw it as an assault on human dignity, a denial of biblical truth, and a rejection of the idea of God's providential design. Many still see it this way, though this is less common. And there is no denying that evolutionists have sometimes used the theory in this way. Moreover, when evolutionary theory began to expand beyond the biological domain to try to account for cultural features such as moral norms, a reductionist spirit was often the dominant research paradigm: sociobiology in the 1970s, which sought to discover the biological origins of social behavior, is an obvious case in point. Yet there is nothing inherently reductionist in evolutionism once its key concepts of heritable genetic variation and natural selection of random mutations are put in wider perspective.

Evolution is usually thought of in biological terms, but the power of the model has encouraged thinkers in other disciplines to expand its reach. Cosmologists today talk of stars and galaxies evolving, anthropologists will talk of the evolution of cultures, and evolutionary robotics provides models of how computers may reprogram themselves to deal with new situations. Karl Popper has argued persuasively for evolutionary epistemology, and there are new disciplines such as evolutionary psychology and evolutionary economics, though evolution's application to ethics and philosophical theology is still in its early stages. The spirit of these expansions is not to reduce the objects of those disciplines to biology or physics but to make use of the power of evolutionary models in explaining and accounting for transformations. Common to all evolutionary approaches are a number of principles, for example, (1) complex systems arise out of less complex ones, (2) modifications are brought about in interactive response to environmental stimuli, (3) transmission mechanisms carry forward successful innovations from one "generation" or stage-instance to another, and (4) evaluation of individual success is measurable by the degree to which an individual both realizes the potential within its generation and makes possible further evolution.

The evolutionary model can be extended downward toward inanimate objects or upward toward cultural and psychological entities. Stars evolve, for example, in the sense that each new stage forces them to develop new energy generation mechanisms. Pressure and gravity fuse hydrogen into helium, which cannot fuse in turn until gravitational collapse raises its temperature, causing rises in the temperature and luminosity of its hydrogen shell, which places pressure on the outer stages of the star, causing them to expand, which in turn cools the outer layers while the core continues to collapse and rise in temperature until it reaches a threshold in its evolution when the temperature is sufficient to fuse helium into carbon, stabilizing the star for a time as a red giant, which in turn will create new conditions requiring new energy sources, etc.

The model can also be extended upward toward the self. The self emerges first as an organizing principle of behavior and locus of control in the central nervous system, later as a superordinate structure of drives and representations (including self-representations) enmeshed in the internalizations and the empathic object relations of social relationship,[17] later as an autonomously reflective self capable of rational and moral choice, later as an entity aware of, aspiring to, and in some measure achieving relationship with a transcendental reality. These stages are not treated as discrete substances but as complexifying transformations: the mind is the body in its conscious state, the self is the mind in its reflective and relational state, and the soul is the self in its spiritual state.

The soul does not arise by the addition of a secret ingredient produced by supernatural agency outside the evolutionary process (perhaps at conception or perhaps at the "quickening" at the end of the first trimester of pregnancy when the mother first begins to feel the baby kick). The grandeur and dignity of the human person lies elsewhere – in its capacity for interiority and the evolutionary leap in its capacities for moral and spiritual life. There is, of course, a sense in which human beings do have something extra that lower animals do not, but the evolutionary model protects us from the temptation to reify this extra into a substantive soul. The extra is in terms of what the organism can do as a result of its new structural organization generated from its specific interaction with the environment, capabilities that are unpredictable from the point of view of prior stages.

The identity of the evolving self is such that it gains its existence in and through its loves and desires, its understandings, and its acts. It has real ontological status, even if it is not a "substance" in the old sense of the word. The image of nature suggested by non-reductive evolutionary naturalism is of one big system of evolution with no upward limit. Continuity is the keynote of downward linkage. We are all – stars, birds, and humans – linked in one great immanent chain of being. Discontinuity (or in more religious terms, transfiguration) is the keynote of upward linkage; our next step in the evolutionary process is always transcendental to our current self-understanding.

At this point it is natural to ask whether evolutionary naturalism implies teleology (i.e. goal-directed variation that contributes to evolutionary selection) throughout nature, guiding the direction of evolution. There are minimalist and maximalist answers to this, and current debates are fierce. It seems to me that the choice of answer is primarily methodological – whether one is seeking to cover the facts with the fewest and least risky metaphysical hypotheses or seeking an account of the facts most congruent with a clear account of religious faith. My preference is for the former, and so I would restrict the concept of natural teleology to the conscious level and up. The reason why the nutcracker evolved is because someone thought it would do a better job of opening nuts than smashing them with a stone. The replication mechanism here is not genes but "memes" – culturally generated information units stored through socially constructed information technology.[18]

At a lower level, natural selection seems quite adequate to the task, but natural selection is only one type of evolutionary selection process; intentional design is another. At preconscious levels, there is still room for at least a quasi-teleological or functional explanation but only in two more restrictive senses. First, in biology it is a useful stand-in concept for a causal history of natural selection. When we say at the level of the genotype or species that the proper function of the heart in mammals is to pump blood, we mean that possession of an efficient means of pumping blood through the body was one of the factors by which mammals were selected for survival.[19] Second, at the phenotypal or individual level, as well as at the pre-biological level, where it is not a question of genotypal replication through a gene pool, teleological explanation still is in order, to explain the way that an individual moves toward complexity (i.e. the combination of integration and differentiation in relation to the individual's environment).[20] But the principle of complexity holds for all stages in the evolutionary process. The dynamic tension between individual and community, for instance, is humanity's way of achieving complexity, the individual providing differentiation and the community providing integration.

## Supervenience

Naturalism relies on the notion of "supervenience," a concept traceable to the moral philosophers G.E. Moore and R.M. Hare.[21] Hare coined the term in 1952 to explain the relation of moral properties to descriptive properties. When we say, for example, that Jennifer is a good person, the property of being good *supervenes* on various character traits and actions of Jennifer. That is, we could not imagine that there could be someone who had all the character traits and actions of Jennifer but differed in this one respect, namely that Jennifer was good and this other person was not. Discussions of supervenience can quickly become very technical, and the term has been used in a variety of ways. One straightforward definition of supervenience runs: "properties of type A are supervenient on properties of type B if and only if two objects cannot differ with respect to their A properties without also differing with respect to their B properties."[22] Some philosophers use the concept to engage in various forms of reductionist "nothing buttery" – the supervening mind is nothing but the brain – but it can also be adapted to chart a middle course between dualism and materialism.

An important distinction to make is between two kinds of supervenience: property supervenience and structural supervenience. Property supervenience is quite amenable to reductionist analysis. For example, when we say that the property of liquidity supervenes upon $H_2O$, we mean *nothing but* that water molecules, when in a certain state, can run down hills. The analysis remains within the realm of physics, and no independent causal power is attributable to the property of liquidity. But when we say that the mind supervenes on the brain, we are talking of structural supervenience. Various features of the brain have cohered into a causally autonomous system. Structural supervenience permits us to talk of two-way causal interaction between the mind and the brain, recognizing that all natural causality is physical in nature, and yet treating the mind and brain as ontologically distinct.

Consider the case of money. How big is a dollar bill? The first answer that occurs to us is something like "about five inches by two inches." But, of course, this is the size of the paper that the dollar bill is printed on, not the dollar bill itself. A dollar bill is part of a system of exchange and is what it is only by being part of that system. The dollar structurally supervenes on the paper. It is not simply identical to any sum of properties of that paper – the green ink, the picture of Washington, etc. A counterfeit dollar bill, no matter how perfectly it replicated those properties, would not be a dollar bill. So the correct analogy is not "the mind is to the brain as liquidity is to $H_2O$," but "the mind is to the brain as a dollar bill is to the paper it is printed on." The mind (like the system of exchange) does not occupy physical space, even though everything that it does it does in and through physical space. The question of how big a mind is is not the same as the question of how big a brain is. Mind is the interior dimension of physical space. It has no spatial locality, even though nothing that it does is done outside of ordinary physical space. Despite its surface oddness, this property is not unique to minds but is a widespread and familiar datum. We can now see the difference between the view of the mind (or soul) offered by non-reductive evolutionary naturalism and that offered by either dualism or materialism. Mind does not occupy its own peculiar space, nor is it located in ordinary physical space (though thoughts may have spatial *content* in their representations). Contra Descartes, however, to say that mind lacks spatiality is not to say that it lacks structure or parts or that it is a simplicity.

In structural supervenience, though supervening states of a system are indeed caused by states of prior or subvening systems, this is so only in the sense that the supervening system requires those prior or subvening states for its activity. The causation involved is of a global sort, i.e. supervenient states arise from and are made possible by states of the supervening system, but the subvenient states are not independent of the operation of the supervening system. The recognition that the structure of the soul or self has a non-reducible role to play in states of the body has important consequences for debates over the meaning of explanation in the humanities and social sciences, for it implies that reductionism is to be rejected not merely on *epistemological* grounds but on *ontological* grounds as well.

A kind of temporary truce between materialists and "friends of the mental" had been achieved in the past by asserting that problems about the relation between the soul and the body were not really about metaphysics but about language (the famous "linguistic turn" in analytic philosophy). It was argued that of course we could not solve the epistemological problems involved because soul talk and body talk were fundamentally different languages. The former was the province of explanation, which looked to causes, while the latter was the province of understanding, which looked to reasons. Such a position was laid out most clearly by Donald Davidson in his theory of *anomalous monism*, which asserted a monism of substance (the physical) and a dualism of description (the physical and the mental).[23] Although such a position gave temporary relief to anti-materialists by assuring them that what they were talking about was indeed irreducible to physics, it eventually undermined their position, since epistemological non-reductionism is fully compatible with both functionalist materialism and the disparagement of soul talk as mere "folk psychology," to be eventually disposed of as we discover more about the brain.

More fundamentally, reductionism should be rejected on *ontological* grounds. The supervenient system has a causal power of its own, even though nothing that it does is done through any other medium than the physical. Souls are real things, really existing in the natural world, although their being is structural rather than substantial. It is not a question merely of how we *interpret* mental representations but of explaining their causal origins and effects. The causal path in the supervenience relation is a two-way street. Even though all the traffic on that street is physical in a local sense, what *kind* of traffic is traveling on the street depends on global features of the system involved, whether it be one billiard ball hitting another, an act of compassion, or an encounter with God. The world of nature is through and through physical in its subvening base, but at the same time it contains selves – active structural entities that are not themselves physical even though constituted by physical components.[24]

Non-reductive evolutionary naturalism specifically denies the dualist claim that there are two kinds of things – one that is spatio-temporal and the other that is only temporal and marked by an essence and power of action unconnected to its body. It speaks instead of evolutionary layers, causally linked from the bottom up but non-reducible to lower level explanation.[25] The ontology of souls is understood not in terms of substances with essences, but of emergent structures generating new principles of operation. The immateriality of the soul is nothing strange, or no more strange than the immateriality of a corporation or a piece of music or a name. It is not the immateriality of souls that give them their special place in the world but their capacity for interiority.

## Interiority

Interiority is the third leg of the picture and the one that may seem least congruent with a naturalistic view of the world. The distinctive features of human souls are their first-person subjectivity, their capacity for self-awareness, and their capacity for personal relationship. These capacities, I think, are usefully described under the idea of interiority. All creatures have these to some degree, but the human capacity for reflexive interiority indicates a quantum leap in both cognitive and spiritual evolution. Interiority is what makes the world have meaning for us instead of merely a syntax. It is what all computational models of the mind leave out. Interiority is the soul's (or self's) way of arranging space so as to distinguish the places it inhabits from those it merely passes through unawares. Souls inhabit the same space as bodies but in an interior way. Houses, nests, shells, corners, friendships, families, communities, rituals are all ways by which the earth's creatures distinguish the inside of the world from its outside. Interiority is what makes intimacy possible. Interiority is not merely subjectivity but self-awareness and relationship. Interiority is where the Transcendent may be encountered.

Naturalists of a more reductive stripe might be tempted to treat interiority as a mere metaphor and say, for example, that a home is simply a physical structure about which a person has certain affective states. But non-reductive evolutionary naturalism takes interiority quite literally; the world really does have an outside and an inside (with very many windows). Experientially we know this quite well, but intellectually it is very difficult not to be bewitched by dualist or materialist ontologies. There is a rhetorical impulse either to reduce interiority to states of subjective consciousness or to banish it from reality altogether because it cannot be discovered by an objective search. But the embodied soul straddles both sides of the world. The soul is the gateway to the world's interior, but this neither mystifies science nor belittles religion. It simply accommodates what we know to be true about ourselves with what we have learned of the external world. Thinking of interiority as a dimension of ordinary space avoids the problems generated by dualism's ontological splitting of the world into two kinds of beings only one of which inhabits space. That is, we can talk of the soul (mind, self) as uncovering the world's inner space while inhabiting its outer space through the body. One advantage of this approach is that it does not limit the self to the boundaries of the skin; our identity is not limited to our biological organism but to the relationships and communities within which we dwell.

## IMPLICATIONS FOR ETHICS

What implications does evolutionary naturalism have for ethics, particularly for ethical thinking that is receptive to spiritual concerns? Some changes will have to be made, both at the meta-ethical level of core concepts and grounding ontology and at the normative level of concrete moral choice. But, I would argue, these changes are not nearly so dire for ethics as many fear and some hope. The theoretical or meta-ethical changes, though apparently radical in their challenge to traditional moral categories, do not in the end force us into the kinds of relativism or immoralism that many have assumed to be inevitable. Just the opposite, in fact – we recover a deeper sense of absolute value and a clearer conception of the centrality of ethics in any meaningful conception of the good life. The normative changes, by embedding us firmly in the natural world and increasing our sensitivity to the evolutionary context, strengthen our capacity for effective moral deliberation by recognizing moral complexities that are systematically denied by more traditional approaches.

## The Meta-ethics of Evolutionary Naturalism

It cannot be denied that evolutionary naturalism has relativistic implications. A naturalistic worldview is incompatible with a realm of pure practical reason in which absolute and universal moral principles can be derived. Principles must be treated as more or less approximate formulations of values that have been found, on the whole, to be worth pursuing and upholding. And when naturalism is given a specifically evolutionary cast, the case for founding principles is weakened further. Not only are many values shaped and conditioned by stage-specific biological facts (consider only sexual mores), but individual selves are also involved in a dynamic evolutionary process, and what might be the right thing to do at one stage of one's evolution need not be right at another.

The idea of intrinsic value, central to much ethical theory, is at stake also. The conviction that persons have unconditional and objective worth in themselves lies behind the notion of moral respect and is frequently invoked in objecting to purely hedonistic or utilitarian conceptions of the right thing to do. But when human beings are conceived of in an evolutionary chain with other creatures, when the very self is conceived of in dynamic terms lacking any substantive existence or noumenal essence, intrinsic value seems to be a very dubious concept. Morality seems to lack autonomous grounding, and moral values seem to be placed on equal par with other values (aesthetic, sensual, etc.).

But the situation is not as bad as all that. Although evolutionary naturalism is incompatible with absolute moral principles (general rules of conduct), it is quite consistent with (and even requires) an absolute dimension to moral values (criteria of worth). Values here are to be thought of as embodied psychological structures through which we perceive, estimate, and respond to the worth of things. They may be manifested in a variety of different ways (ideals, goals, desires, norms, choices, commitments, etc.), and they have both an outer aspect in terms of perception and action, and an inner aspect in terms of the formation of the self.[26] Values have a quite different logic to principles. Principles are subject to universal or existential quantification, e.g. the principle "Don't lie" might apply to everyone. But values are articulated more personally and schematically, e.g. as the ideal "a world without lies." Someone might strive to live by this ideal and encourage others to do likewise, but its logic does not require that it be universal to be moral. Furthermore, values are organized around prototypes and exemplars rather than rules of inclusion or exclusion. One has in mind a clear image, perhaps, of a truthful person, with other cases more or less far from that prototype. Other people might share the value but may have different prototypes.

Some of our values are clearly limited in their scope, depending on particular social and historical circumstances. Others, however, appear to have universal application. Respect for people's dignity, concern for their welfare, and responsibility for what one does are three values that lie at the core of any morally and spiritually viable code. To be sure, these will be manifested differently in different times and cultures, and some people will emphasize one more than the other. Linguistically, these will also be expressed somewhat differently by different cultures. The Japanese concept of *kyosei*, for example, which means living and working together for the common good and doing one's part, combines both concern and responsibility into a single concept. But difference of formulation detracts neither from the empirical universality of these values nor their quality of absoluteness.

The reason why moral values have such a crucial claim on the self is not because of the Kantian idea that they are the purest expression of our practical rationality and our rationality is ultimately the essence of who we are. Rather it is because they form the necessary framework for the deepening of interiority, which is the very life of the self. A self is a local center of interiority. Selves need integrity in order not to fragment. Selves need responsibility (trustworthiness grounded in accountability) if they are to embody core ideals in individual choice and action. Selves need respect for other centers of interiority, for to deny respect to others is ultimately to deny it in oneself. And selves need concern or compassion for others, since selves are essentially relational entities; they can no more survive without empathic community than our bodies can survive without oxygen. The personal recognition of these truths – and all the world's religions declare them in one form or another – is an inevitable part of the self's evolution toward wholeness, growth, and restoration.

Intrinsic value, also, survives the de-substantialization of the concept of the self. To say that our soul or self is non-substantial is not thereby to declare it unreal: that is a prejudice of materialism. Supervenient entities are more than just fictions, and their meaning and reality are not exhausted by the kinds of narratives that we invent about them. They have a way of breaking up our stories, of insisting on their continued presence by going their own way and playing out their own destinies. Further, it is precisely because of interiority that the self has intrinsic worth. On the face of it, this might seem quite odd. On the one hand, intrinsic value is not subject to degree. Being subject to degree means that an item can be measured on a scale other than itself, and it is the nature of intrinsic value not to be externally measurable; all intrinsic value is of identical worth. Interiority, on the other hand, does seem to be a degree concept. Human beings, because their cognitive abilities open up a great range of experience and opportunities for reflection, have a richer interior life than squirrels, which in turn have richer interior lives than mosquitoes. Similarly it does appear that degree of interiority differs among human beings – an adult has more than an infant, a sensitive artist more than a callous murderer. Yet our moral sense draws back from the idea that Jane might be worth more as a human being than John. Similarly, for many of us, the idea that intrinsic value is restricted to human beings is also distasteful and incompatible with our relationships with other animals.

The impasse is a difficult one, although it is more difficult for secular ethics than religious ethics. Among theistic religions, God is the ultimate structure of value, the ultimate interiority. On such a view, we might justifiably value a human being over a squirrel and prefer one kind of human being to another, without thereby denying that they all have intrinsic value. That judgment is always referred to God. Human beings have arrived at an evolutionary stage that produces a particularly intense form of interiority, self-reflection, with all its consequences for personal relationship. Many of our moral categories (justice, freedom, obligation, etc.) assume that capacity as a starting point for moral action. This humanistic outlook is natural and legitimate, but that assumption will not cover all points on our moral compass. It will not cover our relation to animals, to people with major neural incapacities, to infants and the unborn, to evolutionary potential in general, and (in many ways) to God.

Such relationships require an ethics in a transcendental mood, i.e. a religious outlook. In such an outlook, the worth of things flows *from* interiority, rather than being what interiority ascribes *to* things. This is not mere subjectivism, since the self-reflecting subject is put in immediate relationship with that which is beyond and beneath its subjectivity. It does not measure comparative worth, but seeks to live and act at all times within the truth of the world's interiority. The ethical perspective of non-reductive evolutionary naturalism is bifocal, shifting between humanistic and transcendental moods as warranted.

The case for secular ethics is harder. The autonomy thesis, which states that ethics is completely independent of religion, has historically depended on a Kantian establishment of unconditional moral principles known through reason. It is on that basis that Kant argued for the intrinsic worth of persons. A naturalistic rejection of such absolute principles seems to leave the secular mind with the choice between utilitarianism and moral skepticism; in either case, intrinsic value has little foothold. This situation may not be redeemable, but it is at least worth noting that no specific set of religious doctrines is required by the idea of interiority, that a good deal of the practical deficiencies of moral skepticism are often balanced by a vague sense of the sacredness of things or by the sheer necessity of relationship. One can, in fact, be quite religious while insisting vigorously on one's atheism.

## Normative Implications

Consider the imaginary example of Veronica, a sixteen-year-old girl living in Bakersfield, California, who has been offered a scholarship that would enable her to go and study at a good (though not the best) ballet school in New York. She dearly wants to go, but she is the mainstay of support – emotionally, physically, and to some degree financially – of her moderately invalid mother, who declares that she would be lost if Veronica "abandons" her. Her mother is exaggerating somewhat, and arrangements could, with difficulty, be made for her to spend most of her days in a nursing home, and on weekends she could visit a half dozen relatives who would probably be willing to host her on a roster basis. But there is no question that her mother feels that she would be much less happy with such an arrangement, and fears that the institutional life will quickly erode her spirit and will to live. She loves her home, is very close to her daughter, and had for years struggled to provide the money for her daughter's ballet lessons. She begs her daughter not to go, to wait another couple of years until she finishes high school, and then try and find a life for herself in Bakersfield – perhaps eventually marry that boy she has been dating for the past year. Veronica is convinced that she will never be offered this chance again. The idea of living in New York fills her with excitement, and she believes (though somewhat uncertainly and on rather slender external evidence) that she may have a very special gift for ballet. Perhaps she might become a great ballerina. But she loves her mother and is grateful for her courage and care in raising a daughter alone after Veronica's father died when she was just a little girl. The letter says she must give her answer within a week. She is torn. What should she do, assuming that prolonged discussion yields no change in either of their attitudes?

Veronica is in a morally risky situation. If you find the situation too easy to decide, it can be altered by lowering the hoped for gains to Veronica, raising the risks to her mother or vice versa. The first thing to see is that her decision cannot simply be resolved by an appeal to some moral principle; her obligations to herself and her mother conflict. The question remains: what should she do, and why? Those who like myself are committed to what Bernard Williams calls "the concept of the moral"[27] hold that there is a right thing to do no matter how difficult it is to discover, that this right thing to do cannot be treated as simply one good among many (i.e. that the question of what is right must in some way be *ubiquitous* in our decision making), and that it cannot simply be measured by how things turn out. Williams himself thinks that cases like these indicate that we should be skeptical about the centrality of ethics to the good life, since too much of the justification for our conduct depends on luck.

Suppose that Veronica does go to New York and that a month later her mother falls on the steps of the nursing home and fractures her jaw. Should Veronica feel culpable? Or suppose that she stays and marries her boyfriend and they have a wonderful marriage, or a horrible one. Should she feel justified or unjustified? Or suppose that she becomes a great ballerina, or a failure, or is crippled in a subway accident. Suppose she comes to realize that her ballet teacher in Bakersfield was merely flattering her, and that she had no great talent but had been susceptible to flattery. Or suppose that her teacher had great insight and saw her potential even if she did not. A thousand other suppositions could be made. What do they show about what she should do and about what makes her choice right or wrong?

Not a great deal, I believe. The evolutionary perspective is always internal to the agent; a view from nowhere is impossible. She must make her choice now, with the capacities she has and with the information she has. Of course she should strive to estimate consequences and risk with as little self-deception as possible, but it is not these that will determine the rightness of her choice. From the perspective of evolutionary ethics, her imperative is to do that which most honors the interiority of her mother, herself, and the relationship between them. "Honor," here, is a bivalent term, meaning that Veronica should both acknowledge what is true about the past history of their relationship and forward its evolution. In the case as stated, I believe that the right thing for her to do would be to go to New York. She is at a crucial stage in her personal evolution, and this is a remarkable chance. Her mother's begging seems to have an element of selfishness and manipulation about it. A mother should be particularly sensitive to the necessity of letting go of one's children when the time comes. Veronica's leaving may create an opportunity for her to evolve in her relationship with her daughter and to rediscover the capacity to look after herself. There will be costs in the choice, of course, and Veronica has an obligation to mitigate those as much as is reasonably possible. But she should go. If the case were somewhat different, e.g. if instead of a moderate disability her mother had cancer with a year to live, our advice might be different. It is as Confucius says in the *Analects*: "In his dealings with the world, the *junzi (chun tzu)* is not invariably for or against anything. He is on the side of what is right."

## CONCLUSION

Evolutionism without reductionism and naturalism that makes room for interiority provide a common ground on which science, religion, and philosophy can find constructive engagement and much reason to celebrate each other's achievements. This is not so much a separation of spheres, as it was at the beginning of the modern period, but a mutual endeavor. One of the things that naturalism asserts is that nature has an intrinsic order. This we discover through science. But until we have explored the matter through philosophy and religion, we are left to answer the ultimate "Why?" question with the reply "That's just the way things are." But metaphysics and religion may go beyond that – metaphysics by conceptually charting how the immanent points to the Transcendent, and religion by actually experiencing that path at the concrete level of the self. The three endeavors go hand in hand and require each other for sure navigation. This partnership gives confidence to religion and a conscience to science. And it gives to philosophy a much larger task than it has conceived for itself for some time, that of actually embodying the search for wisdom in the world. In the words of the mid twentieth-century French philosopher, Gaston Bachelard, "Logicians draw circles that overlap and exclude each other, and all their rules immediately become clear. Philosophers, when confronted with inside and outside, think in terms of being and non-being ... but in philosophy, all short-cuts are costly."[28]

Much of this chapter has been written in a terminology that is adapted to Western religion more than that of the East. Buddhists, for example, who tend to view the self in terms of the ego, and see transcendence in terms of escaping from the self so understood to selfless-mindedness, may find the notion of interiority awkward. The theist notion of selfhood is different and places the ego further down the evolutionary scale. Religious experience on the theist view is not the escape from selfhood but occurs rather in the innermost depths of selfhood, where God awaits. The terminological differences, growing out of different religious traditions, should not be treated as ultimately conflictual but as different ways of saying the same thing – or at least as material for further discussion.

NOTES

1. John R. Searle, *The Rediscovery of the Mind* (Cambridge, MA: MIT Press, 1992), p. 86.
2. William A. Dembski, *Intelligent Design: The Bridge between Science and Theology* (Downers Grove, IL: InterVarsity Press, 1999), pp. 100–101.
3. At least one writer, however, does take this approach. The distinguished British neuroscientist turned dualist philosopher, Sir John Eccles, has argued that the point of contact must be in the supplementary motor area of the cortex, since this fires even when motor actions are contemplated but not acted upon. See Sir Karl Popper and John C. Eccles, *The Self and Its Brain* (New York: Springer-Verlag, 1977), p. 364.
4. An alternative to substance dualism proposed in the 1970s and 1980s was property dualism, the best known example of which was Davidson's anomalous monism. Though it cannot be argued here, the Cartesian problems remain under this variant. See Jaegwon Kim, "Epiphenomenal

and Supervenient Causation," *Midwest Studies in Philosophy* 9, 1984, pp. 257–270.

5. We must be careful, however, to separate the secular assumptions of many big bang cosmologists from the theory. William E. Carroll notes, "Aquinas would have no difficulty accepting Big Bang cosmology, even with its recent variations, while also affirming the doctrine of creation out of nothing." ("Aquinas and the Big Bang," *First Things*, 97, 1999, p. 20.)

6. For example, Robert Wright, *The Moral Animal: Why We Are the Way We Are: The New Science of Evolutionary Psychology* (New York: Vintage, 1994).

7. Warren S. Brown, Nancey Murphy, and H. Newton Malony, eds, *Whatever Happened to the Soul?: Scientific and Theological Portraits of Human Nature* (Minneapolis: Fortress Press, 1998).

8. Joel B. Green, "Bodies – That Is, Human Lives: A Re-examination of Human Nature in the Bible," in *Whatever Happened to the Soul*, ed. Brown, Murphy, and Malony, p. 156.

9. Ray S. Anderson, "On Being Human: The Spiritual Saga of a Creaturely Soul," in *Whatever Happened to the Soul?*, ed. Brown, Murphy, and Malony, p. 192.

10. Nancey Murphy, "Non-Reductive Physicalism: Philosophical Issues," in *Whatever Happened to the Soul?*, ed. Brown, Murphy, and Malony, p. 147.

11. Trenton Merricks, "The Resurrection of the Body and the Life Everlasting," in *Reason for the Hope Within*, ed. Michael J. Murray (Grand Rapids: Eerdmans, 1999), pp. 284–285.

12. The strong identity thesis (reductionist physicalism) says that the mind *is* the brain, so there is no interaction problem. The weak identity thesis (e.g. anomalous monism) says there is no problem of interaction in the things, which can be described purely physically or purely mentally (it doesn't matter which), but only an incompatibility in the mental and physical languages, which is no real problem at all.

13. John R. Searle, *The Rediscovery of the Mind*, chapter 2.

14. See Thomas Nagel, "What is it Like to Be a Bat?," *Philosophical Review*, 83, 1974, pp. 435–450.

15. See, for example, the discussion by Richard Swinburne, "Personal Identity: The Dualist Theory," in *Metaphysics: An Anthology*, ed. Jasegwon Kim and Ernest Sosa (Malden, MA: Blackwell, 1999), pp. 377–392.

16. David J. Chalmers, "The Hard Problem: Facing up to the Problem of Consciousness," in *Explaining Consciousness – The "Hard Problem,"* ed. Jonathan Shear (Cambridge, MA: MIT Press, 1997), pp. 9–30.

17. For a fuller discussion of psychoanalytic models of the self, see Nathan Tierney, *Imagination and Ethical Ideals: Prospects for a Unified Philosophical and Psychological Understanding* (Albany: State University of New York Press, 1994).

18. Richard Dawkins, *The Selfish Gene* (New York: Oxford University Press, 1976).

19. Karen Neander, "The Teleological Notion of 'Function,'" in *Function, Selection and Design*, ed. David J. Buller (Albany: State University of New York Press, 1999).

20. "*Differentiation* refers to the degree to which a system (*i.e.* an organ such as the brain, or an individual, a family, a corporation, a culture, or humanity as a whole) is composed of parts that differ in structure or function from one another. *Integration* refers to the extent to which the different parts communicate and enhance one another's goals. A system that is more differentiated and integrated is said to be more *complex.*" Mihaly Csikszentmihalyi, *The Evolving Self: A Psychology for the Third Millennium* (New York: HarperCollins, 1993), p. 156.

21. Jaegwon Kim, *Supervenience and Mind: Selected Philosophical Essays* (New York: Cambridge University Press, 1993). See also G.E. Moore, "The Conception of Intrinsic Value," in *Philosophical Studies* (London: Routledge & Kegan Paul, 1922).

22. Terrence Horgan, quoted in *Whatever Happened to the Soul?* ed. Brown, Murphy, and Malony, p. 133.

23. Davidson's theory of anomalous monism was developed in his classic article, "Mental Events," first published in *Experience and Theory*, ed. Lawrence Foster and J.W. Swanson (Cambridge, MA: University of Massachusetts Press and Duckworth, 1970), reprinted in Donald Davidson, *Essays on Actions and Events* (Oxford: Clarendon Press, 1980), pp. 207–227.

24. The Berkeley philosopher, John Searle, though he declares that he has not a religious bone in his body, and though I do not share his property view of minds, presents a view of the mind and its place in nature upon which both the religious and non-religious can agree. Minds are a part of nature, brains cause minds, but mind is not a material thing, and minds are not identical brains, and minds are inherently subjective things; "the ontology of the mental is an irreducibly first-person ontology." (*The Rediscovery of the Mind*, p. 97.)

25. Note that in some evolutionary processes, prior stages become extinct (e.g. Neanderthals), whereas in others they exist contemporaneously (souls and bodies).

26. For a fuller account of the self psychology of valuation, see Nathan Tierney, *Imagination and Ethical Ideals: Prospects for a Unified Philosophical and Psychological Understanding.*

27. Bernard Williams, "Moral Luck," in *Moral Luck: Philosophical Papers 1973–1980* (New York: Cambridge University Press, 1981), p. 39.

28. Gaston Bachelard, *The Poetics of Space* (Boston: Beacon, 1969), pp. 211–212.

*Plate 7* Where the towers of cathedrals, temples, and mosques once presided over the skyline of human towns and cities, now commercial buildings, such as the dramatic art deco spire of the Chrysler Building which reigns over the New York City skyline near the East River, dominate the skylines of contemporary cities.

Photo: *Joseph Runzo*

# 7

# THE LEVELING *of* MEANING: CHRISTIAN ETHICS *in* A CULTURE OF UNCONCERN

*Philip Rossi, S.J.*

Christian practices and beliefs – and, quite probably, the practices and beliefs of most religious traditions – have generally presupposed a deeply rooted human need to have one's own life and the context of one's life make sense in a definitive way. If one accords this quest to find a "final meaning" for human activity a fundamental status in the make-up of human beings, religion functions as an important activity for the satisfaction of this basic human need. Indeed, religion may even be understood to be nothing other than human engagement in such a quest for final meaning.[1] According to this view, meaninglessness, and its concomitant, despair, would eventually loom before persons and communities lacking a framework of such implicitly religious "final" meaning.

Yet what if it were possible for persons to live in ways that are – at least apparently – humanly satisfying, but without a framework of definitive (i.e. religious) meaning? Suppose that the human quest for meaning could be satisfied by a series of discrete, partial episodes of making sense which need not add up to a final, comprehensive framework – or suppose, even more radically, that one – or one's culture – came to accept that the quest for final meaning *need not be satisfied at all.* Suppose most people considered it not at all problematic to hold that life mostly consists – to use a colloquial expression – of "one damn thing after another" and that few, if any, felt that there was any urgency to make of it anything more than that.[2]

Against the background of these seemingly speculative questions, this essay advances for discussion the hypothesis that a set of dynamics for living without a framework for final meaning is, in fact, already operative at a number of levels (theoretical, practical, popular) in the emerging cultures of informational, economic, and technological globalization. These dynamics are unlike those forms of nihilism and atheism that, because they presume the validity or the significance of a human quest for final meaning, are paradigmatically "modern" in their theoretical and practical articulations. Modern nihilism and atheism, like the forms of belief they contest, take final human meanings to adumbrate connections that are more than merely accidental and discontinuities that are not simply random. They are matters enduringly inscribed in the human condition which mark out its depth – even if that depth consists only in the recognition of all meaning as a fragile human construct that is irrevocably shattered at one's death.

In contrast, at least some of the dynamics present in emergent forms of so-called "postmodern" global culture work from a quite different presupposition: meaning *is not and can never be* final; it is only and always a matter of immediacy, contingency and "surface" – the connections that constitute meaning are merely transient links that one just as easily clicks on as clicks off. Since every meaning is evanescent, any meaning will do. One need not regret abandoning one form of meaning for another, or for yet another after that. Meanings have only limited, contingent usefulness, and so are disposable once their usefulness for the moment has run its course.

These dynamics, so the hypothesis runs, offer precisely the possibility of setting aside, without (much) regret, a quest for a life meaning that is unifying and comprehensive, while still finding life satisfaction precisely in whatever transient meaning can be constructed in and from the interrupted and interrupting interplay of life's particularity and contingency. This possibility is not altogether novel. A case can be made that this view was prefigured, in a much earlier age, by the Democritian atomism of Epicureanism, and that, more recently, David Hume eloquently proposed a similar view: an effective cure for the temptation to embark on a quest for final meaning – at least of the kind represented by metaphysical reasoning – is to find some pleasant social diversion that does not purport to exhibit itself as something deeper. Such clear-headed recognition of the absence of final meaning need not lead – as it did for the existentialists of the middle third of the twentieth century – to defiance or despair in the face of a cosmos ultimately indifferent to the fate of any of its particular components. This recognition simply allows one to get on with making one's way through the partialities and contingencies of one's own life with an equanimity that comes from putting aside as pointless bother any quest for a deeper or final meaning in it.

These dynamics can be appropriately called "the leveling of meaning." They arise, I believe, from the convergence of a variety of vectors upon the conditions of human living at the beginning of this new century. Some of these vectors take an economic form that seems driven by a momentum fueled by late twentieth-century global capitalism's dismantlement of its Marxist rival. In this context, the measure of "meaning" is economic loss and gain. As a function of market share, the bottom line, and the maximization of profit, this form of meaning has a far wider field than ever before over which to play as well as many more ways in which to play. Instantaneous transfer throughout a global network of markets has made it possible to catch, at anytime of day or night, just the right movement – up or down – to better one's placement for yet more gain.[3]

Other vectors take a technological form, driven by the exponentially growing possibilities for accessing and organizing information and for global communicative interconnection. In this context, even as meaning accrues in the assemblage of information and through the pathways of its transmission, it is potentially subject at each juncture of its path to re-assemblage and reconfiguration. Meaning arises as a function of coding and decoding, and power resides in mastery of the code.[4]

Still other vectors take social and political forms that variously devolve governing power from the center into more localized bodies or demand due recognition of the practices that mark and sustain the particularity of linguistic, religious, or ethnic identity. Yet even as the forms of political power seem to be edging back to the local and particular, the shaping of the terms of the political discourse giving concrete meaning to the exercise of that power remain entrenched in dynamics that seem systemically to circumvent the possibility of accountability to any genuinely public realm, be it local, national, regional, or global. Political meaning – most notably, but not only, in electoral politics – comes to reside in how policy and personality can be packaged for this particular electorate at this particular time. The temporal horizon for the endurance of political meaning stretches only as far as the next campaign.

Embedded in these vectors (and others that I believe can be identified within the interplay of forces shaping our contemporary world) – so my hypothesis continues – is an implicit account of, if I may modify a phrase appropriated from Charles Taylor, "the making of a postmodern identity."[5] This account, which arises from the context of what Taylor has termed the "fractured horizons" of meaning that are the inheritance of modernity, poses a serious and perhaps even radically new challenge to religious belief and practice – most certainly to those forms that have arisen from the traditions that stretch back to Abraham but perhaps to all that construe our human identity, be it individual or collective, to be in some core sense "spiritual."

The challenge that this account presents is not simply that it is a reductive naturalism, i.e. the view that there is no spiritual ingredient in what it takes to constitute an individual as (a) human (person). The challenge is, rather, that it is a naturalism so seamlessly woven into the fabric of daily practice that this *absence* of a spiritual component in our human make-up is unsurprising. It is taken as a matter of course that human life is solely a matter of contingent particularity that need not add up, individually or collectively, to all that much. Whereas "modern" challenges to religious belief and practice more typically took form as an articulated theoretical denial or indignant protest (be it social or personal) in the face of claims made on behalf of transcendence, the "postmodern" challenge is far more likely to be, in practice, an expression of puzzlement or a shrug of indifference.

This shrug is directed not so much at the content of the claims of belief, but at the very possibility that belief in God – or its denial – is a matter of importance in the business of negotiating one's way through life. As Taylor has succinctly put it, "The threat at the margin of modern non-theistic humanism is: So what?"[6] The shrug of indifference, moreover, is no longer about what may be claimed about God; it is about what we may claim about our own humanity. If it is the case – and I think it is, though the point is arguable – that "modernity" has taught us that we can talk about ourselves and about the world without having to talk about God, then what "postmodernity" in some of its practical forms may be teaching us is to talk about ourselves without having to talk about ourselves as spirit.

I think it important for keeping discussion of my hypothesis on track that I point out that it is not principally concerned with the *intellectual* articulations that so-called "postmodernism" has given to matters such as particularity, contingency, interruptions and otherness. It is even less concerned with urging a program for a countervailing intellectual refutation of claims that are made in a postmodernist mode about these matters. I would, in fact, be willing to argue that such postmodernist articulations are particularly valuable precisely because they draw our attention to an emergent dynamic within our human circumstances which it would be perilous to ignore.

My main concern in articulating this hypothesis is that we attend to how our imaginative and conceptual construal of what it is to be human is affected by practices that are woven into an emergent global culture and affect our daily lives. These practices, on the one hand, enable and encourage us to construe the content of our human satisfactions more and more in terms of the immediacy that arises from the interplay of contingent succession; yet, on the other hand, they also promise us the possibility of having increasing individual control over that interplay. They place us on the brink of beginning to believe that within our hands will soon be nothing less than the possibility of us each achieving our own individual "designer" satisfaction.

I think that what is at issue here can be put in terms of a narrative that, even as it goes back to the formative period of Western philosophy, maintains considerable power as a diagnostic tool for our own circumstances: the myth of the cave told by Plato in the *Republic*. A contemporary retelling of this myth would, I believe, have to acknowledge that the shadows that play upon the wall of the cave have grown in the power they have to captivate human imagination. They have grown in power because we now seem to have gained a capacity to make them almost (shall I use the mantra "virtually"?) indistinguishable from that of which they are shadows. They have also grown in their power because we have willingly been enlisted in their making by the lure that we can make them whatever we want them to be. Unlike in Plato's version of the myth, we need not be chained before the shadow show to keep us engaged in it – we readily stay in the cave, each taking our turn now as shadow-maker, now as shadow-watcher. There is no "outside" beyond the cave to make it manifest that the shadow show is no more than that. Insofar as we have come to believe that the shadow show is sufficient, that we need no outside against which to measure it, such an "outside" has become quite unimaginable – and it is not even all that much of a bother to tune out the occasional noisy chatter of the few odd folks who claim there is.

Perhaps this is all too harsh, especially in light of the fact that other vectors are at work within the dynamics fueling an emerging culture of globalization which make it possible for us to discern more fully the level of enduring human meaning that religious belief and practice have articulated as the locus for the presence and operation of spirit. At its best, the culture of globalization should make possible a more effective concrete recognition of our human interdependence and commonality, even as it allows greater room for expression and recognition of the particularity that makes each human being and set of human circumstances unique. It would be genuinely exhilarating to see processes of globalization deepening and enlarging the range for our discerning the presence of the spiritual at the core of human existence by making it possible for us to affirm both the enduring strength of our human connectedness and the uniqueness of the rich variety of our human differences.

Yet it is also the case that the human knowledge and skills that make it possible for us to enlarge the complexity and the scope of our connectedness with one another have also made it possible for us to level our connectedness down to the linear simplicity of the discrete moments of transactional encounter and exchange in a marketplace that now is global. Our imaginative construal of the content of what connects us begins to be modelled on the *means* that now so easily enable us to make so many connections with one another: encoded packets of instantly transmittable information. Similarly, the knowledge and skills that make possible an articulation of difference as difference in ways that are potentially richer than any that were available in previous eras have also made it possible for us to level any difference down to the contingent coalescence of particularity that wins its meaning not as difference but as effective power against any other congeries of particularity that we perceive as posing a threat to our own particularity.

This duality of possibilities suggests to me that in order to make actual those that a culture of globalization offers for enlarging the realm of spirit, we also need to identify and engage the perilous counter-possibilities of our seriously contracting it. It is important that we recognize the ways that we might very well become willing accomplices to the self-stifling of spirit, a possibility that Charles Taylor has aptly likened to performing "spiritual lobotomy" upon ourselves.[7] How might we prevent that from happening? At this point, I really do not know – and my own perplexity in the face of the possibility that we may be facing the emergence of a culture of unconcern is precisely what has moved me to propose the hypothesis of this chapter for discussion.

If my hypothesis is correct, then an appropriate response on the part of communities of religious belief seems likely to require significant reshaping of both thought and practice in a variety of ways in order to address effectively the challenge presented by an environing culture that levels out all meaning. Just as I am quite sure that there is no one way, no single strategy that communities of religious believers can adopt to deal with these dynamics, I am equally sure that the wrong general strategy would be simply to seek some form of insulation from them – even though there may be circumstances in which creative strategies of protest and resistance may well be fitting. Far more appropriate, I believe, will be strategies that engage these dynamics in such a way as to enable them to become open from within to the possibility that the reality of spirit is so deeply embedded in the human that it simply *cannot* be stifled – no matter how hard we try.

Let me therefore propose the outline of one strategy for discerning and engaging the reality of spirit within the larger cultural dynamics shaping us at the start of the twenty-first century. This strategy emerges from a resource upon which the three forms of the reflective appropriation of experience that have long shaped my work in philosophical and theological ethics have regularly converged: the capacity for exercising *imagination* as *a critical power for the discernment of what is most deeply human.*[8] In proposing imagination as an appropriate resource for countering the leveling of meaning in which the practices of contemporary culture can make us complicit, I am understanding imagination as more than merely "fictive."[9] Imagination is not the mere play of make-believe, a capacity for making up that which will never become actual. Imagination – as it is exercised, for instance, in the oracles of the Hebrew prophets, in the parables of Jesus, or in nonviolent resistance to injustice as practiced by Martin Luther King, Jr. – is rather a capacity to make manifest the deepest inner possibilities that can be made actual as well as to unmask the illusions that constrain us from acting on those possibilities.[10]

In particular, the exercise of imagination that I think will be most needed throughout the century that has just begun is precisely that which makes manifest to us that our own deepest inner possibilities as human are thoroughly spiritual. Imagination must be brought to bear to counter one of the losses that Charles Taylor thinks has taken place in forging the modern self – viz. an increasing inability to articulate our human identity as moral or spiritual in any but a private sense. Such a private construal of our identity as spirit almost inevitably proves too fragile to bear the weight of the quite public moral responsibility for one another in human solidarity, sympathy, and equality which, even in their naturalistic forms, our modern notions of the human self, agency, and experience have placed upon us.[11]

On the cusp between modernity and postmodernity, the task of imagination is also to unmask the illusions that would keep us from acknowledging these inner possibilities. The postmodern has helped to unmask a core illusion embedded in the modern story: that it is within the reach of human power, and human power alone, be it through inwardness plumbed and expressed, or through attunement with nature, or through mastery over nature, to go beyond the conditions of our finitude. Yet, as Taylor argues, much that goes by the name "postmodern" is itself caught in the shadow of an illusion more subtle and far more dangerous, viz. *that our finitude is all there is* (to this I would add: and *it is all the same.*) What makes this illusion dangerous, on Taylor's account, is that it fatally undermines the possibility of acknowledging the full significance of our lives as human – an acknowledgment Taylor holds to be central to the self-interpreting activity that is a key marker of our character as spirit.[12] In the absence of that which stands beyond life, there cannot be an affirmation of life which is both sufficiently robust to acknowledge the plenitude of its goodness and sufficiently sober to recognize humbly that life is neither all that is nor all that matters.[13]

What direction, then, might imagination take to enable a new recognition of ourselves as spiritual, one that enables us to address the leveling of meaning? Taylor suggests that it lies in the fashioning of "new languages of personal resonance to make crucial human goods alive for us again."[14] Although he notes the association that this notion of "personal resonance" has with the "expressive" strand of modernity, he distinguishes it carefully from the radical subjectivism into which much of both modernity and postmodernity have become fully enmeshed. The distinction is needed so that "languages of personal resonance" can effectively relate our human "life goods" to "constitutive goods" whose meaning and reality stand in being beyond the mere projection of immanent human strivings. In this I believe that Taylor seeks to set imagination off on the Augustinian path along which the movement "inward" of the self is drawn into a movement "outward" and "upward" and along which may be encountered the God who brings all such movement into being.

This Augustinian echo suggests that the retrieval – or, indeed, reconstruction – of our selves as spirit/spiritual may be possible only by reference to what is encountered, recognized and respected as truly other as we move in the space that our valuings create. This Augustinian movement provides a theological context in which to read Taylor's otherwise enigmatic descriptions of what it means to be a self: "We are only selves insofar as we move in a certain space of questions, as we seek and find an orientation to the good."[15] On Taylor's account – in contrast to what has become both a typically modern *and* postmodern account – our activities of recognizing and bestowing significance and worth are not confined to a space entirely of immanent human making.

On this account the most illusion-free ways of being a self – i.e. ways of valuing and being valued, of interpreting and being interpreted – thus involve recognition that value and meaning *are not entirely ours to create.* I think it is legitimate to read Taylor's account here as an Augustinian and Hegelian transformation of one of the most powerful postmodern themes: recognition of *the other as the space in which meanings emerge* can now also be seen as the space of spirit, i.e. the space in which otherness can welcome and can receive welcome. Taylor's rendering of this theme also has resonances of "grace," perhaps most clearly sounded in his characterization of the hope needed to chart our course in the wake of modernity, viz. the hope that is "a divine affirmation of the human, more total than humans can ever attain unaided."[16]

Taylor provides little explicit guidance for articulating what this hope means for the project of retrieving a notion of "spirit" by which to interpret our human lives and activities. The very suggestion of grace as the horizon of his project could, I suspect, be easily dismissed as a mere rhetorical flourish – but such a dismissal would be typically modern, for only moderns are likely to consider a rhetorical turn to be "mere." Both premoderns and postmoderns (as Taylor seems well aware) know better than to dismiss the rhetorical in this way. What direction, then, does Taylor expect us to chart for imagination from this echo of grace? How does this horizon of grace as divine affirmation bear upon the possibility of interpreting ourselves constitutively as spirit? At this point I can offer only a suggestion that is as cryptic and as tentative as it is brief: spirit *is* the presence of others welcomed; spirit *is* presence to others welcoming; spirit is, first of all, being in the presence of the Other who welcomes all that is other.

## EPILOGUE: CHRISTIAN ETHICS, IMAGINATION, AND THE RECOVERY OF THE HUMAN AS SPIRIT

If the diagnosis set forth in the main body of this chapter is correct, then the articulation of a Christian ethic for the twenty-first century needs to look critically and creatively at the resources available – both within Christian belief and practice and within the emergent globalized culture – that will enable the re-envisioning of spirit as a constitutive element of the deepest part of our reality as human. The easier part of this task may be locating the imaginative resources that lie within the traditions of Christian belief and practice. One does not have to stand within the ambit of Christian faith to recognize the power that the narratives within Hebrew scripture, the parables of Jesus, or the lives of Francis of Assisi or Mother Teresa have to remind us – sometimes uncomfortably – that what is most deeply human within us (to use Taylor's image) is the "space" we clear (or constrict) for recognizing and acting on the orientation to the good, which, however flawed it may have become, remains firmly embedded within us. When, for instance, we hear or read the story (2 Samuel 12:1–12) of how the prophet Nathan leads King David to recognize the enormity of the betrayal involved in his adulterous taking of Bathsheba, Uriah the Hittite's wife, a chord of self-recognition should strike in our own hearts – we are just as capable of moral self-deception as King David was and we are just as ready to condemn the other's conduct as we are to excuse like conduct of our own – until we are confronted by the humbling insight that we, too, are just as much the very "other" whom we were ready to shun and condemn.

In this retrieval of the imaginative resources that lie within the traditions of Christian belief and practice, Christian ethics must not overlook the two-edged danger they also bear within them precisely in their power to shape our self-understanding. As feminist, African, Latino, African-American, and Asian theologians have vigorously, vividly, and variously reminded those carried along by the mainstream of European and North American theology, uncritically appropriated images can distort theology's understanding of God, humanity, and the world and have misdirected – sometime disastrously – the practices of Christian communities. At the same time, awareness of the power that these resources have to disorient our movement toward what is good in the space of our valuings should not cause us to shrink from the other edge of their dangerous power. This is their capacity to surprise, subvert, and overturn even the most settled understandings we may have of ourselves and of the others we encounter in that space of our valuings. The story of the Syro-Phoenician woman (Mark 7:24–29) hints at how the insistent intrusion of the other – who turns inside out the image of "dog" that Jesus meant to rebuke and repel her – could be dangerously subversive even for Jesus in that it prods him to extend the horizon of his mission.

More challenging for Christian ethics – and, I believe, more urgent – will be the work of discerning the resources within the rapidly shifting kaleidoscope of the emerging globalized culture which will enable an appropriate re-envisioning of "spirit" as a constitutive element of the deepest part of our reality as human. To the extent that globalization is driven solely by a dynamic of the greater production and distribution of information, goods, and services to be consumed, the more likely we will be tempted to shape ourselves solely in the image of *homo consumens*. As one religious educator has noted, "Advertising, society's most potent educational force, teaches [our children] that their hunger for intimacy, security, success and meaning can be satisfied by conspicuous consumption. But if the deepest human needs can be met by owning and consuming products, what is left for religion to provide?"[17] Yet, if it is true, as I claimed above, that the reality of spirit is so deeply embedded in the human that it simply cannot be stifled, then even as we make ourselves complicit in the attempted leveling of all meaning to the surface play of contingencies, there remains something resistant within us that yearns for heights and depths of meaning commensurate with the best aspirations of our being.

Some of this work has already started. For instance, Tom Beaudoin, in *Virtual Faith: The Irreverent Spiritual Quest of Generation X*,[18] seeks to discern how a popular, technologized, and globalized culture has shaped authentic religious meanings for his "Generation X" cohort. Beaudoin's work suggests that it will be increasingly important in the twenty-first century for Christian ethics to attend closely to the concrete and particular ways in which contemporary culture – perhaps even without conscious intent on the part of its makers – encourages or challenges individuals to enlarge their horizons of meaning. So even as a dynamic of the leveling of meaning plays itself out in contemporary culture, it may yet turn out to be a graced occasion for rediscovery of the more enduring truth of the resiliency of human spirit.[19]

## NOTES

1. This understanding of religion in terms of a human quest for meaning – or in terms of what Paul Tillich termed "ultimate concern" – does not require that the "final" meaning satisfying it be construed as that which is robustly "transcendent" of human reality, e.g. the God of the Abrahamic religions. It is thus an understanding of "religion" which is sweeping enough to encompass views and movements (such as Marxism or scientific naturalism) that even explicitly reject the doctrines and practices of those religions – or indeed of any formally religious tradition – insofar as this rejection is made in virtue of some *alternative construal* of what gives human activity and existence its definitive significance.

2. The universality of such a quest for what I call "final meaning" has been recently affirmed in John Paul II's encyclical letter *Fides et Ratio* as a common basis out of which humanity's philosophical and religious dynamisms issue. To that extent, I believe that the encyclical continues primarily to engage philosophy in its "modern" guise. It does not fully articulate the radical challenge posed by the forms of postmodernity which theoretically or practically set aside the presuppositions that human beings (1) necessarily find themselves engaged in such a quest and (2) must eventually attain such final meaning to find life satisfaction.

3. A point made – probably without conscious irony – in a recent television ad for an on-line securities trading service which is set in a meditation class: mantra-chanting students are asked to visualize themselves in soothing and tranquil circumstances. After one student evokes a seaside scene and another the forest, the third imagines himself at his computer making eight-dollar-per-trade transactions – a scene that immediately captures the imagination of the whole class, and the instructor as well, as truly relaxing.

4. Meaning as coding can also be seen at work in the hopes that have been pinned on the successful completion of projects to map the human genome: knowledge of the code of life will provide mastery to determine its future shape. The role of economic incentives in this project, moreover, is hardly peripheral: the U.S. Patent Office has been accepting applications

that would give to those who have deciphered segments of the genome rights over future use of those segments – for instance, in the case that they later provide a basis for new and effective medical therapies.

5. Charles Taylor gives his magisterial work, *Sources of the Self*, the subtitle *The Making of the Modern Identity* (Cambridge: Cambridge University Press, 1989).

6. Taylor, *Sources of the Self*, p. 317.

7. Ibid., p. 520.

8. These forms of "reflective appropriation of experience" are Catholic theology's understanding of grace as the freely given completion of all creation, Ignatius of Loyola's principle of "finding God in all things," and Immanuel Kant's recognition of hope as the critically founded focus for humanity's common moral endeavors.

9. This point is more extensively treated in Philip J. Rossi, S.J., "Imagination and the Truth of Morality," in *Together Toward Hope: A Journey to Moral Theology* (Notre Dame: University of Notre Dame Press, 1983), pp. 37–80.

10. Iris Murdoch is one author who has extensively explored – both in her novels and in her philosophical essays – the power of imagination to bring us *to make real* that which is *good*. For a thoughtful appreciation of her work, see Charles Taylor, "Iris Murdoch and Moral Philosophy," in *Iris Murdoch and the Search for Human Goodness*, ed. Maria Antonaccio and William Schweiker (Chicago: University of Chicago Press, 1996), pp. 3–28.

11. For Taylor's elaboration of this point, see Part IV of his Marianist Award Lecture, *A Catholic Modernity?*, ed. James L. Heft (Oxford: Oxford University Press, 1999), pp. 30–37.

12. Taylor, *Sources of the Self*, pp. 341–343.

13. I take this to be much of the burden of Taylor's argument in Part III of "Iris Murdoch and Moral Philosophy," pp. 18–28.

14. Taylor, *Sources of the Self*, p. 513.

15. Ibid., p. 34. Cf. Taylor, *Human Agency and Language: Philosophical Papers 1* (Cambridge: Cambridge University Press, 1985), p. 3: "[T]o be a full human agent, to be a person or self in the ordinary meaning, is to exist in a space defined by distinctions of worth. A self is a being for whom certain questions of categoric value have arisen, and received at least partial answers."

16. Taylor, *Sources of the Self*, p. 522.

17. James DiGiacomo, "Theology for Teens," *America*, 182(3), 2000, p. 13.

18. Tom Beaudoin, *Virtual Faith: The Irreverent Spiritual Quest of Generation X* (San Francisco: Jossey-Bass, 1998). For an application of Beaudoin's insights to a specific religious context, see Jeremy W. Langford, "Ministering to Gen-X Catholics, Jesus Style," *America*, 182(14), 2000, pp. 6–10.

19. The initial draft of this chapter was written under the auspices of a fellowship at the Institute of Advanced Studies in the Humanities, University of Edinburgh.

*Part III*

# ETHICS AND RELIGION IN ASIA

*Plate 8* A bullock-drawn mobile temple in India, displaying a scene from the Hindu epic the *Ramayana*. Rama, Sita, and Lakshmana see the mysterious golden deer sent to draw Rama and Lakshmana away, making Sita's abduction by the demon king Ravana possible. Rama, an incarnation of Vishnu, is the exemplar of *dharma*, the way of duty. Photo: *Nancy M. Martin*

# 8

# HINDU ETHICS *and* *DHARMA*

*Vasudha Narayanan*

Although scholars have, in general, assumed that the word "religion" is a suitable term to describe the Hindu tradition,[1] it is commonly agreed that there is no category in Hindu thought and literature which is an exact fit for "ethics." The general perception is that there is no formal discipline in Hinduism which has "an internally consistent rational system in which patterns of human conduct are justified with reference to ultimate norms and values."[2] This does not mean that Hindus did not know about ethics or that they were immoral; it is simply that there is no discipline in Indian thought directly congruent with "ethics," just as there is no Western area of inquiry which matches the Hindu category of *dharma.* Many articles and books have been written on Hindu ethics, but by and large they deal with selected aspects of what Hindus call *dharma.*[3]

Hindus today use the word *dharma* (from the root *dhr,* "to sustain, to uphold") to refer to religion, ethics, and moral behavior in general and to their religion in particular. The term *sanatana dharma* (the eternal or perennial *dharma*) has been used to designate the Hindu tradition as a whole in the last two centuries. Indeed Buddhists, Jains, and Hindus all use the term *dharma* to indicate a wide variety of concepts and issues, and the word has some recognition in the Western world as well. In the last two centuries, the texts on *dharma* also formed the basis for formulating the administration of law in India.

As is true with most concepts and words, the meaning of *dharma* depends on the context; further, there have been changes in emphasis over the centuries. The Monier-Williams Sanskrit–English dictionary gives about seventeen meanings: *dharma* means religion; the customary observances of a caste, sect, etc.; law usage; practice; religious or moral merit; virtue; righteousness; duty; justice; piety; morality; sacrifice; and more. When used as a name, Dharma may refer to Yudhishthira, one of the Pandava brothers in the epic story of *Mahabharata* or to Yama, his father. Yama, the god associated most commonly with death today, was known as the presiding deity of *dharma*.

This preliminary set of meanings gives us some indication of the parameters of the concept and practice of *dharma*. The word *dharma* appears in the early vedic texts several times. In many later contexts, it means "religious ordinances and rites," and in others it refers to "fixed principles or rules of conduct." In conjunction with other words, *dharma* also means "merit acquired by the performance of religious rites" and "the whole body of religious duties." Eventually, the predominant meaning of *dharma* came to be "the privileges, duties and obligations of a man [or woman], his [or her] standard of conduct as a member of the Aryan community, as a member of one of the castes, as a person in a particular stage of life."[4] Texts on *dharma* both described and prescribed these duties and responsibilities and divided up the subject matter into various categories.

*Dharma* is said to deal with behavior, justice, and repentance/ atonement rites. Other classifications are more elaborate. Pandurang Kane, the pre-eminent writer of the history of *dharma* in the twentieth century, starts his second volume on the subject with "The Topics of *Dharmashastra*." He cites dozens of traditional books on *dharma* and proceeds to list the domains of this concept. His list covers about twenty-four topics and includes the duties of the classes/castes of society; the sacraments from conception to death; the days when one should not study the *Vedas*; marriage; the duties of women; the relationship between husband and wife; ritual purity and impurity; rituals for ancestors; gifts and donations; crime and punishment; contacts; inheritance; activities done only at times of crises; mixed castes; and more. If one goes through the texts carefully, one will also find discussions on the geographic areas of the world most fit for a human being to lead a righteous and meritorious life (i.e. northern India), and on charity and humanitarian and ecological concerns. Although this list is extensive, it does not exhaust the other areas that the term *dharma* covers. It is obvious that the areas and concerns of what is deemed to be righteous behavior in the Hindu tradition do not fit closely with Western notions of ethics. With abundant caution, then, we begin our discussion of *dharma*, with full cognizance that it intersects with ethics but does not purport to parallel that discipline.

Further caveats are in order. This survey is not in any way exhaustive. Ideally a study of *dharma* and righteousness which pays attention to some Western academic concerns as well as to Indian categories would look at *dharma* in connection with human accountability and responsibility, free will, *karma*, individual and social justice, cycles of time, divine grace, and liberation from the cycle of life and death – but a brief survey cannot do justice to these categories. Secondly, although several Sanskrit texts are examined here – texts that are the *locus classicus* of *dharma* – one must be aware that these were aimed only at high-caste brahmanic males. In many parts and communities of India, these texts were not held as normative, and vernacular texts and local customs vied with dharmic texts for attention. Finally, with regard to areas in which correct behavior is important, Hindus have been particularly concerned with ritual purity and impurity and with auspiciousness and inauspiciousness. In philosophy and in the ordering of Hindus' lives, the two categories that have had overriding importance are *dharma* and liberation (*moksha*).

## SOURCES OF *DHARMA*

The earliest texts on *dharma* are the *Dharma Sutras*. These are part of the *Kalpa Sutras*, which are considered to be an ancillary to the *Vedas*. Thus, the earliest and pre-eminent source for *dharma*, at least in theory if not in practice, is considered to be the vedic corpus. In addition to these texts, many treatises on the nature of righteousness, moral duty, and law had been written by the first centuries CE. This corpus of texts, known as *dharma shastras*, contains the most famous works on *dharma*, and they form the basis for later Hindu laws. Among these the *Manava Dharmasastra*, or the *Laws of Manu*, is the most well known and was probably codified around the first century CE, reflecting the social norms of that time.

The *Laws of Manu*, along with some other texts, lists the foundations for our understanding of *dharma*. *Manu* 2:6 lists these as the *Vedas* (*shruti*); the epics, *puranas*, and other *smriti* literature; the behavior and practices of the good people (*sadachara*); and the promptings of one's mind or conscience. Variations of this list are found in the earliest texts on *dharma* as well.[5] Although these texts deal with common topics, they vary in their opinions and provide plenty of room for interpretation. Since these rule books were written by *brahman* men for other *brahman* men (a very small but influential percentage of society which considered itself the "elite"), they were by no means followed widely. Norms differed all over India according to caste, area, region, gender, and age.

Far better known than the treatises on *dharma* is the narrative literature of the epics and the *puranas* ("ancient lore"). Hindus in India and the diaspora know the epics (the *Ramayana* and the *Mahabharata*) and *puranas*, and they understand stories from these texts as exemplifying values of *dharma* and situations presenting dharmic dilemmas. Rama, the hero of the *Ramayana*, followed his filial path and went into exile; Sita is the paradigm of *stri* (womanly) *dharma*; and so on. The people of these epics are exemplary paradigms to be imitated or avoided. Also influential are the collections of folk tales both in Sanskrit and in the vernacular. Many times the vernacular tales challenge and even subvert the value system found in the Sanskrit works. However, there is a consensus in all these texts that this span of time during which we are living – this span of 432,000 years known as the *kali yuga* – is the worst possible time for *dharma*.

## AGES OF TIME

The *puranas* composed through the first millennium CE, speak about cycles of creation and destruction of the cosmos. These cycles are known as the days and nights of Brahma, the creator god. During each of his days, the creator god brings out the universe periodically and withdraws it into himself. These days of Brahma are divided into many cycles of great eons, which are in turn divided into four *yugas* or eons. A single one of these eons is the basic cycle. The *krita* or golden age lasts 4800 divine years (1,728,000 human or earthly years). During this time, *dharma* is on a firm footing. To use traditional animal imagery, *dharma* or righteousness stands on all four legs. The *treta* age is shorter, lasting 3600 god years, that is, 1,296,000 earthly years; at this time *dharma* is on three legs. The *dvapara* age lasts half as long as the golden age; it is 2400 god years long (864,000 earthly years), and *dharma* is now hopping on two legs. During the *kali yuga*, the worst of all possible ages, *dharma* is on one leg, and things get progressively worse. This age lasts for 1200 god years (432,000 earthly years). We live in this degenerate *kali yuga*, which, according to traditional Hindu reckoning, began around 3102 BCE.

There is a steady decline through the *yugas* in morality, righteousness, life span, and human satisfaction. At the end of the *kali yuga* – still a long time away – there will be no righteousness, no virtue, no trace of justice. When the world ends, seven scorching suns will dry up the oceans, there will be wondrously shaped clouds, torrential rains will fall, and eventually the cosmos will be absorbed into Vishnu. We must keep in mind, however, that although, according to many Hindu systems of thought, it is entirely possible for a human being to end his or her cycle of birth and death through transforming wisdom and/or through devotion, the cycles of creation and destruction of the universe are independent of the human being's attainment of liberation from the cycle of life and death. Regardless of individual morality and *dharma*, we should keep in mind this big picture of the general atrophy of righteousness and moral behavior in this worst age as we discuss the topic.

## SPECIFIC *DHARMA* AND "UNIVERSAL" OR COMMON *DHARMA*

> "*satyam vada, dharmam chara*" ("Speak the Truth; be on the path of righteousness")
>
> (*Taittriya Upanishad*)

*Dharma* is not homogeneous. Some virtues and behavior patterns are recommended for all human beings, whereas others are incumbent according to one's caste in society, stage of life, and gender. Many Hindus in the nineteenth and twentieth centuries have emphasized what has been called the common (*samanya* or *sadharana*) *dharma* for all human beings – what some call the "universal" *dharma*. The epics speak of this universal *dharma* as the *sanatana* or eternal *dharma*. The following are typical examples of virtues that all human beings should have:

> Remembering a good deed and returning it with another; this is *sanatana dharma*.[6]

> Lack of enmity to all beings in thought word and deed; compassion and charity are the eternal *dharma* of the good.[7]

The ultimate importance of eight virtues is extolled in Gautama's *Dharma Sutra*, one of the earliest texts on *dharma*. These are compassion to all creatures, patience, lack of envy, purification, tranquillity, having an auspicious disposition, generosity, and lack of greed. A person with these qualities may not have performed all sacraments but will still reach the ultimate goal of being with Brahman, the supreme being.[8] There are many such lists in the texts on *dharma*, and the individual virtues are also illustrated in the epic narratives.

Although these virtues and recommendations for behavior are considered to be common to all human beings, the texts on *dharma* emphasize the specific behavior enjoined upon people of the four major castes and upon males who are in the various stages of life. There is also considerable discussion of women's duties (*stridharma*). The longest discussions focus on marriages, death rituals, food laws, and caste regulations.

## Food Regulations[9]

Right eating is not just a matter of what one can eat or should avoid; in the texts on *dharma* as well as in orthoprax houses, it involves issues like the caste and gender of the cook (preferably male and high caste, or the lady of the house, except at times when she is menstruating); the times one may eat (twice a day, not during twilight times, eclipses, or a wide variety of other occasions); not eating food cooked the day before; and so on. In earlier times other directives were also in vogue. In attention to detail, some of these regulations equal or even surpass those given in many legal texts of other traditions. The order of food courses in a meal; the direction in which the diner must sit (preferably facing east or north); how much one may eat (the number of morsels depends on the stage of life); the materials out of which the eating vessels should be made; what is to be done with leftover food – are all topics for discussion, and many of these directives and more have been followed for centuries.

There were several strict rules regarding with whom one may dine (best to dine alone!). Silence was recommended for the time of dining except to inquire after a guest's needs. Most texts said – and this was followed until probably the mid twentieth century – that one may dine only with people of the same caste and with people one knew. It was believed in many circles that one shares the sins of the people with whom one dines – especially if one sits in a single row with them. Through the centuries, we see Hindus from many communities visiting shrines of other religious traditions; but many seldom ate with anyone other than their own caste and community. Even until the time of India's independence (when there was a general effort to introduce more "socialistic" and "democratic" practices such as inter-dining), college food services in the hostels (dormitories) in South India were divided along simplified caste lines; most commonly seen were the dining halls for *brahmans,* with separate ones for non-*brahman* (vegetarian) and non-*brahman* (non-vegetarian).

The greatest amount of space in *dharma shastra* discussions of right eating is spent on forbidden foods, which varied between different time periods and between authors. It is generally agreed that most people ate meat, even beef, possibly up to the beginning of the Common Era. It is a matter of some controversy whether Indians ate beef during the time of the *Vedas* and whether the cow was a protected animal; however, it seems to be fairly well accepted that most Indians ate other kinds of meat and fowl then. It is remarkable that a whole culture seems to have slowly given up meat eating – or at least that it ceased to be the norm after the first centuries of the Common Era. During these centuries, *ahimsa* or nonviolence became normative in the many texts on *dharma.*

## Varna-Ashrama Dharma

Although there are common virtues that all human beings should have, the texts on *dharma* speak of context-specific *dharma* that is incumbent on the different classes or castes of society (*varna*). The texts say that male members of the upper three castes – the priestly *brahmans,* the rulers, and the merchants – should ideally go through four stages (*ashrama*) of life. The behavior recommended for each caste and each stage of life is called *varna-ashrama dharma.* The responsibility to behave thus is called *sva* (self) *dharma.* Whenever books describe the decline of the social order in the world, they refer to the abandoning of the duties that are incumbent on one by virtue of one's station in life.

The word "caste" (derived from a Portuguese word to mean a division in society) is used as a shorthand term to refer to thousands of stratified and boundaried social communities that have multiplied through the centuries. The beginnings of the caste system is seen in the "Hymn to the Supreme Person" in the *Rig Veda,* with its enumeration of priestly, ruling, mercantile, and servant classes. From this simple fourfold structure eventually arose a plethora of endogamous social and occupational divisions. The texts on *dharma* specify the names of various subcastes that come from marriages between the various classes. There are more than one thousand *jatis* ("birth groups") in India. Ritual practices, dietary rules, and sometimes dialects differ between the castes.

Deviation from caste practices in past centuries sometimes resulted in one's being excluded from the caste. *Brahmans* were supposed to learn and teach the *Vedas*. The monopoly that they exercised in teaching the *Vedas* orally was jealously guarded, and for centuries these hymns were not written down. The *kshatriya* ("royal") class was the one from which kings and rulers emerged. The men from this community were allowed to learn but not teach the *Vedas*, and their *dharma* was to protect the people and the country. Arjuna, the hero of the *Bhagavad Gita*, is from this class. One famous text is a conversation between the warrior Arjuna and his cousin Krishna (an incarnation of Vishnu, who is considered here to be the supreme being).[10] When Krishna urges Arjuna to do his *dharma*, he is reminding him of the duties incumbent on him by virtue of his birth. The mercantile class (*vaishyas*) was in charge of most commercial transactions. According to the codes of law, they, like the ruling class, had the authority to study but not teach the *Vedas*. They were to rear cattle, trade, and deal with agricultural work. The last class mentioned formally in the *dharma shastra* is the *shudras*, a term that has generally been translated as "servants." The *dharma shastras* say that the duty of a *shudra* is to serve the other classes, especially the *brahmans*. The *Laws of Manu* and the *Bhagavad Gita* tell us that it is better to do one's own *dharma* imperfectly than to do another's well. However, the law books acknowledge that in times of adversity, one may do other tasks, and they list these in order of preference for each class.

Despite these textual injunctions, Manu's advice was apparently not followed in many parts of India. The caste system is far more complex and flexible than the *dharma shastra* descriptions. The Vellalas of South India, for instance, were considered a *shudra* caste technically but wielded considerable economic and political power. They were a wealthy caste of landowners, and the *dharma shastra* prohibitions against *shudras* owning land do not seem to have had any effect on their fortunes. We will see soon that custom and tradition seem to override the literature of the *dharma* texts.

Although these codes of law emphasize the importance of marrying within one's own caste, they recognize that mixed marriages take place quite often, and so go on to list the kinds of subcastes that emerge from various permutations. A marriage is generally acceptable if the male partner is of a higher caste. However, if a woman is higher, the offspring is considered of a lower caste than either parent. The Indian caste system is not a feature of the Hindu tradition alone. It is such a strong social force that non-Hindu communities such as the Christians, Jains, and Sikhs have absorbed parts of it. Nadar Christians from the south, for instance, will marry only people of the same heritage, and one may draw similar parallels all over India.

The code of Manu also contains prescriptions of criminal law, in which the punishment frequently varied with the castes of both the offender and the victim. The gravity of the crime and how heinous the sin was considered to be were dependent on the castes of the perpetrator and the victim. The lower castes faced harsher punishments for the same crime than the higher castes according to this text. But one is not sure whether these prescriptions were followed and enforced. Scholars have shown that the *Laws of Manu* had limited import, that in fact the law was mitigated by learned people, and each case was decided with reference to the immediate circumstances. It was only in the nineteenth century, after the establishment of British rule, that the *Laws of Manu* and other texts received more attention than they had commanded in the previous centuries. The British assumed that these laws were binding, when in fact they had been only one factor among many considerations in the judicial process.

In addition to caste, the texts of law recognized four stages of life, called the four *ashramas,* for males of the upper three castes of society, each with different dharmic responsibilities. First, a young boy was initiated into the stage of a student and during his student years he was to remain celibate and to concentrate on learning. Although in the earlier vedic literature there is some evidence that girls could also become students, it is probable that by the time of Manu in the first century CE this right had been withdrawn. After being a student, a young man was to get married and to repay his debt to society and his ancestors and his spiritual debt to the gods. He earned a living to support his family and other students. Whereas it was a student's *dharma* not to work for a living and to remain celibate, a householder's *dharma* was to be employed and to lead a conjugal life with his partner in *dharma* (*saha-dharmacharini*).

Probably most men never went beyond these two stages, and even the first may have been of a cursory nature for some. The *Laws of Manu*, however, gives details of two more stages – those of a forest dweller and an ascetic. When a man sees his skin wrinkled and his hair gray, says Manu, when he sees his grandchildren (that is, when his children have reached the householder stage and become the economic pillars of society), he may retire to the forest with his wife, lead a simple life, and spend his time in reciting the *Vedas* and in quietude.

The final stage, *sannyasa*, was entered by very few. A man apparently staged his own social death and became an ascetic. His old personality was now dead. The ascetic owned nothing, living off the food given as alms and eating but once a day. He was to spend his time pursuing salvific knowledge and cultivating detachment from life. However, with the increasing popularity of the *Bhagavad Gita*, which stresses detached action even while a person lives in the thick of society, the need to enter formally into the life of a reclusive renunciant was diminished considerably in the Hindu tradition. Still, Sanskrit and vernacular texts on *dharma* extol the importance of becoming an ascetic (*sannyasi*). Indeed, in India one does see such ascetics in ochre or saffron clothes. And though the texts on *dharma* specify that only male members of the upper three classes of society have the right to become ascetics, we shall see that this was sometimes challenged. When a man enters this stage of life, he is considered to be socially dead and is formally disassociated from all his relationships. He is now religiously (and legally today) a new person without connections.

## TEXT AND PRACTICE

It is important to note that the texts on *dharma* were frequently superseded by local practices. Let us consider just one question: can a member of the fourth class, i.e. a *shudra*, become a renunciant? This question was debated by the Supreme Court of India. According to the classical texts of *dharma*, only men of the upper three classes could go through all the four stages of life. *Shudras* and women are usually lumped together in one low category even for apparently trivial issues. For instance, according to Manu, men of the upper classes will sip water three times to purify themselves, but women and *shudras* should sip water only once (*Manu* 5:139). Despite these statements, *shudra* ascetics are seen in the tradition of the theologian Ramanuja (eleventh century) and in many Shaiva orders in South India.

When one *shudra,* traditionally barred from becoming an ascetic, became one, the validity of his action was challenged in the court of law in the case of *Krishna Singh* v. *Mathura Ahir* (AIR 1980 SC 707; 1980 All LJ 299) over a question of the inheritance of some property. It was alleged that a *shudra* cannot become an ascetic, and so the property of the *shudra sannyasi* in question should devolve to the natural relatives and not to the spiritual community. This issue was debated in the High Court of Allahabad and then went all the way up to the Supreme Court of India. In a landmark decision in this case, the Supreme Court of India made it clear that though the orthodox view does not allow *shudras* to become *sannyasis,* the existing practice in India is contrary to such a view and that at the present time a Hindu of any caste can adopt the life of a *sannyasi.* It was further declared that where according to custom or usage a *shudra* can enter a religious order, such usage will be recognized and the ban on *shudras* becoming *sannyasis* stands abrogated by virtue of the mandates embodied in Part III of the Constitution of India.[11]

Because such issues as becoming a renunciant are, for Hindus, governed by personal law, which is derived from Hindu texts, one can reflect on the formal authority of the *dharma* literature and legal commentaries. In *Krishna Singh* v. *Mathura Ahir,* the Supreme Court observed, "In applying Personal Laws of the parties [the judge] could not introduce his concept of modern times, but should have enforced the law as derived from recognized authority sources of Hindu Law, i.e., *smritis* [texts on *dharma*] and commentaries referred to and interpreted in various judgments of the High Courts except where such law is altered by usage or custom as modified or abrogated by statue."[12]

What the Supreme Court of India declared here is very important. The Court articulated an understanding that has been applied all over the country for centuries: although the *dharma* and legal texts are important, local custom and tradition are even more important. When dispensing justice, kings and other rulers traditionally favored custom over texts. What it is necessary to prove is that the usage has been acted upon in practice for such a long period and with such invariability as to show that it has by common consent been submitted to as the established governing rule of the district concerned. The diversity of the Hindu traditions, rather than the uniform straitjacket of a dharmic text, is showcased in this context. The Supreme Court asserted that indeed a *shudra* could become a *sannyasi,* and therefore the natural relatives could not be his heirs.

We see the importance of custom over text in other areas also. Although the texts on *dharma* state several times that a woman is dependent on male relatives, we see that women in many areas of India, especially if they were from the so-called "lower castes," exercised considerable independence. Many women have donated money to charitable institutions and to temples in their own name, as the many hundreds of temple inscriptions attest.[13] Although *brahman* widows seldom remarried in most areas of India, the custom was quite prevalent in parts of Gujarat.[14] The notion of what was right and wrong, therefore, was not just incumbent on scriptural injunctions but also on local practice and custom.

## MORAL PARADIGMS

Many stories in the *puranas* do not make a direct correlation between goodness of character and piety. The *puranas* are filled with stories of demon men and women who show intense devotion to a deity and practice severe austerities to receive certain divine favors. Such favors may include being invulnerable to death at the hands of human beings or beasts, long life, etc. Having received these favors, the characters then terrorize human beings. A typical story is that of Mahisha, a buffalo demon, who had practiced austerities and received a divine boon that he would not be killed by a man or a god. He proceeded to ravage the earth and was eventually destroyed by a *woman* deity – one of the categories of people he did not seek to be protected from when he got his original boon from the gods. Although stories such as these do not relate ethical behavior with devotion to a deity, we will soon see the connection between devotion and liberation.

Epic narratives and *puranas* in the Hindu tradition do portray other characters who have served as moral exemplars for centuries. As in any other culture, characters are selectively chosen and held as moral ideals. Rama, the great hero of the *Ramayana* and an incarnation of the deity Vishnu, is considered to be one such person. He is hailed as the paragon of virtue and as one who struggles to lead a dharmic life. Many of Rama's actions are taken at face value – thus he is an ideal son who obeys his father and goes into exile, an ideal husband who loves his wife Sita, and an ideal monarch. The other characters in the *Ramayana* are also said to embody behavior that is to be followed or shunned; thus one is to emulate the fraternal affection seen between Rama and his brothers and not the wrath that Vali shows to his brother Sugriva. Ravana, the demon king of Lanka, has many virtues; yet his lust for Sita causes his downfall. Similarly, in the *Mahabharata*, Yudhishthira, who is the embodiment of *dharma* itself, has one weakness – a penchant for gambling.

On the other hand, Krishna, another incarnation of Vishnu, is understood to be one whose actions were right for him but not for others. Although there is a popular saying, *krishnam dharmam sanatanam* (Krishna's *dharma* is eternal), he is not held as one whose behavior is to be followed. It is Krishna's advice, especially that given in the *Bhagavad Gita*, which is to be followed, not his actions. One way of interpreting stories of Krishna is to understand them as having a symbolic, spiritual value; thus his dancing the moonlit night away with the many cowherd girls is said to portray the relationship between the human being and the deity. The Hindu use of multiple interpretive strategies like these was frequently missed by outside scholars in earlier centuries, leading to misperceptions of Hindu ethics and allegations of apparent lack of morality in the Hindu tradition.

Hindus have wrestled with many ethical issues over the centuries. The caste system is one issue that has frequently been questioned and which is subverted in folktales and in hagiographic narratives. Whereas early and popular understanding of caste connect it to being born in a particular family, some conversations in the *Mahabharata* link caste to human character and propensity and not to biological birth. Interpretations given by A.C. Prabhupada, the founder of the International Society for Krishna Consciousness (the "Hare Krishna" movement) in the West, follow this line of reasoning.

Stories like Rama's treatment of his wife Sita in the *Ramayana* have also troubled some Hindus. Rama's behavior is paradigmatic, as we saw earlier, yet there are one or two instances that have been grist for multiple interpretations in the last two millennia. Although Rama shows his love for Sita in most of the narrative, toward the end a question is raised about her chastity. Sita has been held captive by Ravana, and after an epic battle Rama has rescued her. He now feigns disinterest toward her, and Sita, saddened by his behavior, steps into fire. The god of fire returns her unharmed as proof of her chastity, but women have seen this as a paradigmatic instance of the victim being blamed. There have been many interpretations of this story, with questions about and rationalizations of

Rama's behavior. Not all of them are orthodox; nevertheless, this dynamic continuous tradition of interpretation has kept these questions alive and the epic ethics flourishing for centuries.

## *DHARMA* AND LIBERATION

*Dharma* is one of the main categories of Hindu life and thought; *moksha* (or liberation) is another. However, though *dharma* in many contexts focuses on order in this world, *moksha* leads one away from existence in this world. *Dharma* frequently refers to actions that promote righteousness, order, and well-being in this world; the realms of monetary success and power encompassed by the term *artha* as well as the sensual love denoted by *kama* are also of this world. *Moksha*, on the other hand, generally refers to liberation from the cycle of life and death and is otherworldly in character.

Many texts and theologies have, however, seen *moksha* and *dharma* as part of the same continuum. The *Bhagavad Gita*, makes it clear that if one does one's *dharma*, that is, perform one's daily work without any attachment to the reward, it will lead to liberation. Is there a connection between *dharma* and *moksha*, or are they fundamentally opposed to each other, pointing in different directions and having different aims? Books on *dharma* say that one is to be married at a certain age, beget children (especially sons), perform acts of righteousness and ritual actions, and so on. However, to obtain liberation, one is advised to be detached from all of these worldly actions. Scholars such as Daniel Ingalls and J.A.B. van Buitenen have offered different opinions on whether *dharma* and *moksha* are part of a continuum or are like parallel lines which never meet.[15]

The word *dharma*, as we saw at the beginning of this essay, has many meanings; in some contexts *dharma* is, indeed, considered a path to liberation. Although some injunctions of *dharma* are directed to worldly order, others seem to lead away from it, toward liberation. In a famous liturgical work called the *Thousand Names of Vishnu* (*Vishnu Sahasranama*), the protagonist, Yudhishthira, asks, "What is that *dharma* that you consider to be highest of all?" Bhishma, the elderly statesman to whom this question has been addressed answers, "The best among all *dharmas* is to have devotion to the Lord whose eyes are like lotus flowers [Vishnu] and praise his qualities." Devotion to the deity has been seen as a way to liberation, and the classical text that speaks extensively about this is the *Bhagavad Gita*. This text also deals with unselfish action as the ideal action. In the course of the *Bhagavad Gita*, Krishna describes three ways to liberation (or as some Hindus believe, three aspects of one way to liberation) from the cycle of births and death: (1) the way of action, (2) the way of knowledge, and (3) the way of devotion. Each way (*marga*) is spoken of also as a discipline (*yoga*).

The way of action (*karma yoga*) entails the path of unselfish action; one must do one's duty, but it should not be done either for fear of punishment or in hope of reward. The right action should be done without expectation of praise or blame. For example, one is to study or do good acts because it is correct to do so – because it is one's duty (*dharma*) to do so, not because other people will reward and praise one for it.

Acting with expectation of future reward leads to bondage and unhappiness. On one level, such actions instigate further action and thus further *karma* is incurred, for one is never satisfied when one reaches a goal. One may long for a promotion, for more money, or to be loved by a particular person, and when one acts with these goals in mind, one may meet with disappointment and react with anger or grief. Even if one is temporarily successful, the goal that has been reached is replaced with another. Thus the thirst for material success is never quenched. Instead, one succeeds only in accumulating more *karma*, which leads to further rebirth.

Indeed, on one level (according to other books of the Gita's time), even the *karma* one gets from performing good deeds is ultimately bad and causes bondage because to enjoy the good *karma* one has to be reborn. A later Hindu philosopher calls good *karma* "golden handcuffs." Therefore, one is to act according to one's *dharma*, but Krishna urges Arjuna to act without any attachment to the consequences. Evil will not touch such a person, just as water does not stick to a lotus leaf. All actions are to be offered to Krishna. By discarding the fruits of one's action, one attains abiding peace.

The third way is the most emphasized throughout the *Bhagavad Gita*: the way of devotion (*bhakti yoga*). If there is a general amnesty program offered to those who sin, those who have a karmic overload, it is through the way of devotion:

> Even if a sinful person adores me with exclusive devotion
> He must be regarded as righteous ...
> quickly his soul becomes righteous and
> he gets eternal peace ...
> My devotee is never lost.
>
> (*Bhagavad Gita* 9:30–1)

In verses like these, it is implied that by divine grace a sinful person becomes virtuous.

Ultimately, Krishna makes his promise to Arjuna: if one surrenders to the Lord, he will forgive the human being all sins:

> Letting go all *dharma*, take refuge in me alone;
> I shall deliver you from all sins; do not grieve.

(Bhagavad Gita 18:66)

In this context, *dharma* is interpreted as ritual actions or as actions of atonement. Others interpret it as the fruit of one's action; giving them up is said to lead one to the highest good. These are held to be almost the last words of the *Bhagavad Gita*, and thus the ultimate teaching of this work.

## NEW REPRODUCTIVE TECHNOLOGY AND THE HINDU TRADITION

How do we move from such understandings of *dharma* and *moksha* to the ethical dilemmas of new reproductive technology? Not only are the ethical issues surrounding reproductive technology still being debated, but some of their basic logic may at first seem to run contrary to the *smriti* literature dealing with *dharma*. Books on *dharma* written about two thousand years ago by Manu and others emphasized the importance of married couples having children. Many Hindus today accept advances in reproductive technology, such as artificial insemination, as a means toward this goal. Since considerable importance is placed on biological descent, the husband is generally the only acceptable donor. Sperm banks as a source are sometimes rejected by "higher" castes, who value the perceived purity of their lineage. For similar reasons, adoption of an unknown child may be unacceptable for caste-conscious Hindus.

The Hindu epics and *puranas* offer stories about supernatural means of conception and giving birth. In the *Mahabharata*, a hundred embryos are grown in separate containers by a queen called Gandhari. In other texts, an embryo is transplanted from one woman to another; Krishna's brother Balarama is transplanted into another womb when still in an embryonic stage. Divine potions are consumed, and children are born miraculously. Deities are invoked to fertilize the woman if the husband cannot procreate. Even though these tales that could legitimate the new reproductive technologies are generally not invoked, the technologies seem to have been accepted easily.

What about abortion? In ancient India society was patrilineal and patriarchal. By having male children, one was fulfilling one's obligations to one's forefathers. In time, wedding gifts to a daughter became a significant financial burden. Because of both these factors, male children were more welcome in many Hindu families. Though abortions are done for a number of reasons, a growing recent trend has appeared related to sex selection. Sonograms and amniocentesis are performed to ascertain the sex of the unborn, and female fetuses are aborted. Statistics available from many parts of India, for instance, show that in recent years there has been a dramatic drop in the number of live births of girls.

According to the texts on *dharma*, the unborn fetus has life. According to popular belief and stories from the *puranas*, the fetus is even capable of hearing conversations that take place around it and learning from them. Thus, according to popular belief and the texts on *dharma*, the fetus is an entity. One would logically think, then, that terminating its life would be ethically reprehensible according to the texts on *dharma*; yet abortions are conducted legally in India. Laws permitting abortion were enacted and accepted without any strong dissent from religious leaders or prolonged editorial, legislative, or judicial debate. Thus, despite the *dharma* texts' vehemence in condemning abortion, and despite notions of embryonic life, *karma*, and so on, decisions about abortions are less likely to be made according to scriptural injunctions than according to how much a child, particularly a female child, is wanted by the couple.

The religio-legal texts that condemn the willful killing of a fetus have very limited bearing on daily life. Many Hindus are not even aware of the *dharmasastras'* pronouncements, and many who are so aware apparently find it easy to ignore them. In other words, the *dharma* texts simply have not had the compelling authority that religious law has had in some other religious traditions. Just as there were selective ways in which the caste system played out in Hindu societies through the centuries, despite the rigid pronouncements of the texts on the duties of each caste, birth technologies have been used selectively by Hindus.

Hindu *dharma*, thus, has been and continues to be a dynamic tradition, reinventing itself constantly, but within certain parameters. As in any other tradition, incongruous practices may exist side by side. The same rocket scientist who works with NASA may also be doing ancestral rituals on new moon days; the woman who utilizes new reproductive technology may also have ritually purifying baths after every menstruation. In transmitting and adapting the old and in assimilating the new, the tradition lives up to its name of the eternal or *sanatana dharma*.

## NOTES

1. Notable exceptions are J.F. Staal, *Rules without Meaning: Ritual, Mantras and the Human Sciences* (New York: Peter Lang, 1989), and S.N. Balagangadhara, *The "Heathen in His Blindness": Asia, the West and the Dynamic of Religion* (Leiden: E.J. Brill, 1994).

2. Barbara A. Holdrege in her survey article, "Hindu Ethics," in *A Bibliographic Guide to the Comparative Study of Ethics*, ed. John Carman and Mark Juergensmeyer (Cambridge: Cambridge University Press, 1991), pp. 12–69. For the importance of moral behavior in Hindu thought, see Pandurang Vaman Kane, *History of Dharmasastra* (Poona: Bhandarkar Oriental Research Institute, 1974), vol. 2, part 1, pp. 3–11.

3. See, for example, S.K. Saksena, "Moral Philosophy of India," in *Studies in the Cultural History of India*, ed. Guy S. Metraux and Francois Crouzet (Agra: Shiva Lal Agarwala, 1965); Sanat Kumar Sen, "Indian Philosophy and Social Ethics," *Journal of the Indian Academy of Philosophy*, 6(1–2), 1967, pp. 63–74; Balbir Singh, *Hindu Ethics: An Exposition of the Concept of Good* (New Delhi: Arnold Heinemann, 1984); Purusotamma Bilimoria, "Indian Ethics," in *A Companion to Ethics*, ed. Peter Singer (Oxford: Basil Blackwell, 1991), pp. 43–57.

4. Descriptions and definitions of *dharma* in this paragraph have been taken from Pandurang Vaman Kane, *History of Dharmasastra* (Poona: Bhandarkar Oriental Research Institute, 1974) vol. 2, part 1, pp. 1–3.

5. *Baudhayana Dharma Sutra* 1.1.1–6; *Gautama's Dharma Sutra* 1.1.1–6; see translation in Patrick Olivelle, *Dharmasutras: The Law Codes of Ancient India* (New York; Oxford University Press, 1999).

6. *Ramayana*, Sundarakanda 1.

7. *Mahabharata*, Santi Parva 160.21. For more examples, see also Pandurang Vaman Kane, *History of Dharmasastra*, vol. 2, part 1, pp. 5–9.

8. *Dharma Sutra of Gautama* 8.22–24; in Olivelle, *Dharmasutras*, pp. 90–91.

9. The discussion on food is based on the extensive writings of Kane, *History of Dharmasastra*, vol. 2, part 2, pp. 757–799.

10. The *Bhagavad Gita* is eighteen chapters long and was probably composed just before the Common Era. It is a part of the *Mahabharata*.

11. Vasudha Narayanan, "Renunciation and the Law in India," in *Religion and Law in Independent India*, ed. Robert Baird (New Delhi: Manohar, 1993), pp. 279–292.

12. Ibid.
13. See Leslie C. Orr, *Donors, Devotees, and Daughters of God: Temple Women in Tamilnadu* (New York: Oxford University Press, 2000).
14. Vatsala Mehta, "The Hindu Widow with Special Reference to Gujarat" (MA thesis, Deptartment of Sociology, University of Bombay, 1956).
15. Daniel H.H. Ingalls, "*Dharma* and *Moksha,*" *Philosophy East and West,* 7, 1, 1957, pp. 41–48; and J.A.B. van Buitenen, "*Dharma* and *Moksha,*" *Philosophy East and West,* 7, 1, 1957, pp. 33–40.

*Plate 9* Jain practitioners at Ranakpur Temple in India prepare the sandalwood paste and other elements needed to offer ritual devotion to the *tirthankaras* (ford crossers) or *jinas* (victors) honored in Jainism. Devotion to the *jinas*, not as deities but as exemplary embodiments of the goal toward which all living beings (*jivas*) aspire, is coupled with ethical action and asceticism in the Jain path toward purification and liberation. Photo: *Nancy M. Martin*

# 9

# PUSHING THE BOUNDARIES
*of* PERSONAL ETHICS:
THE PRACTICE *of* JAINA VOWS

*Christopher Key Chapple*

The aim of this volume on ethics and religion is to examine how religions and religious precepts can affect ethical and moral decision making. In this chapter, I will explore the voice of Jainism, a minority faith in India which has developed a highly specialized and personalized system of ethics that emphasizes the importance of nonviolent behavior as key to optimal human behavior and, ultimately, the liberation of one's soul. A summary overview will be given of Jaina ethical practices as they relate to Jaina metaphysics, which emphasizes the pervasiveness of countless individual souls throughout the cosmos. Then the life story and work of Haribhadra (700–770 CE) will be discussed as an example of applying the principles of nonviolence when thinking about the views and opinions of others. This chapter will conclude with a discussion of how the highly individualistic ethics of Jainism might contribute to broadening our view of relationships, both interpersonal and between humans and the nonhuman world.

## PROHIBITIONS: THE INDIAN CONTEXT

The religions and cultures of India are well known for their prohibitions in matters of food and sex, which are organized according to caste. As noted many years ago by Vincent Smith, caste is the most vital principle of Hinduism, dominating Indian social life, manners, morals, and thought. It consists [of] ... about 3,000 hereditary groups, each internally bound together by rules of ceremonial purity, and externally separated by the same rules from all other groups ... The most essential duty of the member of a caste is to follow the custom of his[/her] group ... particularly in relation to diet and marriage. Violation of the rules on those subjects, if detected, usually involves unpleasant and costly social expiation and may result in expulsion from the caste, which means social ruin and grave inconvenience.[1]

As Dumont, Marriott, Khare,[2] and many others have noted, one's status in Hindu society depends upon one's ranking, as expressed through caste or *jati*. Status can also be found in religious identity for Muslims, Christians, Sikhs, Parsis, and Jainas. In some instances, members of these faiths effectively function as a subcaste within their own caste in the form of a community of co-religionists. In other instances, caste differences can be found *within* non-Hindu religious groups in India, particularly the Muslims, Christians, Sikhs, and Jainas.[3]

These distinct identities, Hindu and non-Hindu, are defined and maintained by what one eats, with whom one eats, with whom women are allowed to marry, conceive, and bear children, and the occupations that one pursues. In modern urban India and even among the immigrant communities of Indians in Africa, North America, and Britain, these restrictive traditions regarding diet and marriage persist. The South Asian caste sensibility perpetuates itself through codes, symbols, and expectations that flow through Indian culture regardless of barriers such as Western individualism which threaten to detour its power but in fact only slightly modify it. The persistent maintenance of caste and religion through observant orthopraxy has been well documented in contemporary field studies in India and in studies of more ancient traditions.[4] Social identity in India revolves around adherence to codes and behaviors related to the exchange of food, marriage, and occupation.

For Hindu populations who are mainly concerned with caste and for Muslims and Christians who seek to distinguish themselves from other groups, the rules of "ceremonial purity" serve to emphasize differences and establish certainty regarding one's place in society. The Hindus prohibit the eating of beef; Muslims prohibit the eating of pork; Christians eschew all such prohibitions and hence establish themselves as radically other than

Hindus or Muslims. The Hindu prohibitions stem from the brahmanical edicts found in the *Dharmashastras*. The Muslim law was established in the Qur'an and *hadith*, with roots in the Jewish tradition of law. Christian attitudes toward food and gentile fraternization arise from the teachings of St. Paul. In each instance, the code for daily life can be traced back to a religious authority and serves to cement community ties.

## JAINA IDENTITY

Within this overarching culture that includes multiple castes and religions, the Jaina subculture has developed its own systems of identity and community maintenance.[5] With the assistance of a unique philosophy of the pervasive nature of life and a resultant system of rigorous ethical observances based on nonviolence, Jainas have retained an identity distinct from the more popular mainstream traditions of India.

Jainism has been identified for over 2500 years as a way taught by the *sramanas*, the renouncers, as opposed to the Hindu way of the *brahmans* or priests. This path of renunciation arose from the terrain of what Mircea Eliade calls the proto-Yoga meditative traditions within India and perhaps stems from the Indus Valley civilization.[6] Jainism's sister renouncer traditions, Buddhism and the meditation systems mentioned first in the Upanishads and then codified by Patanjali as the Yoga tradition, developed their own philosophical perspectives, though some common ethical and ascetic practices, particularly an emphasis on non-injury to life, are shared by each system. Whereas the observance of purity codes in the non-renouncer traditions primarily serves to cement group identity and foster a sense of belonging, for the renouncer traditions the purity codes move one away from the group and ultimately dislodge one from all possible identifications. Buddhists, Yogis, and Jaina monks and nuns enter into their respective ascetic paths (*marga*) in search of release from the karmic constraints and bonds (*grantha, bandha*) that perpetuate attachment within the realm of rebirth (*samsara*) and suffering (*duhkha*).

Among these renouncer traditions, Jainism includes some of the strictest purity laws and vows. These ethical ascetic vows serve to define and distinguish Jainas from other religious groups in India. By choosing not to engage in certain occupations, by rejecting certain foods as impure, and by strictly observing endogamous marriage patterns, Jainas have forged a distinct identity within the larger ambit of India for nearly three millennia. Furthermore, a hierarchy of vows serve to delineate differences in status between the lay and monastic communities within Jainism.

Although the early history is difficult to ascertain, most scholars agree that the earliest historical evidence of Jainism can be traced to Parshvanatha, who flourished around 850 BCE and taught a system of four purities. According to early Jaina texts, he gathered thousands of both lay and monastic followers, specifically 16,000 monks, 38,000 nuns, 164,000 lay male disciples, and 327,000 lay female disciples.[7] He was succeeded approximately three hundred years later by Vardhamana Mahavira, also known as the Jina, who likewise gathered thousands of followers. Mahavira taught five vows that foster purification: nonviolence (*ahimsa*), truthfulness (*satya*), not stealing (*asteya*), sexual restraint (*brahmacharya*), and nonpossession (*aparigraha*). These vows also appear in identical form in the *Yoga Sutras* of Patanjali and in slightly revised form in the Buddhist tradition.

Adherence to these precepts in some ways parallels the sorts of observances that solidify caste identity. For instance, many dietary rules can be linked to the precept of nonviolence; Hindus increase their purity status by following an increasingly rigorous vegetarian diet. Sexual restraint helps ensure that castes do not intermix and helps reinforce the endogamous marriage system that has been developed among the castes and religious traditions of India. On a general level, the same society-based observance of these rules has helped maintain Jaina lay identity. However, as we will see, the monks and nuns intensify the practice of these vows to an extent that goes far beyond concerns of maintaining one's group status, and purity is defined almost exclusively by living according to an ethic of radical nonviolence.

## JAINA APPROACHES TO NONVIOLENCE

Approximately one or two generations after Mahavira (*c.* 400 to 500 BCE), the earliest texts of the Shvetambara sect of Jainism arose: the *Acharanga Sutra* and the *Sutrakritanga*.[8] In this early material we find statements of basic Jaina teaching:

> All beings are fond of life; they like pleasure and hate pain, shun destruction and like to live, they long to live. To all, life is dear.

> Living beings should not be slain, nor treated with violence, nor abused, nor tormented, nor driven away.[9]

A great sage, neither injuring nor injured, becomes a shelter for all sorts of afflicted creatures, even as an island, which is never covered with water.[10]

I renounce all killing of living beings, whether subtle or gross, whether movable or immovable. Nor shall I myself kill living beings nor cause others to do it, nor consent to it.[11]

All beings, those with two, three, four senses, plants, those with five senses, and the rest of creation, experience individually pleasure or displeasure, pain, great terror, and unhappiness. Beings are filled with alarm from all directions and in all directions.[12]

He who injures does not comprehend and renounce the sinful acts; he who does not injure comprehends and renounces the sinful acts. Knowing them, a wise man should not act sinfully towards animals, nor cause others to act so, nor allow others to do so.[13]

The *Acharanga Sutra* represents the earliest systematic discussion of nonviolence in India (and perhaps throughout the world) and advocates a variety of practices to insure its observance. These rules, which number into the hundreds, delineate a way of life for Jaina monks and nuns which sets them apart from virtually all other religious orders. In addition to refraining from killing or eating any forms of animal life, monks and nuns are urged not to injure the earth or water, not to kindle or extinguish fires, and not to "act sinfully to plants."[14] The mendicant is even charged with avoiding harm to bodies borne by wind, which presumably include insects and microoganisms (*nigoda*).[15]

To facilitate this life of harmlessness, the *Acharanga Sutra* lays out a series of disciplines to be followed. These include constant wandering, except in the rainy season,[16] a sloughing off of all possessions, and utmost care in all one's activities to avoid harm to even the smallest forms of life. This commitment is reflected in numerous passages that specify actions to be avoided by monks and nuns:

A monk or nun should not wipe or rub a wet or moist alms-bowl. But when they perceive that on their alms-bowl the water has dried up and the moisture is gone, then they may circumspectly wipe or rub it.[17]

I shall become a Sramana who owns no house, no property, no sons, no cattle, who eats what others give him; I shall commit no sinful action; I renounce to accept anything that has not been given.[18]

A monk or nun might wish to go to a mango park; they should then ask the landlord's or steward's permission. Then they might desire to eat a mango. If the monk or the nun [should] perceive that the mango is covered with eggs, living beings, etc., they should not take it, for it is impure.[19]

A monk or nun, seeing that the ground is infected by eggs or living beings should not ease nature on such an unfit ground. But if the ground is free from eggs or living beings, then they may ease nature on such a ground.[20] (Several dozen other places to avoid defecation or urination are also listed.)

A monk or nun should not resolve to go where they hear the sounds of ... drums ... nor where three or four roads meet ... nor to places where buffaloes, bulls, horses, etc., fight ... nor to places where story tellers or acrobats perform ... nor to places where quarrels, affrays, riots, conflicts between kingdoms, anarchical or revolutionary disturbances occur ... nor to places where a young, well-attended girl, well attired and well ornamented is paraded, or where somebody is led to death ... A monk or a nun should not like or live, desire for, or be enraptured with, sounds of this or the other world, heard or unheard ones, seen or unseen ones.[21]

A Nirgrantha [renouncer] eats and drinks after inspecting his food and drink; he does not eat and drink without inspecting his food and drink. The Kevalin [jina] says: If a Nirgrantha would eat and drink without inspecting his food and drink, he might hurt and displace or injure or kill all sorts of living beings.[22]

A mendicant who is fitted out with one robe and a bowl will not think: I shall beg for a second robe.[23]

These few passages convey a sense of the life of rigor experienced by the Jaina monks and nuns. Their possessions are limited to the clothes on their backs and the bowl from which they eat. The most advanced monks of the Digambara sect renounce even clothing and bowl. Monks and nuns are not allowed to take up a permanent abode. They must avoid places that provide potential sensual distractions. They are restricted in the types of food they may accept and must carefully inspect all food to make certain that it harbors no obvious additional life forms. They must take care to make certain that their excretions do not injure any life forms.

The raw physicality of this asceticism can be seen in the scrupulous attention to where one places one's body, what one places in one's body, and where the tracings of one's body may be deposited. The observance of the five vows – not to cause harm, not to lie, not to steal, not to engage in sexual activity, and not to possess – to this extent leaves one in a state of raw corporeality, a state wherein one's skin and little else defines identity and personhood. Ego for such persons will remain only in vestigial form; presumably, advanced monks and nuns have effectively deconstructed the *karma* that constituted their pre-renouncer selves.

As noted above, following these various rules advances one along the spiritual path. It also results in the living presence of a group of exemplars for highly rarefied moral behavior. The daily prayer recited by Jaina laypeople includes reverence for the *jinas* (the great teachers), the *siddhas* (the liberated ones), the teachers, and the monks and nuns. Jainas hold high esteem for these four groups and seek to model their own lives after the moral and ethical example set by their adherence to the extremely rigorous vows, some of which have been listed above. Though laypeople are not expected to emulate the lifestyle of the renouncers, it provides a moral compass for their own behavior. To make sense of this orientation, however, it is important to explore the underlying cosmology and metaphysics that inform the practices of the monks and nuns.

## JAINA COSMOLOGY AND SPIRITUALITY

In the fourth or fifth century of the common era, Umasvati, a thinker lauded by both the Shvetambara and Digambara Jainas, provided an integrated philosophical, cosmological, and ethical account of Jainism, explaining the foundations for Jaina observance, and undoubtedly compiling materials from earlier textual and oral traditions, many of which have been lost.[24] In his text, the *Tattvartha Sutra*, Umasvati describes a many-tiered universe populated with an infinite number of eternal, uncreated souls (*jivas*) that, with few exceptions, find themselves mired in the trappings of *karma*. According to the configuration of their *karma* – which Jaina tradition describes as physical, sticky, and colorful – a soul may take life in various embodiments: as an elemental body dwelling in earth, water, fire, or air; as a plant; as an insect; as an animal, human, hell being, or god. Through millions of years of switching corporeal, infernal, or heavenly forms, all beings at one time have been related to one another (a primary argument used against sexual activity is that by definition all such intimacy proves incestuous).[25] Because the violent activities in which most people engage result in an accumulation of ever thickening layers of *karma*, the soul returns again and again in a cycle of birth and rebirth, mired in vacillating experiences of pleasure and pain. Only in human form, and only through the strict observance of purificatory ethical and ascetic vows, can one hope to ascend beyond the earthly realm, beyond the heavenly realm, into a state of eternal consciousness and knowledge (*kevala*).

In this sophisticated, analytical text, Umasvati catalogues the possible manifestations of karma into 148 subcategories or *prakritis*. He asserts that only by the observances of the vows and other austerities such as fasting can the *karma* be purged (*nirjara*).

Inflow [of *karma*] is inhibited by guarding, careful movement, morality, reflection, conquering hardships, and enlightened conduct. (9.2)

Austerities wear off karma as well as inhibiting it. (9.10)

He further describes fourteen stages (*gunasthana*) through which the Jaina practitioner ascends, from the lowest phase of worldliness, to the fourth phase of provisional insight, to the fifth stage of commitment to observe nonviolence and the rest of the vows, through increasing states of purity up to the fourteenth and final state of bodiless enlightenment (*ayogi kevala*).

Fourteen hardships – hunger, thirst, cold, heat, bites of flies and mosquitoes, travel, learning, lack of intelligence, lack of gain, sleeping place, injury, ailment, touch of thorny grass and dirt – occur at the tenth stage of spiritual development which is attended by subtle flickering greed, the eleventh stage which is attended by suppressed passions and knowledge-covering karma, and the twelfth stage which is attended by eliminated passions and knowledge-covering karma. (9.10)

Omniscience arises when deluding karma is eliminated, and, as a result, knowledge-covering, intuition-covering and obstructive karma are eliminated. (10.1)

There is no fresh bondage because the causes of bondage have been eliminated and all destructive karmas have worn off. (10.2)

The elimination of all types of karma is liberation. (10.3)

When all karmic bondage is eliminated, the soul soars upwards to the border of cosmic space. (10.5)[26]

In this system, the steady observance of the vows, the fencing in and girding of one's soul, and the expulsion of karmic residue result in a gradual spiritual ascent. Whether one begins from the depths of hell and moves upward into the middle realm or begins from the heights of heaven and descends from bodiless splendor into the human domain, it is through one's bodily efforts in the human realm that *karma* can be purged. These observances of purity – extreme care with the intake of food, extreme care with the dispersal of one's bodily fluids, extreme care in one's social interactions – seek not so much to define and clarify one's social standing in relation to other caste groups as to directly benefit the state of one's soul (and the souls of others). The more assiduously one applies the austerities (*tapas*) mandated by scripture, the higher one's spirit ascends.

Although the *Acharanga Sutra* and other early Jaina texts mention *karma* and its dispersal, their primary focus resides in explicating the day-to-day observances required for those committed to the lifelong quest for liberation. The *Tattvartha Sutra*, on the other hand, articulates a theoretical context through which to interpret the rigorous asceticism practiced by Jaina monks and nuns. In the process, it provides a cosmology that integrates and accounts for Jaina ethical behavior. As Joseph Runzo has argued in the opening essay of this volume, metaphysics drives ethics. The Jainas provide a perfect example of this insight, having developed their ethical ascetic regimen out of their unique metaphysical vision.

## CONTEMPORARY EXAMPLES OF JAINA ETHICS AND ASCETICISM

Anthropologist James Laidlaw has provided some ethnographic descriptions of Jaina asceticism which elucidate the contemporary reality of Jaina worldview and practice. He uses the example of the monsoon season:

> The monsoon rain shows us something of what the world is really like. With the rains, all kinds of swarms of insects come briefly into existence. They are everywhere, and it is impossible not to kill some. They live for a while, and they die. And Jainism teaches that even though we cannot see it, this is happening all the time on an even smaller scale in water, air, fire, and soil. Although our lives last a little longer, they are just the same, and they are part of this awful, endless cycle. Next time we might be one of these insects, or a fire body, which is born and dies again, doubtless in unspeakable agony, in an instant.[27]

By seeing multiple life forms suffusing all that surrounds us, and recognizing that harm to them has a deleterious effect on one's own soul as well as theirs, the Jainas, particularly the monks and nuns, develop a heightened sensitivity to the need to observe nonviolence. As Laidlaw notes,

> A great deal of the discipline which renouncers live under makes sense in the light of this vision. They must learn to sleep lightly, and not to move in their sleep. If they do, they should perform a penance. Whenever they sit down, they should lightly sweep the floor to remove any creatures that are there. They should always move slowly, and never wave their arms about, for the air is full of creatures who are killed whenever one moves, and one should try to minimize this. For the same reason, they should talk as little as possible, and always in a soft voice.[28]

The list of prohibited foods is quite extensive, and at various times of the month or year, particular groups of Jainas will refrain from eating milk products and leafy vegetables, above and beyond the normal prohibitions against meat, honey, and, depending upon the strictness of one's community, root vegetables such as carrots and potatoes.

Earlier in this chapter, the five vows of Mahavira were mentioned: (1) nonviolence, (2) truthfulness, (3) not taking anything that is not freely offered, (4) sexual restraint, and (5) nonpossession. To these are added seven additional ethical observances, bringing the total of primary vows to twelve. These additional seven are: (6) setting a limit on one's travels; (7) limiting the number of "ornaments, soaps, perfumes, and foods" one uses; (8) detailed practices for observing nonviolence, including not digging in the earth and not leaving containers of liquid uncovered; (9) daily performance of prayer and meditation; (10) even further restricting one's range of travel for a day or two; (11) devoting an entire day to religious activities; and (12) being "hospitable to uninvited guests."[29]

In contemporary practice, the tenth vow has been glossed with various suggestions. For instance, in one contemporary pamphlet consulted by Laidlaw, fasting is recommended, along with a list of fourteen additional subvows: avoiding all seeds; limiting the number of different substances one eats; avoiding sugar, salt, oil, *ghee*, curd, milk; limiting one's shoes and socks; avoiding *paan*, betel nut, cardamom; limiting the number of clothes one wears; avoidance of flowers or perfume; limiting the vehicles one uses; limiting the items of furniture one uses; avoiding or limiting creams and oils applied to the body; avoiding sexual relations and flirtations; limiting travel; limiting the number of times one bathes and uses water; limiting the amount of food eaten.[30]

## LAY LIFE IN JAINISM: APPLIED LESSONS IN NONVIOLENCE

It is important to note that laypeople comprise the largest group within the Jaina community, as has been the case throughout Jaina history. Although these individuals have not committed themselves to the minute vows governing all aspects of bodily and mental activity, they nonetheless observe a way of life that sets them apart from the vast majority of other Indians. In fact, Dumont and others have speculated that vegetarianism was adopted by high-caste Hindus in imitation of the Jainas, in an attempt to appropriate some of the status and spiritual energy generated by the observance of nonviolence.[31]

In addition to an all-pervasive commitment to vegetarianism within the Jaina lay community, the strict ethical code modeled by the monastic community of Jainas inspired the lay community to pursue limited forms of livelihood: government and farming are acceptable but not desirable occupations; writing, arts, and crafts are encouraged; and commerce is the most desirable, provided that trade is not conducted in tools of violence such as weapons or in animals or animal products.[32] Today, Jainas are prominent in many of India's largest industries, including the major newspapers, the pharmaceutical, automotive, and textile industries, and in the diamond-cutting business.[33] As a result of this proclivity for business, the Jaina community is probably the wealthiest subgroup in Indian society, with the approximately seven million Jainas (one percent of the population) controlling a large share of India's economy.

The Jaina theory of *karma* plays a central role in the formulation of the Jaina way of life. One's karmic composition determines one's actions and orientations. However, it must be kept in mind that according to Jainism, the individual is one hundred percent responsible for their own karmic composition. Agency lies squarely in the hands of each individual; no creator god can play a role in the Jaina metaphysical system. Hence, having been reminded since childhood of the inescapable effects of one's action, both positive and negative, the Jaina individual seeks to cultivate the path of lightening and purifying their karmic load. The Jaina niche within Indian society paves an easy path, in that the hereditary occupations of Jainas lend themselves to embracing clearly prescribed ethical options. This does not, however, compromise the need of the individual to confront specific ethical dilemmas. Several Jainas have served as kings, requiring that they command armed forces, and some individual Jainas have been known for their bravery in battle, fighting in defense of their king. Monks and nuns, because of their more rigorous vows, would never serve in the military.

Though perhaps more reminiscent of the Levitican code (with a heavy dose of Pelagianism) than the Christian teachings of *agapé* or the European Enlightenment insistence on the dignity of all persons, the Jaina worldview has resulted in a care for harmlessness to life which has had profound influence on ethical thinking in India and elsewhere. Beyond the various monastic and lay requirements regarding vegetarianism, avoidance of killing, and entering into professions that minimize violence, Jaina thinkers have additionally extended the nonviolent ethic to their dealings with other philosophers and religions. As C. Ram-Prasad discusses in detail in chapter 16, the Jainas were unwilling to dismiss the views of others in a facile way, and hence developed a tradition of learning the philosophical arguments of various competing traditions. The *Sutrakrita*, one of the earliest Jaina texts, includes summaries of non-Jaina systems of thought. In the fifth century, Siddhasena's *Sanmati Sutra* investigated various viewpoints, and stated they are invalid when asserted in an absolutist manner. In the eighth century, Haribhadra composed several texts that accurately represent the positions of the Charvakas, the Buddhists, and others. In the thirteenth century, Mallisena's *Syadvadamanjari* offered a comprehensive critique of non-Jaina philosophical schools and religious practices. I will leave the philosophical discussion of many-sidedness or multiplism to C. Ram-Prasad. However, the life story of one of its early advocates, Haribhadra (c. 700–770 CE) helps contextualize the urgency for developing this philosophy of toleration and mutual respect.

## THE LIFE OF HARIBHADRA: A TEST OF TOLERANCE

One of the great thinkers of the Shvetambara Jaina tradition was Haribhadra. His writings have been influential in the development of Jaina thought and practice. He provides some of the first summaries of non-Jaina thought in the form of doxographies, which even today are used as a textbook to familiarize students with the various strands of Indian thought, particularly Vedānta, Samkhya, and various forms of Buddhism.

Phyllis Granoff has conducted extensive research on the various biographical accounts of his life, which give us a sense of the role Haribhadra played in the development of the Jaina scholarly tradition.

Before looking at some of the stories of Haribhadra's life, I first want to make some general observations about religion and violence. As various scholars have noted, religion, though professing to bring out the highest and best of human potential, has often been the reason for tremendous violence and even warfare. Religious conviction galvanizes a sense of righteousness within individuals and groups. This staunchness of belief can yield various predictable and sometimes unpleasant results. Having decided that one's own faith is the correct one, one can enter a crusade to convert others. Or, alternatively, one might claim an exclusivity of faith and prohibit non-group members from joining. In either case, this level of identification sets up a condition that is conducive to fighting. Those who do not embrace one's own faith can be referred to as "infidels" and pressured into aligning their views and religious commitment with the dominant one, or those who were not born into one's faith can be seen as outsiders, not admissible into the fold. Either situation results in a charged atmosphere that can lead to violence. This often becomes compounded with economic, political, linguistic, and ethnic issues. One can find numerous examples in history, from the suppression of the Jews and Christians under the Romans to the split between Catholics and Protestants in Europe and the current tension between Hindus and Muslims in South Asia. Religious identity, even more than nationalism, often gives people a sense that their particular faith is worth dying for – and killing for.

Haribhadra lived in such a time when there was great religious creativity and tension, with competition between various Hindu, Jaina, Buddhist, and Tantric organizations. Though scholars are uncertain about the precise date of his life (and if in fact there was only one Haribhadra), we do know that he lived during the second part of the first millennium of the common era. In the stories that have been passed down through the generations regarding his life, we get an impression of an individual deeply interested in the quest for knowledge, whose quest led him through personal tragedy to a genuine concern for promoting a type of inter-religious understanding grounded in nonviolence. Drawing on the research of H.R. Kapadia[34] and Granoff, I will summarize the primary accounts of his life and then discuss how his commitment to nonviolence shaped his later scholarship.

In the twelfth century, a series of stories arose that roughly include the following basic storyline. Haribhadra was born into the *brahman* caste of the Hindu faith. He was a brilliant scholar and excelled in all branches of Hindu erudition. He was so proud of his knowledge that he tied a gold plate around his abdomen to prevent his body from exploding due to his abundance of learned scholarship. He was also quite zealous in his commitment to win in every debate, carrying a "spade, a net and a ladder in his desire to seek out creatures living in the earth, in water and in the ether in order to defeat them with his great learning."[35] He proclaimed that he would become the pupil of anyone who told him something he did not already know.

One day Haribhadra heard a Jaina nun reciting verses that he did not understand. The nun, Yakkini, explained that her song gave praise to the departed teachers of the Jaina faith. He became her student and eventually became a Jaina. In his quest for knowledge, he encouraged two students (possibly nephews) to infiltrate a Buddhist monastery and learn the philosophy taught there for purposes of refutation. The student spies were caught and, although the details vary from story to story, irate Buddhists eventually killed them. Haribhadra, out of rage, then argued against Buddhism, defeating various monks in debate. These Buddhists then were sent to their deaths, in one account being boiled alive in oil. After witnessing the terrible demise of his one-time adversaries, Haribhadra repented. In his later years, he wrote many texts that extol the virtues of Buddhism, possibly to atone for his earlier sins or perhaps to gain patronage from Hindu kings who took a disdainful view of Buddhism.

This story can be seen as a story of conversion to one of the cardinal precepts of human rights: the right to hold one's own religious beliefs. The later works of Haribhadra abound with praise for non-Jaina faiths and the desire not to impinge upon the views of others. For instance, the *Yogadrishtisamuccaya* states that

> There is no distinction
> in regard to the essence of omniscience.
> In this all principles are known
> and one is firm and notable in one's conduct. (108)
> Essentially, there is no distinction
> between the great souls who have attained omniscience,
> although they are called by different names.
> This is perceived by the great souls. (109)

Devotion can be directed to either one god or many gods.
Just as the devotion itself remains the same regardless,
So also omniscience is single
regardless of whom or how many have obtained it. (110)

He even makes the statement that all approaches to the quest lead ultimately to the same goal. Using language common to Hinduism, Buddhism, and Jainism, he writes,

The highest essence of going beyond *samsara* is called *nirvana.* The wisdom gained from discipline is singular in essence, though heard of in different ways. (130)
Pervasive Shiva, Highest Brahman, Perfected Soul, Thusness:
With these words one refers to it, though the meaning is one in all these various forms. (131)[36]

The first two epithets for the culmination come from competing Hindu schools; the third comes from the Jaina tradition (among others); the fourth is a distinctly Buddhist term. Hence, Haribhadra seeks to establish a commonality among, in the phrase used by William James, "varieties of religious experience."

The Jainas were able to put this skill in tolerating the religious views of others to good use. For a millennium they were able to co-exist with the Muslim community in North India, during which time their Buddhist counterparts disappeared, having been forcibly removed from the monasteries. One Shvetambara Jaina sect, the Sthanakvasi, arose in the middle of the fifteenth century in Gujarat, a region increasingly influenced by the Islamic faith. This particular group, founded by Lonka Saha, eschewed all worship of the Jina image, somewhat in keeping with the Muslim insistence on iconoclasm.[37]

## THE JAINA VISION OF NONVIOLENCE:
## AN ETHIC OF RELATIONSHIPS

Nonviolence in the Western context requires an essential recognition of the dignity of all humans. In Jainism, it requires a recognition of the divinity within all things of nature, including the water, the air, and the bodies of the earth. This most extreme example of nonviolence can provide inspiration for deepening and extending the Western view of nonviolence. One Jaina describes her decision to become a nun as follows:

she walked into the kitchen. There was a cockroach in the middle of the floor, "and I just looked at it and suddenly I thought, 'Why should I stay in this world when there is just suffering and death and rebirth?'"[38]

For this nun, the interconnectedness of life moved her to take up a lifestyle commitment binding her to the path of nonviolence. If an entire community of people can see even the cockroach as an integral expression of the plight of all things, and, by extension, see even an insect as a potential human being, then cannot the common person, regardless of faith, be educated to expand his or her ethical view?

The practice of Jaina vows could lead some to speculation that Jainism is a form of extremism that bears little or no relevance to contemporary ethical concerns. Is there too much obsession with maintaining one's purity by not killing any living being? Is the thorough description of the world as being fraught with potential violence that must be avoided accurate? How can one be successful in respecting other beings in light of always watching out for one's own behavior?

One thing that must be remembered regarding the Jaina tradition is that the taking on of the many vows and practices listed above is voluntary. For laypeople these vows are also largely temporary. Even the degree of one's vegetarianism is negotiable, subject to an escalation of one's observance on a periodic cycle. Hence, though the tradition has developed numerous texts, manuals, and guides for how best to practice the cardinal virtue of nonviolence, this does not constitute a universal social code to be followed by all Jainas at all times. Nor is there an expectation that all of humanity should follow the most rarefied practices.

Contrary to some popular misinformation, it is not even the case that Jainas reject military service, a hallmark of the Christian pacifists.[39] There have been prominent Jaina kings in both the south (Karnataka) and the north (Gujarat, most notably Kumarapala) who maintained armies, as well as examples of Jaina soldiers. Laidlaw poses the question, "Surely 'non-violent' Jains should not be soldiers?" He receives the following response:

> No, Jain religion does not say you should be a coward. Jains are heroes. Religion first teaches you about duty. So if it is part of your duty to go to the front in war, you should do that. It is different for renouncers, but laymen should do that duty. There were always Jain warriors, and they were very religious. Jain warriors used always to stop when the time came for *samayik* [meditation], and perform their *samayik* on horseback.[40]

Depending on time and place, different precepts will guide people along distinct paths. The highest ideal can be found in the most rigorous practices of nonviolence, to which monks and nuns bind themselves perpetually but to varying degrees, and which laypeople take up on an occasional basis. But the world at large cannot be expected to adopt these practices wholesale; the forces of *karma* are simply too great.

On the one hand, this seems deterministic and fatalistic. If the highest good can only be embraced by a select few, and the actions of these select few are limited to their immediate day to day activities, then how can this tradition even hope to marshal society toward nonviolent attitudes? The Buddhists and Hindus have long argued that Jainism holds an extreme view that is impractical; Christians, from the colonial British missionaries to modern day Southern Baptists, have condemned the Jaina religion as utterly bereft of hope. In one memorable encounter, I saw Janet Gyatso, now Professor of Buddhist Studies at Amherst College, pose this standard criticism to the great Berkeley Jaina scholar Padmanabh S. Jaini. Jaini replied simply, if you think this tradition is impractical and irrelevant, please visit and spend time with those human beings, monks and nuns in particular, who have dedicated their lives to the Jain observances. He commented that their simplicity and commitment evoke a profound spirituality, and, having visited with some of these leaders in India, I support his observation.

But does this convey a moral message? Does the life of a few isolated individuals hold a message for society at large? Laidlaw has commented that "Jain ascetics is an ethics, much more than it is a moral code,"[41] emphasizing the Jaina emphasis on personal decision making over and above following externally prescribed rules. But does this utter personalization of ethical behavior render Jainism impotent against the many ills of society and deprive it of any relevant voice on such topics as human rights or child labor laws or environmental issues?

I would argue that this is not the case. In the course of Indian history, Jainas have exerted an active social conscience. They successfully convinced the first Buddhist monks to cease their wanderings during the rainy season, to avoid harm to the many insects and plants that sprout during the monsoons. The Jaina community has developed and implemented lay codes, mentioned above, for assuring an integration of nonviolent values into the workplace. Jainas have lobbied against nuclear weaponry. The head of the Terapanthi Shvetambara sect, Acharya Tulsi, took a public stance on numerous issues, with campaigns against the ostracism of widows, child marriages, and ostentatious funeral practices. He sought to heal the rift between North and South India in the 1960s and sent many disciples to the Punjab during the 1970s and 1980s to help quell the rampant terrorism during the height of the Hindu–Sikh rift.[42]

Jainism challenges ethicists to cast their net more broadly to include more than just human concerns. In Jainism, as well as Hinduism and Buddhism, the human being is not just a human being, but includes a long, incalculable history of past births not only as human beings but as animals and, according to the Jainas, elements and plants and microorganisms. Jainism inherently acknowledges the interdependence of humans and the environment and sees a continuity between all life forms and the life form of the human. James Kellenberger argues in chapter 3 of this volume that ethics proceeds from relationships. In the Jaina view, any declaration of ethics or the sanctity of human life must by definition be extended to relationships with life forms that could be or have been human, that is, the entire spectrum of living reality. Hence, nonviolence, though it can refer to human–human relations, needs also to refer to species–species relationships and human–earth relationships.

In conclusion, the Jaina vision of the all-pervasive nature of life can contribute a great deal to current discussion of rights and responsibilities. At the recent Parliament of the World's Religions in Cape Town, Baba Vaswani, a Hindu leader steeped in the Jaina and Gandhian values of nonviolence, proclaimed the following: "The eighteenth century brought to us the liberation of men. The nineteenth century brought to us the liberation of slaves. The twentieth century brought to us the liberation of women. And the twenty-first century will bring to us the liberation of nonhuman animals." Though we know that many parts of the world are still fighting the battles begun in the eighteenth century, the challenge he put before us indicates that the Jaina message advocating respect for life in all its forms still holds currency in the contemporary climate for an expansion of our definition of ethics.

## NOTES

1. Vincent A. Smith, *The Oxford History of India*, 3rd edn (Oxford: Clarendon Press, 1958), pp. 61–62.

2. Louis Dumont, *Homo Hierarchicus: The Caste System and Its Implications*, trans. Mark Sainsbury (Chicago: University of Chicago Press, 1970); McKim Marriott, "Hindu Transactions: Diversity without Dualism," in *Transaction and Meaning*, ed. Bruce Kapferer (Philadelphia: Institute for the Study of Human Issues, 1976); R.S. Khare, ed., *The Eternal Food: Gastronomic Ideas and Experiences of Hindus and Buddhists* (Albany: State University of New York Press, 1992).

3. The Jainas include groups of merchants and groups of laborers who would be considered *vaishyas* and *shudras* according to the brahmanic caste system. They also include endogamous marriage groups such as the *osvals*, and are divided into two primary sects, the Shvetambaras and Digambaras. See Marcus Banks, *Organizing Jainism in Indian and England* (Oxford: Oxford University Press, 1992).

4. For in-depth studies of contemporary observances, see Lawrence A. Babb, *The Divine Hierarchy: Popular Hinduism in Central India* (New York: Columbia University Press, 1975) and Gloria Raheja, *The Poison in the Gift: Ritual Prestation and the Dominant Caste in a North Indian Village* (Chicago: University of Chicago Press, 1988). For studies of caste and hierarchy in ancient India, see Dumont, *Homo Hierarchicus*; Ariel Glucklich, *The Sense of Adharma* (Oxford: Oxford University Press, 1994); and Brian K. Smith, *Classifying the Universe: The Ancient Indian Varna System and the Origins of Caste* (Oxford: Oxford University Press, 1994).

5. See Banks, *Organizing Jainism in India and England*; Michael Carrithers and Carolyn Humphrey, eds, *The Assembly of Listeners: Jains in Society* (Cambridge: Cambridge University Press, 1991); Kendall W. Folkert, *Scripture and Community: Collected Essays on the Jains* (Atlanta: Scholars Press, 1993); V.A. Sangave, *Jaina Community: A Social Survey* (Bombay: Popular Book Depot, 1959); John Cort, ed., *Open Boundaries: Jain Cultures and Communities in Indian History* (Albany: State University of New York Press, 1998); and James Laidlaw, *Riches and Renunciation: Religion, Economy, and Society among the Jains* (Oxford: Clarendon Press, 1995).

6. Mircea Eliade, *Yoga: Immortality and Freedom*, 2nd edn, trans. Willard R. Trask (Princeton: Princeton University Press, 1969).

7. Hermann Jacobi, *Jaina Sutras*, Part I (Oxford: Clarendon Press, 1884), pp. 161–164.

8. Paul Dundas, *The Jains* (London: Routledge, 1992), pp. 20ff.

9. Jacobi, *Jaina Sutras*, Part I, p. 39.

10. Ibid., p. 61.

11. Ibid., p. 202.

12. Ibid., p. 11.

13. Ibid., p. 12.

14. Ibid., p. 11.
15. Ibid., p. 14.
16. Ibid., p. 136.
17. Ibid., p. 170.
18. Ibid., p. 171.
19. Ibid., p. 174.
20. Ibid., p. 180.
21. Ibid., pp. 183, 184, 185.
22. Ibid., p. 204.
23. Ibid., p. 71.
24. Umasvati, *That Which Is: Tattvartha Sutra*, trans. Nathmal Tatia (New York: HarperCollins, 1994).
25. See Phyllis Granoff's "Jain Stories Inspiring Renunciation," in *Religions of India in Practice*, ed. Donald S. Lopez, Jr. (Princeton, NJ: Princeton University Press, 1995), pp. 412–417.
26. Umasvati, *That Which Is: Tattvartha Sutra*.
27. James Laidlaw, *Riches and Renunciation: Religion, Economy, and Society among the Jains* (Oxford: Clarendon Press, 1995), p. 157.
28. Ibid., p. 158.
29. bid., p. 180.
30. Ibid., p. 182.
31. Louis Dumont, *Homo Hierarchicus*, p. 149.
32. Padmanabh S. Jaini, *The Jaina Path of Purification* (Berkeley: University of California Press, 1979), p. 171.
33. Michael Tobias, *Life Force: The World of Jainism* (Berkeley: Asian Humanities Press, 1991).
34. H.R. Kapadia, *Sri Haribhadrasuri* (1963).
35. Phyllis Granoff, "Jain Lives of Haribhadra: An Inquiry into the Sources and Logic of the Legends," *Journal of Indian Philosophy*, 17(2), 1989, p. 112.
36. Translations from the *Yogadrishtisamuccaya* are by the author, based on the edition of K.K. Dixit (Ahmedabad: Lalbhai Dalpatbhai Bharatiya Sanskriti Vidyamandira, 1970).
37. Jaini, *The Jaina Path of Purification*, p. 310.
38. Laidlaw, *Riches and Renunciation*, p. 157.
39. Tobias, *Life Force: The World of Jainism*.
40. Laidlaw, *Riches and Renunciation*, p. 155.
41. Ibid., p. 191.
42. Muni Prashant Kumar and Muni Lok Prakash, "Anuvrat Anushat Saint Tulsi: A Glorious Life with a Purpose," *Anuvibha Reporter*, 3(1), 1997, pp. 33–36.

*Plate 10* The exquisite "water temple" of Chamei-ji extends out over the waters of Lake Biwa, east of Kyoto, Japan. The unification of nature and religion in this particular Zen Buddhist embodiment of the Mahayana tradition demonstrates the harmony of the interconnectedness of all things. Photo: *Joseph Runzo*

# 10

# PRACTICES *of* PERFECTION: THE ETHICAL AIM *of* MAHAYANA BUDDHISM

*Dale S. Wright*

On 15 April 1991, an unusual article appeared in the *Los Angeles Times* entitled "We Are the Beaters; We Are the Beaten." This brief piece by the well-known Vietnamese Buddhist monk Thich Nhat Hanh amounts to a startling response to the brutal beating of Rodney King by officers of the Los Angeles Police Department earlier that year, witnessed on television all over the world. What is startling about this newspaper article is that amidst all the finger pointing and blaming and criticizing that filled the press and the minds of the people of Los Angeles at that time, Thich Nhat Hanh was the only one to step forth and say, boldly, "I am to blame; I am responsible, and here is what will need to be done." Since this Buddhist monk does not even live in Los Angeles, much less the United States, that is a surprising admission. But once we begin to probe Buddhist ethics, you will, I think, see the point. In this essay, I will use Thich Nhat Hanh's newspaper article as exemplary of the ethical aim, or goal, or intention of Mahayana Buddhism, interpreting it in relation to the classical principles of Buddhist thought generally and more specifically in relation to an articulation of "the six perfections," a central ethical doctrine in the *Vimalakirti Sutra*, a Mahayana scripture from the second century BCE. Since a specifically *Buddhist* ethics cannot be understood without reference to several basic principles of Buddhist thought, we begin there.

## BASIC BUDDHIST PRINCIPLES

We begin with four early Buddhist ideas that, although certainly not unchanging in the history of Buddhism, do constitute the building blocks from which virtually all later Buddhist philosophical systems were built. The first is a premise, the reason why Buddhism came to be in the first place. This is that human life in all of its forms entails suffering, universally and inevitably, not just among the downtrodden like Rodney King but for every one of us. Buddhism arises as an answer to suffering, as a response based upon understanding that reorients and in certain ways overcomes the suffering and awkwardness that all of us feel throughout our lives. The next three ideas provide the essentials for that understanding, constituting as they do the starting point for Buddhist meditation.

After *dukkha*, the Noble Truth of suffering that *marks* all human existence, the second idea is impermanence, the Buddhist principle that nothing remains the same over time. Simply stated, the early Buddhists recognized that all things are in process, in flux, changing from one state or condition into another endlessly, and that failure to recognize this, and to adjust one's life accordingly, inevitably leads to poor judgment and to forms of clinging and attachment that are doomed to failure in a world of change. Unless we explicitly understand movement and transformation as inevitable in every dimension of the world, both planning on it and allowing for some degree of unpredictability, we will suffer the consequences of this refusal. Third, early Buddhists were eager to add that change is not random, and that at least one principle is visible within it: that all things arise and change over time dependent on other things. Several important realizations follow from the Buddhist principle of "dependent arising": that all things depend on others as their cause or condition; that nothing, therefore, stands alone, independently; and that the inability to comprehend in a very practical way the "relationality" or "relativity" of everything is another source of misjudgment and hence universal suffering.

The fourth and final Buddhist idea that we will employ in understanding Buddhist ethics is the counter-intuitive and, to some extent, outrageous idea that there is "no self," no soul or fundamental ground to a human life, no single dimension to a human being that is permanent, stable, and that undergirds all the other less essential elements of life. What prompts this denial of the self in Buddhism are the implications of the doctrines of impermanence and dependent arising. If, like all things, I arise dependent on a variety of conditions and change continually throughout my life depending on what other conditioning factors appear, including my own choices, then it would follow that there simply is no self, if by "self" we mean something stable over time that constitutes the real me as opposed to other clearly changeable factors like my body, my thoughts, my feelings, and so on.

There is another motive for this denial of a center to self, however. This is that, from a Buddhist point of view, nothing leads more directly to suffering, to unwise decisions, to emotional clinging, to intellectual attachments, than "selfish" behavior and thinking, and nothing leads more directly to such behavior than the understanding that I am a distinct and independent self and that this rock bottom state of affairs requires me to focus primarily on my own interests, to secure myself and see that only good things come my way. Thinking otherwise – that there is no such self or essential nature, and that, like all things, I exist relative to innumerable factors beyond me and change continually along with changes in the world – and meditating on this thought, I just might begin behaving otherwise. This, in short, is why Thich Nhat Hanh does not mind shouldering the blame for violent criminals and violent cops in a city half-way around the world from where he lives. He hopes that, even if in some minute and infinitesimal way, some new, perhaps less violent, situation in Los Angeles will arise dependent on his having taken such a stand. So having introduced what I will put forward as the fundamental principles of Buddhist ethics, let us return to the story.

## "I AM THOSE POLICEMEN"

Thich Nhat Hanh begins the article by recalling the pain he had felt watching the video clip of the beating, how, like probably all of us, he could almost feel the blows of the police clubs. But then, "looking more deeply," he says, "I was able to see that the policemen who were beating Rodney King were also myself." Why would a pacifist monk, and one of the gentlest human beings in the world, picture himself as an angry, club-weilding policeman intending to inflict pain and suffering upon a man prone on the ground with powerful blows from his club? Because that anger, that violence, is not the product of these individuals; it is produced daily by our society and by the world each day and absorbed by all of us as individuals to varying degrees. The individuals who enact the violence are extensions of current anger and hatred in the society at large; they are more products of it than they are producers. It is not simply that the police are our employees, hired guns to do our dirty work; although that is certainly true, it is more important to recognize from Thich Nhat Hanh's Buddhist point of view that they are our social products, the outcome of the forms of consciousness available in our time and place. Their acts arise dependent on our acts, and vice versa, and there is simply no escaping this inextricable interdependence. Therefore he writes: "We are co-responsible . . . That is why I saw myself as the policemen beating the driver. We all are these policemen."

Thich Nhat Hanh then proceeds to clarify the Buddhist point of view from which he writes:

> In the practice of awareness, which Buddhists call mindfulness, we nurture the ability to see deeply into the nature of things and of human beings. The fruit of this practice is insight and understanding, and out of this comes love. Without understanding, how can we love? Love is the intention and capacity to bring joy to others, and to remove and transform the pain that is in them.[1]

This practice of mindfulness is better known as meditation, and the author demonstrates, in principle at least, the outcome of his own practice. Developing understanding and love for others through insight meditation, he quite naturally extends himself to include others within his domain of responsibility. Therefore, he proceeds as follows:

> From the Buddhist perspective, I have not practiced deeply enough to transform the situation with the policemen. I have allowed violence and misunderstanding to exist. Realizing that, I suffer with them, for if they do not suffer, then why would they do what they did? Only when you suffer much do you make other people suffer; if you are happy, if you are liberated, then there will not be suffering in you to spill over to others.[2]

This is what I meant earlier by Thich Nhat Hanh's willingness to take the blame. *He* did not practice meditation deeply enough to do what? To change these officers whom he has never even met? On an individualistic understanding of separate selves, this is clearly absurd. But on his Buddhist understanding, where there simply is no isolated and unaffected self, it makes perfect sense. Obviously Thich Nhat Hanh has no magical control over the individual acts of other human beings. But he does have proportionate control over the kind of influence on the world that he exerts on his own, and he knows very well that each of us, in every one of our acts, leaves a deposit on the spirit of the world, and that the world as it is in any given moment is simply the sum total of these imprints large, small, and of all shapes.

Picturing the problem with the Los Angeles Police Department, and violence in the world generally, as *our* problem, and not just a limited problem of a couple of bad cops, he goes on to say what needs doing:

> Putting the policemen in prison or firing the chief of police will not solve our fundamental problems. We have all helped to create this situation with our forgetfulness and our way of living. Violence has become a substance of our life, and we are not very different from those who did the beating. Living in such a society, one can become like that quite easily. Daily, we are being trained like those who did the beating: to accept violence as a way of life, and as a way to solve problems. If we are not mindful – if we do not transform our shared suffering through compassion and deep understanding – then one day our child will be the one who is beaten, or the one doing the beating. It is our affair. We are not observers. We are participants.[3]

Thich Nhat Hanh is what Mahayana Buddhists call a *bodhisattva,* literally, an "enlightened being," one who through extensive meditation on selflessness, on dependent arising, on change and suffering, has been transformed in such a way that he can meaningfully live as though the real problem is not just *his* suffering, but suffering itself, all of it as it is experienced all over the world. A *bodhisattva* is one who, having been transformed in this way, makes a commitment to seek enlightenment, an awakening from suffering and illusion, not just for his own benefit but for everyone equally. Ultimately, our individuality is relative and fleeting, and to focus all of our energies on it is the greatest of all illusions for human beings. Those whose lives are memorable, and most significant over time, are those who either by historical accident or by methodical practice have penetrated this illusion. Martin Luther King, Jr. is clearly a modern example of this form of greatness, of selflessness on behalf of something far greater than his own pleasure, and it is no accident that he could also see this capacity in the then youthful Thich Nhat Hanh, whom King nominated for the Nobel Peace Prize for his work in Vietnam.

## VIMALAKIRTI AND THE *BODHISATTVA* IDEAL

Allow me now to present a classical example of a *bodhisattva*, an exemplary human being as projected in the minds of early Mahayana writers who imagined in their time what true human greatness might be. The example I have chosen is Vimalakirti, who, whether he ever actually lived or not, is, as described in the *sutra*, clearly the projection of an ideal. Unlike Thich Nhat Hanh, Vimalakirti was a layman, and in that respect more like most of us. But he was also an extremely wealthy and prominent citizen of his city and therefore a good test case for the practices of selflessness that we have placed before us. If you are not a monk or nun, and must therefore live in the world of worldly activities, how could you possibly actualize the kind of understanding that we see in Thich Nhat Hanh? Chapter 2 of the *sutra* is devoted to describing Vimalakirti, and to my mind, this is one of the great segments of Buddhist literature.

Vimalakirti is introduced in the second chapter of the *sutra* as a great man living as a wealthy and prominent citizen of the city of Vaishali in India. He was known for his superior understanding of Buddhist teachings, for his compassion for all living beings, and for his eloquence. It says that he was praised, honored, and commended by everyone, including the Buddha. As a sample of the kinds of character traits that the *sutra* attributes to him, I offer the following few selections:

> In order to be in harmony with people, Vimalakirti associated with elderly people, with people of middle age, and with the youth, yet always spoke in harmony with the Dharma. He engaged in all sorts of businesses, yet had no interest in profit or possessions. To train living beings he would appear at crossroads and on street corners, and to protect them he participated in government ... To develop children, he visited all the schools ... He was honored as the businessman among businessmen because he demonstrated the priority of the truth. He was honored as the landlord among landlords because he renounced the aggressiveness of ownership. He was honored as the warrior among warriors because he cultivated endurance, determination, and fortitude. He was honored as the aristocrat among aristocrats because he suppressed pride, vanity, and arrogance ... He was compatible with ordinary people because he appreciated the excellence of ordinary merits.[4]

And that is just a sample of Vimalakirti's virtue. What the author of the *sutra* has done is, based upon his own training in the various disciplines of Buddhist thought and practice, to project an ideal layman to provide a clearly defined literary embodiment of the highest trajectory of Buddhist practice. Here the whole history of Mahayana Buddhist practitioners has been given a clear glimpse of at least one version of the ideal goal.

It is worth my pointing out at this juncture that what I am concerned with here is an ideal. It is another, and open, question whether anybody has ever truly lived up to this ideal. This is a historical question about what in fact has happened in the history of Buddhist societies. My question is not so much who has actually lived what way in Buddhist history as what in any given time and place it was possible for Buddhists to imagine as an ideal of human excellence. Ideals are always cultural projections, the highest aspirations imaginable by a group of people, and they are always undergoing modification through history. Moreover, ideals are by definition unattainable; that is, whenever you find yourself in a position to actualize what you set out to accomplish, at that point you will also find yourself able to conceive more profound and more sophisticated goals to set out before you. Having an ideal is always understanding the gap between what you are and what at that particular point you could imagine yourself being. Move toward it, and your imagination will have been deepened and your target suitably altered.

In Vimalakirti's case, somewhat in contradistinction to much of the Buddhist tradition before him, what we have is an ideal of worldliness. Rather than allowing the contemplative side of Buddhism to seduce him into withdrawal from the messiness and virtuelessness of the ordinary world, Vimalakirti dives into the world, and uses it as the basis of his own practice. He is pictured, contrary to much of the earlier Buddhist tradition, as spending time with gamblers, prostitutes, drunks, and shysters, not to mention children, government officials, policemen, and the homeless. In their midst, he maintains equanimity, poise, wisdom, and most of all compassion. When engaged in business, he shows what it would mean to conduct business in full awareness of the impermanence of all things and the emptiness of personal desire, self-interest, and possessiveness. The aspiration guiding his numerous activities is no less than a transformation of the world, and in view of this lofty goal, he simply smiles in tenderness when the rest of us scurry past him in our various small-minded and selfish pursuits.

## THE PRACTICE OF THE SIX PERFECTIONS

What does Vimalakirti do or practice in order to develop and sustain this level of magnanimity? He practices the "six perfections," a set of ideals articulated in most early Mahayana Buddhist *sutras* as the basis for the *bodhisattva*'s life. Here is how the *Vimalakirti Sutra* introduces these six ideals in its effort to place Vimalakirti concretely before our minds and imagination; you will find one sentence each for the perfection of generosity, the perfection of morality, the perfection of patience, the perfection of energy, the perfection of meditation, and the perfection of wisdom.

> His wealth was inexhaustible for the purpose of sustaining the poor and the helpless. He observed a pure morality in order to protect the immoral. He maintained tolerance and self-control in order to reconcile beings who were angry, cruel, violent, and brutal. He blazed with energy in order to inspire people who were lazy. He maintained concentration, mindfulness, and meditation in order to sustain the mentally troubled. He attained decisive wisdom in order to sustain those who had little understanding.[5]

This same sequence of six appears throughout the *sutra*. Vimalakirti strives to perfect his generosity, his morality, his patience, his energy, his meditation, and his wisdom, but notice that in each case the *sutra* gives his rationale: why does he perfect himself in these ways? The *sutra* says, "In order to sustain the poor and helpless, in order to protect the immoral, to reconcile beings who are cruel, angry, violent, and brutal, to inspire those who were lazy, to sustain the mentally troubled and those who had little understanding." Why does he practice these forms of self-transformation? Clearly *not* on behalf of his own greatness. In fact, in each case, the word "his" that I have added is inappropriate. What Vimalakirti seeks is not so much "his" generosity, morality, and so on, but the development of generosity, morality, patience, energy, meditation, and wisdom in the society itself and among all human beings; that is his goal, almost as if there truly is "no self" that should be or could be thus cultivated. Thinking, as Buddhists would, that all things change, including people, and that all such changes arise dependent on various alterable conditions and causes, Vimalakirti proceeds as if his own striving in this way can change the world.

So, "blazing with energy," as the *sutra* describes him, Vimalakirti shoots out every morning on his way to the school to work with children, or to the city council meeting to weigh in on the quality of decisions that are being made on the people's behalf, or to the encampment of homeless people or the police station. He honestly thinks that if he is deeply generous, impeccable in moral standing, always kind and patient, full of energy, profound in meditative mindfulness, and penetrating in wisdom, this will somehow rub off on others, and that through this process the whole society will be transformed. At least, this is what the *sutra* encourages us to think about our own lives. Considerable concern is expressed in the *sutra* about the quality of our aspirations – what is it that we seek in life? Unless our aspirations demonstrate profound under-standing of the impermanence of all things, the relativity of all things, and our own lack of a predetermined essential nature, we are vulnerable to poor judgment, feelings of insecurity, and to the likelihood of seeking something ultimately unsatisfying and unworthy of our efforts. Therefore, the *sutra* shows us the example of Vimalakirti, and has him instruct the other *bodhisattvas* in the importance of the quality of their own aspirations. The reason for this, again, is not that they are *our* aspirations, but that "living beings with inferior aspirations will be inspired by lofty goals,"[6] that is, that humanity as a whole would be enlightened in some way and to some degree.

This cannot be accomplished, however, if the virtuous go about their business in the spirit of moral superiority. Vimalakirti refuses to separate himself from the poorest and humblest of citizens, because, on the Buddhist principles we have introduced here, they simply are not separate. Vimalakirti's most famous and most impressive deeds show the mastery of what the *sutra* calls "non-duality," the recognition that ultimately there are no separate and distinct selves, and that what each of us come to be arises dependent on the others; it is not an individual attainment and cannot in wisdom be comprehended through "dualistic" modes of conception.

Therefore, when Vimalakirti is out seeking to enlighten sinners, the *sutra* makes a point of having him acknowledge his own complicity in the crimes of criminals. As it says, "Only those guilty of the five deadly sins can conceive the spirit of enlightenment and attain Buddhahood."[7] The *sutra* does not bother to explain this cryptic remark. We already know from what we have read up to that point that Vimalakirti *himself* has not committed these sins; he has not murdered, stolen, and so on, and is not enlightenment a condition in which one would not commit such sins? Yes, enlightenment is a condition in which you the individual will not do these things. But it is also a condition in which you the individual will see clearly the illusions of individuality, recognizing in a very practical way the sense in which what others do *we* have done, and that the interdependence of all beings ties us in one way or another to every act ever performed. Therefore, when the *sutra* says, "Only those guilty of the five deadly sins can conceive the spirit of enlightenment and attain Buddhahood," we can take it to be saying, "Only those who realize the truth of 'no self' and who profoundly grasp the ultimate interdependence of all beings can conceive the spirit of enlightenment and attain Buddhahood."

Some pages later, a *bodhisattva* friend of Vimalakirti, in what would have been an excellent description of Vimalakirti, says, "When there is thorough knowledge of defilement, there will be no conceit about purification."[8] Conceit about one's own state of purity is a sure sign of impurity. It implies a profound misunderstanding, from the Buddhist point of view, of what a "self" is; it fails to recognize that all attainment of greatness is best understood as the accomplishment of the culture, the society at large, a family, an educational system, and not just *my* attainment. On the principles set forth in the *sutra*, the best way to overcome such pride is not just the practice of humility; it is rather the thoroughgoing effort to understand all "defilement," that is, all human failure, as *my* failure. Hence, we see Thich Nhat Hanh in 1991 writing publicly in the *Los Angeles Times*, "I have not practiced deeply enough to transform the situation with the policemen ... We are these policemen."

The Buddhist teaching of the "six perfections" is the primary training ground of the *bodhisattva*. An unusually large and sophisticated literature on these six, in both theory and practice, has developed in the two-millennium history since their emergence. But in order to give you some sense of this, let me elaborate a bit on just one of them, the first perfection, the "perfection of generosity" or the "perfection of giving."

## THE PERFECTION OF GIVING

The "perfection of giving" is a positive correlate to the negative prohibition on stealing, on taking what is not yours or demanding more than you deserve. As a positive ethical demand, beyond what you should refrain from doing, it asks the *bodhisattva* practitioner to set aside questions of personal gain and extend a compassionate hand in offering what may not even be deserved in any standard sense of justice. Just as biblical texts establish in no uncertain terms what "Thou shalt not do," they also suggest an ideal in its positive dimension: "Love your neighbor as yourself." "Loving your neighbor as yourself" would require an exceptional degree of selflessness, an ability to recognize that ultimately there is no such separation between us. Otherwise, although we might in fact love our neighbor, it would never amount to the kind of concern and affection that we invariably show to ourselves.

Realizing this, when Vimalakirti attempts to define "perfect generosity," he must articulate several dimensions of this perfection. Here is his most succinct version:

> The giver who makes gifts to the lowliest poor of the city, considering them as worthy of offering as the Buddha himself, the giver who gives without any discrimination, impartially, with no expectation of reward, and with great love – this giver, I say, fulfills the perfection of giving.[9]

Two points in this initial definition warrant explication. Giving is perfected when we can do it impartially, without discrimination, and when we are just as eager to give to the poor who cannot reciprocate as to a friend, or family member, or superior who can and may repay the gift. Vimalakirti's requirement, therefore, is that a pious Buddhist's offerings to the Buddha, from whom great reward might be anticipated, be extended to every sentient being without discrimination. To make this clear Vimalakirti adds the words "with no expectation of reward." Reward comes in many forms, and Vimalakirti is clear in including them in his articulation of giving. We may give because the other may give back the same thing in equal or greater proportion. We may give in order to be thought well of, to be loved, or in order to enhance our reputation for generosity. Or we may give in order simply to think well of ourselves, to clear our conscience, to accumulate good *karma*, or to enhance our self-help program of perfection. But by Vimalakirti's account, all these versions of giving "in order to" fall short of perfect giving. That does not mean, of course, that Vimalakirti would suggest that they should not be done. Giving of almost any sort qualifies as a "practice" and as one step toward the perfection of giving even if the act itself does not fulfill the ideal. Vimalakirti then goes on to add another dimension to the ideal: the giver whose act has been perfected gives "with great love." Love is the motive that most readily qualifies an act as perfect giving. Loving your neighbor as yourself can easily be seen to lend itself to the spirit of giving. When we give a gift to ourselves, our love is unquestionable. What would it mean to extend that same spirit of generosity to others, and how would we ever manage it?

The *sutra*'s answer to this is that "equanimity" is the key, and that equanimity is attained through the realization of the selflessness and relationality of all of reality. Therefore when Manjushri, the *bodhisattva* of wisdom, asks Vimalakirti, "What is the equanimity of the Bodhisattva?" our hero responds, "It is what benefits both self and others."[10] Both self and others are benefited when the *bodhisattva* is able to treat all things equally, in just proportion, and does not favor his or her own self as the rest of us tend to do. Since "equanimity" and "peacefulness" are treated in the *sutra* as equivalents, the *sutra* can go on to claim that the perfection of generosity "is consummated in peacefulness."[11] And when Manjushri asks, "What is the great joy of the Bodhisattva?" Vimalakirti does not hesitate to turn the question back to the practice of giving: "It is to be joyful and without regret in giving."[12]

Making this same point in his recently released book, *Ethics for the New Millennium*, the Dalai Lama writes,

> Looking back over my life, I can say with full confidence that such things as the office of Dalai Lama, the political power it confers, even the comparative wealth it puts at my disposal, contribute not even a fraction to my feelings of happiness compared with the happiness I have felt on those occasions when I have been able to benefit others.[13]

Since, as the Dalai Lama writes elsewhere in the book, the "principle characteristic of genuine happiness is inner peace,"[14] that explains why the *Vimalakirti Sutra* would claim that the perfection of generosity is consummated in peacefulness, in an equanimity that is not out of accord with the equality and relatedness that both the Dalai Lama and the *sutra* recommend as the character of the world. In any case, all of us can sense, I think, what the Dalai Lama means when he links feelings of happiness to acts of generosity. For the rest of us, even a momentary act of pure giving – a truly unselfish moment – is invariably accompanied by a sense of exhilaration, a sense of expansion out beyond ourselves. The sense of warmth and joy that ensues, even if just momentary, contrasts sharply with our usual perception of narrowness, the sense of being inextricably confined to ourselves and nothing beyond. In the act of giving we expand, which is the very meaning of magnanimity.

Giving is perfected, then, when we give not because we must but because we want to. And wanting to give can become the norm in our lives only through a fundamental transformation of our self-understanding. This transformation in perspective reorients the point of life. Therefore when Vimalakirti says that "the Bodhisattva should live for the liberation of all living beings,"[15] he makes clear that the perfection you pursue is not *your* perfection; it is just perfection as seen from the vantage point of equanimity.

Since all acts can be inspired by the perfection of giving, that includes acts of receiving as well. In breaking down all dualism, Vimalakirti includes the dualism between an active giving and a passive receiving. Neither activity nor passivity can encompass either act successfully. Therefore, when receiving a gift, *bodhisattvas* like Vimalakirti, Thich Nhat Hanh, and the Dalai Lama practice mindfulness; they *give* concentrated, thoughtful attention both to the gift itself and to the giver. They make sure to give the giver all that they can so that whatever love and selflessness has inspired the gift will be given back, and multiplied several-fold. Giving the gift of genuine gratitude is enabled by a sense of deep, primal gratitude that accompanies the realization of no self and dependent arising. In fact, since we are not self-created, our very lives are a gift. You do not have to be religious, much less Buddhist, to realize that we owe our very existence to forces and events beyond us. This level of gratitude is inspired by a readiness and an ability to understand everything that comes to us as a gift, rather than as our achievement. And if everything is a gift, no attitude will pervade our daily lives as much as a profound sense of thankfulness. Nothing less than this overarching sense of gratitude could adequately explain the fact that what *bodhisattvas* give, in the end, is themselves.

## ETHICS AND THE PERFECTION OF WISDOM

Generosity and a willingness to give in large measure are never quite enough, however. We may have deep feelings for the suffering of others and be moved to help them and still end up acting in such a way as to be ineffectual or to make things worse. Even with the noblest of intentions we too can create even more suffering for others. Wise ethical discernment is essential to any form of well-honed generosity. Without clear thinking and moral intelligence our kindest acts may come to be resented, or inappropriately taken advantage of, thus doing harm to the recipient. A broad range of skills are required in addition to the requisite feelings in order to succeed in perfect giving. In addition to intelligence or wisdom, perceptual skills are important. It is not helpful, for example, to be generous in spirit if we are insensitive or oblivious to the needs of others. The person who is so entrapped in himself or herself that they never notice when others are in serious need will not have developed the kinds of mindfulness that Vimalakirti's practice of generosity demands. Attentive skillfulness, what bodhisattvas call upaya, or "skill-in-means" is important as a correlate to the kind of self-understanding that makes possible any intention to give selflessly.

The bodhisattva's upaya or "skillfulness" is typically the last word in matters in Mahayana Buddhist ethics. This is true because upaya includes and is based upon a realization that no understanding we have of these matters, no matter how sophisticated, will be either true or effective in all circumstances. The bodhisattva's "skill," in other words, includes a deep sense of the relativity and impermanence of all modes of understanding. Although Vimalakirti may be quite satisfied with his account of perfect giving, if he lacks a thorough sense of the limits of its applicability, and the possibility that he may turn out to have been wrong, then he will have failed in the sixth perfection, the perfection of wisdom, and in the skills of upaya. If all things are impermanent, and arise to be what they are dependent on changing circumstances, that would imply that there is no fixed goal for all times and places, or for all human beings. And if in response to the question "what is our true nature?" Buddhists posit "no-self nature" because all natures are dependent and change over time, that leaves open the question of what an adequate goal might be.

If the character of human enlightenment is not defined in advance by a fixed human nature, then that opens up a range of possibilities for self-transformation. In fact, this is a good way to understand the history of Buddhism, or any tradition for that matter, as a precious repertoire of images of human excellence set before us as an inheritance for our use in creative, critical imagination. If "no self" means that who we are is not a given, then it must be a product, a work of art, which each of us can either take upon ourselves or fail to do so. And since "perfection" is never attained before death intrudes – that is – the task is open and never complete, it is never too late to begin anew. As a Tibetan monk once said to me: resting on your past accomplishments is as dangerous as resting while walking in a snowstorm. The result is that you freeze up and never move again. Therefore, the *bodhisattvas* consulted here posit persistence and adaptability as the requisite virtues for an ethics based upon impermanence and lack of self-nature.

## NOTES

1. Thich Nhat Hanh, "We Are the Beaters; We Are the Beaten," *Los Angeles Times,* 15 April 1991.
2. Ibid.
3. Ibid.
4. Robert Thurman, trans., *The Holy Teaching of Vimalakirti* (University Park, PA: Pennsylvania State University Press, 1976), p. 21.
5. Ibid., p. 20.
6. Ibid., p. 79.
7. Ibid., p. 66.
8. Ibid., p. 73.
9. Ibid., p. 21.
10. Ibid., p. 57.
11. Ibid., p. 39.
12. Ibid., p. 57.
13. Dalai Lama, *Ethics for the New Millennium* (New York: Riverhead, 1999), p. 61.
14. Ibid., p. 55.
15. Thurman, trans., *The Holy Teaching of Vimalakirti,* p. 58.

*Plate 11* This vibrant stylized porcelain mural in Canton, China, represents the complementary forces of the yielding, dark, cool feminine *yin* associated with the moon, earth, and water and the assertive, bright, fiery, masculine *yang* associated with the sun (in the upper right) and heaven and epitomized by the dragon. In Chinese thought these forces of *yin* and *yang* are not oppositional but rather must be balanced for cosmic harmony. Photo: *Nancy M. Martin*

# 11

# CONFUCIANISM: CONCERN and CIVILITY

*John H. Berthrong*

Each of the great and enduring Eurasian axial-age civilizations and religious traditions has encountered the acid rains of modernity in a unique way.[1] Nonetheless, the defining motif of the Confucian encounter with the Western form of modernity after 1839 resulted in extreme dislocation of both the Confucian worldview and its social praxis.[2] As Wm. Theodore de Bary has remarked (and a host of other Western and East Asian scholars have attested), in a short space of time at the beginning of the twentieth century the Confucian tradition lost most, if not all, of its major functional social and spiritual roles in Chinese culture.[3]

The traditional Confucian social world rested on three firm foundations. First, Confucian theory and practice dominated the structure and functioning of literati families in terms of cultural and social praxis. Second, Confucian scholars dominated the educational system that provided a steady flow of candidates for the imperial civil service. It is crucial to remember that education in the Confucian tradition, at its best, was not merely the transmission of information – it was a commitment to the transformation and reform of the person, family, community, state, and even the world and cosmos. Third, educated Confucians, all of whom had passed through the examination system, completely dominated all levels of formal and informal government in China, save for the ruling ethnic Manchu imperial elite.[4]

However, by the 1920s, all three of these patterns of Confucian family life, education, and government service and policy formation were eroded beyond recognition. The Confucian establishment had been disestablished; even more, the whole Confucian project was under severe and often warranted attack as a failed program that exposed China and the rest of East Asia to the less than tender mercies of the imperial Western powers. Many informed observers wondered if Confucianism would, or should, survive as anything more than an object of historical research and popular ridicule. A perfect example of such a warranted critique was and is offered by feminists concerning the role Confucianism played as a public ideology in the subordination of women to patriarchal domination.[5]

However, the reports of the death of the Confucian way proved premature. Even in its most trying moments, a group of scholars, now known as the New Confucians, set about reviving, reforming, and transforming Confucianism. The basic shared assumption of the New Confucians was that there was something worth rescuing in the Confucian tradition from the wreckage of late imperial Chinese society. The burning question is: just what is to be saved? And how will what is saved be promoted?

## CONFUCIAN HABITS OF THE HEART AND ROOT METAPHORS

Moreover, even before trying to answer the question of what is to be saved and how to save it, we must address the question of defining the domain of *what* Confucianism is. The now commonplace answer to the question of Confucian self-definition is the observation that "Confucianism" is a Western neologism invented by the early Christian scholar-missionaries in order to define what they discovered about the traditions of the Ming and Qing literati scholars. Lionel Jensen has recently developed an extensive argument that "Confucianism" as an intellectual construct was the co-creation of the early Jesuit missionaries and their Chinese literati dialogue partners.[6] The general and historically broad Chinese referent would be *ru* (or *ju*). However, as any scholar of Chinese intellectual history knows, the definition of *ru* lies on contested ground. Nonetheless, at least from the Song period on, scholars of a ruist persuasion cultivated a keen sense of identity when writing about the difference between their tradition and those of Buddhists, Daoists, and other heterodox thinkers and movements.[7]

What makes the depiction of the *ru* tradition difficult is that the term describes so many different social realities. Gilbert Rozman has suggested that we must sort out the functional roles of the *ru* in order to be clear about our terminological referents.[8] For instance, there is a great deal of difference between and among what Rozman calls the "reformist" wing of the Confucian world and the equally impressive imperial state ideology, which also consistently claimed to be within the lineage of the First Sage and Teacher of the Ten Thousand Generations. However, Rozman points out that there was constant tension between the reformist Confucian scholars and the government's use of Confucian themes in service to state policy from the very beginning of the traditon in the Warring States period. The question becomes even more complicated when we try to factor in movements such as popular forms of "Confucian" practice at the regional, local, and family levels of society. The vast expanse of elite, popular, and folk "Confucian" praxis forces some scholars to note that "Confucianism" then simply becomes a term for all things Chinese.

One way to address this terminological question is to ask about the nature of Confucian identity or, in the felicitous words of Robert Bellah and his colleagues, to ask what are the Confucian "habits of the heart." The evocation of habits of the heart, it should be noted, does not demand an ahistorical catalog of essential core beliefs, praxis, doctrine, or even texts at the center of the Confucian mind-heart. Such a search does not necessarily need to acknowledge a hegemonic ontological presence or even a logical or substantial essence to Confucian life. Moreover, habits can change over time. Some Christian theologians such as Hans Küng, for instance, have argued that the Christian tradition is a family of such habits of the heart transformed synchronically through a series of dramatic paradigm shifts. The continuing Christian family resemblance is strong enough to sustain a common lineage.

## Mapping the Contours of Tradition with Cognitive Metaphor Theory

One of the more promising approaches to the question of identity formation and the mapping of a heuristic hypothesis about the contours of the Confucian tradition is the cognitive metaphor theory of George Lakoff and Mark Johnson.[9] Recently Lakoff and Johnson have summarized their two-decade project in *Philosophy in the Flesh*.[10] The basic argument for metaphoric philosophy, at least for the purposes of this chapter, rests on two foundations. Much of Lakoff and Johnson's elaborate theory is based on evidence derived from second-generation cognitive science and collateral trends in linguistic research. The second source derives from Lakoff and Johnson's engagement with and critique of modern Western philosophy. Although their project arises from Western cognitive science and linguistics, they are sensitive to its implications for cross-cultural intellectual dialogue.

One main theme of the Lakoff and Johnson position is that metaphors are the basic building blocks of human cognition and self-reflective activities. Metaphors are not just literary devices; metaphors help human beings move between and among diverse domains of human query, feeling, and action. In short, philosophy is built on metaphors, not the other way around. I suspect that this would not have been news to many Daoists and Confucians.

Not the least of cognitive metaphor theory's appeal to comparative studies lies in its promise to facilitate an escape from the "prison of language." Although language is obviously the medium of most cultural communication, metaphor theory asks us to attend to the complex cognitive terrain of concept formation. Lakoff and Johnson provide a complex argument about how we develop our conceptual maps of the world based on a realistic account of human interaction with the world. We are, in Lakoff and Johnson's terms, embodied creatures, and many of the essential ways we engage the world are derived from our neural hardwires (to borrow a computer metaphor). Hence, Lakoff and Johnson argue that "Philosophically, the embodiment of reason via the sensorimotor system is of great importance."[11]

To make a very long story short, philosophic theories about the *Dao* as a way or a metaphor for the proper path of human conduct connect with very basic forms of cognitive sensorimotor prototypes. Lakoff and Johnson hypothesize that our ability to form categories rests on our cognitive ability to compare and contrast various basal sensorimotor domains. We experience in one domain and map these experiences onto other domains. "The cognitive mechanism for such conceptualizations is conceptual metaphor, which allows us to use the physical logic of grasping to reason about understanding."[12] The conclusion here is that we cannot reason without recourse to metaphors, and that metaphors are what assist us to move cognitively from one domain of experience to another.

In their earlier work, *Metaphors We Live By*, Lakoff and Johnson offer the following definition of metaphor: "*The essence of metaphor is understanding and experiencing one kind of thing in terms of another.*"[13] This early definition still captures the main contours of what Lakoff and Johnson take to be the cognitive function of metaphors. Moreover, I interpret the notion of "thing" very widely in terms of this definition. Actually, in *Philosophy in the Flesh,* Lakoff and Johnson are at pains to reject any reductionistic or overly substance-oriented understanding of "thing." In their later work they tend to use the language of "domain" in place of "thing." I have argued elsewhere that such an interpretation helps to make sense of the processive or generative sensibilities of a great deal of Chinese philosophy.[14]

## Defining Qi *and Other Root Metaphors*

A classic case of this of sensibility is quickly uncovered in the attempt to translate the term *qi* (or *ch'i*).[15] A.N. Whitehead once remarked that a metaphysical concept is one that never takes a holiday. It is a concept that is assumed to underlie all possible exemplifications of reality in the broadest possible sense of what any philosopher deems to be real. Anyone who has struggled to translate *qi* quickly encounters frustration in terms of selecting an appropriate English term. The problem stems from the fact that the Chinese philosophic tradition seems to conjoin in the one graph *qi* elements that are usually separate domains in classical Western discourse.

An attentive reader will notice that I am here talking about the whole of the Chinese philosophic tradition. As we learn more and more about the development of Chinese philosophy and religion from its first flowering in the Warring States period to its conclusion in the Qing dynasty, we realize that this philosophic development is much more complicated than has previously been assumed. The easiest way to see the grand development is to use the Buddhist image of a series of waves upon the ocean of thought. There is little doubt that the Sinitic world forms one of the most successful, enduring, and distinctive prototypes of Eurasian high civilizations. Although there is no easy or even possible way to develop a complete catalog of the essential features of just what constitutes the unique Sinitic cultural domain, it is also hard not to recognize it when we see it. Like pornography, it is difficult to define but easy to notice. Moreover, a great deal of postmodern critical and philosophic literature has been devoted to the deconstruction of the viability of ideas of ontological essence, substance, or the hegemonic reading of Whitehead's perfected philosophic dictionary (also known as the "fallacy of the perfect dictionary"). Whitehead, though not often thought of as a devotee of critical postmodernism, argued that there is no such thing as a perfected dictionary of philosophic usage against which we can check our definitions of terms.

Nonetheless, few would argue that there is not a vast, protean, and rich Sinitic sea in which the waves of Confucian, Daoist, and Buddhist high culture float upon a pan-Chinese ocean of meaning. A simple thought experience provides an illustration: think of the great Dutch masterpiece known as *Night Watch* and then think of a grand northern Song landscape painting. Both are supreme examples of the genius of painting at two ends of the Eurasian world. I doubt that anyone would maintain that we will fail to spot the different cultural sensibilities embedded in the pictures. We float in different bodies of water. Moreover, as Sarah Allan has demonstrated, the metaphor of water is a pervasive feature of early Chinese thought.[16]

Yet great oceans do have many waves, and the waves can be differentiated one from another. In the Sinitic sea, one of the most distinctive common features is revealed in the various interpretations of *qi*. The difficulty in translating *qi* arises from the fact that it includes the Western cultural domains of matter, substance, mind, action, vapor, and force. One of the more amusing and revealing early cross-cultural encounters between Neo-Confucianism and early modern Western philosophy emerged in the attempt of the Jesuit missionaries to teach their Chinese literati friends about Western philosophy and theology. At one point the Jesuits reasoned that they would have to teach the Chinese basic Aristotelian logic because the Chinese seemed incapable of making what seemed to the Jesuits basic intellectual distinctions. For instance, the Neo-Confucian scholars asserted *xin* (the mind-heart) was both rational and emotive and mental and material. The Jesuits were shocked that the Confucians were subject to such an elementary category mistake. Something could be mental or material, but not both at the same time and in the same place.

That *qi* intersects the domains of mind and matter, the spiritual and the physical, is now commonplace for students of Chinese thought. A perfect example of the formulation of a pan-Sinitic perspective on *qi* is found in Harold Roth's new examination of the "Inward Training" chapter in the *Guanxi.* Roth argues that not all new finds in early Chinese thought are necessarily uncovered via archaeology. He contends that the "Inward Training" is a perfect example of an early and foundational text of the emerging Daoist tradition which has been overlooked because it was encapsulated in a later anthology. The exact nature of Roth's argument about how to situate the "Inward Training" within the matrix of the world of early Daoist thought need not detain us.[17]

Roth notes that our Western distinction between energy and matter is "blurred." He chooses to translate *qi* as either vital energy or vital breath depending on the context. Roth cites the fact that our earliest encounters with *qi* find it representing either the vapors or steam that arises when we heat liquids and only slightly later as the living breath of creatures. This leads some scholars, with merit, to translate *qi* as vapor. Yet the philosophic extension of the metaphor of breath as the vapor of life expanded outward toward the more abstract notion of vital energy makes sense in the overall context of the development of early Chinese thought. *Qi*, as Roth explains, points us in the direction of a cosmos informed by the constant flux of the interaction of matter and energy in ever changing patterns, or what Roger Ames and David Hall have defined as the field and focus frame of early Chinese cosmology.[18]

Roth's elegant translation of the "Inward Training" make this point about the vast domains of *qi* beautifully:

I

The vital essence of all things:
It is this that brings them to life.
It generates the five grains below
And becomes the constelled stars above.
When flowing amid the heavens and the earth
We call it ghostly and numinous.
When stored within the chests of human beings,
We call them Sages.

II

... Therefore this vital energy
Cannot be halted by force,
Yet can be secured by inner power.
Cannot be summoned by speech,
Yet can be welcomed by the awareness.
Reverently hold onto it and do not lose it:

This is called "developing inner power."
When inner power develops and wisdom emerges,
The myriad things will, to the last one, be grasped.[19]

This may be Daoist in a technical sense as defined by Roth, but it is also a beautiful exposition of the graph *qi* as it comes to play a major role in the pan-Sinitic Chinese philosophic world. Many other terms also come to mind: *ren* (or *jen*) as the primary Confucian virtue, *Dao* as the way or path of conduct and even reality as such, and *de* (or *te*) as the power of virtue. All of these terms became part of the rich metaphoric and rhetorical world of early Chinese philosophic and religious discourse.

From the position of cognitive metaphor theory as developed by Lakoff and Johnson, philosophy grows out of the manipulation of patterns of complex cognitive metaphors. These complex cognitive metaphors, such as those associated with the *Dao* as the process of moving along a path, become crucial parts of the emerging cultural sensitivities Bellah calls the "habits of the heart."[20] Stephen Pepper in 1942 gave the name of "root metaphor" to the rich metaphors that reside at the center of the philosophic imagination.[21] Pepper suggests that most philosophic systems have a root metaphor, their own habit of the heart, that controls the development and logic of their particular philosophic endeavor. One paradigmatic example for the rich history of Western philosophy is the notion that the world is a machine. Another root metaphor is that of a form, that the world is governed by certain patterns of abstract forms. Or the world is organic, such that examples from the plant and animal worlds provide vivid metaphors that govern organic philosophic visions.

As we shall see, cognitive metaphor theory focuses attention on certain aspects of the Confucian project. For instance, habits of the heart can be manifested in different ways and times and yet retain their metaphoric roots. The early world of Confucius is remarkably different from the southern Song ethos of Zhu Xi, yet both men are recognized as great Confucian masters. As the old Buddhist and then Neo-Confucian adage put it, the metaphor is one but its manifestations in the rivers and lakes are many.

## "Concern Consciousness" and the Interpenetration of Religion and Ethics

The twentieth-century philosopher Mou Zongsan (1909–1995) made the following suggestion about one such Confucian habit of the heart which gives a clue about the enduring root metaphor of the Confucian way.[22] In contradistinction to the Greek habit of "wonder" or the search for the answer to the how and why of the world, and the Semitic and Indic sense of awe before the power and mystery of the world which evokes faith and prayer, the Confucian habits of the heart are always governed by what Mou called "concern consciousness." The prototypical Confucian asks: how are things properly related and how ought people to be concerned about their relations with their own persons and other persons? Because of this, Mou reasoned, it was not difficult to see why many Western intellectuals believed Confucianism to be a form of social ethics. Of course, if we take Mou's insight seriously, it is appropriate to apply the label of "social ethics," but if we were to stop here, we would miss a much deeper point that Mou was trying to make.

Mou is actually suggesting a very interesting root metaphor at this point. From the perspective of Pepper's analysis of Western philosophic root metaphors, Mou's vision of concern consciousness comes closest to the Western metaphor of purposive action (which is also Whitehead's root metaphor according to Pepper). At the level of the habits of the heart, it makes sense to notice the incurably social field for all Confucian thought. But within the field of concern, the truly basic question is: how are the things of the world related to each other? This can be translated into Pepper's metaphor of a purposive action – at least for the Confucian version of the metaphor. The Daoists contest this Confucian metaphor and adopt a commitment to *wu-wei* or uncontrived action. However, it is important to note that what is still at the root of the vision is how to envisage the relationship of things, events, and persons. The argument, therefore, between Daoists and Confucians is a family debate within a shared cultural world of prototypical root metaphors.

Mou also affirmed a strong religious dimension within the expanse of the Confucian way.[23] Although it is not an organized religion in the Western sense of Judaism, Christianity, or Islam, Mou argued that if we fail to recognize the religious or spiritual dimensions of the Confucian tradition, we miss an important element of the tradition as it has developed over time. In Mou's terms, Confucianism has both vertical and horizontal dimensions. The vertical, according to Mou, is that part of the tradition we can label "spiritual" if need be. When we are in tune with the vertical axis, we are in tune with the workings of the *Dao* itself. We have become fully actualized. Zhang Cai's famous *Western Inscription* is a perfect example of such a Confucian appeal to the vertical or depth dimension of reality, a reality and experience that can only be called deeply spiritual.

The horizontal dimension is that of mundane life. Mou argues that every great religion has both a vertical dimension and a horizontal set of teachings that help us navigate the mundane world. However, it would be a mistake to think of the mundane as without spiritual moment. As Herbert Fingarette so aptly noted, for Confucius the secular is the sacred.[24] There is no split between some other world and this world. Our actions in this world, how we relate to the quotidian, are the measure of the sacred in concrete daily life. This is yet another reason why Confucian teachings are often so closely linked to the cultivation of humane virtues and the establishment of civility between and among people. In traditional Confucian terminology, this is the realm of *li* or ritual.

## CONFUCIANISM FOR THE TWENTY-FIRST CENTURY

If Mou is correct about the root metaphor of concern consciousness, or even suggestive at this point, then the next question to ask is: how will the Confucian vision of concern consciousness (purposive action) manifest itself in new rivers and lakes in the modern world? There is no simple answer to this question short of prophecy, which is notoriously inaccurate in predicting the evolution of societies and philosophic systems. Therefore, I will change gears and report on certain recent conversations about the future of Confucian thought at two conferences in Beijing and Qufu in October 1999.

The conferences, held to commemorate the 2550th birthday of Confucius, were sponsored by the International Confucian Association and assembled over 290 scholars to discuss the future of the Confucian way in what is now called "post-Confucian" East Asia. Discussion focused on these two sets of themes: the vertical and horizontal nature of the tradition and the role of concern and civility in the formulation of New Confucian philosophic and social visions for a just and harmonious world.

Civility is here understood to be a reflection of the range of social arrangements traditionally called rituals. The first and favored way to address these issues turned on another famous Confucian conceptual pair, namely that of *nei* or inner and *wai* or outer. The second modal pair of Confucian concepts was that of *sheng* or sage and *wang* or king. When these two dipolar pairs are linked, we have the notion of the king without and the sage within. This has always been one way to express the unity of personal self-cultivation and social concern beyond the person. The sage is the icon of perfected personhood; but the true sage can also be a true king, namely, someone who plays a role in the constitution of civil society.

In diverse ways these two polarities came up again and again for discussion. The prime affirmation about the anticipated union of the inner sage and outer king was that neither pole was complete without the other. In fact, the major source of concern for many of the presenters at the conference was the fact that the outer or kingly aspects of the Confucian tradition were not being articulated by contemporary Confucian thinkers in anything like the richness they deserved from a revived, reformed, and transformed Confucian teaching for the modern world. There seemed to be a consensus that the New Confucians had only been (relatively) successful in revamping the inner or sagely dimensions of the tradition. They had addressed the domain of concern (especially education and scholarship) but not that of civility (ritual in the broadest sense) within the larger public order.

However, even the claims for inner transformation were contested. Many scholars noted that what this really meant was that there had been a revival of exemplary Confucian scholarship by members of the second and third generations of the New Confucian movement. Clearly there has been and continues to be a major revival of study of and respect for the Confucian tradition throughout the domain of Cultural China. Serious historical, philosophic, philological, ethical, and aesthetic work is being done on the sources of the Confucian tradition. Critical editions of classical texts from the most recent archaeological finds to re-editions of the great works of the Neo-Confucian era have been printed in large numbers. Departments of philosophy and the even newer departments of religious studies in Chinese universities are continuing research about the Confucian traditions in all their historical diversity and richness. A philosopher such as Mou Zongsan is accepted as someone who has contributed mightily to the intellectual renovation of Confucian studies.

Nonetheless, there is another side to the debate. This has to do with what is called "public policy" in Western ethical discourse. What do Confucians now have to say about the burning social issues of the day? What do Confucians have to say about feminism and the changing role of women in modern society? About the economy? About democratic forms of government? About human rights? About whether or not there is really something called "Asian rights" as opposed to the international human rights regime? Many at the conference affirmed that any fully functional New Confucianism must develop a contemporary form of social thinking that will allow not only scholarly study of tradition but also reasoned applications of the root metaphors of the tradition to the modern world. Therefore, many scholars deemed it accurate that only one half of the Confucian way has been addressed by the New Confucian movement.

Conference participants also pointed out with some irony that Buddhists are ahead of Confucians in some aspects of social outreach. The modern Buddhist reformation has spread from places like Taiwan and Hong Kong back to China itself. This is now not only a tradition of meditation and ritual but an engaged form of social praxis that has become the patron of education, medicine, social relief, and ecological reflection. In short, the Buddhists are showing how a classical religious tradition can function in the modern world, and the New Confucians must now do likewise.

New Confucians, in short, will remain Confucians. The grand root metaphors of the tradition still lie at the heart of revived Confucian discourse. The best guess is that Confucianism will yet again find a way to affirm both the need for concern consciousness as a purposive act in terms of self-cultivation, scholarly achievement, and personal virtue along with the formulation of new forms of interpersonal civility. Ritual will change, but it will still beckon us toward a more civil future. Humaneness will remain the Confucian benchmark for personal integrity. The dream of the unity of sage and king, of inner and outer dimensions of human life in a generative cosmos, will be secure in Confucian education and social praxis.

## NOTES

1. For three assessments of the impact of "modernity," see Eliot Deutsch, ed., *Culture and Modernity: East–West Philosophic Perspectives* (Honolulu: University of Hawaii Press, 1991); Andre Gunder Frank, *ReOrient: Global Economy in the Asian Age* (Berkeley: University of California Press, 1998) and the issue of "Multiple Modernities," *Daedalus*, 129(1), 2000. All three works help to focus attention on the very usefulness and definition of modernity in the pursuit of comparative global philosophy and religious studies. Perhaps modernity is not singular; we may live in a world of multiple modernities.
2. My definitions of worldviews, their classic texts, and social praxis as a form of self-reflection about the world are derived from David Tracy's masterful

account of the contemporary state of Christian theology. See David Tracy, *The Analogical Imagination: Christian Theology and the Culture of Pluralism* (New York: Crossroad, 1981).

3. For short expositions of the glories and problems of Confucian theory and praxis, see Wm. Theodore de Bary, *The Liberal Tradition in China* (New York: Columbia University Press, 1983) and *The Trouble with Confucianism* (Cambridge, MA: Harvard University Press, 1991).

4. This is a fairly accurate statement for the Chinese political world during and after the Song dynasty. Although some emperors, such as Huizong (1100–1126) of the Song, were personally inclined toward Daoism, no one doubted the dominance of the Confucian literati in government service.

5. Personal and random conversations on both sides of the Pacific have convinced me that the most difficult challenge facing the New Confucian reform movement will be to persuade women that there is something of genuine worth for them to be found and encouraged in the Confucian tradition. However, Confucianism is not alone among the axial age intellectual movements in facing this challenge of addressing the full humanity of women. See Chenyang Li, ed. *The Sage and the Second Sex: Confucianism, Ethics, and Gender* (Chicago: Open Court, 2000) for a varied collection of sober opinions about women and Confucianism.

6. Lionel M. Jensen, *Manufacturing Confucianism: Chinese Traditions and Universal Civilization* (Durham, NC: Duke University Press, 1997).

7. Evidence of this is abundant in the writings of Zhu Xi (1130–1200) and many of his disciples and students. A perfect example is found in the philosophic dictionary of Ch'en Chun (1159–1223). Ch'en knew that he was a *ru*/Confucian and believed that he understood where his differences lay in conversation with Buddhists and Daoists. See Ch'en Chun, *Neo-Confucian Terms Explained (The Pei-hsi tzu-i)*, trans. and ed. Wing Tsit-chan (New York: Columbia University Press, 1986).

8. Rozman suggests a number of different categories for a functional description of the Confucian tradition. For instance, he notes that, especially in Japan, we need to include Merchant Confucianism along with other forms of elite reflection on the Confucian way. See Gilbert Rozman, ed., *Confucian Heritage and Its Modern Adaptation* (Princeton: Princeton University Press, 1991).

9. I owe some of my reflections on the use of Lakoff and Johnson to a set of stimulating discussions with P.J. Ivanhoe (Michigan University) and Edward Slingerland, (University of Southern California). Of course, neither of my friends are at all responsible for my use/misuse of their advice.

10. George Lakoff and Mark Johnson, *Philosophy in the Flesh: The Embodied Mind and Its Challenge to Western Thought* (New York: Basic Books, 1999).

11. Ibid., p. 43.

12. Ibid., p. 45.
13. George Lakoff and Mark Johnson, *Metaphors We Live by* (Chicago: University of Chicago Press, 1980), p. 5; italics in the original.
14. John H. Berthrong, *Transformations of the Confucian Way* (Boulder: Westview, 1998).
15. The meaning of this basic metaphysical concept of Confucianism is also discussed in detail by Mary Evelyn Tucker in chapter 16 of this volume, particularly in regard to its implications for ecological ethics.
16. Sarah Allan, *The Shape of the Turtle: Myth, Art, and Cosmos in Early China* (Albany: State University of New York Press, 1991).
17. Roth's thesis will, no doubt, prove controversial in the field of Daoist studies and the broader examination of the origins of Chinese philosophy. In short, Roth claims that the "Inward Training" is one of the foundational texts of Daoism and, in fact, is very close in worldview to the *Laoxi*. See Harold D. Roth, *Original Tao: Inward Training (Nei-yeh) and the Foundations of Taoist Mysticism* (New York: Columbia University Press, 1999).
18. David L. Hall and Roger T. Ames, *Thinking from the Han: Self, Truth, and the Transcendence in Chinese and Western Culture* (Albany: State University of New York Press, 1998).
19. Roth, *Original Tao*, pp. 46–48.
20. Robert N. Bellah et. al., *Habits of the Heart: Individualism and Commitment in American Life* (Berkeley: University of California Press, 1985).
21. In Pepper's first list of root metaphors in the Western philosophic tradition he found four such metaphor systems. In the 1960s he added one additional root metaphor, namely that of a purposive action, to the other four. Pepper has become persuaded that Whitehead's philosophy actually represented a unique type, the metaphor of purposive action, rather than a mixture of other types of what Pepper called "pure" root metaphors. See Stephen C. Pepper, *World Hypothesis: A Study in Evidence* (Berkeley: University of California Press, 1942) and *Concept and Quality: A World Hypothesis* (La Salle, IL: Open Court, 1967).
22. The best short introduction to this aspect of Mou Zongsan's corpus is *Zhongguo zhexue de tezhi* (The uniqueness of Chinese philosophy) (Taipei: Student Publishing Company, 1994). This short collection of semi-popular lectures on the development of Chinese philosophy outlines Mou's theories about the place of Chinese thought in world intellectual history.
23. Other members of Mou's generation of the New Confucian movement also recognized a spiritual dimension to Confucianism. Tang Juni has also written eloquently about the spiritual and religious dimensions of Confucian thought and culture.
24. Herbert Fingarette, *Confucius – The Secular as Sacred* (New York: Harper & Row, 1972).

*Part IV*

# ETHICAL ISSUES ACROSS RELIGIOUS TRADITIONS

*Plate 12* These stained-glass windows from the great Norman cathedral of Norwich, England, articulate the view, inscribed above the chivalrous knight in armor, that "the path of duty is the way to glory." On the left is a scene from the trench warfare of World War I, in which millions of young European men were slaughtered under horrific conditions. Photo: *Nancy M. Martin*

# 12

# "THAT WAS THEN ...": DEBATING NONVIOLENCE *within* THE TEXTUAL TRADITIONS *of* JUDAISM, CHRISTIANITY, AND ISLAM

*Daniel L. Smith-Christopher*

The present industrialized western civilization is a two-faced coin ... a bright and brilliant face and an ugly one ... The bright face is its scientific and material advancements, and the capacity to employ these achievements to improve human life. Its ugly face, on the other hand, is the failure to intelligently pursue peace.

(Ustadh Mahmoud Mohamed Taha)

This study is offered as a contribution to thinking about a particular aspect of religious ethics with regard to issues of war, peace, and personal behavior, namely nonviolence as a religiously based personal commitment that is seen by its advocates to be reasonably based on the reading of the sacred texts of the religious traditions in question.

It (almost) goes without saying that the three rich heritages of textual analysis and interpretation in Judaism, Christianity, and Islam are quite different in both tradition and method, however one might try to generalize about "People of the Book." How these people actually *read* their books, in other words, is not so simple. Furthermore, I need to clarify at the outset that although I clearly have a personal interest in the arguments put forward in this study as both a Christian and a pacifist, I am not here concerned with the validity of the arguments I am citing. I am rather interested in asking questions about methodology and the use of texts as a preliminary to evaluating the validity of the arguments. It would thus be a misunderstanding of my task in this essay to engage someone like myself, who is certainly not qualified to deal with the qur'anic and rabbinic materials, in discussions about *the validity or lack thereof* of Schwarzschild's rabbinic or Taha's qur'anic arguments, especially if those engagements are based on my inevitably cursory summaries of their thought. In short, as a Christian in a nonviolent theological tradition, I would *like* for these arguments outside my own Christian tradition to be valid, since I have a particular fondness for interfaith dialogue where nonviolence is a shared premise of the discussion, but I am hardly the best judge of traditions that are not my own. What I am particularly concerned with here are questions of methodology and procedure, and on this matter I do not think that generalizations are impossible – on the contrary, they may even be suggestive, and I offer this study as an attempt to defend that premise.

## "THAT WAS THEN . . .": DEVELOPMENTAL ARGUMENTS AND SCRIPTURES

### *"Commentorial Strategies" and Nonviolence in the Hebrew Bible, the Christian Bible, and the Qur'an*

In his masterful study of how the canonical texts in a number of religious traditions are used in commentaries written about them (including the use of classic Confucian texts compared with Western use of the Bible), John Henderson pointedly noted that commentary traditions begin to sound more similar the further they are removed from their respective scriptural texts:

> The very act of canonization had systematic consequences that were in part independent of the peculiarities of the canonical text. One may thus contrast the great variety among the classics or scriptures in various premodern traditions with the increasing uniformity of the commentorial presuppositions and procedures that grew out of attempts to interpret these texts.[1]

Included in his observations about commentary traditions across religious boundaries was an interesting set of assumptions shared by the commentators. Among them were the following:

1. A text is considered to be comprehensive and all-encompassing.[2]
2. A canon is well-ordered and coherent, arranged according to some logical, cosmological, or pedagogical principles.[3]

3. Contradictions are only apparent.[4]

Following this, there are three further "lesser assumptions" operative for the commentators: they assume that classics are (4) moral, (5) profound, and (6) contain nothing superfluous.

The impact of these shared assumptions leads to a profound similarity of methodologies or strategies in the work with texts over time. Among the more common strategies that Henderson suggests are:

1. The idea that there is meaning behind the literal meaning or obvious/ apparent sense. This results in ideas suggesting that these *apparent* meanings are present merely to teach lesser people, as an allegory, or as an accommodation.
2. The use of deletion or expurgation. This involves declaring a passage inconsistent and thus unlikely.
3. The idea of a "canon within a canon"–an emphasis on what is considered the "most important parts." The canon is clear on "central points." Obscurities promote closer study.

I want to suggest that in the case of arguing within a textual tradition about nonviolence, especially where there are clear examples of violent behavior and/or admonitions within the text in question, we can cite examples of all three strategies. But this study derives from my own observations that there is one interesting similarity in the strategies of textual interpretation in certain Jewish, Christian, and Islamic defenses of nonviolence as a normative interpretation of the ethical teachings of their respective sacred texts. As examples, I would like to cite the late Professor Rabbi Steven Schwarzschild, especially his further comments following a reading of Maimonides; Ustadh Mahmoud Taha's text *The Second Message of Islam*; and a sampling of some classic twentieth-century Christian essays from important advocates of Christian pacifism. Let us begin with the latter, since reflection on these types of arguments gave rise to my interest in the comparative cases.

## *Christian Nonviolence and the Problem of War in the Old Testament*

Christian nonviolence as a doctrinal position is widely known from the traditions of the so-called "Historic Peace Churches" (Quakers, Mennonites, and the Church of the Brethren). There have been, however, notable examples of advocates of Christian nonviolence from within larger denominational traditions, and it is among these that I have selected some samples. Although there is a rich variety of theological and biblical arguments used to defend Christian nonviolence as a teaching from the Gospels applicable to modern Christian life, there was an important tendency in the polemics of the mid twentieth century which we can identify best by simply citing a number of examples.

In a classic defense of Christian pacifism issued by the Fellowship of Reconciliation in 1958, Culbert Rutenber entitled his fourth chapter "But the Old Testament Says ..." In this chapter, Rutenber takes a directly developmental position with regard to the problem of warfare and violence in the Hebrew Bible, which is known to Christians as the Old Testament:

> At the beginning of the last chapter, we noted that the Old Testament was provisional and preparatory to the New Testament. The very terms "Old" and "New" indicate the relation of lower to higher, as the entire book of Hebrews is written to prove. The new covenant has made the old one obsolete, says the author of Hebrews (Heb. 8:13).[5]

> Thus God taught the Hebrews the law of absolute justice: an eye for an eye and a tooth for a tooth. This was a great advance over the jungle ethics of revenging a blackened eye or a knocked-out tooth with any retaliation you could get away with. But it wasn't the kind of conduct that God was ultimately trying to establish. Ultimately, the love that does not even seek just retribution is the will of God (Matt. 5:38ff).[6]

This is an excellent example of a straightforward argument to the effect that "That was then ... this is now."

More nuanced arguments, furthermore, essentially amount to the same strategy. In his critically sophisticated treatment of the Gospel passage about "Love your Enemies," John Piper cannot apparently avoid observing that

> As a source, the Old Testament alone cannot entirely account for the understanding of enemy love in the New Testament paraenesis. The followers of Jesus had heard a new word which guided them in the proper use of the old word.[7]

In his classic text from 1960 which served to introduce the issue of Christian nonviolence as a historically grounded testimony in Christian church history to more than two generations of graduate students, Roland

Bainton argues that the teaching of Jesus was so radically different than what proceeded it that

> The whole scale of the classical virtues was thereby altered ... many Hebrew concepts were transformed. The covenant, which God swore to the fathers to destroy their enemies from before their face became in the mouth of Jesus "the new testament in my blood". The apocalyptic doomsday of Judaism, when God would annihilate the enemies of Israel, became the day when wrath would be pronounced upon those who had not clothed the naked.[8]

Finally, we can cite an important text that has been influential, along with André Trocme's *Jésus-Christ et la révolution non violente* (Jesus and the nonviolent revolution),[9] in the articulation of the modern Anabaptist theologies of war and peace, the French Protestant Jean Laserre's "War and the Gospel." Lasserre, who in 1962 approached the same issue of the warlike texts of the Old Testament, asked,

> What guidance can we draw from [the Old Testament] on the problem of war? From the point of view of the Christian ethic a study of the Old Testament is bound to be disappointing, because – as already pointed out – Old Testament texts cannot be normative for Christians, except when they can be interpreted Christologically; and this is particularly true for ethical questions. That is why I had to begin with the New Testament ...
>
> But here is the brutal fact: one can say by and large that the Old Testament ignores that respect for human life, that unconditional love, that non-violence, which as we have seen forms the general climate of the New Testament. There is a striking contrast here between the two parts of our Bible.[10]

The procedures here are only different in how they manage a developmental view. Typically, the change is made on the basis of the authority of Jesus himself. In short, when Jesus said about some older traditions, "You have heard, but now I say," this is taken to validate the possibility of interpreting Christian ethics as superseding certain aspects of older Hebrew tradition.

As I indicated, this form of articulating the issue was more common in the middle of the twentieth century than it is now. More recent discussions, building on the more recent fashions of critical biblical analysis, tend to emphasize the diversity of theological perspectives in the

Old Testament, including attitudes about war and peace. Interestingly, this point is often made in arguments *against* the use of the Bible to defend a Christian pacifist position, such as the study by T.R. Hobbs, whose epigram to the entire book is the Ecclesiastes quote "To everything there is a season," which although not originally intended to be an ethical maxim, ends up being so for Hobbs.[11] John Wood, on the other hand, in his analysis *Perspectives on War in the Bible*, uses the precise same argument to establish that New Testament nonviolence clearly had a Hebrew legacy to draw upon, if not all the diverse views of the Old Testament.[12] This argument from diversity, incidentally, was anticipated in Jacob Enz's older book, *The Christian and Warfare: The Roots of Pacifism in the Old Testament.*[13]

What is intriguing, however, is how much this developmental, textual perspective resembles arguments that can be cited from an Islamic and a Jewish source.

## Mahmoud Taha and The Second Message of Islam

Mahmoud Mohamed Taha, often referred to by French journalists as "the African Gandhi," was the founder of a movement in the Sudan known as the "Republican Brotherhood." Taha himself graduated from the Engineering School of Gordon Memorial College, now the University of Khartoum, and worked briefly for the Sudan railways, before entering private practice in the 1940s. As he became known for his religious and social leadership, beginning already in anti-colonial struggles in the Sudan, Taha's teachings and practice were increasingly perceived as a threat to the conservative forces of Northern Sudan, which sought to impose a repressive and regressive version of *shari'ah* law throughout the Sudan – including the largely Christian and animist Southern Sudan, where there have been long periods of serious warfare between sides defined along faith lines. The noted international human rights theorist, Abdullahi Ahmed An-Na'im, who was Taha's disciple, writes,

> One cannot exaggerate the importance of his humane and liberating understanding of Islam as an alternative to the cruel and oppressive interpretation underlying recent events in Iran, Pakistan, and Sudan, and the equally negative traditionalist view prevailing in Saudi Arabia and other parts of the Muslim world.[14]

Taha, then, was a critic of this repressive tradition in its Sudanese manifestations, advocating democracy, equality for men and women, and equal rights for non-Muslim Sudanese *all as values of Islamic faith.* As the Republican Brotherhood movement grew, Taha became a focus of contention for the increasingly repressive Numieri regime, and Ustadh Taha was eventually executed by that regime, not long before the regime itself fell. Many of the disciples of Taha were forced to leave the Sudan and are presently active throughout the world. Among them is An-Na'im, who is also the translator of Taha's most central text, *The Second Message of Islam*, from which we draw our present examples of Taha's thought.

Taha spends a good deal of his argument in *The Second Message of Islam* establishing the notion of development in religious understanding, not so much as development in the understanding of humanity but rather as development that is a rational manifestation of God's plan of care for humanity as it passes through different stages. The religious understanding appropriate for Adam, he writes, was not the same, nor on the same level, as the religious insights revealed by Muhammad. From a series of discussions along these lines, Taha proceeds to conclude that

> it would be a gross mistake to assume that the Islamic Shari'a of the seventh century is suitable, in all its details, for application in the twentieth century ... Muslims maintain that the Islamic Shari'a is perfect. That is true, but its perfection consists precisely in the ability to evolve, assimilate the capabilities of individuals and society, and guide such life up the ladder of continuous development, however active, vital, and renewed such social and individual life may be ... the perfection of the Islamic Shari'a lies in the fact that it is a living body, growing and developing with the living, growing and developing life, guiding its steps and charting its way toward God, stage by stage.[15]

Having established the general principle of change as inherent in revelation, Taha can then proceed to his main argument about the "second message." The central argument is a difference between teachings associated with Mecca and those later associated with the conquest of Medina. In explicating this difference, Taha engages in interesting textual analysis, which is not entirely different from critical biblical analysis when he argues that

> The Qur'an itself is divided into two parts: one of al-iman and the other of al-islam, in the sense that the former was revealed in Medina, while the latter was revealed earlier in Mecca. Each class of texts has its

own distinguishing features, reflecting the fact that the medinese Qur'an pertains to the stage of al-iman, while the Meccan Qur'an pertains to the stage of al-islam. For example, those parts of the Qur'an which use the phrase "O believers" with the exception of Surat al-Haj (Ch. 22), are Medinese, as are verses where the hypocrites are mentioned or reference is made to Jihad.

The Meccan Qur'an, on the other hand, is distinguished by several features. For example, every chapter which mentions prostration, or opens with the alphabetical letters, is Meccan with the exception of Surat al-Baqarah and al'Imran (Chs. 2 and 3), which are Medinese. Again, any chapter which uses the phrase, "O, mankind", or "O, Children of Adam" is Meccan, with the exception of Surat al-Baqarah and al-Nisa (Chs. 2 and 4).

... The Meccan and Medinese texts differ, not because of the time and place of their revelation, but essentially because of the audience to whom they are addressed. The phrase "O believers" addresses a particular nation, while "O mankind" speaks to all people.[16]

For Taha the difference is critical. The Meccan teachings are eternal, the Medinese teachings are for the historical context ... or in other words, "that was then."

Reflecting on the teachings associated with the Meccan experience, then, Taha concludes,

This was Islam's original and fundamental principle. The propagation of Islam began with the verses of persuasion in Mecca where the verse, "Propagate the path of your Lord in wisdom and peaceable advice, and argue with them in a kind manner. Your Lord is more knowledgeable of those who stray from His path, and He is more knowledgeable of the guided ones (16:125) and many other similar verses were revealed. This approach was continued for thirteen years, during which time much of the Miraculous Qur'an was revealed, and many men, women, and children were transformed under the guidance of the new discipline. The early Muslims curtailed their own aggression against the unbelievers, endured hurt, sacrificed their comforts sincerely and self-denyingly in the cause of spreading their religion, without weakening or submitting. Their lives were the supreme expression of their religion and consisted of sincere worship, kindness, and peaceful coexistence with all other people.[17]

Thus we see how it is that Taha, the avowed Muslim advocate of nonviolence who went to his death before renouncing that commitment, can stand on qur'anic grounding for his commitment to absolute nonviolence. An-Na'im summarizes helpfully:

[T]he main thesis of Ustadh Mahmoud regarding the evolution of Islamic law may be summarized as follows. Islam, being the final and universal religion according to Muslim belief, was offered first in tolerant and egalitarian terms in Mecca, where the Prophet preached equality and individual responsibility between all men and women without distinction on grounds of race, sex, or social origin. As that message was rejected in practice, and the Prophet and his few followers were persecuted and forced to migrate to Medina, some aspects of the message changed in response to the socioeconomic and political realities of the time. Migration to Medina was not merely a tactical step, but also signified a shift in the content of the message as well ...

In the Medina stage God was responding ... to the potential and actual needs of human society at that stage of its development. To that end, some aspects of the earlier level of revelation and Sunnah were subjected to repeal or abrogation from the legal point of view, although they remained operative at a moral/persuasive level ...

... what is revolutionary in his [Taha's] thinking, however, is the notion that the abrogation process was in fact a postponement and not final and conclusive repeal. Once this basic premise is conceded a whole new era of Islamic jurisprudence can begin.[18]

## Steven Schwarzschild as Jewish Advocate of Nonviolence

The late Professor Rabbi Steven Schwarzschild was a founding member of the Jewish Peace Fellowship in the U.S.A., as well as a widely known Jewish philosopher who was, by his own identification, a Kantian "disciple" of Herman Cohen. Schwarzschild is mainly known for his often complex philosophical essays, but not incidentally he was also the author of the entry on "Peace" in the *Encyclopedia Judaica*.[19] My observations with regard to Schwarzschild's arguments in connection to textual arguments must remain informal, unfortunately, since they are based on class notes rather than formal writings. I was among the small group of students who sat in on Professor Schwarzschild's engaging seminar on "The Peace Ethics of Judaism," which he offered while Lecturer in Residence at the University of Notre Dame (I was, at the time, a student at the nearby Mennonite seminary). It was the only occasion when Schwarzschild articulated, beyond two important but brief essays he published, many of his views on the subject of nonviolence, Jewish history, and Jewish tradition, although in a form that would be comprehensible to a class of Christian graduate students.

In the comments that follow, however, I try to take seriously Schwarzschild's assertion that his pacifism is argued on the basis of Jewish tradition and is not an imported notion foreign to Judaism (an important note, incidentally, given the frequency with which Jewish writers assert that "there is no pacifism in Judaism"). I will cite two interesting examples of Schwarzschild's use of rabbinic arguments dealing with questions of war and peace. These are not offered as comprehensive arguments on a Jewish defense of nonviolence – a project that Schwarzschild never undertook[20] – but rather are offered simply as comparative cases in line with my other comments on Ustadh Taha's textual methodology, and the more commonly known textual strategies illustrated from a variety of classic Christian defenses of nonviolence from biblical sources.

The first example is Schwarzschild's references to R. Yochanon Ben Zakkai, who was the youngest student of perhaps the greatest rabbinic teacher of the pharisaic movement, R. Hillel. R. Yochanon Ben Zakkai appears to have left Jerusalem for Galilee between 20 and 40 CE, as a young man, because he had a son there. Neusner notes that R. Yochanon had returned to Jerusalem during the tenure of Gamaliel I as head of the pharisaic party.[21] By 65 CE, it is further clear that R. Yochanon Ben Zakkai was a major spokesperson for the Pharisees in their disputes with the Sadducees. R. Yochanon Ben Zakkai is famous for reflecting a generally nonviolent ethic, often argued to be typical of first-century pharisaic thought.[22]

What I am specifically interested in citing is the tradition, drawn from the rabbinic sources, of R. Yochanon Ben Zakkai opposing a capital case.[23] According to the tradition, R. Yochanon Ben Zakkai was asked to judge a case involving a capital crime. According to the Mosaic law in Deuteronomy (17:6–9; 19:15, etc.), capital crimes require two valid witnesses for a conviction. R. Yochanon Ben Zakkai, discovering that the alleged crime had taken place under a fig tree, quizzed the two witnesses as to the shape of the figs on the tree. When they could not answer, R. Yochanon Ben Zakkai judged their testimony to be invalid, thus not allowing the case to proceed to punishment. This case, so reminiscent in Christian eyes of Jesus with the adulterous woman in the Gospel of John, is an illustration of how a methodological move – in this case the invalidation of required witnesses – was seen as an illustration of rabbinic loathing of any killing, even if it was considered permissible in ancient Jewish tradition. As Louis Finkelstein writes, quoting other pharisaic traditions,

> Citing R. Tarfon and R. Akiba, "Had we been members of the Sanhedrin when it had the power of capital punishment, no man would ever have been executed by it."[24]

The case of R. Yochanon Ben Zakkai, however, would not be so notable were it not for the fact that scholars have been able to trace a consistent line of tradition associated with this first-century rabbinic leader which clearly establishes his interest in what has been called the "quietist" tradition[25] of early rabbinic Judaism. For example, one must keep in mind the following famous incidents also recorded in the rabbinic literature:

1. R. Yochanon Ben Zakkai's opposition to the Jewish revolt against Rome, and his acting on this opposition by actually making a separate peace with the Roman officials, whereupon he was allowed to establish the rabbinic academy in Yavneh.[26]
2. The famous teaching in which R. Yochanon Ben Zakkai, noting the tradition that metal must not touch stones used to make altars for sacrifice to God, further elaborated an earlier suggestion that this was because swords were made from metal, and thus the substance of "death" (e.g. swords/metal) should not be in contact with "life" (the atonement of the altar of sacrifice). To this tradition, R. Yochanon Ben Zakkai added the observation that if stones that make peace are kept from metal, so ought *people* who make peace be kept from the metal of swords.[27]
3. R. Yochanon Ben Zakkai famously commented favorably on the leniency of the exemptions from military activity enumerated in Deuteronomy, chapter 20.[28]

As noted, the association of R. Yochanon Ben Zakkai with the virtual pacifism of many first and second century rabbinic teachers has been established in a variety of studies, but what we are interested in here is Schwarzschild's use of this tradition to illustrate Jewish *halakhic,* that is "legal," moves that deal with earlier Hebrew biblical traditions considered problematic or even contradictory to a later commitment to Jewish nonviolence.

This is even more sharply drawn in Schwarzschild's comments on the traditions of "required wars" and "optional wars" in the writings of the *Mishneh Torah*, a comprehensive statement of Jewish belief and practice written by the famous medieval Jewish philosopher Maimonides. In his chapter "On Kings and Wars" (Book 14), Maimonides, as is well known,[29] established a difference between wars that were required by God's command in history (e.g. Milchemet Mitzvah), and wars that are "optional," that is, wars that must be examined and tested to determine whether they can be conducted according to Jewish ethical tradition (e.g. Milchemet Reshut).

Among the "required wars" noted by Maimonides are:

1. the war against the Seven Nations, that is, the wars leading to the original conquest of the "promised land" by Joshua;
2. the wars to exterminate Amalek (Exodus 17:8–16 and Deuteronomy 25:17–19 are the key texts);
3. wars in defense of Israel.

"Optional wars," on the other hand, are defined as those wars conducted by a decision of the Sanhedrin – the famous ruling council of all Jews, which does not at present exist.

Schwarzschild argued that Maimonides himself already considered the first two categories of "required wars" to be historically *closed*. Quite literally, these were wars conducted in single historical circumstances, and no longer operative in ethical consideration thereafter. Since there is no longer any Amalek or Seven Nations, these required wars are historically, and thus ethically, sealed.

A somewhat different approach to Maimonides on this point is provided by a recent essay of Avi Sagi. Sagi notes that many rabbis tried to deal with the offensive aspects of the command to totally destroy Amalek. For example – taking a related issue – despite the command in Deuteronomy 23:4 (23:3 in Christian Bibles: "No Ammonite or Moabite shall be admitted to the assembly of the Lord, even to the tenth generation, none of their descendents shall be admitted to the assembly of the Lord"), an Ammonite convert is mentioned in rabbinic tradition in the Talmud (M. Yad. 4.4). How can this be? Sagi notes that many rabbis pointed to the historical events of 722 BCE, when the Assyrian Empire conquered and exiled many from Palestine, but also Transjordanian countries like Ammon, Moab, and Edom. Therefore, the original populations are hopelessly mixed together, and, since we can no longer be certain who is a descendent of whom, the prohibitions against the Seven Nations are historically closed.[30] Sagi observes,

> This analysis shows that halakhists, facing a tension between a canonical text they recognize as compelling and their own beliefs, can resort to a transitional principle. Supports of the practical model use an "empirical" fact cited in the sources – "the commingling of the nations" – as a vehicle for their moral intuitions. Aware of their limited ability to reinterpret the canonical text so as to make halakhic norms accord with the moral views, they rely on a fact that allows them to restrict the scope of a ruling about which they have moral reservations.[31]

But Maimonides, states Sagi, reasoned differently. He suggests that other moral rules are *paramount,* and that the command to kill Amalek is *subsidiary.* Thus, not killing children for sins of fathers *also* applies, and offering *peace* in the first instance *also* applies. But, since the killing of Amalek had to do with fear of their influencing Israel toward idolatry, states Sagi, "Once these fears become groundless, however, the ruling requiring that 'thou shalt save alive nothing that breathes' may be considered irrelevant." Maimonides, so argues Sagi, makes the text subsidiary to "basic moral assumptions." The method is, however, inescapably textual in orientation.[32]

But how does Schwarzschild, the avowed pacifist, go forward from the suggestions initiated by Maimonides? This can be illustrated by Schwarzschild's further questions about the remaining moral bases for war cited in Maimonides, namely, "defense of Israel" and "optional wars called by the Sanhedrin."

First, Schwarzschild raises the question of the definition of "Israel" in the ruling about wars to "defend Israel." Who, he asked, is "Israel"? How many Jews make up "Israel"? Schwarzschild argued that when this question is raised in many rabbinic traditions, the answer is fully stated "indisputably" that only when *all* the Jewish people are reassembled in the Holy Land can this come into force. Therefore, this is seen as a reference to the messianic age, the coming era of the kingdom of God. War, in short, is pushed into the eschaton, or as Schwarzschild put it, this point is "De-operationalized by Messianization." And, he added, since the messianic era is characterized by global peace, this potentiality for warfare in removed (noted in chapter 12, paragraph 5 of the *Mishneh Torah,* "In that era there will be neither famine nor war").

Schwarzschild's de-operationalization of "optional wars" operates in precisely the same manner: any optional wars would need the decision of the Sanhedrin, and the required Sanhedrin will not be gathered before the messianic era (the ability to grant the requisite qualifications for a rabbi to sit on the Sanhedrin having been suspended since the eighth century). Schwarzschild granted that his reading of Maimonides pushes beyond Maimonides' own conclusions on the matter, particularly with regard to the nature of messianism, but is methodologically well within the tradition. He often replied to those Christians who wondered if his interpretative strategies were beyond the pale with the words "I give expression to the historic voice of Judaism, not my own pacifism."

Before leaving this example, I would mention that Sagi, in his study of rabbinic responses to the texts about Amalek, tried to argue for the notion that a sense of morality overrides wooden adherence to the letter of the text. But I would take issue with Sagi's conclusions, precisely because the rabbinic methodology (whether inherently motivated by a higher moral sense or not) illustrated here involves contrasting *texts*. In short, the methodology illustrated by R. Yochanon Ben Zakkai, Maimonides, and Schwarzschild's comments is consistent in that it contrasts values *derived from texts*. The method, in short, is what Henderson would call "commentorial." And all three examples illustrate the method of argument involving the conclusion "that was then ..."

## INITIAL CONCLUSIONS

Having stated at the outset that my purpose here is not a formal evaluation of the arguments summarized, it remains to suggest why this exercise is important. I would argue that the most significant element of this study is to show that nonviolence is a value that can be shown to derive from a close reading of the sources of each of the three traditions represented here. In other words, I consider it already highly significant that nonviolence can be shown to be a religious and ethical value in Islam and Judaism which is not a foreign import. This is particularly important given the frequently encountered notion that nonviolence (or pacifism) is an import from Christianity, or from late twentieth-century ethical maturity about war in the nuclear age, or an import from a romanticized fascination with Gandhi. This preliminary conclusion is already important because of the religious issues associated with contemporary intra-ethnic conflict. Peace, in short, can be seen to be as clearly implied from the same religious traditions that are often held responsible for fanning the flames of conflict.

Beyond this, however, there are interesting differences to note. The Christian strategies differ significantly from both the Islamic and Jewish strategies of Taha or Schwarzschild. The Christian strategies are arguably evolutionary. Perhaps influenced by the rationalism of critical biblical analysis, the Christian arguments appear to focus on a developmental *understanding* of the intentions of God as revealed in Jesus. In each case, Jesus is seen as divinely empowered and thus able to abrogate and change, but the language of the Christian theologians is liberally seasoned with terms suggesting improvement or advance, such as "transformed," "changed," and "new" versus "old," etc. In short, Christians seem unable to argue in a manner that does not imply error at one stage that is corrected at a later stage.

Taha, on the other hand, is far more concerned with identifying what he argues is God's strategic assignment of wisdom that is *appropriate to the times*. Change, in this case, is assigned to God's temporary postponements (to use An-Na'im's term) of what is the generally recognized divine intention. Mecca (significantly, I think), in Taha's thought, precedes Medina with the general plan for all humanity – Medina later temporarily suspends this. The clear change in ethical instruction is suggested to be introduced by God as a result of human failures but is also seen as part of more fully enacting the original intentions. It is the priority of Mecca, in Taha's thought, that allows his strategy to differ from the Christian strategy, since the latter is not as able to point to an "originally clear intention" that preceded the more problematic passages of the Hebrew tradition. However, Millard Lind's famous arguments in *Yahweh is a Warrior* resemble Taha's strategy by positing an original notion of the God of the Hebrews fighting without human involvement, until Israel foolishly chose a king to engage in conventional warfare.[33]

Schwarzschild's rabbinic arguments are perhaps the easiest to accept, largely because of the commentorial freedom afforded him within the rabbinic tradition. In other words, his strategic questions about the nature of "Israel" or the ability of the Sanhedrin to determine legitimate wars are the kind of questions that are typical of rabbinic exegetical method. Indeed, one could say that the essentially "commentorial" tradition of Judaism is so deeply an imbedded value in Jewish historical tradition that

Schwarzschild faced few methodological difficulties and faces lack of agreement only on the conclusions he draws rather than his interpretative strategies. Furthermore, Judaism suffers less from the authoritarianism of either Islam or Christianity, so that different perspectives derived from different strategies of interpreting the tradition are far less threatening – except insofar as they are complicated by questions surrounding Zionism.

Also, in comparison with both Islam and Judaism, the Christian arguments seem incomplete and somewhat crude. They raise, for example, unanswered questions about the role of the Old Testament in Christian ethical thought generally, and have a faint whiff of Marcionism about them (Marcion being the early heretic who advocated removing the entire Old Testament as scripture and "Marcionism" being a frequent accusation against Christian advocates of nonviolence). Christianity, it appears, although inherently developmental in that Abraham clearly precedes Moses, who clearly precedes Jesus, seems uncomfortable with other implications of such developmentalist approaches to the relation to the two Testaments. "Evolution," it appears, continues to ring foul in (especially more conservative) Christian ears, suggesting flaws in earlier understandings of God, and yet the Christian versions of developmentalism seem unable to escape this implication entirely.

## SOME CHRISTIAN REFLECTIONS

Drawing on the Sufi Taha and the Rabbi Swartzschild, Christians might reflect on a developmentalism that is not evolutionary and thus appears less compelled to demean its own religious tradition. However, it needs to be admitted that Christianity already presumes a developmentalism of a sort – the basic notion is not a foreign import into the discussion simply to save the day for an argument for nonviolence. Any suggestion otherwise risks becoming an argument in bad faith.

Secondly, a commentorial developmentalism, far from being disrespectful of the text as sacred scripture, can be seen to be precisely within the textual tradition and thus honoring the textual tradition – if for no other reason than to affirm that the text points to the fact that *God is interested in us in our time and context* and is not a passive observer. This is a critique that carries more power in Protestant circles, I would suggest, where there has always been a deeply held suspicion of Christianity's own tradition through the centuries, at least up to the point at which the

Protestant reformers chartered new courses. Indeed, it is particularly the case that a Protestant argument against some form of developmentalism can often appear to be sawing off the branch upon which one is sitting.

Third, developmentalism simply does not make much sense if one central point is missed, namely that the need for a developmental perspective is raised by close reading of the texts themselves. Part of the problematic presumptions in arguments against nonviolence as a Christian ethical standard is that it is often not granted, at the outset, that the problem of the canon is raised by the New Testament itself. The motivation to work out the meaning of scripture from the perspective of nonviolence is not an attempt to import a foreign value into textual discussion – rather it arises from respectful reading of the scriptures themselves.

Finally, a personal observation. Although I am not prepared to embrace developmentalism of some variation as the main, *or only,* viable manner in which to defend a Christian theological commitment to nonviolence from reading scripture, I am also not prepared to jettison this approach as without value. The dangers of a full-blown, anti-Semitic supersessionism must always be guarded against, but that does not invalidate the entire methodological approach of a developmental perspective, any more than certain dangers of supersessionism invalidate the rabbinic method itself. I am more comfortable, at this point, with theological arguments that pay attention to the diversity of the Old Testament or Hebrew Bible witness, and therefore the possibilities of arguing for nonviolence as a Hebrew virtue already initiated and developed within the diverse traditions that pre-date the New Testament. In short, I do not believe that nonviolence was new to the New Testament, nor do I believe that there *is* a *single* Hebrew perspective on war and peace in the canonical texts. To suggest other directions of approaching this issue, however, would take us in an entirely different line of historical, textual, and ethical polemics, with its own problematics.

NOTES

1. John Henderson, *Scripture, Canon, and Commentary: A Comparison of Confucian and Western Exegesis* (Princeton: Princeton University Press, 1991), pp. 5–6.
2. Ibid., p. 89.
3. Ibid., p. 106.
4. Ibid., p. 115.

5. Culbert Rutenber, *The Dagger and the Cross: An Examination of Christian Pacifism* (Nyack: Fellowship Publications, 1958), p. 71.

6. Ibid., p. 72.

7. John Piper, *"Love Your Enemies": Jesus' Command in the Synoptic Gospels and in the Early Christian Paraenesis* (Cambridge: Cambridge University Press, 1980), p. 34.

8. Roland Bainton, *Christian Attitudes Toward War and Peace* (Abingdon: Nashville, 1960), p. 54.

9. Andre Trocme, *Jesus and the Nonviolent Revolution,* trans. W. Shanks and M. Miller (Scottdale: Harold Press, 1973).

10. Jean Lasserre, *War and the Gospel* (Scottdale: Herald Press, 1962), p. 59.

11. T.R. Hobbs, *A Time for War: A Study of Warfare in the Old Testament* (Wilmington, DE: Michael Glazier, 1989).

12. John Wood, *Perspectives on War in the Bible* (Macon, GA: Mercer University Press, 1998).

13. Jacob Enz, *The Christian and Warfare: The Roots of Pacifism in the Old Testament* (Scottdale: Herald Press, 1962).

14. Abdullahi Ahmed An-Na'im, in Mahmoud Mohamed Taha, *The Second Message of Islam,* trans. Abdullahi Ahmed An-Na'im (Syracuse: Syracuse University Press, 1987).

15. Mahmoud Mohamed Taha, *The Second Message of Islam,* p. 39.

16. Ibid., p. 125.

17. Ibid., p. 133.

18. An-Na'im in Taha, *The Second Message of Islam,* p. 21.

19. See Steven Schwarzschild, "The Religious Demand for Peace," in *Judaism,* 15, 1966, pp. 412–418; and Schwarzschild, *The Pursuit of the Ideal: Jewish Writings of Steven Schwarzschild,* ed. Menachem Kellner (Albany: State University of New York Press, 1990).

20. But for adumbrations, see Steven Schwarzschild, "Shalom," in *The Challenge of Shalom,* ed. M. Polner and N. Goodman (Philadelphia: New Society Publishers, 1994), pp. 16–25.

21. Jacob Neusner, *A Life of R. Yochanon Ben Zakkai* (Leiden: E.J. Brill, 1962); and Neusner, *The Development of a Legend: Studies in the Traditions Concerning R. Yochanon Ben Zakkai* (Leiden: E.J. Brill, 1970).

22. On this point, see Louis Finkelstein, *The Pharisees: The Sociological Background of Their Faith* (Philadelphia: Jewish Publication Society of America, 1940), pp. 286–291; Reuven Kimmelman, "Non-violence in the Talmud," *Judaism,* 17 1968, pp. 316–334; Jacqueline Genot-Bismuth, "Pacifisme Phariseien et Sublimiation de L'Idee de Guerre aux Origines du Rabbinisme," *ETR,* 1, 1981, pp. 783–789.

23. Neusner, *A Life of R. Yochanon Ben Zakkai;* and Neusner, *The Development of a Legend.*

24. Finkelstein, *The Pharisees*, p. 286.
25. Jacob Neusner, *From Politics to Piety: The Emergence of Pharasaic Judaism* (New York: Prentice Hall, 1973), p. 91.
26. Neusner, *A Life of R. Yochanon Ben Zakkai*, pp. 115–116.
27. Neusner, *The Development of a Legend*, pp. 16–17.
28. Ibid.
29. See Eliyahu R. Touger, *The Laws of Kings and Their Wars* (New York and Jerusalem: Maznaim, 1987).
30. Avi Sagi, "The Punishment of Amalek in Jewish Tradition: Coping with the Moral Problem," *Harvard Theological Review*, 87, 1994, p. 339.
31. Ibid.
32. For an important discussion of the continued use of the Amalek metaphor in contemporary politics, see the work of Gerald Cromer, particularly "Amalek as Other, Other as Amalek: A Case Study of Secondary Othering." This essay, soon to be published, was graciously provided by the author.
33. Millard Lind, *Yahweh is a Warrior: The Theology of Warfare in Ancient Israel* (Scottdale, AZ: Herald Press, 1979).

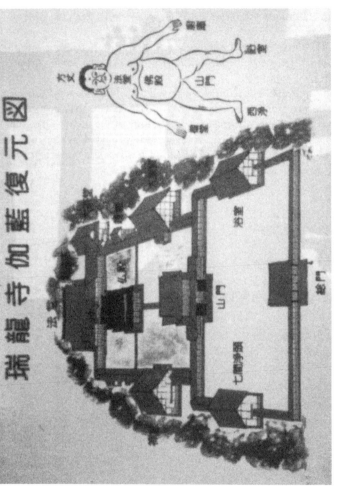

*Plate 13* This diagram at the entrance to the Zuiryu-ji temple in Tahaoak, Japan, shows the relationship of the parts of the temple to the parts of the human body. This points to the Japanese view of the integrative sanctity of human life, though not in the Western theistic sense that the body is the "temple" for the soul. Photo: *Joseph Runzo*

# 13

# FROM *AGAPÉ* TO ORGANS: RELIGIOUS DIFFERENCE *between* JAPAN AND AMERICA IN JUDGING *the* ETHICS OF THE TRANSPLANT

*William R. LaFleur*

Please don't take
    your organs to heaven.
       Heaven knows
          we need them here.
            (American automobile bumper sticker)

What I take up here is part of a larger project, one where I examine the reasons why much of Japan's religious community – that is, persons with varying combinations of Buddhist, Shinto, and Confucian sensitivities – not only has expressed strong doubts about the morality of excising organs from putatively dead bodies for the purpose of transplantation but also has been attempting to express more global reservations about the trajectory taken by "advanced" biomedicine, especially in America, during recent decades.[1] My larger study considers how the views of Japan's bioethicists, often interestingly different from their American counterparts, are given expression and makes a comparative analysis.

Here, however, although I make frequent reference to Japanese materials for their heuristic value, the principal focus is on the till-now largely ignored question of how it happened that in North America the doing of cadaveric transplants, so contentious an issue in Japan, not only received a relatively swift sanction from most religious organizations but even today is a procedure often promoted through church and synagogue homilies and active campaigns. Although other studies have touched on this issue, it is the sole focus of this one. Moreover I here offer my own hypotheses – new ones I believe – concerning how and why this ready acceptance came into being.

The central of these is that the Christian embrace of the new transplant technology is best seen as contingent rather than necessary and that, looked at historically, it took place at what was, at least from the perspective of this new technology's promoters, a specific and perhaps even unique window of opportunity in time. It was both a time in which older religious sentiment against corpse desecration had been brought into question as being inadequately ethical and one in which *agapé* was being put forward as the quintessence of Christianity. Consequently, with traditional reserve about corpse maltreatment under theological review, the willed transfer of body organs from a putative corpse to a needy recipient was easily valorized as a remarkably concrete expression of exemplary gift giving in the agapeic mode. Although materials of theology and theological ethics will be included in what I look at here, my own method of inquiry will be that of the historian of religions and ethics.

We may not, of course, assume that the modes of handling the bodies of the dead were in human history determined simply by religious ideas. Relative wealth and specific historical or local conditions were often heavy players. The sarcophagi of kings and rich merchants contrast sharply with the mass graves of peasants. Moreover, in times of famine, war, or epidemic the sheer number of new corpses undoubtedly forced communities of the still alive to adopt manners of disposal that these same persons would have deemed unacceptable in more normal times. As recently as 1918 an epidemic of influenza caused the death of so many people in Philadelphia that extant documentary film records the more-or-less routine collection of bodies along city streets.

One conclusion to be drawn from the fascinating research on death and burial practices that has been carried out by historians such as Philippe Ariés is that the sheer diversity of such practices and the changing valorizations within European history make it impossible to identify anything that could qualify as *the* Christian perspective on such matters. There were no constants. Although mass graves had been common even for Christians until the eleventh century, there occurred then, according to

Ariés, "a return to the individuality of the grave and its corollary, the positive value attached to the dead body."[2] In the later Middle Ages there were many instances of the flesh being cut away from the bones and of bones and flesh being buried at separate sites. And this occasioned a papal ban on such practices. In a historical note with special relevance to the present study, Anne Marie Moulin detects a certain irony when she notes that Pope Boniface VIII in 1299 "forbade the cutting up of remains – evisceration – in short, all the practices that are now necessary for the transplantation of organs."[3]

If within Christianity it was the case that acts disrespectful of the bodily integrity of the corpse were increasingly seen as objectionable, such acts were *a fortiori* forbidden within Judaism – and had long been so. The interesting and important question that arises, then, is that of how things changed both for Christians and for many Jews during the twentieth century. The evidence of such change having occurred comes from the fact that during the weekend of 13–15 November 1998 "churches and synagogues across the United States encouraged their faithful to sign donor cards."[4] This was, of course, responding to encouragement from organ transplant organizations eager to correct what was seen as a serious lack of donors in America.

The story of such change is, of course, not exactly the same for Christians and for Jews, and among the latter there remains even today a fair amount of theological and emotional resistance to cadaveric transplantation. One theological problem faced by *both*, however, was that of reconciling the removal of organs with concerns about the need for bodily integrity at the time of bodily resurrection. Although he himself supports organ donation by Jews, Elliot N. Dorff explores in some detail how the resurrection is cited as a factor in at least the explanations offered by many Jews – many of them otherwise totally secular – for why they resist any cutting of the cadaver. He calls attention to a discrepancy:

> The fact that so many Jews object to autopsies and to organ donation
> on the grounds of their incompatibility with a belief in resurrection
> means ... that a far higher percentage of Jews believe in life after death
> than are willing to admit that they do.[5]

Although comparative data might suggest that also for Jews there may be much more going on here than can be explained by Dorff's reference to a discrepancy between "the popular belief that impedes donation and the rabbinic disgust with this belief,"[6] my point here is simply that, for both Jews and Christians, traditional ideas of bodily resurrection have in our times had to be reckoned with – and perhaps even significantly reinterpreted – so as to make acceptable the excision of a cadaver's organs.

It is not yet clear that twentieth-century efforts by Christian clergy and many Jewish rabbis will be fully successful in convincing their respective constituencies that organ removal for transplant need pose no *real* problem in contexts of future bodily resurrection. Although, for instance, in 1988 the Southern Baptist convention, in order to address this problem, stated that "complete resurrection of the body does not depend on bodily wholeness at death," ordinary adherents may perhaps need to be forgiven for harboring the view that a truly *physical* resurrection might be at least facilitated by keeping the *physical* parts (or what is left of them) as contiguous as possible.

Nevertheless, a trend of the twentieth century can be seen in multiple efforts to see as acceptable certain treatments of the corpse that had earlier been deemed religiously objectionable. Cremation for Catholics is a salient example. Consistent with what had been a stance since at least the time of Charlemagne, as late as 1886 the Catholic Church explicitly forbade its adherents from undergoing cremation. Yet in 1963 the Second Vatican Council, partially in response to the fact that Catholics in Tokyo were caught between this ecclesiastical prohibition and a municipal law that forbade anything other than cremation within that city, removed the interdiction for Catholics – while insisting that ashes should not be scattered on the sea or earth or in the air. In parts of East Asia this change undoubtedly began to alter what had been seen as one of the most concrete, ritualized indices of core difference between Christians and Buddhists.[7]

It was, however, the decades of the 1950s and 1960s that were, I argue, crucial for making the changes under review here. Not only were there official moves at this time to declare that resurrection doctrines did not disallow organ removal, but it was then that new, more technical ways of measuring a body's vital signs appear to have convinced some religious authorities to cede over to medicine whole territories that up to that point had been considered religion's own. This was shown when in 1958 Pope Pius XII in an encyclical, *The Prolongation of Life,* stated that any pronouncement determining the point of death was not a matter for the church but for the physician.[8] It is, I surmise, probable that Japan's Buddhists would, if asked, have balked at making a comparable concession. To them, we may assume, to relinquish the right to say things about dying and death would be somehow equivalent – in a cultural way not without its economic entailment – to "giving away the store."

Yet for most American Christian denominations organ donation and the cadaveric transplant were not just things to be tolerated. They were, on the contrary, given an extraordinarily warm embrace. The technology, of course, was welcomed in the same way as its immediate antecedents – namely, with language about being "miracles" of the modern sort. But to that was added the all-important fact that the transplant involved a higher level of interpersonal (or, at least, intercorporeal) relations than had been the case in most medicine, except for the blood transfusion, up to that point in time. My central point here is one concerning a *unique historical convergence*. That is, what was an unusual time of opportunity for a new medical technology to gain the immediate blessing of most of the American religious community also happened to be a somewhat exceptional time in the history of modern theology – namely, one in which the concept of *agapé* was being much bandied about and many in the Christian community were eager to show that theological concepts were not just mental constructs but could be made concrete in inter-human relationships and social praxis. The result of this was that the pre-death donation of one's own cadaveric organs was seen as an especially exemplary instance of Christian *agapé* in action.

Although *agapé* was a Greek term of significance in the New Testament, it seems clear that until the twentieth century it had not been singled out to designate and tag the kind of love deemed *specific* to Christianity. Although it is quite likely that with Kierkegaard's *Works of Love* of 1847 the quest to locate a specific and unique mode of Christian love took off in earnest, the term *agapé* as *the* term to designate that specificity gained prominence only with Anders Nygren's *Agape and Eros*, a work of 1930 but not available and widely known in America until its appearance in English translation in 1957. In an excellent overview of these matters published in 1972, Gene Outka signalled at the outset the formative importance of Nygren's study, one that "first distinguished what he took to be two radically different kinds of love. [Nygren] so effectively posed issues about love that they have had a prominence in theology and ethics they have never had before."[9]

It is far from my purpose to enter here into the complex theological and ethical debates about *agapé*.[10] What does interest me is what I see as the profound cultural significance of the specific *time frame* – that is, from the late 1950s until the early 1970s – during which discussions both of agapeic love and how it might be societally implemented first played a large role in American intellectual and religious life. My point is that talk about *agapé* was very much in the air in and around the year 1967 when Dr. Christiaan Barnard performed the world's first heart transfer out of the body of a putative cadaver in South Africa. Impressive is the alacrity and intensity with which explicit connections were at that time drawn between one of that epoch's most salient theological discussions and its newest, most awesome medical technology. In a word, the transplant seemed to have been made for *agapé* and *agapé* for the transplant.

## JAPAN AND THE *AGAPÉ* BOOM

I need first, however, to recall what has been the outside stimulus for my exploration of these developments in America – that is, the Japanese materials that hinted in the first place that the American process in this was wholly contingent and in no way necessary or morally superior. It is interesting to note that already in 1958 an essay by Itô Osamu in *Shisô*, Japan's premier intellectual journal of the time, explicitly brought up the relationship of *agapé*, so prominent then in Western discussions, and Japanese culture. Itô suggested that it would be a mistake to assume – as some in Japan apparently had been assuming – that what Christians meant by "love," something theoretically directed to anyone without distinction, was roughly equivalent to terms found in the works of Confucianism or Buddhism.[11]

But if some thinkers were suggesting that the gap between Japan and the West was one that ought to be filled by a deeper Christianization of the East Asian archipelago, other Japanese, especially when thinking concretely about the ethics of organ transplants, held that the traditional Japanese position is the more reasonable, that *agapé* is an unrealizable ideal, and that Japan's religious and cultural difference from Christian societies is one worth retaining. A discussion of comparative notions of "love" enters, for instance, into Ogiwara Makoto's *Nihonjin wa naze nôshi zôki ishoku o kobamu no ka* (Why is it that the Japanese reject "brain death" and organ transplantation?). Although he perhaps generalizes too broadly to all of Christianity, Ogiwara is, I suggest, basically right concerning a concept of love in Christianity holding sway *at that point in time* – the late 1960s through the 1980s – in America when organ transplants were deemed an adequate, even an exemplary, expression of such love. In a book that argues against the notion that a "higher" concept of universalizable love should sweep away all cultural objections to cadaveric transplants, Ogiwara wrote

> When we Japanese hear the word "love," we link it to matters of the heart, to feelings, and to emotion. The notion of "love for the neighbor" in Christianity, however, does not put the same degree of emphasis on the emotional element and in its stead prioritizes love as expressed in acts of volition. Of course the emotional element is also important, but that is not the whole story. In Christianity the question becomes: Is not the real evidence of love's presence shown in actual deeds? Is it not rather meaningless to be only saying *with the mouth* that love is present?
>
> Love so conceived, I suggest, is not love based on sentiment or the emotions. It has nothing to do with the kind of natural emotion that springs up when we say about another person that we like or love him or her. No, rather, this is a kind of love that is an act of the will. Therefore in some sense love as conceived in Christianity is one which is *produced* by humans [in contrast to love that would arise naturally and spontaneously]. It is love that is un-natural. When Jesus demands "Love your enemies and pray for those who persecute you," he is requiring something that is not emotionally possible.[12]

Ogiwara gives articulation to something I have found to be common in Japanese discussions of these matters, namely, an affirmation of the Confucian principle of parent–child relations as the best paradigm of love because it is also the one that is most realistic.[13] Along with this comes a skepticism about the *emotional* likelihood of being able to prioritize a willed "love" for an unknown and anonymous person (the "neighbor" of the *agapé* concept) over the existing power of bonds to persons to whom one is already related.

This is not to deny the possibility of altruism[14] but rather to express doubt about the wisdom of constructing an ethic that would implicitly denigrate or downgrade existing structures of interpersonal bonding, especially those of close familial relations. It is, in a word, to reaffirm a Confucian preference and to insist that the Kierkegaardian concept of love is not only unnatural but also, from this perspective, *unethical*. That is, there is not only doubt that we can emotionally exclude all sense of "personhood" from how we respond to the still-present corpse, but also the additional problem that it is close interpersonal ties, especially those of near kin, which make exercises in premature mental distancing seem deeply problematic, impious, and even wrong. Such redefinitions may look good as high-wire acts of the mind. But they run counter to our natural emotions and, in truth, our emotions are not to be dismissed or denigrated in the making of moral judgments.[15] The parents, told that their child is now suddenly "brain dead" owing to an accident, will not only "naturally" but also *rightly* reject the suggestion that "he" or "she" be "harvested." To many Japanese, then, the cutting into the body and removal of organs of a freshly "dead" member of the family will, even if for an altruistic purpose such as a transplant, seem not only highly "unnatural" but also an act that transgresses some of the best-known norms and values of what is meant by "love" in Japanese society.

## JOSEPH FLETCHER'S "AGAPEIC CALCULUS"

By contrast to this strong Japanese resistance to the cadaveric transplant, its acceptance on the clerical level in the United States was relatively fast and easy. Yet, even in America this acceptance was not a foregone conclusion. In fact, given evidence that the late 1960s witnessed a renewed spate of criticism of medicine, the degree to which the Christian community readily embraced the transplant is itself suggestive of the power there of the *agapé* rationale. Christians may, that is, have been more, not less, receptive than others to this and other "miracles" of modern medicine. In a fascinating and important study that focuses on the evidence of wide public anxiety about misdiagnosed death and premature burial during much of the modern period, Martin S. Pernick notes that, in fact, the late 1960s was a period of revived suspicion of medical expertise in America and as such marked a downturn in trust.

> The nineteenth-century premature burial panic had been ended by a unique period of public enthusiasm for medical science, and public deference to the judgement of doctors. This era of deference was an almost unprecedented aberration in the history of American medicine. By the end of the 1960s, the medical profession once again faced public criticism on a variety of issues, including the question of defining death.[16]

Given this, it is surprising, then, that *so little* of this criticism in the late 1960s and beyond came from within the context of American Christian communities. Aside from a few exceptions, the representatives of American Christianity – perhaps in contrast both to critics in academia and to the objections raised by orthodox Jews – not only continued to show deference to medical science but seemed almost eager to sanction the new technique of the transplant.

The reasons for this are, no doubt, multiple. In a recent essay Courtney S. Campbell explicitly asks why, at least among American fundamentalists (at that time being reconfigured as "evangelicals") there was no raising of serious questions about the 1968 "Report of the Ad Hoc Committee of the Harvard Medical School to Examine the Definition of Brain Death." This report, of course, was the document that provided the (still rather) deeply problematic equation between death and "brain death," thus giving scientific legitimacy to the removal of inner organs of persons defined thereby as "dead."

In answer to the question Campbell raises about the whereabouts of fundamentalists on this issue, her own thesis is that 1968 was simply too early a date for the sensitivities of these Christians to be alert and watchdogging a public policy issue such as this. She writes,

> The time frame is very important. One cannot speak of a politically mobilized and socially active fundamentalist movement until after the *Roe v. Wade* decision legalizing abortion in 1973, some five years after the report of the Harvard committee.[17]

This attitude toward new developments in medicine as ethically unproblematic appears to have continued even after American evangelicals became politically active and mobilized.

One part of the explanation for this may lie in the tendency of the evangelical movement to focus its criticisms somewhat narrowly – even though intensely. From this movement's beginning until the present it has been legalized abortion that has served as its well-known *bête noire*. In matters of science it has been the presence of Darwinism in public education and, more recently, the prospect of human cloning that have been the objects of criticism. On virtually all other issues of science and medicine, by comparison, evangelicals have not issued concerns that have registered significantly in the public domain. In fact, as David F. Nobel shows, in most matters of advanced science the evangelical form of American Christianity has been not only receptive but ready to supply both support and advocacy.[18] It would appear, then, that questions having to do with "brain death" and what might be ethically problematic about cadaveric transplants were ones that fell outside the ambit of the evangelicals' attention. The contrast here with its problematization among communities of American Jews, the orthodox most especially, can be instructive. It was also the case that evangelicals seem to have been no way inclined to doubt that the donation of organs was morally and religiously right and worthy of praise. To match the "miracle" of modern medicine with individual acts of self-giving donation was clearly, they assumed, to express Christian love.

For America's more liberal Christians, however, the response to questions about the ethics of the transplant followed, I wish to show, a more intellectually ambitious and interesting trajectory. It is among them that an affirmation of the transplant as a quintessential social expression of *agapé* gained its fullest rationalization. Once again the matter of "time frame" is crucial. The person of central importance in this process was Joseph Fletcher (1905–1991), the author in 1966 of *Situation Ethics: The New Morality*, a widely read reinterpretation of Christian ethics, and – very importantly – someone widely recognized today as one of the founders of the subfield of bioethics. It was Fletcher who in print made the explicit link between *agapé* and organs. It was also Fletcher who became the best-known public advocate for *all* types of new biotechnology – as shown in the range of his writings and culminating in his 1988 book, *The Ethics of Genetic Control: Ending Reproductive Roulette*.

But it was also Fletcher, I suggest, whose overall intellectual career itself gave expression to the greatest conceptual problem for the relationship between Christianity and the ethics of this technological trajectory. The nub of this problem was the antinomy between one project that strove to isolate and prize what was *unique* in Christianity and another that so emphasized the infusion of secular thought into Christianity that the latter's distinctiveness would be virtually liquidated. In the earlier part of his career – that is, that part of it that had a profound impact on the Christian embrace of new medical technologies – Fletcher seems not to have recognized that he was moving simultaneously in two incompatible directions. One part of him was raising high the unique importance of *agapé* as the essence of what is of value in Christianity. However, another part, especially as spurred on by the interests shown already in his *Morals and Medicine* of 1954, wanted a Christianity so deeply relevant to contemporary social issues that it should and would happily "update" its tradition by massive transfusions from secular sources. One project was Kierkegaardian but the other, as will be seen below, was utilitarian to the core. It seems likely that Fletcher's gradual awareness that these were incompatible and that he would opt to be a utilitarian rather than a Kierkegaardian – or, in fact, even a Christian – was what shaped the changes in his professional career and public stance. He who had had his strongest impact upon American Christianity during the days when he had been teaching at the Episcopal Theological School in Cambridge, Massachusetts, eventually made a break with Christianity and with religious perspectives more broadly, a move defended publicly on the Dick Cavett television show in the early 1980s.

It is, however, the earlier Fletcher, the one interested in the linkage between *agapé* and medicine, who had a profound impact upon the acceptance of cadaveric transplant techniques by American Christianity. Again what I call the temporal "window of opportunity" is very significant here. Fletcher's *Situation Ethics*, his most important work and one widely read and discussed in America, was published in 1966. Christiaan Barnard's performance of what was called "the miracle at Cape Town" was an event of December 1967. During 1968 Fletcher became the most conspicuous Christian public proponent of such transplants and his "Our Shameful Waste of Human Tissue: An Ethical Problem for the Living and the Dead" was published in 1969.[19]

The trajectory of how Fletcher moved from Kierkegaard to the transplant is in many ways the most fascinating part of this story. Although his *Situation Ethics* was the subject of extensive controversy among theologians and ethicists, there was very little objection to that part of the book that discussed *agapé* – perhaps because much of what Fletcher said there seemed to merely re-express what had become the "common sense" within much of American Protestantism. Latching on strongly to the Kierkegaardian emphasis on volition – to the virtual exclusion of emotion – as what is central to love in Christianity, Fletcher wrote,

> *Agapé's* desire is to satisfy the neighbor's need, not one's own, but the main thing about it is that *agapé* love precedes all desire, of any kind. It is not at all an emotional norm or motive. It is volitional, conative.[20]

Explicitly acknowledging his own debt to the Danish philosopher in this matter, he wrote, "According to Søren Kierkegaard, to say that love is a feeling or anything of that kind is an unchristian view of love."[21] It seems clear that at this point Fletcher was interested in isolating and prizing what was unique and uniquely Christian about *agapé*. The fact that this formulation relegated emotion – and, by implication, its expression in interpersonal affective ties – to what was at best without value and at worse an impediment to *agapé* had massive importance for how transplants to anonymous recipients would be valorized as "Christian."

Yet it is also important to note precisely *how* Fletcher saw this ideal articulated in modern professional life. Having pursued the Kierkegaardian trajectory so as to disallow any attention to "lovability" in the object of real love, Fletcher explicitly used the physician and nurse as exemplars of *agapé* translated into the routine of daily work. Ignoring the fact that these medical professionals are also constrained by both law and the code of medicine to practice as they do, Fletcher had no difficulty seeing continuity between the crucifixion and the hospital:

> Where were there ever more unlovable men than those who stood around the cross of Jesus, yet he said: "Forgive them"? Paul gave this its cosmic statement: "While we were yet sinners Christ died for us. (Rom. 5:8). Non-reciprocity and nondesert apply even to affection-love: Reuel Howe explains why "my child, your child, needs love most when he is most unlovable." Good medical care prescribes "t.l.c." (tender loving care) every hour on the hour, whether doctors or nurses *like* the patient or not.[22]

This selection of medical practitioners, however routinized in fact their practices may be, as *the* models of such intentional love suggested Fletcher's growing readiness to give his unequivocal blessing to procedures and developments in the medical field. As one of the first to be recognized as a bioethicist in America, Fletcher showed a distinct proclivity for cheerleading rather than for close inspection and wariness *vis-à-vis* medicinal practices.

Already in *Situation Ethics* we can detect the direction – specifically in making a move that, we may assume, would likely have been anathema to Kierkegaard. That is, in making Christian ethics "situational", he did so largely by stuffing it with the perspective and values of utilitarianism. Few moves in modern ethical discourse, I believe, have had such a profound impact on bioethics in general and on the valorization of cadaveric transplants in particular. Through it he radically redescribed the concept of Christian *agapé* so that, as long as the inconsistencies went unnoticed, it could come to serve as *the* religious rationale for removing the organs of a person described as "brain dead." Again it may be instructive to note that this articulation of a marriage between *agapé* and utilitarianism had already been put into place by Fletcher and inserted into the public domain a year before the first cadaveric transplant.

Much of what had always been appealing in utilitarianism had been expressed in its preoccupation with avoiding *waste*. This reference to "waste" became crucial both for transplantation's initial rationale and for subsequent decades of rhetoric aimed at a general public being repeatedly told that organs not reused would be organs foolishly squandered. Of course, in history human bodies and body parts had been reused before. Although controversial, whole corpses had in modern times been used for anatomy lessons, and Tibetans had traditionally made implements out of human bones – in part so as to serve as ready-to-hand *memento mori*. And as part of their larger nefarious designs Nazis had, of course, reused the body parts of people they had murdered.

Fletcher gravitated easily to the notion that the organs of the deceased would be wasted if not recycled. Strategic reutilization and the avoidance of waste had become core values for him – so much so that he made an "updating" of Christianity via the utilitarianism of Jeremy Bentham and John Stuart Mill an explicit part of what he meant by making Christian ethics situational. This involved putting out a religious welcome mat for acts of calculation. In *Situation Ethics* he wrote,

> Justice is Christian love using its head, calculating its duties, obligations, opportunities, resources ... Justice is love coping with situations where distribution is called for. On this basis it becomes plain that as the love ethic searches seriously for a social policy it must form a coalition with utilitarianism. It takes over from Bentham and Mill the strategic principle of "the greatest good of the greatest number."[23]

In what seemed easy to Fletcher but looks retrospectively now like it might have actually been an ominous leitmotif for the kind of torturous calculations that have become part and parcel of organ transplants during more recent decades, Fletcher wrote of "distribution" as the remaining core problem.

Once Christianity could be convinced to "use its head," Fletcher saw it as necessarily bringing about a marriage between quantitative analyses and love – but a love now narrowed down so as to be made up entirely of the volitional, and decidedly not the emotional, element. Love acts of pure will and not tainted by emotion were, this formulation asserts, to be put into praxis by calculations aimed at benefiting the maximum number at the minimum cost. *Agapé* was to be linked in eternal union with computational analysis. Skilled at constructing neologisms, Fletcher for this purpose coined the term "agapeic calculus" – that is, what he defined as achieving "the greatest amount of neighbor welfare for the largest number of neighbors possible."[24]

## PHYSICIANS RATHER THAN FATHERS?

Although Fletcher did not refer to what follows (and may, in fact, have been unaware of it), the choice of Jeremy Bentham (1748–1832) by Fletcher for praise becomes especially fascinating when viewed in terms of the longer Western trajectory toward acceptance of transplant techniques. Through the precise manner in which he willed the disposition *of his own corpse* and how he articulated the significance of his own decisions, Bentham was probably no match as both foreshadower and valorizer of the direction taken.

As part of her larger project of studying the social history of whose corpses were confiscated for anatomical dissection and of the injustice that was often part of procurement efforts, Ruth Richardson collaborated with Brian Hurwitz to look at the role of Bentham in this process. In a period in English history during which not only were corpses of the indigent often stolen and sold but some persons, it has been proven, were even murdered for the prices their cadavers might fetch, Bentham was, commendably, among those deeply disturbed by the fact that the bodies of the poor were dissected so that physicians might, through what they had learned, more readily correct the illnesses of the rich who could afford their services. He, therefore, in a way that cohered exactly with his own utilitarian philosophy, directed that his own corpse be made *useful*. He directed that it, first, be available for use in an anatomy lesson and, thereafter, be properly prepared so that it could be put on ongoing public display as what Bentham referred to as an "auto-icon." Envisioning the development of a wider public trend, he saw the corpse as till-then overlooked and thereby "wasted" whereas it had the potential to become an *objet d'art*. Cadavers, rightly and efficiently reused, could make the efforts of the sculptor expendable. Richardson and Hurwitz note that

Bentham's quirky vision of the uses of human taxidermy included the erection of temples of fame and infamy in which auto-icons would take the place of carved statuary or waxwork: "so that every man be his own statue."[25]

These authors go on to detect a motif of narcissism in this part of Bentham's utilitarian project.

Where, however, the direction of Bentham's values becomes especially interesting for ethical analysis lies in that place at which his entirely praiseworthy interest in ensuring that not only the bodies of the poor be used for dissection got linked up with his categorical abhorrence of anything smacking of traditional religious respect for the body of the recently deceased. Richardson and Hurwitz write,

> Lacking religious belief, Bentham viewed the human carcass as matter created by death. As an eighteenth-century rationalist, he found little difficulty in addressing the problem of how this matter might be best disposed of with a view to maximising the "Felicity of Mankind." Death was a waste of resources.[26]

Here was *in nuce* a prefiguring of the dilemma that Fletcher would eventually seek to resolve by abandoning religion when later in life he had come to think of religion's values as inferior to – and even inimical to – those of the ethical dimension. In other words, that with which Bentham had begun was that with which Fletcher felt compelled, for the sake of consistency, to end.

It is not my intention here to solve the vexing problem of the degree to which utilitarian values and procedures for judgment may or may not be compatible with religion and the ethical values expressed in the various religions. My own hunch is that the compatibility on a deep level may be rather slight. In another context I examine the extensive degree to which a *critique* of utilitarianism, both explicit and implicit in Anglo-American medical ethics, has long been a major part of how Japanese thinkers, in both religion and philosophy, have sought to construct an alternative view of the bioethical enterprise.

Yet what I wish to emphasize here is how the utilitarian abhorrence for waste seems to have resonated especially within Anglo-American Protestantism. It resulted in a fairly widespread interest, one both new and strikingly modern, in exploring how the human body after death might *still prove useful* to the human community. The assumption in such a search was that the traditional use to which the new corpse had always been put – that is, as the concrete focus point for ritual gatherings and the reaffirmation of human community in ways consonant with the analyses of Durkheim – no longer made sense. That is, the traditional concern for the bodily integrity of the corpse was assumed to have no detectable *ethical* import. Consequently, this traditional use was thus seen as constituting a flagrant example of a waste of time and resources. Therefore, once it came to be assumed that the expression of true *agapé* required something more noble and decidedly "Christian" than what was present in the traditional disposition of the corpse, many of the leaders of American Christianity were primed not only to accept one or another version of a Fletcherian "agapeic calculus" but also to praise and promote cadaveric donation.

Japan's Buddhists, in part because so much of Confucianism had been absorbed into their thinking about ethics, not only did not follow this trajectory but for the most part found it completely unpersuasive.[27] I suggest there may be value in trying to see how deeply something like the "agapeic calculus," especially when translated into specific choices, would have gone against the grain of traditional Confucian values. If it was already the case that many Japanese found unacceptable the notion that "love" might require an act like "[Jesus] Christ's rejection of his own mother,"[28] even more repugnant would have been Fletcher's readiness to augment this outlawing of sentiment and his own preference for impersonality with a fully rational calculation.

The Confucian-Buddhist would have found morally repugnant a strategy that would elevate the calculation of results to the point where primary human relationships would go by the board. Cold and virtually "inhuman" would, then, be the judgment passed on the author of *Situation Ethics* when he wrote,

> [When you can only carry one out of life-threatening danger and] ... the choice is between your father and a medical genius who has discovered a cure for a common fatal disease, you carry out the genius if you understand *agapé*.[29]

In addition to the fact that the making of such a calculated choice would be highly unlikely to occur in real situations, what is interesting here is that Fletcher's selection of the "medical genius" as the person unquestionably more worthy of rescue than one's own father is itself part of a calculation. Fletcher's selection here not only reaffirms the high public status given the medical profession in America of his time but itself makes maximum use of that profession's public prestige to help him make what he himself, it seems, sensed to be a hard sell as arguments go. His provision of a concrete hypothetical case shows that Fletcher wanted, at least intellectually, to cash in on what Pernick has referred to as that era's "public enthusiasm for medical science." It is difficult to imagine any profession other than that of the medic – attorney? politician? scholar-educator? – as capable of helping Fletcher conduct with rhetorical success the difficult, perhaps impossible, thought experiment he wished to carry off here.

These problems notwithstanding, Fletcher's role in the process of radical secularization of bioethics did not prevent his formulations and phrases from contributing substantially to the American religious community's perception that organ transplants are fundamentally expressive of the highest possible form of human altruism, one that with little difficulty might be interpreted as deeply *religious*. This is by no means to say that Fletcher's work was mere ruse. It is, however, to suggest that many in America's religious organizations, both Christian and Jewish, appear to have been less than circumspect or ready to engage in careful analysis when provided with what appeared to be acceptable reasons for sanctioning the latest in medicine. It is also to suggest that they appear to have paid inadequate attention to the writings of Paul Ramsey, another early bioethicist, who was Fletcher's most trenchant critic at the time, a thinker who challenged Fletcher repeatedly for faulty reasoning and for misconstruals of Christianity. Ramsey was a severe critic of the growing enthusiasm for utilitarianism and deplored what he saw as the reduction of persons to "an ensemble . . . of interchangeable . . . spare parts" in which "everyone [becomes] a useful cadaver."[30]

Finally it needs noting that, at least until the present, the terminology and slogans used in America to promote organ transplantation and organ donation have been heavily indebted to the rhetorical linkages made by Fletcher and those who adopted his viewpoint. Language about avoiding the "waste" of organs, about the high virtue of donation to an anonymous recipient, about life itself as the most precious thing a giver could possibly give, and about such acts as expressions of supreme love were and remain common. The term *agapé* need not be used. Yet it and the trajectory of interpretation it took in America are infused deeply into public rhetoric about organ donation. A currently available promotional poster states "Organ transplantation – The Ultimate Gift," a phrase that makes most sense when viewed in the historical context traced here. It would seem to be no accident that "ultimate" can signify both what is temporally *final* in terms of the volitional acts one can perform in a lifetime and *highest* in terms of religious and/or ethical value. When scratched even only lightly, such a phrase, even when passed off as secular, reveals close to its surface the notion of *agapé* and how it has played a role in American public discourse about the ethics of advanced medical technologies.

## NOTES

Comments both from participants in the conference at Chapman University and from William Londo in Kyoto at an early stage in the development of this paper have been very helpful to me, and I here express my gratitude.

1. It is important to note that it is the excision of organs from *cadavers* that is at issue here; the Japanese have been much less resistant to the transplantation of kidneys etc. from living donors. In addition, I here refer to the *putative* dead because of the ongoing concern, one intensified by fairly recent neurological research, that persons defined as "brain-dead" are sometimes, in fact, not only still alive but capable of recovered consciousness. The shakiness of the view that "brain-death" equals death has, of course, been a major part of Japanese skepticism about the excision of organs from putative cadavers all along.

2. Philippe Ariés, *The Hour of Our Death*, trans. Helen Weaver (New York: Alfred A. Knopf, 1981), p. 208.

3. Anne Marie Moulin, "The Ethical Crisis of Organ Transplants: In Search of Cultural 'Compatibility,'" *Diogenes*, 172, Winter 1995, p. 79.

4. *Japan Times*, 15 November 1998.

5. Elliot N. Dorff, *Matters of Life and Death: A Jewish Approach to Modern Medical Ethics* (Philadelphia and Jerusalem: Jewish Publication Society, 1998), p. 238. See also Elliot N. Dorff, "Choosing Life: Aspects of Judaism Affecting Organ Transplantation," in *Organ Transplantation: Meanings and Realities*, ed. Stuart J. Youngner, Renée C. Fox, and Laurence J. O'Connell (Madison: University of Wisconsin Press, 1996), pp. 168–193.

6. Dorff, *Matters of Life and Death*, p. 235.

7. In 1967 during a visit to Seoul I was shown a hillside burial site by a Korean Christian. With obvious pride he commented that such sites of interment would not be so easily found in Japan, where Buddhist cremation was still the common practice. He went on to cite this as evidence that Korea was becoming a Christian country. Two decades later, however, on another visit to Korea I learned that the extensive usage of prime land for burials had come under public criticism as ecologically unwise.

8. David Lamb, *Death, Brain Death, and Ethics* (Aldershot: Avebury, 1996), p. 52.
9. Gene Outka, *Agape: An Ethical Analysis* (New Haven: Yale University Press, 1972) p. 1.
10. To Nygren the older, largely Catholic, notion of love as a kind of *eros* directed to God had to be replaced with a more specifically New Testament kind of love. He held that *agapé* was very different and virtually an act of the will alone. But a Catholic scholar would later comment, "Such love has its place, but Christian life would be impoverished if this love were its exclusive ideal." Edward Collins Vacek, S.J., *Love, Human and Divine: The Heart of Christian Ethics* (Washington: Georgetown University Press, 1994), p. 231. More recently Joseph Runzo shows how religion is impoverished even if the explicitly *erotic* element is denied; see his "Eros and Meaning in Life and Religion," in *The Meaning of Life in the World Religions*, ed. Joseph Runzo and Nancy M. Martin (Oxford: Oneworld, 1999), pp. 186–201.
11. Itô Osamu, *"Kindai nihon ni okeru ai no kyogi"* (Misconceptions in "love" in early modern Japan), *Shisô*, July 1958.
12. Ogiwara Makoto, *Nihonjin wa naze nôshi zôki ishoku o kobamu no ka* (Why is it that the Japanese reject "Brain-death" and organ transplantation?) (Tokyo: Shinyôsha, 1992), pp. 151–152.
13. See William R. LaFleur, "Love's Insufficiency: Zen as Irritant," in *Love, Sex, and Gender in the World Religions*, ed. Joseph Runzo and Nancy M. Martin (Oxford: Oneworld, 2000), pp. 47–48, n.3, where I show that already in medieval Japan the paradigm of love was the affective one of the parent-child relationship.
14. Ogiwara and others must be seen as responding to the quasi-theological American debate about the possibility of agapeic love. Theirs was *not* a concern to react to the later American debate, one largely introduced by E.O. Wilson and sociobiology, about the possibility, extent, and meaning of altruism once Darwinian factors and animal behavior are brought into the picture. On this interesting but latter debate, see Elliott Sober and David Sloan Wilson, *Unto Others: The Evolution and Psychology of Unselfish Behavior* (Cambridge MA: Harvard University Press, 1998).
15. Very recent work in advanced neurology strongly supports this view. See, for instance, Antonio R. Damasio, *Descartes' Error: Emotion, Reason, and the Human Brain* (New York: Avon, 1994).
16. Martin S. Pernick, "Back from the Grave: Recurring Controversies over Defining and Diagnosing Death in History," in *Death: Beyond Whole-Brain Criteria*, ed. Richard M. Zaner (Dordrecht and Boston: Kluwer, 1988), p. 57. For details on the controversy, see Renée C. Fox and Judith P. Swazey, *The Courage to Fail: A Social View of Organ Transplants and Dialysis* (Chicago: University of Chicago Press, 1978), especially pp. 78ff.

17. Courtney S. Campbell, "Fundamentals of Life and Death: Christian Fundamentalism and Medical Science," in *Definition of Death: Contemporary Controversies*, ed. Stuart J. Youngner, Robert M. Arnold, and Renie Schapiro (Baltimore and London: Johns Hopkins University Press, 1999), pp. 194–209, quotation p. 199. I am grateful to Professor Youngner for directing me to Cambell's essay.

18. David F. Nobel, *The Religion of Technology: The Divinity of Man and the Spirit of Invention* (New York: Penguin, 1999), pp. 194–200.

19. Joseph Fletcher, "Our Shameful Waste of Human Tissue: An Ethical Problem for the Living and the Dead," in *Updating Life and Death*, ed. Donald R. Cutler (Boston: Beacon, 1969), pp. 1–30.

20. Joseph Fletcher, *Situational Ethics: The New Morality* (Louisville: Westminster John Knox Press, 1966), p. 104.

21. Ibid.

22. Ibid., p. 109.

23. Ibid., p. 95. Again on p. 115: "Our situation ethic frankly joins forces with Mill; no rivalry here. We chose what is most 'useful' for the most people."

24. Ibid, p. 95.

25. Ruth Richardson and Brian Hurswitz, "Jeremy Bentham's Self-Image: An Exemplary Bequest for Dissection," *British Medical Journal*, 295, 1987, p. 196.

26. Ibid., p. 196.

27. See, for instance, Kaji Nobuyuki, *Chinmoku no shûkyô: Jukyô* (Silent religion: Confucianism) (Tokyo: Chikuma Raiburarî, 1994), especially pp. 218ff. The author, a scholar, is also a Buddhist priest.

28. Imai Jun, "*Ai to nihonjin*" (Love and the Japanese) in *Nihon shisôshi kôza: Nihonjinron* (Lectures on Japanese intellectual history: theories of Japanese-ness), ed. Furukawa Tesshi and Ishida Ichirô (Tokyo: Yûzankaku, 1983), p. 25.

29. Ibid., p. 115.

30. Paul Ramsey, *The Patient as Person: Explorations in Medical Ethics* (New Haven: Yale University Press, 1970), pp. 208–209.

*Plate 14* In this mural from a village temple in Gujarat, India, a devotee comes to the great god Shiva with Indra, the ancient supreme Vedic god, on the right. Indra makes the sign of *abhaya* (protection and reassurance) as he rides the royal elephant. The waters of the sacred Ganges spring from Shiva's hair as he holds the trident, symbol of his threefold role as creator, protector, and destroyer, and the drum, symbol of the originating sound of the universe, *om*. He, too, makes the sign of *abhaya*. Photo: *Nancy M. Martin*

# 14

## DOGGED LOYALTIES: A CLASSICAL INDIAN INTERVENTION *in* CARE ETHICS

*Vrinda Dalmiya*

### A CROSS-CULTURAL RETHINKING OF ETHICAL CARE

The ethic of care as it appears in Western discourse is coded as a "feminine" ethics. Whether or not this involves the essentializing move of casting *all* women as caring, historically the moral voice of care in the West has emerged in and through activities and experiences of *women* in traditional society. It can be traced to the research of developmental psychologist, Carol Gilligan, who discerned a unique style of moral decision making in her female subjects struggling with real life moral dilemmas.[1] According to Gilligan, their "different voice" of care and responsibility stemmed from a construction of self-identity that was grounded in interrelations rather than the "autonomous" self of the Kantian tradition. Many commentators have lauded this as a significant intervention in dominant ethical theorizing based on the reality of women's lives and experiences.

The move to considering the perspective of care as a *feminist* motif, however, has proven much more problematic.[2] It is feared that caring may be too closely bound to oppressive constructions of femininity to effectively challenge traditional stereotypes of women – which, after all, is the feminist agenda. My chapter speaks to this ambivalence toward a feminist care ethics in the West but does so by retrieving a notion of ethical caring found in the East – more specifically, in two stories from the *Mahabharata*.[3] The methodological point here is that unless the key concept of "care" is itself restructured, any liberatory ethic based on it is bound to fail. Locating ethical care in a completely different cultural context as in the *Mahabharata* may help us negotiate such a re-evaluation.

Interestingly, the protagonists of ethical caring in the stories that I use are *not* women: in one, it is a parrot and, in the other, no less than the male warrior Yudhishthira. The self-styled *opponent* to the voice of care in both stories is the god Indra. Thus, the fault lines between an ethic of care and a "traditional" ethic fall not between females and males but between the human realm on the one hand and an ideal divine sphere on the other. Caring is not gender coded here but cast as a fundamental aspect of social and inter-species relationships. With that, let us turn to the two narratives.

The first occurs in the *Anushasana Parva* of the *Mahabharata* when Yudhishthira asks the dying Bhishma to explain the meaning of cruelty.[4] The answer comes in the form of a parable. A poisonous arrow got lodged in a huge tree owing to the inaccurate aim of a careless hunter. As the poison spread, the tree began to wilt, gradually shedding its leaves and fruit. One parrot living in a hollow of that tree did not fly off and take refuge in the other flourishing trees of the forest. It stayed on, shriveling away along with its host, becoming gradually emaciated and songless. Indra, intrigued by this bizarre behavior, appeared disguised as a *brahman* and lectured the parrot on the virtues of instrumental rationality. "Aren't you being utterly stupid?" he asked. "Look at the greener foliage elsewhere that can protect you from the scorching sun; notice the ripe fruit on other trees that can appease your hunger. Go somewhere else so that you can live in happiness." The parrot replied,

> I was born in this tree and have lived here all my life. This tree has camouflaged me from hunters and has nourished me with its fruit. I cannot leave it now. It is cruel not to be sympathetic to those who are loyal [*bhakta*]. Why are you trying to weaken my bond with the tree [*anukrosha*] by sympathizing with me?

The end of the story holds no surprises. Pleased by the moral excellence of the parrot, Indra granted eternal life to the tree, and the parrot did live happily after all.

The second episode is much more familiar and occurs in the *Mahaprasthanika Parva*[5] at the very end of the *Mahabharata* when

Yudhishthira and his brothers leave for the "final journey" to heaven. The other Pandavas gradually got eliminated along the way, and Yudhishthira trudged along alone, followed only by the stray dog that had attached itself to the group. Indra appeared in his chariot with much bugle-blowing fanfare (clearly without a disguise this time) to escort Yudhishthira to heaven. Yudhishthira was ready but wanted to bring the dog along with him. Indra recoiled in horror. Remember that dogs are pollutants in traditional Indian society and Indra was headed toward heaven, the purest of all places. Dogs just did not belong there. He pleaded with Yudhishthira:

> O King! You have won immortality and a status equal to mine; all the felicities of Heaven are yours today. Do cast off this dog. In this there will be no cruelty.

Yudhishthira remained unswayed. They had reached the end of the world. He saw in the helpless gaze of the dog, trembling in the stark, desolate surroundings, an appeal not be abandoned. Filled with compassion (*anukrosha*), Yudhishthira, was not able to disregard this silent cry for the sake of his own happiness. Dismayed by this unexpected obstacle to his mission, Indra lost his temper and railed:

> Not only is this concern for a dog not required of you as a paragon of justice, but it seems that you, who have been able to renounce everything – the love of kingdom, the love of a wife and brothers – have morally stumbled at this last moment and become ensnared and blinded by the irrational love [*moha*] for a dog!

Refusing to be shamed, Yudhishthira retorted,

> O Indra, I think the sin of abandoning one who is loyal [*bhakta*] is greater than many other sins put together. I cannot leave the dog behind.

Of course, there is a happy ending even to this apparent impasse. Yudhishthira did not lose the glories of heaven. The dog revealed himself as *dharma* in disguise and explained the entire incident as a final test of moral worth – a test that Yudhishthira passed yet again, with flying colors, because of his "intelligence and compassion [*anukrosha*] for all creatures."

## *ANUKROSHA*: A "DIFFERENT VOICE" IN THE *MAHABHARATA*

The tropes of (1) contextuality, (2) emotionality, and (3) a non-contractual interrelational selfhood are clear in these stories, and consequently

I construe them as echoes of the "different voice" that Gilligan discovered through her female subjects. Both the parrot and Yudhishthira appeal to the peculiarities of their circumstances in order to resist the course of action that Indra rationally computes for them like a math problem, using the received system of moral principles.[6] Indra is very much like Gilligan's male subject, Jake. He quickly constructs the parrot's and Yudhishthira's situations as a dilemma involving conflicting principles – one's own life versus loyalty (in the parrot's case) and a right to enjoy one's moral deserts versus loyalty (in Yudhishthira's case). Having done this, he orders the principles in a rational hierarchy (where loyalty is deprioritized), and thus there is no question in his mind as to which principle should guide action.

Now it may be contended that the resistance of our protagonists signifies a simple quarrel about *which* principle should be regarded as universally valid – arguing (against Indra) for the superiority of the maxim "Do not abandon the loyal" rather than for a rejection of principled morality *per se*. Given the number of times betrayal is actually condoned in the *Mahabharata*, this is hard to concede, but is there anything in the stories themselves to block such an interpretation? The point is important because it highlights the drawback in conceiving of care ethics as entailing a complete rejection of rules and principles. Our stories indicate that principles work in a very different way in a care perspective rather than being absent altogether.

Loyalty *emerges* as having categorical force for Yudhishthira when he looks at the trembling dog and is filled with *compassion* for it. For the parrot this happens because it has constructed a historical narrative – "I was born in this tree, I have always lived here, this tree has nurtured me," etc. – through which it comes to *experience* itself as connected with the tree. Both these experiential grounds for their decision are called *anukrosha* or "crying after" – a concept we shall return to later. The relationships between the parrot and the tree and between Yudhishthira and the dog thus acquire a moral tone only when they are *experienced* in a particular way. The very identification of someone as "loyal" and hence requiring moral reciprocation is dependent not on objective relations between the parties concerned but on whether they happen to evoke a kind of emotional response.

Indra, even though cognitively aware of the connections (between the parrot and the tree and between Yudhishthira and the dog), did not construe their situations as involving "betrayal of the loyal" because these facts failed to move him emotionally. He stresses the *absence of cruelty* (in abandoning the tree and the dog) and not the ethicality of betrayal. Thus, if and when loyalty emerges as a moral principle, it is because of an immersion in a certain kind of experience. Indra clearly derides this as *moha* – a befuddled state of mind. Since there can be no universalizable conditions for evoking such feelings, we have here a built-in contextualization.

Just as experience of relationality is not rule bound, the relationality itself is also not contractual. The parrot *was born* in that particular tree and *found* itself in a context that it did not actively choose. Yudhishthira, too, did not ask or maybe even want the dog to tag along with him, but it so *happened* that they were together. The parrot and Yudhishthira structure their own existential dilemmas as a struggle to maintain a web of relations that they had not entered into voluntarily. Since their articulation of this struggle is in moral terms – not to speak of the fact that their victory is ultimately lauded as an ethical victory – we find here the moral voice of Gilligan's female subject, Amy.

## TWO PROBLEMS

Now these Indian samples of the care perspective seem only to deepen the problems that feminists have with care. I shall deal here with what I consider to be two of their most central objections.

The first objection is that caring roles are the *cause* of oppression of women rather than a means to their liberation. In the parrot we may see the many women who, driven by loyalty, cannot extricate themselves from abusive relationships. Yudhishthira reminds us of wives and mothers who give up all their ambitions to satisfy the needs of their loved ones. Of course, both our care givers are ultimately rewarded by divine intervention. But this promise of an otherworldly recognition could well be a ruse to keep the worldly *status quo* intact. The worry here is logical. The care perspective emphasizes embeddedness of selves in social networks. But these networks may constitute the very power structures responsible for exploitation. Thus, without the notion of an autonomous selfhood – of a self that can take control of her life from a space outside social relations – there can be no emancipation. An ethic of care, in prioritizing relationships, works against autonomy and hence against freedom.

According to the second more Kantian worry, interpersonal caring is deemed too arbitrary and restricted to ground a *public* morality. What if, like Indra, we just do not feel any compassion when we encounter wilting trees, frightened dogs, or even people who look different from us? Can we realistically found an ethic on so variable a foundation as the experience of connectedness? *Anukrosha* may be sufficient to regulate dealings with those with whom we come in face-to-face contact but leaves those in the wider public domain outside the sphere of moral considerability.[7] The problem here is psychological: given the very real limits on our ability to care, an ethic of care is bound to be limited to the domestic realm, with nothing to contribute to a public morality.

I attempt a solution to both these problems by looking at how the concept of *anukrosha* works in our two narratives. Thus my hypothesis is that juxtaposing "care" with *anukrosha* could help us toward a more robust ethic of care after all.

## ANUKROSHA, SELFLESSNESS, AND AUTONOMY

What exactly is *anukrosha*? Etymologically the word means a crying out that "follows" (*anu*) someone else's "cry" (*krosha*). The translations of "sympathy," "compassion," or even "empathy" suggest a re-enacting or mimicking of another's mental state. However, Yudhishthira would not be much of a moral agent if he ended up feeling as scared as the dog and nothing else besides. Though accepting the importance of apprehending or even feeling the reality of others, we need a distancing so as to determine their "good." It should be remembered that what a person feels and wants is often quite contrary to what is good for him or her. Simply reverberating the feelings of the other is at best only the beginnings of *anukrosha* as an ethical stance.

Care ethicists have pointed out that genuine care must extend beyond the realm of feeling, into *action*.[8] "Caring for" in the sense of sympathizing with people must be intertwined with a "*taking* care" or an active engagement with bringing about their good. But the dynamic of the stories we have looked at suggests an extension of care along another dimension, that is, into the realm of *critical inquiry*. Remember that Indra applauds Yudhishthira for his "*intelligence* and compassion."

*Anukrosha* appears to be as much an affair of the head as of the heart. It is lauded as a moral excellence only *after* the dialogue with Indra, when it is made quite clear that the parrot and Yudhishthira are going against traditional expectations but they decide to do so nevertheless. Through that exchange, then, spontaneous compassion or an upsurge of feeling is transformed into a self-consciously and critically adopted stance. Now this extension of *anukrosha* into critical self-reflection is not as *ad hoc* as it might seem to be. After all, the primary connotation of *anukrosha* is to step outside ourselves and "take on the point of view of others" – to feel, for example, the dog's fear when we are not afraid ourselves. Universalizing this core attitude of adopting perspectives other than our own in any given situation would require considering our *caring attitude* itself from alternative perspectives. It would mean seriously entertaining criticisms that our initial care is *in*appropriate, is foolish or in bad faith. Thus care, as the injunction to step out of ourselves and into the worlds of others, yields the self-reflexive move of "*caring* about care" or entertaining critical points of view on our caring.[9] This is possible only in an atmosphere where others are willing and allowed to engage us in debate.

My argument here is that this dimension of *anukrosha* suggests a rethinking of the notion of autonomy. Autonomy is important in feminist agendas as signifying the absence of coercion, which, in turn, is suggestive of self-control. For a decision to reflect the true self, actions must be uncoerced, but it is also important that they not be motivated by ignorance, bad faith, impulsive abandon, or simply blind social conditioning. Ethical *anukrosha* thus ensures the self-critical perspective that is the positive condition for genuine autonomous and authentic choice.[10]

However, the nagging worry remains that mere critical reflection on a relationship, particularly when this involves questioning implicit power structures, is ineffective in transforming it. *Maintaining* relationships even when they are problematized is the overriding message of the parrot and Yudhishthira (as of any care practitioner). Care autonomy, then, seems quite consistent with exploitation of the care-giver – the motif of Yudhishthira willing to give up a lifelong goal and, even more poignantly, the parrot ready to perish for a relationship.

Let us look at the starker situation of the parrot. *Is* the parrot really choosing to sacrifice its self-interest? True to the temper of care ethics, the parrot's narrative self-construction is one in which it is essentially a self-*in-relation-to-the-tree*. Thus, the exclusive disjunctions between itself and the tree, between egoism and altruism, break down. Prioritizing tree interests is not really a sacrifice of the self of the parrot because tree interests are made *part* of its own interests to begin with. However, a hard-hearted critic may maintain that such inclusivist reformulations of apparently conflicting interests are not always possible.

But even if we allow that on some level the interests of the tree are radically irreconcilable with the interests of the parrot, is the parrot's construction of a relational selfhood necessarily *forgetful* of these parrot interests that are different from tree interests? Note its final plea to Indra: "Why are you trying to weaken my bond with the tree [*anukrosha*] under the guise of *sympathizing with me*?" What this seems to indicate is a genuine struggle: here the parrot is not only aware of but actually feels the motivational pull of an alternative identity – an identity constructed by Indra in which the parrot is constructed as being *independent* of the tree. We have here not someone who cannot imagine a different life for itself but one who struggles to remain loyal to a choice (of identity-in-relation) in spite of being aware of alternatives and having the choice to embrace them.

Thus, one way of looking at the situation is to see the parrot as underscoring for us the deep pathos of genuine moral dilemmas – the reality of "moral remainders" that refuse to erase unchosen alternatives. Although the essence of morality is "not hurting," there is an honest recognition that "no matter what, someone will get hurt." Moral maturity in the care perspective is a three-step process.[11] Beginning with an instinctive preoccupation with our self interests, we move to a total absorption in the interests of the other and then, finally, to a realization that self interests are as important. Ethical excellence consists in trying to balance the two and respond with *honesty* while taking full *responsibility* for the inevitable pain that is caused by any choice.

Western feminists have been absorbed with justifying the ethicality of decisions in which the choice involves having to hurt *others*. Gilligan's female subjects in her "abortion decision study" mostly struggle with justifying an option that they fear will be characterized as "selfish" by society; "taking control" is articulated by them as their decision to go ahead in spite of the possible social condemnation. But should we balk at claiming ethicality for a decision that, at this third stage, assumes the responsibility to hurt *oneself* instead (everything else being equal)? This would follow only if situations where it is inevitable that *someone* will be hurt are automatically construed as situations where it is inevitable to *protect oneself* – which reverts back to an atomistic selfhood and universalism that care ethics has been committed to negating all along.

What is problematic from a feminist point of view is the assumption that there is a *special merit* in the parrot's choice – a choice that aligns itself to interests of the others at Gilligan's third stage of moral development. It may even be argued that if a godlike figure in a traditional story endorses a parrot-like behavior, it amounts to establishing that behavior as being worthy of emulation. But is it the actual choice being lauded or the *deliberative practice* leading to that choice? A patriarchal society would need to glorify the actual ("altruistic" or other-regarding) choice of the parrot for its own ends – but there is nothing within care ethics itself to suggest this. In fact, open-endedness and contingency of ethical choice are emphasized by both traditions: Yudhishthira's gloss of the ethical way is: "Wise men disagree, traditions conflict, the real nature of *dharma* is hidden in the cave."[12] Gilligan's Amy seems to echo this in commenting,

> If both the roads went in totally separate ways, if you pick one, you'll never know what would happen if you went the other way – that's the chance you have to take, and like I said, it's just really a guess.[13]

Yet, it is noteworthy that the *Mahabharata* characters choose what is traditionally regarded as "selflessness," whereas Gilligan's subjects argue overwhelmingly for what is usually called "selfishness." An explanation for these widely different conclusions yielded by a care methodology might be that moral authenticity is particularly threatened in different ways in the two traditions. Gilligan and her subjects work in a milieu shaped by an individualism about human nature and a conventional morality that attempts to secure an other-directedness in spite of this. Practitioners of care ethics here have to be overly careful to establish the *ethicality* of "selfishness" that not only goes against conventional morality but is consistent with what a human being is supposed to be "naturally." Establishing the *autonomy* of an apparently "selfish" choice is important because, given the received ontology of human nature, it is easy *not* to see it as such and to regard the decision as being merely reflexive.

Classical India, on the other hand, worked with a more communitarian idea of human nature with conventional morality consisting of rigid shastric injunctions of *svadharma* to ensure self-fulfillment within the matrix of a social good. Indra's admonitions are aimed to make the two ethical agents see their "own good" as following from the structures and principles already in place. In this atmosphere, the parrot and Yudhishthira are hard pressed to show that their decisions of apparent self-sacrifice are *ethical* even though going against established rules. The *autonomy* of selflessness needs to be foregrounded in a culture where humans are regarded as "naturally" other-regarding. It is fascinating that Yudhishthira, who had passed one of the earlier moral tests (akin to Gilligan's second stage?) by defining the "moral path" as a convention – that which is "followed by great or great many people,"[14] takes a stand at the end of his life *against* the Greatest of Elders, Indra himself. In doing this, he achieves ultimate moral maturity and an ethical autonomy even though the choice appears to be very much like a traditional selflessness already in place.

Juxtaposing the ways care methodologies tend to work in the two traditions leads to an important development of the perspective of care itself. Care in any *one* tradition is the process of negotiating a moral dilemma and articulating a course of action that one can live with and can claim responsibility for. But this may lock us into a notion of ethical agency grounded in an undifferentiated and unitary subjectivity – in an integrity that is the yearning for a clear and central principle of self-construction. However, if the difference in care reasonings of Gilligan's subjects and the characters of the *Mahabharata* can be mapped onto a *single* subject as an *internal* tension, then we get not a simple value pluralism but a "decentering of subjectivity" itself. This alone, according to some contemporary feminists, can initiate the continued re-negotiation of the boundaries of the self which is necessary for hearing genuinely "different voices."[15] Can a woman, thus, eat her cake of self-flourishing as well as keep her faithful dog? Whether or not she can, as an authentic centerless subject, she must feel the pull of both.

## EXPANDING THE CIRCLE OF MORAL CONSIDERABILITY

Let us now turn to the second objection. If feelings of interconnection engendered by *anukrosha* are the basis of morality, then people and entities with whom we do not happen to feel interconnected would be left out of the ethical domain. Does not an ethic of care restrict the moral domain to the very genuine limits of our psychological feelings of care?

Once again, looking closely at the notion of *anukrosha* may help us out. Yudhishthira is clearly drawn to the dog by something akin to pity – seeing the dumb appeal in the dog's eyes, he is moved to respond. The parrot's *anukrosha* for the tree is not a direct response to a perceived *pain* (of the tree) but rather is a decision or commitment to stand by it because of a certain articulated causal history. The parrot feels *indebted* to the tree and Yudhishthira experiences something like what Cora Diamond has called "*fellow feeling.*"[16] Yet *both* the parrot and Yudhishthira construe their respective decisions as "standing by those who are *bhaktas* [those who have served]." However, notice that "loyalty" for Yudhishthira is doing what the dog wants him to do even though the dog has not favored him in any way. But it is unclear if the tree particularly wants the parrot to stay with it, though clearly the parrot has been served well by the tree in the past.

This, I think, creates an interesting possibility. The root idea of *anukrosha* common to the two cases implies (1) a sense of commitment that may or may not be grounded in feeling the pain of the other and (2) a notion of a *bhakta* or "someone who has served" as a person from whom one may or may not have directly benefited or contracted a gain. Thus, it seems possible to bring into the realm of moral considerability peoples and entities with whom I have no face-to-face contact or for whom I do not feel anything, those from whom I have not directly gained in any way and those who do not directly expect anything from me. The minimal sense of *anukrosha* is the parrot's commitment grounded in an indebtedness and an attempt to give back something that is not being asked for. This relationship, when interpreted as "care," has the resources for widening the sphere of ethics to all things – living and non-living – and is based on a shift in the motivational force of care from feelings of compassion to an acknowledgment of *indebtedness* that need not be paid back contractually.

The actual working out of this may be quite complicated and harks back to other motifs in the classical Indian tradition. The *Satpatha Brahmana* articulates an intriguing idea of "a debt to death" in this way:

> Man, so soon as he is born, is to be regarded, his whole person, as a debt owed to death. When he performs sacrifice, he is purchasing himself back from death.[17]

In simple terms, this means that the existence of anything is sustained by resources that have to be consumed and, hence, existence or life itself is constituted by contributions of "death." We are born with debts that we have not voluntarily contracted. Note that a congenital debt in this sense is also a debt to things I may never have encountered. Construing this natural dependence on resources as a "*debt* to death" introduces a form of life structured around an *acknowledgment* of dependence on all things – which acknowledgment we have identified as the heart of *anukrosha*. The relation between Yudhishthira and the dog and between the parrot and the tree is an inter-species commitment to the interrelationality of all things, which is thereby also indicative of the recognition-transcending width of the moral sphere.

Now, although recasting *anukrosha* through the meta-narrative of debt can extend the sphere of moral considerability, it may seem to do so at a price. Debt is a deontological notion, and the imperative to repay debts is a universal maxim. Have we not thereby defined *anukrosha* out of the realm of contextualized "care"? In fact Sarah, one of Gilligan's subjects in the abortion study who does not "feel good" about having a second abortion, reasons quite explicitly *against* any feelings of indebtedness in a way that situates "care" in direct opposition to indebtedness:

> I would not be doing myself or the child or the world any kind of favor having this child. *I don't need to pay off my imaginary debts to the world through this child*, and I don't think that it is right to bring a child into the world and use it for that purpose. (My emphasis)[18]

In order to argue for the compatibility of the debt idea and care, remember that the kind of indebtedness in the Indian texts does not demand repayment to any particular person/child in any particular way through a specific course of action. In fact, "repayment" of a congenital debt *cannot* be strictly reflexive. The particular entities that have made my existence possible may not be around for me to pay back or may be forever beyond my grasp. The intentional object of indebtedness is the group/collection of entities that have nurtured me – which in effect is the set of all that there is. Since debts ought to be repaid, I am expected to contribute to the existence of all kinds of things because they have contributed to mine. But it is impossible to repay everything and everyone – and the very process of "giving back" makes me incur even more such debts. Since I can never be debt free, a negotiation is opened up as *to which particular debts to which particular entities I can repay. How* I pay back a debt and *when* is decided by me through a context-sensitive balancing act.

What emerges is a richly textured and nuanced view of moral life. I am *forced* to take the moral claim of everything seriously – the dogs and the trees – but there are no fixed recipes given for action *vis-à-vis* any particular one of them. The debt deontology that introduces the universalist constraint requires finer grained contextualization in deciding the specific relations to specific others that could constitute a "paying back." And the notion of *anukrosha* is a layered notion involving both these dimensions. Non-cruelty is the heart of *dharma*. When someone is going to get hurt anyway, when all creditors cannot be repaid, virtuous people listen to the voice of tradition and the voice of self-interest and allow their "heart's outcry" to decide which hurt to avoid. A heart that hears all these intersecting voices and claims, acting intelligently without claiming to *know* the correct ethical way, exemplifies the *dharma* of caring. The parrot and Yudhishthira are moral exemplars just because they manage to do this.

## NOTES

I am grateful for comments from Arindam Chakrabarti and Jim Tiles on an earlier draft of this chapter.

1. Carol Gilligan, *In a Different Voice: Psychological Theory and Women's Development* (Cambridge, MA: Harvard University Press, 1982).
2. See for example, Sarah Lucia Hoagland, "Some Thoughts about 'Caring,'" in *Feminist Ethics*, ed., Claudia Card (Lawrence: University of Kansas Press, 1991).
3. The *Mahabharata*, one of the epics of India, is a complex text with stories within stories. The central tale, however, is about the Kuru clan and a great war fought between the Kauravas (led by Duryodhana) and the Pandavas (led by Yudhishthira). Yudhishthira, as the son of Dharma, exemplifies righteousness which is put to test on many occasions. The contrast between Yudhishthira's moral sense and the duties imposed on him by tradition is a recurrent theme in the *Mahabharata*. I have referred to the Sanskrit text of the critical edition of the *Mahabharata* edited by V.S. Sukthankar et al. (Poona: Bhandarkar Oriental Research Institute, 1944) and the translation by P.C. Roy (Calcutta: Oriental Publishing Company, undated). My renderings are not verbatim quotations or translations. Thanks to Arindam Chakrabarti for help with the Sanskrit.
4. *Mahabharata*, XIII/5.
5. *Mahabharata*, XVII/3.
6. Gilligan, *In a Different Voice*, p. 26.
7. This criticism has been developed in detail by (among others) Daryl Koehn, *Rethinking Feminist Ethics: Care, Trust and Empathy* (London: Routledge, 1998).
8. Such an extension is spoken of by both Nel Noddings, *Caring: A Feminine Approach to Ethics and Moral Education* (Berkeley: University of California

Press, 1984), and Joan Tronto, *Moral Boundaries: A Political Argument for an Ethic of Care* (New York: Routledge, 1993).

9. See the debate between Harry Frankfurt and Annette Baier on this. Harry Frankfurt, "The Importance of What We Care About," *Synthese*, 53, 1982, pp. 257–72; Annette Baier,"The Importance of What We Care About: A Reply to Frankfurt," *Synthese*, 53, 1982, pp. 273–290.

10. For a discussion of feminist versions of autonomy, see Grace Clement, *Care, Autonomy and Justice* (Boulder: Westview, 1996).

11. See Gilligan, *In a Different Voice*, chapter 3.

12. *Mahabarata*, III / Appendix 1, p. 1089.

13. Gilligan, *In a Different Voice*, p. 32.

14. *Mahabarata*, III / Appendix 1, p. 1089.

15. See Bonnie Honig, "Difference, Dilemmas, and the Politics of Home," in *Social Research*, 61, 1994, pp. 563–597.

16. Cora Diamond, "Eating Meat, Eating People," in Diamond, *The Realistic Spirit: Wittgenstein, Philosophy, and the Mind* (Cambridge: Bradford / MIT Press, 1996), pp. 319–334.

17. *Satpatha Brahmana* III, 6, 2, 16. See Raimundo Panikkar, ed. and trans., *The Vedic Experience: Mantramanjari – An Anthology of the Vedas for Modern Man and Contemporary Celebration* (Delhi: Motilal Banarsidass, 1977), p. 393.

18. Gilligan, *In a Different Voice*, p. 92.

*Part V*

# GLOBAL VIEWS OF
# RELIGIOUS ETHICS

*Plate 15* Mother Teresa of Calcutta distributing medallions of Mary to children in Tihuana, Mexico in 1989. Today more than five hundred houses of the Order of the Missionaries of Charity, which Mother Teresa founded in 1948 in India, care for the blind, the aged, the dying, and the lepers in the poorest sections of cities worldwide. Photo: *Valerie Reed and N. Prasad*

# 15

# CHRISTIAN SOCIAL ETHICS *in* A *global* CONTEXT

*Brian Hebblethwaite*

Five questions set the agenda for this chapter. Does Christianity as such contain a social ethic? What, if anything, is distinctive or indeed unique about Christian social ethics? Is there some basic common ground between Christian social ethics and the social ethics of other religions? Is this common ground shared by secular social ethics? And, if so, what, if anything, is the importance of the religious or the Christian dimension, context, or motivation for social ethics today worldwide?

## DOES CHRISTIANITY CONTAIN A SOCIAL ETHIC?

I should say, first, what I mean by "social ethics" in this connection. I do not mean any and every way in which human beings relate to one another. I restrict the term to the structural and institutional ways in which our common life is ordered, that is to say, to the political and economic aspects of what Ernst Troeltsch wrote about in his great work, *The Social Teaching of the Christian Churches.*[1] Hence the importance of my first question. Everyone knows that Christianity has much to say about the virtues, about interpersonal relations, about the family, and about the fellowship of Christians. But is it also, essentially, concerned with the economic order and with the structures of political life? Troeltsch himself was skeptical about this. In a late essay, translated as "The Social Philosophy of

Christianity" (1922), Troeltsch declared that "Christianity has a social philosophy that was derived, for the most part, from the social philosophy of late antiquity, and that has been continually modified. But it has no social theology, that is, no social theory springing directly from its religious idea, either directly as dogma or indirectly as logical consequence."[2]

That may strike us as a pretty implausible remark. What about the Christian socialism of F.D. Maurice, Charles Kingsley, and J.M. Ludlow in mid nineteenth-century England? Was that not an attempt to apply the Christian gospel to the condition of the working class in 1848 and to create a Christian alternative to revolution? What about the social gospel of Walter Rauschenbusch and his colleagues in America in the later part of the nineteenth century? Was that not an attempt to realize, at least in part, the kingdom of God on earth and to implement Christian teaching about the "brotherhood of man" in the world of business and politics? What about the more radical teaching of the religious socialists in Switzerland and Germany around 1900, who influenced the young Karl Barth to the point of proclaiming that socialism was a predicate of the gospel?

Well, Troeltsch was extremely scathing about the phenomenon of Christian socialism. "The transmutation of workers' socialism," he wrote,

> "into a Christian socialism and its new promise of the salvation of the world and of the establishment of the Kingdom of God is a fantastic, dilettante notion, in comparison with which the old Christian natural law is the very quintessence of wisdom. The great problem of socialism, that is inescapable for our generation, namely, the control of unrestrained individual and national freedom and the creation of a universal planned economy for the civilized nations, simply cannot be solved by religious ideas. The problem is, rather, a scientific and a practical-political one that only the deepest professional knowledge and superior political leadership can resolve."[3]

There appear to be two main reasons behind Troeltsch's position in this essay. One is his conviction that Christianity is primarily a religion of redemption, centered on the forgiveness of sin and growth in personal holiness. From this, he allows, proceed communal forms that "rest on the principle of a mature, free, conscious decision by the adult individual, on the conscious union of those intent upon the service of God." As is well known, Troeltsch sees these communal forms as taking sometimes a church form, sometimes a sect form. Any wider, more universal social ethic is, according to Troeltsch, either taken over from the social philosophy of late antiquity, like the natural law idea, which he ironically dubbed the "quintessence of wisdom," or constitutes a "fantastic, dilettante notion," like so-called Christian socialism.

And yet the final paragraph of Troeltsch's essay seems to put a question mark against all that has gone before. "It remains true," he says, "that such immense problems" – the practical-political ones just reserved for the professionals – "are not to be solved without moral renewal and deepening, without kindness and justice, without a sense of solidarity and a readiness for sacrifice, without a basically believing outlook on life and the world." "This task," he avers, "had best be kept separate from the first" – the practical politics – "and pursued with the aid of the available religious and ethical resources of the various denominations, groups, philosophies, and worldviews that are being driven to rapprochement by conditions themselves" – an interesting throw-away line to which we shall return. A little later he goes on, "Self-restraint, consideration for others, a feeling for the solidarity of nations, and respect for human rights, must be inculcated in people's minds, and the spirit of obligation to a more-than-human truth and justice must be aroused. That is task enough in itself, without any need for religion to embroil itself in dilettante social philosophy or amateur social ethics. The spirit it can thus awaken will then on its own redound to the benefit of social and political reconstruction, which in turn will have more and more occasion to call for such a spirit."[4]

I think we are bound to question Troeltsch's sharp disjunction between these two tasks – the practical-political task on the one hand and the (apparently) religious task of infusing society with all these values. Surely values such as justice, solidarity, consideration for others, self-restraint, a readiness for sacrifice, and respect for human rights have socio-political implications and consequences if taken seriously; and surely these values are inseparable from what Troeltsch earlier referred to as "the conscious union of those intent upon the service of God." It would be interesting to have been able to press Troeltsch on just this question of how Christianity as a religion of redemption is related to the values – undeniably social values – that he lists at the end of the essay. Clearly he does not think these values to be the exclusive prerogative of Christians – he speaks of the ethical resources of a variety of groups and worldviews. But he does seem to think them to be bound up with "a believing outlook on life and the world." All the same, one might suppose that just such values are implicit in Christianity as a religion of redemption. Redemption, it might be urged, is not just a matter of the redemption of individuals but holds out hope for the redemption of society and the sanctification of the world. I shall return to this theme later.

Troeltsch may have reason to dismiss Christian socialism as a fantastic dilettante notion – though there are plenty of Christian ethicists who would still think otherwise – but in any case Christian socialism is not the only way in which Christian ethics has tried to deduce socio-political implications from the Christian gospel and from fundamental Christian doctrines. Consider the case of the Christian Social Union in England, founded in 1889 by Charles Gore and Henry Scott Holland, precisely in order to apply the religion of the Incarnation to the social, economic, and political problems of the day. The attempt, characteristic of Anglicanism ever since, to derive a social ethic from the doctrine of the Incarnation would be a strong counter-instance to Troeltsch's insistence that "Christianity has no social theory springing directly from its religious idea, either directly as dogma or indirectly as logical consequence." Members of the Christian Social Union did, of course, tend to speak of themselves as Christian socialists but in a much looser sense than their nineteenth-century predecessors who had incurred such scorn from Troeltsch.

The same is true of William Temple, who in his 1942 book *Christianity and Social Order* appealed to both natural law and Incarnation in insisting on the church's right to interfere in politics, where sin has distorted the structures that shape human lives.[5] In connection with these basic elements of Christianity, Temple singles out the principles of God's purpose of love, the dignity of humans made in God's image, and the destiny of humans in God's creative intention. In light of these principles, Temple moves on to set out certain broad objectives that should shape policy making – a secure family, educational opportunity, a fair wage, participation in the common good, sufficient leisure, and liberty of worship, speech, and association. These are examples of what were called in contemporary ecumenical ethics "middle axioms" – midway between general principles and specific policies. In an appendix, Temple does declare what particular policies he personally would endorse, and they turn out to be more or less those of the Labour Party; but it is interesting to note that, in a foreword to the 1976 re-issue of Temple's book, Edward Heath, the former Conservative prime minister, though praising Temple's overall approach, observes that he "too readily accepted that his objectives could only be achieved through the Labour Party rather than by setting out to galvanize sympathizers into action in their own parties wherever they could be found in the body politic."[6]

Consider also the dominant figure of Reinhold Niebuhr, whose criticism of the social gospel for its naïveté and utopianism led him to develop a more sophisticated and nuanced approach to social ethics, which became known as Christian realism, and which nevertheless represented an attempt to bring to bear the love ethic of the gospel upon political and economic life as a source of both criticism and inspiration. Increasingly this led Niebuhr to endorse the principles of democracy, with its checks and balances, as well as those of social justice. Later in this chapter, we shall consider criticisms of Niebuhr for accommodation with secular liberalism and with Stoic ethics – criticisms reminiscent of Troeltsch's disavowal of the specifically Christian inspiration of the church's social philosophy. But in his own terms, Niebuhr's Christian social ethics is firmly based on the love commandment of the gospel and its application in a sinful world.

Troeltsch's dismissal of specifically Christian theological grounding of general social ethics may further be countered by reference to the Lutheran tradition of the orders of creation and the Anglican development not only of incarnational but of sacramental and Trinitarian theological inspiration for social-ethical commitment.[7] In the Lutheran tradition we have Emil Brunner's exposition of the *orders* of creation, Dietrich Bonhoeffer's articulation of the *mandates* through which the claims of Christ on all humankind are mediated, and Hans Dombois' and Ernst Wolf's emphasis on the *institutions* that provide the context for faithful obedience to God's command. All these positions are open to criticism from a theological perspective. Wolfhart Pannenberg, for example, questions the ahistorical nature of talk of orders, mandates, and institutions and invites us to develop, instead, an eschatological ethic, involving a vision of the coming kingdom of God which inspires continuing social reform.[8] But this too is a thoroughly theological social ethic.

Two further names may be mentioned here – in the first place, that of the mature Karl Barth, who may have moved beyond his earlier Christian socialism but who was still, at the end of his life, drawing out the social ethical content of the command of God the reconciler. The very last part of the unfinished *Church Dogmatics* contains an exposition of the Lord's Prayer's, "Thy kingdom come," under the heading "*fiat justitia*."[9]

In the second place, there is the Dutch systematician Hendrikus Berkhof, who, in his book *Christian Faith*, applies the Reformation principles of justification and sanctification beyond their primary reference to the redemption of individuals (as stressed by Troeltsch) to the renewal of the world.[10] He speaks of the sanctification of the world by analogy with the sanctification of the individual. This takes place where *structures* are transformed in such a way as to allow for the readier transmission of God's holy love. Berkhof is bold enough to claim that some such penetration of the world by the Spirit is discernable in the movements for democracy and social justice that have come from the Christian West.

It is in this connection that contemporary reflection on the theological grounding of human rights and of "the structures of responsible life" – to use Bonhoeffer's highly influential phrase – may be thought to reinforce the view that – *pace* Troeltsch – Christianity does indeed have a social theology. I find this judgment confirmed by study of the social teaching both of the Roman Catholic Church and of the World Council of Churches.

The papal encyclicals, from *Rerum Novarum* in 1891 to *Centesimus Annus* in 1991, and especially Vatican II's 1965 Pastoral Constitution on "The Church in the Modern World" (*Gaudium et Spes*), constitute a very solid body of social teaching on work, rights, duties, co-operation, state intervention, economic development, workers' participation, the removal of structural sin, justice, peace, and ecological concern – teaching explicitly derived from basic Christian theological principles such as natural law, God's design in creation, human dignity, sociality, and the common good. Increasingly, the ethics of the gospel are stressed more than natural law, but it must be remembered – against Troeltsch – that, in the context of Catholic social teaching, natural law is a thoroughly Christian theological notion. As expounded by St. Thomas Aquinas, natural law is written into the created order and reflects the eternal law of God.

It is interesting that, in a recent British statement of Catholic social teaching – the 1996 statement by the Catholic Bishops' Conference of England and Wales, entitled *The Common Good and the Catholic Church's Social Teaching* – although the natural law tradition is not rejected, we get a much more Christ-centered and person-centered approach, deriving "ways of structuring society which facilitate true human development and correspond to moral principles and demands" specifically from the dignity of the human person in the light of the gospel. The common good, it is declared, cannot exist without human rights, solidarity, subsidiarity (much could be said about that), and the preferential option of the poor. These are described as "the basic building blocks of Catholic social teaching."[11]

Roman Catholic social teaching has, of course, been radicalized in Latin American liberation theology with the help of what Troeltsch would certainly have regarded as the alien importation of Marxist theory. But in writers such as Gustavo Gutierrez this is constantly subject to theological control; and, in any case, Marxism itself can be regarded as in large part a secular product of the Christian centuries.

Turning to the World Council of Churches, we note that social ethics has been one of the chief concerns of the ecumenical movement from its pre-war "Life and Work" days, through the early General Assemblies of the World Council itself, when the emphasis was on "The Responsible Society," up to the more radical Assemblies of later decades under the themes "A Just, Participatory and Sustainable Society" and, latterly, "Justice, Peace and the Integrity of Creation." The theology governing these orientations has, in the opinion of many, grown weaker over the decades.[12] But certainly in the immediate post-war period fine work was done for the World Council by Christian ethicists such as John C. Bennett, Heinz-Dietrich Wendland, and Roger Mehl.

Bennett was one of the World Council's chief exponents of the theory of "the responsible society." He argued that both natural law and the Christian love ethic point in the direction of a democratic state with a mixed economy, involving both private enterprise and state intervention to ensure welfare. His response to the criticism that this was not a realistic goal for rapidly changing nations in the Third World is interesting: "The experience of nations in which there has been a continuous development of institutions of political participation of all the people and of institutions which protect the rights of persons surely has meaning for the political goals of the rapidly changing societies."[13] Wendland's conviction of the need for continuing reform of social institutions is derived from his theology of the Lordship of Christ, although it also has a natural law foundation. This latter was, of course, denied by Barthians such as Roger Mehl, who nevertheless defended the idea of the responsible society as a parable or analogy of the order of love which is the law of the kingdom of God.

The idea of middle axioms, indicating policy directions without necessarily specifying particular policies was much in vogue at this time and is still defended by Ronald Preston today. It is attacked by the Scottish ethicist, Duncan Forrester, on the grounds that Christian social ethics cannot be restricted to what is acceptable to most rational people of goodwill.[14] On such a view there would be no place for Christian prophecy on specific issues. Preston admits that there are indeed boundary situations that call for prophecy, not consensus, but much of the time the method of seeking middle axioms is a good one.[15] In any case the middle axiom method is not primarily directed at consensus. It derives policy guidelines from Christian principles and then looks for points of contact and comparable commitments wherever it can find them.

In the face of all this evidence, it would, I think, be hard to deny that Christianity contains a social ethic, springing directly from its religious ideas, disputed though those ideas and their application may be.

## WHAT, IF ANYTHING, IS DISTINCTIVE OR INDEED UNIQUE ABOUT CHRISTIAN ETHICS?

A social ethic based on the principles of natural law, the orders of creation, the divine image, human dignity, or even the love commandment is hardly going to be the private property of Christians, though the last of these – the love commandment – may indeed contain a special, sharpened sense of what love means in the context of the story of Christ and his cross. But even when a social ethic is derived from more exclusively Christian doctrines – from justification and sanctification, from the Lordship of Christ, from the religion of the Incarnation, from the sacramental principle, from the doctrine of the Trinity, or from specifically Christian eschatology – it does not follow that the principles, and middle axioms, derived have no points of contact or common features with ethical norms derived from other systems. The context may be different, the motivation may be different, the spiritual resources made available may be different, but the quest for social justice, with its concomitant rights and responsibilities, may still be shared.

Instead of pursuing this topic at the general level, I propose to look now at two contemporary writers who insist on the distinctiveness and incommensurability of Christian social ethics, namely Stanley Hauerwas and John Milbank, and then, in the next section, at one who is engaged in the project to secure consensus on a global ethic and agreed moral code for economics and politics worldwide, namely, Hans Küng.

Stanley Hauerwas has made a resolute attempt to bring out the distinctiveness of Christian ethics in a series of books stressing the way in which Christian character is formed and schooled in the specifically Christian community, the church. Living by the gospel and by the stories – biblical, historical, and contemporary – that shape this particular community, the church bears witness to a better way than can be found in the endemically violent world. For the church is the peaceable kingdom, or at least its anticipation. And for Hauerwas, as for John Howard Yoder, pacifism is of the essence of the Christian community, or should be.

From this position, Hauerwas mounts a sharp attack on the dominant post-war American tradition in social ethics from the Niebuhrs, through Paul Ramsey, to James Gustafson. This may be found in chapter 2 of Hauerwas's book *Against the Nations*, a chapter entitled "On Keeping Theological Ethics Theological."[16] He accuses Reinhold Niebuhr there of accommodation with liberalism and with specifically American values and of seeking "to develop social strategies which people of goodwill could adopt even though they differed religiously and morally." Niebuhr is alleged to have "continued liberal theology's presumption that theology must be grounded in anthropology" – a criticism that echoes Barth's critique of Schleiermacher. H. Richard Niebuhr, too, though remaining more overtly theological than his brother, is held by Hauerwas to have "continued the liberal project by demonstrating how it reflects as well as describes the human condition."

Paul Ramsey's Christian realism, according to Hauerwas, was another attempt to use Christian ethics "to sustain the moral resources of American society." Despite Ramsey's critique of consequentialism and his appeal to the just war tradition more as a means of control and restriction than of justification of war, Ramsey's rejection of pacifism in the name of realism is dismissed with scorn by Hauerwas as un-Christian. Again, Hauerwas questions James Gustafson's attempt to articulate Christian principles and values in terms that will be persuasive to non-religious people. For Gustafson, this approach is based on the belief that God's purposes are for the well-being of humans and creation; but for Hauerwas, this empties Christian ethics of anything specifically Christian and smacks, again, of accommodation to secular liberal values.

The more one considers this position, the less plausible it seems. Indeed at one point, Hauerwas produces a most palpable non-sequitur. Having accused Reinhold Niebuhr of grounding theology in anthropology, he continues, "Thus, his compelling portrayal of our sinfulness, which appeared *contra* liberal optimism, only continued the liberal attempt to demonstrate the intelligibility of theological language through its power to illuminate the human condition."[17] But, quite evidently, the power to illuminate the human condition is something totally different from grounding theology in anthropology. Niebuhr, no more than Schleiermacher, in fact turns theology into anthropology. Niebuhr's genuinely Christian realism derives from his theology, and it is this that illuminates the human condition. The fact that secular liberals could learn from Niebuhr without appreciating his theology does not make the theology redundant. For, as Gustafson makes clear, what actually promotes human well-being reflects God's will in creation whether that is recognized or not, and Christians should rejoice in the scope this gives for co-operative endeavor between those of any faith or none. It may well be that a liberal temper, a spirit of tolerance, a respect for human rights, and a sense of responsibility for the common good are all better understood in the framework of Christian theological ethics, but the very substance of that understanding leads us to expect points of contact, consensus on basic humane values, and a willingness to co-operate.

It is most unfair of Hauerwas to accuse the Niebuhrian tradition of attempting to provide theological endorsement of American values. Americans have no monopoly of concern for liberality, democracy, and human rights, as is clear from the pressures that made for their restitution in the countries of the former Soviet Union – with the churches playing a significant role in making that possible – as Pope John Paul II observes in his 1991 encyclical, *Centesimus Annus*. I have already drawn on Catholic social ethics and that of the earlier Assemblies of the World Council of Churches to counter Troeltsch's dismissive remarks about Christian social theology. The same points may be made against Hauerwas's exclusivism.

The charge of sectarianism leveled by Gustafson against Hauerwas is, admittedly, unfair. Hauerwas's defense against this charge in the introduction to his book *Christian Existence Today* makes clear his genuine concern for the wider world.[18] The church, like the people of Israel, is to be a light to the nations, not an inward-looking sect preserving itself from the wicked world. Hauerwas certainly hopes that the values of the peaceable kingdom manifested in the life of the Christian community will have some effect on the way the world's violence is tempered in spheres like the care of the mentally disabled or the welcoming of strangers. But it is difficult to see how, on Hauerwas's view, the church can have anything to say, theologically speaking, about the ordering of society in general. It is all very well to declare that "the Church does not have a social ethic, it is a social ethic," but that does seem to entail the restriction of explicit social ethical concern to the Christian community itself, with at best some spin-off effect on certain spheres of wider social life. At worst, this communitarian concentration has the effect of denying points of contact with the ethics of other religions and with secular ethical concern.

A striking example of this is drawn to our attention by David Fergusson of the University of Aberdeen in an excellent recent book, *Community, Liberalism and Christian Ethics.*[19] He refers to an essay by Hauerwas on nuclear disarmament in *Against the Nations,* in which Hauerwas describes concern for survival as a basis for disarmament as "idolatrous." Fergusson comments, "to describe an argument against nuclear weapons based on concern for the future of life on this planet as 'idolatrous' is to depict secular arguments in the worst possible light. While not only unfair to much that is sane and decent outwith the church, this characterization of an alternative position renders allies as foes and hinders the process of making common cause."[20] That sums up the seriousness of my own objection to Hauerwas.

This objection is equally telling against the even more extreme position of John Milbank. In an essay reprinted in *The Word Made Strange* on "The Poverty of Niebuhrianism," Milbank mounts an increasingly sharp critique of Reinhold Niebuhr for simply taking over a Stoic natural law ethic and endorsing an individualistic liberalism more characteristic, again, of American society than of the Christian tradition.[21] It is not surprising, Milbank holds, that secular politicians influenced by Niebuhr tended to ignore Niebuhr's theology – his depiction of the effects of original sin and his appeal to the love ethic of the gospel – since his allegedly "realistic" analyses and remedies are already, in fact, of secular liberal inspiration.

This criticism of Niebuhr's so-called "Christian realism" is pressed home through the assertion that every alleged "realism" is a linguistic and cultural construct (including that of natural science) and a true Christian realism must see everything entirely in the light of Christ's cross and resurrection. "Either," writes Milbank, "the entire Christian narrative tells us how things really are, or it does not. If it does, we have no other access to how things truly are, nor any additional means of determining the question."[22] The sheer unrealism – indeed fantasy – of this rhetoric is manifest in what follows this last quotation. "It is of course," declares Milbank, "quite simply impossible to be a Christian and to suppose that death and suffering belong to God's original plan, or that the struggle of natural selection (which one doubts is even proven as a full account of evolution) is how creation as creation rather than thwarted creation genuinely comes about."[23]

My objection to this is not simply that it willfully dismisses any attempt by Christian theologians to rethink the doctrines of creation and fall in the light of modern science. Much more seriously, to say that to embrace an anti-realist position in respect of everything except the Christian "meta-narrative" is to absolve oneself from the responsibility of looking at and thinking carefully about the good aspects – indeed the Christian provenance – of Enlightenment liberalism and its stress on human rights. It is to ignore the Christian articulation, already mentioned, of natural law theory in the Thomistic tradition. It is to disparage any attempt to discern the law of God in creation and the work of God's Spirit in religion, culture, and morality worldwide. Moreover it is totally to ignore the difference between what Bonhoeffer referred to as matters of penultimate concern and matters of ultimate concern. The ethics of the eschatological kingdom of God can only be effective this side of eternity in gradual, partial, and approximate forms, and the structures of responsible life in present circumstances are not only a proper but an essential aspect of Christian social ethics. And where the ethics of other religions are concerned, it is not encouraging to discover that Milbank's disparagement of Hinduism in "The End of Dialogue"[24] is based largely on Nirad Chaydyri's readable but tendentious book *Hinduism*, which, as my colleague Julius Lipner pointed out in a review, is like relying on a book about Christianity by Bertrand Russell to learn about the Christian faith.

Let us consider a little more closely two issues that emerge from reflection on the exclusivist, communitarian theologies of Hauerwas and Milbank: the issue of liberalism and the issue of pacifism. The undiscriminating nature of wholesale condemnation of Enlightenment liberalism is clear. This was already a demerit in Barth's powerful indictment of nineteenth-century Protestant theology from Schleiermacher to Ritschl.[25] (At least Barth took those whom he was criticizing seriously and treated them with respect – and one has to allow that Hauerwas, if not Milbank, treats Reinhold Niebuhr with respect.) There are, of course, dark sides to Enlightenment liberalism – its excessive individualism, its excessive rationalism, its failure to insist on human responsibilities as well as human rights in respect of the common good, and, above all, its failure to cope with the rising tide of nationalism. (That is equally if not more true of communitarianism.) But the failure of the communitarians to do justice to the positive features of initiative and creativity, the fostering of democratic accountability, and, above all, the spirit of liberality and the humane values that lie behind so much social reform – from the abolition of slavery to the abolition of capital punishment – the failure of the communitarians to do justice to all this and to the possibilities of co-operation and consensus is evident. It is all very well for Milbank to cite Augustine's negative view of the earthly city; but Augustine was writing at the time of the fall of the Roman Empire – a totally different setting from that of the modern world, which is, in so many respects, a product of the Christian centuries.[26] And it was all very well for Barth to prophesy against National Socialism and the German Christians' connivance with its fatal allure. But to tar the whole world of modernity with that brush is equally unfair. Barth, as always, was greater than the logic of his exclusivism should allow. He went on to speak quite positively of "other lights" in world religion and ethics, with which, presumably, Christian ethics – based on the command of God – could be expected to co-operate.[27]

The issue of pacifism needs special attention, too. Certainly the Christian gospel is a gospel of peace and goodwill toward all God's children. And the spirit of peacefulness is indeed of the essence of true Christianity. One hopes, with Hauerwas and Milbank, that this spirit will characterize the church and bear witness to the eschatological peace of God's kingdom. But again this can only take effect in the world gradually and partially as qualities of restraint, non-vindictiveness, compromise, and co-operation come to replace the vendetta mentality of earlier and, alas, some contemporary societies. But Christians cannot require pacifism of all church members, still less can they insist on pacifism as public policy. Nor can they condemn outright the police, the army, and the state's defense ministry as wholly outside the concerns of Christian ethics. I am reminded of Bonhoeffer's sharp words in his book *The Cost of Discipleship*: "If we took the precept of non-resistance as an ethical blueprint for general application, we should indeed be indulging in idealistic dreams ... To make non-resistance a principle for secular life is to deny God by undermining his gracious ordinance for the preservation of the world."[28]

Christian social ethics has three principle areas of concern: first, the form of Christian life in the Christian community itself (this is what the communitarians concentrate on pretty exclusively); second, the gradual permeation of the wider society by Christian values (this is what Troeltsch emphasizes at the end of the essay discussed above, though not exclusively in Christian terms); and third, the structures of responsible life in society at large (this is the sphere of both Catholic and Protestant concern with natural law, the common good, the orders, mandates or institutions that embody the basic principles reflecting God's will in creation). If pressed on the question of the distinctiveness of Christian ethics, one will undoubtedly look first to the church, as Hauerwas and Milbank do. But if, as C.H. Dodd once wrote, the God of our redemption is the same as the God of creation, it follows that the forms of Christian life and community cannot be without analogies and points of contact elsewhere.[29] Even the church must expect to find parallels and "other lights" in other places. Nor will Christian values often have to permeate and change a totally alien environment. This may be so at times. Augustine and Karl Barth were faced, at crucial periods in their lives, with just such challenges and the need to see that the church of God remained the church of God and nothing else. But at other times and perhaps at most times in the world today, the various denominations are surely called to join forces, as Troeltsch suggested, with other groups, philosophies, and worldviews, to pool their religious and ethical resources in order to awaken and foster values of which Christians do not have a monopoly.

The distinctiveness of Christian ethics in this sphere is, as I said before, more a matter of specifically Christian motivation, inspiration, and resources than of a unique and incommensurable content. The same is even more evidently true of the third area of concern – the structures of responsible life which Troeltsch was skeptical about as matters of Christian theological derivation. If, against Troeltsch, we do see them as directly implied by theologies of Trinity, incarnation, sacrament or eschatology, this does not render them incommensurable with analogous commitments from other sources. On the contrary Christians have further theological reasons based on God's law in creation for expecting and hoping to find such analogies worldwide.

## IS THERE SOME BASIC COMMON GROUND BETWEEN CHRISTIAN SOCIAL ETHICS AND THE SOCIAL ETHICS OF OTHER RELIGIONS?

I turn, then, to my third question – clearly to be answered in the affirmative. The work of Hans Küng in this connection, over the last decade, is much to be commended. With remarkable energy and commitment, he has publicized both the need for and the possibility of basic agreement among the religions of the world on a global ethic for politics, economics, and business worldwide. The *need* is captured, in slogan form, by the opening sentences of his 1990 book *Global Responsibility: In Search of a New World Ethic*: "No survival without a world ethic. No world peace without peace between religions. No peace between the religions without dialogue between the religions."[30] The importance of the religions as a major factor on the world scene, for good or ill, has become increasingly apparent in the so-called "postmodern" period, when the all-sufficiency of Enlightenment rationalism has so palpably broken down. Given the evident power of the religions to foster or support discord, tribal enmity, and intercommunal atrocity, it is essential to seek out their positive spiritual resources for promoting peace, solidarity, justice, and truthfulness on a global scale. The possibility of securing a consensus on these matters is shown by the fact that the vast majority of the delegates at the 1993 Parliament of the World's Religions in Chicago were prepared to sign the declaration "*Toward a Global Ethic,*" drafted by Hans Küng.[31]

The basic principle underlying this consensus is expressed in the Golden Rule – "do as you would be done by" – versions of which are to be found in every major religion. From this the declaration derives four irrevocable directions for ordering human behavior – commitment to a culture of nonviolence and respect for life, commitment to a culture of solidarity and a just economic order, commitment to a culture of tolerance and a life of truthfulness, and commitment to a culture of equal rights and partnerships between men and women.

In his 1997 book, *A Global Ethic for Global Politics and Economics,*[32] Küng notes how this approach has been taken up by a number of international commissions, notably the Interaction Council of former presidents and prime ministers in their 1996 *Universal Declaration of Human Responsibilities,*[33] designed to complement the United Nations *Declaration of Human Rights.* Küng stresses again the importance of the religions in motivating and resourcing this sense of global responsibility. There are two reservations that may be expressed about this whole approach. Such declarations may seem little more than pious platitudes, leaving all the practical problems of implementation unresolved; and they may, in any case, seem to set out only minimal agreed conditions for life together on this planet.

Certainly there is much scope for hard work on the more detailed implementation of these broad directives. But agreement on principles and broad directives is not to be undervalued. Küng points out how important such international agreements as the Geneva Convention, the United Nations *Declaration on Human Rights*, and the Helsinki Declaration have been in setting standards and inspiring protest and action worldwide. The Chicago Declaration and the *Universal Declaration of Human Responsibilities* – especially if the latter were to be adopted by the United Nations – could well have comparable effect. All the same, there remains much to be done toward securing consensus on more specific middle axioms and more specific policies.

The relatively minimal nature of the agreed framework should also not be undervalued. The directives are in fact of very far-reaching scope with respect to disarmament, negotiated settlements, social justice, openness and honesty, ecological concern, and, notably, the equal rights of men and women. And such a framework of basic minimum conditions for human flourishing allows for the fostering of many different cultural and religious forms of life within that agreed framework. The religions do not have to seek consensus on every aspect of their total visions of life, provided the agreed global ethic – the minimum framework – is respected.

It is interesting to compare these recent efforts to secure consensus on shared values with Troeltsch's remarks at the end of the essay I referred to at the beginning of this chapter. The values Troeltsch mentioned – self-restraint, consideration for others, a feeling for the solidarity of nations, respect for human rights, and a readiness for sacrifice – are very similar to the values affirmed and urged by the Chicago Declaration and that of the Interaction Council. Moreover Troeltsch did not see these values as simply Christian values. He said they should be "pursued with the aid of the available religious and ethical resources of the various denominations, groups, philosophies and world views that are being driven to rapprochement by conditions themselves." Much that has happened since Troeltsch's time has reinforced this last point. As Küng points out, "globalizations of the economy, technology and the media – including, not least, information technology – require a globalization of ethics, in the sense of a necessary minimum of shared ethical values." Conditions are indeed driving the religions toward rapprochement. But Küng's main point is that the terms of that rapprochement can actually be found in all the major religions themselves, as the Chicago delegates were willing to acknowledge.

## IS THIS COMMON GROUND SHARED BY SECULAR SOCIAL ETHICS?

But now we must briefly consider my fourth question of whether this common ground is shared by secular social ethics. I shall be considering the specifically religious motivation of the global ethics project in my final section. But clearly the analysis of the need for a global ethic, offered not only by the Interaction Council but also by the Chicago Declaration, is of universal import, and the set of common values agreed to be required for human flourishing in the world today is as apparent, one hopes, to the United Nations as it is to the Parliament of the World's Religions. We recall that the Niebuhrs, Ramsey, and Gustafson were all concerned to expound Christian social ethics in terms that even non-religious people would find illuminating and persuasive. It was this that Hauerwas objected to; but the following passage from Gustafson, quoted disparagingly by Hauerwas, is in fact far more telling than anything Hauerwas himself has to offer: "The Christian community is not [we might substitute, the religions are not] ... the exclusive audience. Since the intention of the divine power for human well-being is universal in its scope, the historically particular medium through which that power is clarified for Christians [we might add, or other religious communities] also has universal significance. The theologian engaged in the task of 'prescriptive' ethics formulates principles and values that can guide the actions of persons who do not belong to the Christian [we might add, or any other religious] community." Their statements "will be persuasive to non-religious persons only by the cogency of the argument that is made to show that the 'historical particularity' sheds light on principles and values that other serious moral persons also perceive and also ought to adhere to."[34]

Not only, as we have seen, do Christian social ethicists have theological reasons for expecting the will of God in creation to be apparent, anonymously, to non-religious people. They can also rejoice that the influence of Christianity on world history has contributed to the greater recognition and reception of Christian values, albeit in secular form. In the book already mentioned, David Fergusson quotes the German systematic theologian Eberhard Jungel as saying, "The Church may be thankful that its spiritual goods now exist in secular form. For example, the secular respect for freedom of conscience, the secular assertion of the inviolability of the dignity of the person, the secular commitment to protect handicapped human life, universal schooling and many other achievements of the modern constitutional state are secularized church treasures."[35]

There is much room for debate on how far these secular achievements are in fact products of the Christian centuries and how far other religions have had comparable resources and comparable effects. Interesting questions also arise over how far the encounter and interaction of the religions in the modern period have enabled the various faiths to discover such values latent in their own traditions. Be that as it may, and notwithstanding the fact of some disputed areas between religious and secular social ethics – over such issues as abortion or population control, for example – the large degree of consensus manifest in the declaration of the Interaction Council is very striking.

## THE IMPORTANCE OF THE RELIGIOUS OR THE CHRISTIAN DIMENSION, CONTEXT, OR MOTIVATION FOR SOCIAL ETHICS TODAY

This brings me to my final question: if consensus and common ground can be found not only among the religions but also between the religions and secular social ethics, what, if anything, is the importance of the religious or the Christian dimension, context, or motivation for social ethics today worldwide? Granted the increased perception, including secular perception, of the need for a global ethic, the question still remains about what resources are available for motivating people and societies to adopt, affirm, and realize these values in the actual organization of global politics and economics. The secular answer can only be in terms of peer-group pressure, education, and socialization within a predominantly utilitarian framework. People have to be persuaded that it is in their long-term interest to respect the framework of rights and responsibilities that constitute the basic minimum conditions of human flourishing in the one world of global communication and interaction.

But this is a relatively weak basis for interpreting the inviolability of human rights and the inexorable demand for human beings and for states to act responsibly toward one another. The religions are much better placed both to account for these absolute values and to make available unconditional resources towards their implementation. Ernst Troeltsch, we recall, associated the values under discussion with "a basically believing outlook on life and the world" and with "the spirit of obligation to a more-than-human truth and justice." Hans Küng, in commenting on the Chicago Declaration, asserts that such a global ethic "must penetrate to a deeper ethical level, the level of binding values, irrevocable criteria, and inner basic attitudes." To this end, "it must have a religious foundation, even if all men and women are to be addressed, including those who are not religious." "For those with a religious motivation," he adds, "an ethic has to do with trust . . . in an ultimate supreme reality, whatever name this may be given."[36]

We have seen that the Niebuhrs, Gustafson, and Jungel were more willing to rejoice in secularized value systems, freed from their religious provenance, though they themselves, as Christian ethicists, continued to provide theological accounts of their foundation. The Interaction Council – a less overtly religious body than the Parliament of the World's Religions – was content simply to appeal to the religions among other groups to commit themselves to a common global ethic. Inevitably, they could end with no more than an invitation to commitment.

Interestingly, a "First Conference on a Global Ethic and Traditional Indian Ethics," held in New Delhi in 1997, was more explicit about the need for religious motivation. According to their report, "participants observed that ethical principles which refer to and arise from the ethical domain alone may not be sufficient to ensure discharge of ethical responsibilities. It is spirituality, the dynamism of faith, which has through the ages empowered and spurred individuals and groups to live up to ethical standards."[37] We may conclude that, at this basic minimum level of rights and responsibilities, though the need for a global ethic can be perceived and urged across the borders of the religious and the secular, it is the religions that can best provide the motivation and the spiritual resources to sustain it.

Finally, I return to the perspective of specifically Christian social ethics and make two further points. First, Christian social ethics is not only concerned with the basic minimum framework of values necessary for life together on this planet. It will have a great deal to say about the much deeper aspects of Christian ethics than those which reflect the basic minimum. Its ethic of forgiveness and reconciliation, although one may hope to find some echoes and parallels elsewhere, involves a much richer conception of the dynamics of human life under God than can be expected universally. Similarly, Christian ethics will have much else to say about the ethics of vocation and about works of supererogation. This will apply not only to individuals but to institutions and organizations that embody the love ethic of the gospel. Other religions will have higher and deeper dimensions with, no doubt, very different content. There is less pressure for consensus at these levels than there is at that of the basic minimum framework.

Second, in Christian social ethics the religious motivation and the spiritual resources making for commitment at the basic level of the rights and responsibilities affirmed in a global ethic will continue to stem not only from beliefs in natural law and human dignity, but also from the gospel of the Incarnation, the sacramental principle, the social theology of Trinitarian belief, and from specifically Christian eschatology – the vision of the kingdom of God in the communion of saints. Again, other religions will have their own, often very different, beliefs and resources by which to motivate and sustain commitment to a global ethic. Agreement on a framework of shared values for politics and economics worldwide does not entail any conflation or homogenization of the beliefs and spiritualities that sustain that agreement.

## NOTES

1. Ernst Troeltsch, *The Social Teaching of the Christian Churches*, trans. Olive Wyon (London: Allen & Unwin, 1931).
2. Ernst Troeltsch, *Religion in History*, trans. James Luther Adams and Walter F. Bense (Edinburgh: T. & T. Clark, 1991), p. 212.
3. Ibid., p. 232.
4. Ibid., pp. 233f.
5. William Temple, *Christianity and Social Order* (London: Shepheard-Walwyn and SPCK, 1976), originally published in 1942.
6. Ibid., p. 2.
7. One thinks here of the work of Kenneth Leech, *The Social God* (London: Sheldon Press, 1981).
8. Wolfhart Pannenberg, *Ethics* (Philadelphia: Westminster Press, 1981), p. 28.
9. Karl Barth, *The Christian Life* (Edinburgh: T. & T. Clark, 1981), pp. 260–271.
10. Hendrikus Berkhof, *Christian Faith* (Grand Rapids: Eerdmans, 1979).

11. *The Common Good and the Catholic Church's Social Teaching* (London: Catholic Bishops' Conference of England and Wales, 1996), p. 3.

12. See Ronald Preston, *Confusions in Christian Social Ethics: Problems for Geneva and Rome* (London: SCM Press, 1994).

13. John Coleman Bennett, *Christian Ethics and Social Policy* (New York: C. Scribner's Sons, 1946), p. 381.

14. Duncan B. Forrester, *Beliefs, Values and Politics: Conviction Politics in a Secular Age* (Oxford: Clarendon Press, 1989), chapter 2.

15. Ronald H. Preston, *Church and Society in the Late Twentieth Century* (London: SCM Press, 1983), appendix 2.

16. Stanley Hauerwas, *Against the Nations: War and Survival in a Liberal Society* (Minneapolis: Winston Press, 1985).

17. Ibid., p. 31.

18. Stanley Hauerwas, *Christian Existence: Essays on Church, World, and Living in Between* (Durham, NC: Labyrinth Press, 1988).

19. David Fergusson, *Community, Liberalism and Christian Ethics* (Cambridge: Cambridge University Press, 1998).

20. Ibid., p. 73.

21. John Milbank, *The Word Made Strange: Theology, Language, Culture* (Oxford: Blackwell, 1997), chapter 10.

22. Ibid., p. 250.

23. Ibid., p. 229.

24. Gavin D'Costa, ed., *Christian Uniqueness Reconsidered: The Myth of a Pluralistic Theology of Religions* (Maryknoll, NY: Orbis, 1990), chapter 13.

25. Karl Barth, *Protestant Theology in the Nineteenth Century: Its Background and History* (London: SCM Press, 1972), originally published in German in 1952.

26. Milbank, *The World Made Strange*, pp. 236f.

27. Karl Barth, *Church Dogmatics* (Edinburgh: T. & T. Clark, 1961), IV, 3, 1, pp. 139–165.

28. Dietrich Bonhoeffer, *The Cost of Discipleship* (London: SCM Press), pp. 129f.

29. C.H. Dodd, *Gospel and Law* (New York: Columbia University Press), p. 79.

30. Hans Küng, *Global Responsibility: In Search of a New World Ethic* (London: SCM Press, 1991), p. xv.

31. Hans Küng and Helmut Schmidt, eds, *A Global Ethic and Global Responsibilities: Two Declarations* (London: SCM Press, 1998).

32. Hans Küng, *A Global Ethic for Global Politics and Economics* (London: SCM Press, 1997).

33. See note 31.

34. Quoted in Hauerwas, *Against the Nations*, pp. 37f.

35. Quoted in Fergusson, *Community, Liberalism, and Christian Ethics*, p. 156.

36. Küng and Schmidt, ed., *A Global Ethic and Global Responsibilities*, p. 57.

37. Ibid., p. 132.

*Plate 16* View across the Imperial Summer Palace or Yiheyuan (the Garden of Cultivated Harmony), north-west of Beijing, built in 1888, with serene Lake Kumming on the left and Longevity Hill on the right. The integration of nature and civilization into one harmonious whole displays Confucian ideals. Photo: *Nancy M. Martin*

# 16

# CONFUCIAN COSMOLOGY *and* ECOLOGICAL ETHICS: *qi, li,* AND THE ROLE OF THE HUMAN

*Mary Evelyn Tucker*

In our search for more comprehensive and global ethics to meet the critical challenges of our contemporary situation, the world religions are emerging as major reservoirs of depth and insight, particularly with regard to the pressing environmental crisis of our times.[1] Although the scale and scope of the crisis are subject to debate, few people would deny the seriousness of what we are facing as a planetary community immersed in unsustainable practices of production, consumption, and development. Clearly the world's religions have some important correctives to offer in this respect.

There is a growing realization that attitudinal changes toward nature will be essential for creating sustainable societies, in addition to new scientific and economic approaches to our environmental problems. Humans will not preserve what they do not respect. What is currently lacking is a moral basis for changing our exploitative attitudes toward nature. We have laws against homicide but not against geocide or biocide. Thus, we are without a sufficiently broad environmental ethics to alter our consciousness about the earth and our life on it. Consequently what should concern us is this: to what extent can the religious traditions of the world provide us with ethical resources and cosmological perspectives that can help us deal with these pressing environmental issues? What insights from the world religions might be brought to bear on the re-envisioning of the role of the human in relation to the natural world in order to form the basis for the necessary attitudinal change?

The dynamic and holistic perspective of the Confucian worldview may have significant contributions to make in this regard, enlarging our sense of ethical terrain and moral concerns and providing a rich source for rethinking our own relationship with nature and the meaning of virtue in light of the environmental crisis we are facing. Confucianism's organic holism can give us a special appreciation for the interconnectedness of all life forms and renew our sense of the sacredness of this intricate web of life. Moreover, the Confucian understanding of the dynamic vitalism underlying cosmic processes offers us a basis for reverencing nature. From a Confucian perspective, nature cannot be thought of as being composed of inert, dead matter. Rather, all life forms share the element of *qi* or material force. This shared psycho-physical entity becomes the basis for establishing a reciprocity between the human and nonhuman worlds.

In this same vein, in terms of self-cultivation and the nurturing of virtue, the Confucian tradition provides a broad framework for harmonizing human life with the natural world in its doctrine of the human as a child of heaven and earth, as well as in its understanding of virtues as having both a cosmological and a personal component. Thus nature and virtue, cosmology and ethics, knowledge and action are intimately linked for the Confucians in China, Korea, and Japan. This chapter will give a broad outline of the development of the Confucian tradition and then concentrate on three major themes of *qi, li,* and the role of the human and their implications for ecological ethics.

## OVERVIEW OF THE CONFUCIAN TRADITION

The Confucian tradition encompasses the diverse forms of Confucianism in China, Korea, Japan, Vietnam, Hong Kong, Taiwan, and Singapore. To see Confucianism as a singular tradition is problematic owing to its geographic spread, its historical development, and its varied expressions ranging from local and familial Confucianism to imperial state Confucianism.

Originating in the first millennium BCE in China, the tradition includes the transmission of Confucianism to different East Asian cultural and geographical contexts and its resulting transformations. In accounting for its spread and its appeal, one can point to the spiritual dynamics of the tradition and examine the ways in which it interacted with native traditions in China and across East Asia. For example, Confucianism intermingled with Daoism and Buddhism in China, with shamanism in Korea, and with Shinto in Japan.[2] Such borrowing between and creative interaction among religious traditions in East Asia needs to be more fully studied. Indeed, the so-called unity and syncretism of the traditions of Confucianism, Daoism, and Buddhism in China should be noted, especially in the Ming (1368–1644) and Qing (1644–1911) periods.

Acknowledging this vital cross-fertilization of religions in East Asia, we can also identify three major historical periods of Confucian thought from its beginnings to the present. The first stage is that of classical Confucianism from the sixth century BCE to the tenth century CE. This is the period of the rise of the early Confucian thinkers, namely, Confucius and Mencius. It is also when Confucianism became state orthodoxy under the Han Empire (202 BCE to 220 CE) and began to spread across East Asia. The second period is the Neo-Confucian era from the eleventh to the early twentieth century. This includes the great synthesis of Zhu Xi in the eleventh century and the important contributions of Wang Yangming in the fifteenth and sixteenth centuries. The final period is that of New Confucianism, beginning in the twentieth century, which Tu Weiming has called the "Third Epoch of Confucian Humanism."[3] In this era there has been a revival of Confucianism under the leadership of scholars who came to Taiwan and Hong Kong after Mao took power in 1949. Fifty years later in October 1999 two major conferences were held by the International Confucian Society in Beijing and in Confucius' birthplace, Qufu, to explore the future of the Confucian Way. These conferences marked the 2540th anniversary of Confucius' birth.[4]

This acknowledged founder of the Confucian tradition was known as the sage-teacher Kongzi (551–479 BCE).[5] His name was Latinized by the Jesuit missionaries as "Confucius." Born into a time of rapid social change, Confucius devoted his life to re-establishing order through rectification of the individual and the state. This involved a program embracing both political and religious components. As a creative transmitter of earlier Chinese traditions, Confucius, according to legend, compiled the appendices to the *Classic of Changes* and compiled the other Classics, namely, the *Classic of Documents, Odes, Rites,* and the *Spring and Autumn Annals.*

The principal sayings and teachings of Confucius are contained in his conversations recorded in the *Analects.* Here he emphasized the cultivation of moral virtues, especially humaneness (*ren*), and the practice of civility or ritual decorum (*li*).[6] Virtue and civility were exemplified by the noble person (*junzi*) particularly within the five relations, namely, between ruler and minister, parent and child, husband and wife, older and younger siblings, and friend and friend. The essence of Confucian thinking was that to establish order in the society one had to begin with harmony, filiality, and decorum in the family. Then, like concentric circles, the effect of virtue would reach outward to society. Likewise, if the ruler was moral, it would have a "rippling down" effect on the rest of society.

At the heart of this classical Confucian worldview was a profound commitment to humaneness and civility. These two virtues defined the means of human relatedness as a spiritual path. Through civility, specifically filiality, one could repay the gifts of life both to one's parents and ancestors and to the whole natural world. Through humaneness one could extend this sensibility to other humans and to all living things. In doing so, one became more fully human. The root of practicing humaneness was considered to be filial relations, and its extension from one's family and ancestors to the human family and the cosmic family was the means whereby these primary biological ties provided a person with the roots, trunks, and branches of an interconnected spiritual path. The personal and the cosmic were joined in the stream of filiality. From the lineages of ancestors to future progeny an intergenerational spirituality and ethics arose. Through one's parents and ancestors one became part of human life. Reverence and reciprocity were considered a natural response to this gift of life. Analogously, through reverence for heaven and earth as the great parents of all life, one realized one's full cosmological being. Great sacrifices were made for the family, and utmost loyalties were required in this spiritual path.[7]

Confucian thought was further developed in the writings of Mencius (385?–312? BCE) and Xunzi (310?–219? BCE), who debated whether human nature was intrinsically good or evil. Mencius' argument on the inherent goodness of human nature gained dominance among Confucian thinkers and gave an optimistic flavor to Confucian educational philosophy and political theory. This perspective influenced the spiritual aspects of the tradition as well because self-cultivation was seen as a natural means of uncovering this innate good nature. Mencius contributed an understanding of the discipline of self-cultivation, by identifying the innate seeds of virtues in the human and suggesting ways in which they could be cultivated toward their full realization as virtues.

Confucianism culminated in a Neo-Confucian revival in the eleventh and twelfth centuries CE which resulted in a new synthesis of the earlier teachings. The major Neo-Confucian thinker, Zhu Xi (1130–1200), designated four texts as containing the central ideas of Confucian thought. These were two chapters from the *Classic of Rites* – namely, the "Great Learning" and the "Mean" – and the *Analects* and the *Mencius.* He elevated these Four Books to a position of prime importance over the Five Classics mentioned earlier. These texts and Zhu Xi's commentaries on them became, in 1315, the basis of the Chinese civil service examination system, which endured for nearly six hundred years until 1905. Every prospective government official had to take the civil service exams based on Zhu Xi's commentaries on the Four Books. The idea was to provide educated, moral officials for the large government bureaucracy that ruled China. The influence, then, of Neo-Confucian thought on government, education, and social values was extensive.

Zhu Xi's synthesis of Neo-Confucianism was recorded in his classic anthology *Reflections on Things at Hand* (*Jinsilu*). In this work, he provided, for the first time, a comprehensive metaphysical basis for Confucian thought and practice. In response to the Buddhists' metaphysics of emptiness and their perceived tendency toward withdrawal from the world in meditative practices, Zhu formulated a this-worldly spirituality based on a balance of cosmological orientation, ethical and ritual practices, scholarly reflection, and political participation. The aim was to balance inner cultivation with outward investigation of things.

Unlike the Buddhists, who saw the world of change as the source of suffering, Zhu Xi and the Neo-Confucians after him affirmed change as the source of transformation in both the cosmos and the person. Thus Neo-Confucian spiritual discipline involved cultivating one's moral nature so as to bring it into harmony with the larger pattern of change in the cosmos. Each moral virtue had its cosmological component. For example, the central virtue of humaneness was seen as the source of fecundity and growth in both the individual and the cosmos. By practicing humaneness, one could effect the transformation of things in oneself, in society, and in the cosmos. In so doing, one's deeper identity with reality was recognized as forming one body with all things. As the "Mean" stated it, "being able to assist in the transforming and nourishing powers of Heaven and Earth, one can form a triad with Heaven and Earth" (chapter 22).

To realize this cosmological identification, a rigorous spiritual practice was needed. This involved a development of poles present in earlier Confucian thought, namely, a balancing of religious reverence with an ethical integrity and ritual propriety manifested in daily life. For Zhu Xi and later Neo-Confucians such spiritual practices were a central concern. Thus interior meditation became known as "quiet sitting," "abiding in reverence," or "rectifying the mind." Moral self-discipline was known as "making the will sincere," "controlling the desires," and "investigating principle."[8] All of this was expressed in ritual decorum.

Through conscientious spiritual effort and study, one could become a noble person (*junzi*), or even a sage, who was able to participate in society and politics most effectively. In the earlier Confucian view the emphasis was on the ruler as the prime moral leader of the society, but in Neo-Confucian thought this duty was extended to all people, with a particular responsibility placed on teachers and government officials. Although ritual was primary in earlier Confucianism, spiritual discipline became even more significant in Neo-Confucian practice. In both the early and later tradition, major emphasis was placed on mutual respect and reciprocity in basic human relations.

With this basic understanding of Confucian tradition, let us now turn to a deeper exploration of the concepts of *qi* and *li* and Confucian understandings of the role of the human, in order to consider more fully the possible implications of Confucian cosmology for environmental ethics.

## QI

The Chinese have a term to describe the vibrancy and aliveness of the universe. This is *qi* (or *ch'i*) which is translated in a variety of ways in the classical Confucian tradition as spirit, air, or breath, and later in the Neo-Confucian tradition as material force, matter energy, vital force. It describes the realization that the universe is alive with vitality and resonates with life. What is especially remarkable about this ancient and enduring realization of the Chinese is that *qi* is a unified field, embracing both matter and energy. It is thus a matrix containing both material and spiritual life from the smallest particle to the largest visible reality. *Qi* courses through the universe from the constituent particles of matter to mountains and rocks, plants and trees, animals and birds, fish and insects.

All the elements – air, earth, fire, and water – are composed of *qi*. We humans, too, are alive with *qi*. It makes up our body and spirit as one integrated whole, and it activates our mind-and-heart, which is a single unified reality in Chinese thought.

In other words, *qi* courses though nature, fills the elements of reality, and dynamizes our human body-mind. It is the single unifying force of all that is. It does not posit a dichotomy between nature and spirit, body and mind, matter and energy. *Qi* is one united, dynamic whole – the vital reality of the entire universe.

The implications of this unified view of reality quickly become apparent to us. One wants to know and experience this *qi* more fully. This is why most of the martial arts and exercises like *taiqi* (or *ta'i ch'i*) aim to cultivate and deepen *qi*. Humans for all their blindness are intelligent enough to want to taste and savor this marvellous aliveness of the universe. They want to harmonize their most basic physical processes with *qi* – thus the dynamic coordination of breath and movement is at the heart of the Chinese physical arts. And arts they are – this is not just a physical toning of the body or building up of muscles. This is a spiritual exercise filled with potency for health of mind and body – a coordinated and aesthetically pleasing dance of the human system in and through the sea of *qi*.

One way to visualize *qi* is as a vast ocean of energy, an infinite source of vibrant potency, a resonating field of dynamic power – *in* matter itself, not separate from it. For *qi* once again is matter-energy, material force. This is the important contribution of Chinese thought to world philosophy. It is an insight of particular significance for our contemporary world which has been broken apart by the Enlightenment's separation of matter and spirit, of body and soul, of nature and life.

From the perspective of *qi* the news is this: the world is alive with a depth of mystery, complexity, and vibrancy that we can only begin to taste and never fully exhaust. The sensual world *is* the spiritual world. The dynamism of each particular reality begins to present itself to us: the oak tree in our yard radiates an untold energy; the snow-covered mountains in the distance are redolent with silent *qi*; the rivers coursing to the ocean are filled with the buoyancy of *qi*.

One of the earliest Confucian writers, Mencius, speaks of the great floodlike *qi*. This is what I am evoking here. We are flooded, surrounded, inundated by *qi*. We walk around completely unconscious most of the time that this ocean of energy is here – sustaining us, nourishing us, and enlivening us. *Qi* is the gift of the universe – the endlessly fecund life source unfolding before us and around us in a daily miracle of hidden joy. It is the restorative laughter of the universe inviting us into its endless mystery.

As we return to the Chinese sources to sift through the texts and commentaries to learn more about *qi*, what becomes apparent is that the notion of *qi* is not constant but evolving. Nor is it unified and consistent. It is rather a multivalent idea that begins to reveal something of its shape and function only when seen from a variety of perspectives and texts.

In the classical Confucian tradition *qi* tends to refer more generally to the spirit that animates the universe, the breath that enlivens humans, and the air that connects all things. Even from its earliest articulation, however, it would be fair to say *qi* was never seen as an entity apart from matter. Rather, it is embedded in the natural and the human world. It animates and nourishes nature and humans. The very Chinese character for *qi* is said to represent the steam rising from rice, suggesting the nourishing and transforming power of *qi*. Like food, *qi* maintains life and human energy. Benjamin Schwartz observes, "The image of food even suggests the interchange of energy and substance between humans and their surrounding environment."[9] The idea of *qi* as having the properties of condensation and rarefaction like steam suggests the same.

As the later Han and Neo-Confucians began to articulate their cosmological understanding, the unity of *qi* as matter-energy became more evident. Dong Zhongshu, the leading Han Confucian, described *qi* as a "limpid colorless substance" that fills the universe, "surrounds man as water surrounds a fish," and unites all creation.[10] The Neo-Confucians, however, developed the notion of *qi* to refer to the substance and essence of all life. It pervades and animates the universe as both matter and energy.

For the Neo-Confucian Zhang Zai the vibrancy of material force originates in the Great Vacuity that contains the primal, undifferentiated material force. As it integrates and disintegrates, it participates in the Great Harmony of activity and tranquillity. This perspective affirms the unified and real processes of change, not seeing them as illusory as the Buddhists might nor as a product of a dichotomy between non-being and being as the Daoists would. There is instead a dynamic unity of *qi* as seen in its operations as substance emerging in the Great Vacuity and as function operating in the Great Harmony.

## LI

*Li* is the inner ordering principle of reality which is embedded in the heart of *qi*. The Chinese character for *li* suggests working on the veins in jade, which one needs to discover and carve adeptly. *Li* is comparable to a *logos* principle whereby all of reality is imprinted with structure and intelligibility. It is both pattern and potential pattern and thus gives reality its intricacy of design as well as its thrust toward directionality and purpose. It is a revealing and concealing sensibility for human consciousness. We seek to find its mark, its imprint in the flow of the natural world around us as well as in the unfolding of our lives. As Thomas Berry says so often, we have become autistic to perceiving this vast intelligibility of the universe and thus have become ungrounded and rudderless, locked in our own self-referential cages.

It is, however, the universe that is calling to be read and to be heard in the deep patterning of its particularities. The beauty of *li* is that it brings us into contact with the myriad forms of life – the ten thousand things as the Chinese say – with a penetrating clarity. This is because *li* is both normative principle and intelligible pattern. As pattern it gives us entry into understanding nature and its complex workings. As principle it gives us a grounding for a morality that arises from the very structure of life itself. The moral dimensions of the universe are in the depths of matter revealing itself to us as *li*.

*Li* is principle and pattern – both a moral and a natural entity bringing together our profound embeddedness in a universe of meaning and mystery. The allure of the universe lies in seeing and experiencing that meaning and mystery before us, behind us, and all around us. We are drawn forth into a sense of the breadth and depth of *li* as manifest in the phenomenal world in great diversity and particularity. All of this breadth and depth of inner ordering is gathered up in the Great Ultimate (*taiji*) – that which contains and shapes and generates all principles and patterns in the universe.

As one of the principal Neo-Confucian thinkers, Zhu Xi (1130–1200), says, "The Supreme Ultimate is merely the principle of Heaven-and-Earth, and the myriad things."[11] Another leading Neo-Confucian, Cheng Yi (1033–1107) says, "Principle is one (in the Great Ultimate); its manifestations are many (in the world)."[12] They use the analogy of the moon shining in the water in the irrigated rice fields on a terraced mountain side. There are many moons that are reflected but only one full moon in the sky. *Taiji* is like this full moon. It is the Great Ultimate or the Supreme Ultimate. It refers to a pole star – guiding, illuminating, and alluring. For the Cheng brothers *li* was like a genetic code and thus identified with the creative life principle (*shengsheng*).[13]

The creative dynamics of this great container of principles are cosmological, namely, there is an interaction of non-being and being or the unmanifest and the manifest. This is seen in the interaction of the *wuji* (non-ultimate) and the *taiji* (Great Ultimate). Some of the most interesting arguments and discussions in Chinese thought have arisen among thinkers who are commenting on this complex interaction.

Some would say that the Daoists want to maintain a dichotomy between non-being and being, emphasizing the dynamic creativity of non-being as the source of all life. Others would say the Buddhists want to maintain the ultimate emptiness of non-being and the illusory quality of being. The Neo-Confucians struggled to assert the importance of the dynamic continuity between these two forces (non-being and being). Indeed, they would maintain that the very creativity of the universe is revealed in this dialectical interaction. For the Confucians the complementarity of these creative forces is at the heart of all cosmological processes. The vast changes and transformations of nature in the endless flow of *qi* become clear in this interaction. That is because all reality, all *qi*, is imprinted with *li*. Discovering this patterning in the fluid material force of the universe is the challenge for humans.

As *li* is unveiled, humans can discern the appropriate patterning for both their individual and their collective lives. The universe unfolds according to these patterns of deep structure embedded in reality. Social systems are established according to these patterns, agriculture is conducted in harmony with these patterns, politics functions in relation to these patterns, and individuals cultivate themselves in response to these patterns.

## THE ROLE OF THE HUMAN

For the Neo-Confucians humans receive *li* from heaven. Their heavenly endowed nature is thus linked to the patterning throughout the universe. By the same token, humans are composed of *qi*, the same dynamic substance that makes up the universe.

Humans are thus imprinted with unique and differentiated *li* embedded in *qi,* the material force of their own mind-body. *Li* guarantees the special and different qualities of each human being, and *qi* establishes the material and spiritual grounds for subjectivity, thus uniting humans with one another and with the vast world of nature. In other words, *qi* as vital force is the interiority of matter, providing the matrix for communion and exchange of energy between all life forms.

Humans, then, are given a heavenly endowed nature that joins them to the great triad of heaven, earth, and other humans. Though this is a gift of the universe from birth, it is understood as something to be realized over a lifetime. This realization occurs through the process of self-cultivation which is at the heart of Confucian moral and spiritual practice. This process of actualization is not abstract or otherworldly but rather concerned with the process of becoming more fully human. In doing this, one penetrates principle and perceives pattern amidst the flux of material force in ourselves and in the universe at large. The goal of our self-cultivation is to actualize and recognize the profound identity of ourselves with heaven, earth, and the myriad things.

Because the *qi* that we are each given may vary in its purity or turbidity, self-cultivation is necessary. Evil, imperfection, loss, and suffering are thus part of the human condition. Confucians, however, believe that one's heavenly endowed human nature is essentially good and thus perfectible. To illustrate this, Mencius uses the example of a child about to fall into a well (*Mencius* II A 6). The instinct of any person is to save the child from harm, not for any exterior reasons but owing to a naturally compassionate heart. The key to the goodness of human nature is a profound sympathy or empathy which all humans have. Indeed, affectivity is what distinguishes humans in the Confucian worldview. As Mencius says, "No one is devoid of a heart sensitive to the suffering of others" (*Mencius* II A 6). Because of this basic sympathy, Confucians affirm that at the level of our primary instincts we will tend toward the good. Mencius uses wonderfully evocative images from nature to illustrate this, like water flowing naturally downhill (*Mencius* VI A 2). Like wind blowing over grass, people are inclined toward the good and respond to the good because they are imprinted with the good.

From these examples Mencius goes on to describe the basic seeds implanted in human nature which when cultivated become the key virtues for living a fully humane life. The seeds are compassion, shame, courtesy, modesty, and a sense of right and wrong (*Mencius* II A 6, VI A 6). These seeds need to be watered and tended so they will grow and flourish into the primary Confucian virtues of humaneness, righteousness, propriety, and wisdom. The images used to describe the growth and cultivation of virtue are derived from the agricultural patterns and seasonal cycles of humans dependent on nature. Consequently, I am inclined to use the metaphor of "botanical cultivation" when speaking of Confucian moral and spiritual practice.

The aim of such practice is to allow the seeds or tendencies of our deepest human spontaneities to be nourished and to flourish. Mencius suggests that this should be as clear as tending trees in one's garden: "Even with a *tong* or a *zi* tree one or two spans thick, anyone wishing to keep it alive will know how it should be tended, yet when it comes to one's own person, one does not know how to tend it. Surely one does not love one's person any less than the *tong* or the *zi*" (*Mencius* VI A 13). In this same spirit our actions should develop a naturalness based on the rhythms of the cosmos itself. From seeds in the soil to seasons and their cycles, to the flow of rivers and the thrust of mountains, we are part of the rhythms of the universe and need to nourish our original nature.

If one develops these seeds, it is like "a fire starting up or a spring coming through." The moral power that results from this cultivation of virtue is boundless: "When these (seeds) are fully developed, one can take under one's protection the whole realm within the Four Seas, but if one fails to develop them, one will not be able even to serve one's parents" (*Mencius* II A 6).

The key is to tend, to activate, and to align our deepest spontaneities with the dynamic patterns of change and continuity in nature. Thus self-cultivation needs to be an organic process. As Mencius suggests, we need to nourish our floodlike *qi* with integrity (*Mencius* II A 2) and to recover our original mind-and-heart (*Mencius* VI A 11). However, this cannot be a forced process. Mencius uses the example of the man from Sung who planted rice seedlings. In his desire to see them grow quickly, he pulled at them too soon, and they withered. As Mencius observes, "There are few people in the world who can resist the urge to help their rice plants grow" (*Mencius* II A 2). Others leave them unattended or do not bother to weed. How to nurture and nourish is the art of cultivation both in nature and in humans.

Mencius also uses the example of Ox Mountain, where, owing to deforestation and overgrazing, the mountain becomes denuded (*Mencius*

VI A 8). Erosion sets in, and the ecosystem is destroyed. People are inclined to think this has always been the nature of the mountain. Improper cultivation of ourselves and of the land results in waste and loss. As Mencius says, if one is not restored by the natural rhythms of the day and night but dissipates one's energies and becomes dissolute, people will think that dissolution is one's essential nature. However, he insists that nourishment is the key: "Given the right nourishment there is nothing that will not grow, and deprived of it there is nothing that will not wither away" (*Mencius* VI A 8).

These examples are so simple, clear, and timeless. They are as appropriate for our day as for Mencius', since their natural imagery restores us to the deeper rhythms of our being in the universe. In this context, self-cultivation does not lead toward transcendent bliss or otherworldly salvation or even personal enlightenment. Rather, the goal is to move toward participation in the social, political, and cosmological order of things. The continuity of self, society, and cosmos is paramount in the Confucian worldview.

Thus self-cultivation is always aimed at preparing the individual to contribute more fully to the needs of the contemporary world. For Confucians this implies a primacy of continual study and learning. Thus education is at the heart of self-cultivation. This is not simply book learning or scholarship for the sake of careerism. It is education that leads oneself out of oneself into the world at large. More than anything, then, the role of the human is to discover one's place in the larger community of life. And this community is one of ever expanding and intricately connected concentric circles of family, school, society, politics, nature, and the universe. We are embedded in a web of relationships, and one fulfills one's role by cultivating one's inner spontaneities so that one can be more responsive to each of these layers of commitments.

For Confucians this is all set within the context of an organic, dynamic, holistic universe that is alive with *qi* and imprinted with *li*. Thus finding one's role is realizing how one completes the great triad of heaven and earth. As we rediscover our cosmological being in the macrocosm, our role in the microcosm of our daily lives will become more fulfilling, more joyful, more spontaneous. The pace and rhythm of our lives will be responsive to the rhythms of the day, the changes of the seasons, and the movements of the stars. The great continuity of our being with the being of the universe will enliven and enrich our activities. By attuning ourselves to the patterns of change and continuity in the natural world, we find our niche.

We thus take our place in the enormous expanse of the universe. We complete the great triad of heaven and earth and participate in the transforming and nourishing powers of all things. In so doing, we will cultivate the land appropriately, nurture life forms for sustainability, regulate social relations adeptly and fairly, honor political commitments for the common good, and thus participate in the great transformation of things. This will be manifest as our own inner authenticity resonates with the authenticity of the universe itself.

This holistic and dynamic understanding of the world and the role of humans which we find in Confucianism could bring us far in the revisioning so necessary for dealing with our current ecological crisis and is but one example of the potential benefit of tapping the resources of the world religions in our endeavor to formulate a more comprehensive and global ethics.

## NOTES

1. This has been one of the main objectives of the Harvard conference series and edited volumes on "Religions of the World and Ecology." See www.hds.harvard.edu/cswr/ecology and www.environment.harvard.edu/religion

2. For example, in Japan Confucianism linked itself to Shinto during the seventeenth century, was separated from it by the nativists of the eighteenth century, and was rejoined to Shinto again in the late nineteenth century. Japanese Confucianism as a worldview and a form of spiritual cultivation remains part of many of the new religions in Japan and deserves further study. See, for example, Helen Hardacre, "The World View of the New Religions," in *Kurozumikyo and the New Religions of Japan* (Princeton: Princeton University Press, 1986), pp. 3–36.

3. See Tu Weiming's article with this title in *Confucianism: The Dynamics of Tradition,* ed. Irene Eber (New York: Macmillan, 1986), pp. 3–21. John Berthrong has outlined six periods of Confucianism which separate out the Han, Tang, and later Qing evidential learning. See John Berthrong, *All Under Heaven* (Albany: State University of New York Press, 1994), pp. 77–83; 191–192.

4. John Berthrong discusses these conferences in detail in chapter 11 of this volume.

5. The following nine paragraphs have appeared in slightly different form in "An Ecological Cosmology: The Confucian Philosophy of Material Force,"

in *Ecological Prospects: Scientific, Religious and Aesthetic Perspectives,* ed. Christopher Chapple (Albany, NY: State University of New York Press, 1994), pp. 108–110.

6. John Berthrong has translated *li* not only as ritual but as civility so as to encompass the area of politics and human rights.

7. Likewise, often great distortions were demanded by parents or in-laws, and this dark side of Confucianism was highlighted in the New Culture Movement of the twentieth century. See, for example, the novel *Family* by Ba Jin. (Pa Chin, *Family,* trans. Wade Giles [New York: Doubleday, 1972].)

8. For a discussion of Neo-Confucian spiritual practice, see Wm. Theodore de Bary, "Neo-Confucian Cultivation and Enlightenment," in *The Unfolding of Neo-Confucianism,* ed. Wm. Theodore de Bary (New York: Columbia University Press, 1975), pp. 141–216.

9. Benjamin Schwartz, *The World of Thought in Ancient China* (Cambridge: Harvard University Press, 1985), p. 180.

10. Wm. Theodore de Bary, *Sources of Chinese Tradition* (New York: Columbia University Press, 1960), p. 466.

11. Ibid., p. 701–702.

12. In *I-chuan wenji* (Collection of literary works by Cheng Yi) 5:12b.

13. Wm. Theodore de Bary, *Sources of Chinese Tradition,* p. 689.

*Plate 17* Images of three Jain *tirthankaras* (ford crossers) or *jinas* (victors) in a temple in Osian, Rajasthan, inspire practitioners on the journey toward purity, their meditative posture and open eyes signifying the omniscient and dispassionate state of one who has won release from the bonds of *karma*.
Photo: *Nancy M. Martin*

# 17

# MULTIPLISM: A JAINA ETHICS OF TOLERATION *for* A COMPLEX WORLD

## C. Ram-Prasad

"**M**ultiplism" is simply a neologism to capture the metaphysics and the normative method of the Indian religion of Jainism. Let me begin by making a brief and introductory distinction between this term and the standard notion of pluralism; for the most obvious and first response to the introduction of this neologism might well be to ask how it is any different from pluralism. Whereas a pluralist metaphysics would take reality to consist of many, autonomous truths/principles, multiplism holds the further, stronger thesis that these truths together, integratively, constitute a totality. And whereas a pluralist ethics would take there to be many, autonomous theories/value-sets as a matter of fact, multiplism claims that there is a further, higher-order meta-theory or overarching value to these several theories/value-sets. The important point to note here is that this does not make the Jaina doctrine simply a monism into which all differences are eventually assimilated. The Jainas insist that the plurality of theories or value-sets they deal with are incommensurable, incapable of simultaneously being true in each other's system. Immediately, the following objection arises: if Jainas hold that theories that are irreducibly incompatible somehow can be integrated or held together within some overarching principle, are they not committed to contradiction?

This chapter tackles the following issues. What is the ethical relevance of the Jaina doctrine, such that it is worth examining? What exactly are the historically specific details of this doctrine? How should we interpret these doctrines, such that a defensible concept of multiplism is explicated? Finally, as the preceding paragraph indicates, how is multiplism, for all its potential relevance and application to ethics, to be rescued from the acute problems that seem to beset it? I hope to present the Jaina philosophy in such a way as to present a complex but sustainable understanding of how to approach intellectual conflict, carrying with it an account of toleration that could yield a model for the cultural world that we all now inhabit.

## CONFLICT, TOLERATION, AND THE RELEVANCE OF JAINA PHILOSOPHY

The incontrovertible fact of intellectual conflict is our starting point. There simply is a variety of views and actions consequential on those views. These are in conflict, in the sense that to hold one view is both to hold other views mistaken and to find the actions (broadly understood) consequential on those other views unacceptable. It is the diversity of views and the pervasiveness of conflict between them that call for multiplism. They do so by prompting two questions:

> *Question 1* (Q1). Why are things this way? What is reality like, such that a conflicting diversity of views exists?

> *Question 2* (Q2). What is to be done? How should we, who are part of that diversity, approach that reality?

In brief, multiplism holds, in respect of these questions, the following answers:

> *Answer 1* (A1). Reality is irreducibly multiple in itself; it yields multiple, incompatible truths; it is not just the case that finally there is only one true view of reality and all others are wrong.

> *Answer 2* (A2). We should tolerate conflicting views as genuinely incompatible truths, and not just put up with them until they can be corrected or discarded.

The metaphysical doctrine given as an answer to Q1, although conceptually interesting, seems to me less pressing on our attention than A2. It is here that a practical ethics is adumbrated and the thinking and attitudes necessary for such an ethics are explored. What we have in Jainism is a way of thinking about intellectual conflict and consequently a way of responding to conflict that are probably unique. We already know what the final Jaina position is: it is that which I have termed "multiplism." The two major tasks of this chapter now have to be undertaken. The first is a historical examination of the details of Jaina philosophy. The second is an elaboration of the relevant aspects of this philosophy to yield justification for the prescription in A2. Such elaboration must provide both some guidance on toleration and a defense of the coherence of this philosophy.

## NON-ONESIDEDNESS (MULTIPLISM), CIRCUMSCRIBED VIEWPOINTS, AND CONDITIONALITY: THE THREE CENTRAL CONCEPTS OF JAINA PHILOSOPHY

Jaina multiplism takes the form of the claim that no single truth-telling "point of view" can present a total or determinate description of reality. This is, literally, the doctrine of "non-onesidedness." The complexity or manifoldness of reality is thought to be beyond any single systematic description. An example of this doctrine is the Jaina enunciation of both substantialist and anti-substantialist ontological arguments. The developed Jaina position, as given by the philosopher Siddhasena (sixth century CE), involves a description of reality as both having an essence (literally, "own nature") and being eternally in flux-ridden modification. He argues that it is not possible to make a commitment to only one of these models. There is a defensible ontology of being, in which an element can be interpreted as a substance or as possessing essence. But equally, there is an ontology of becoming, in which an element is perpetually modified.[1] Since both can be defended, neither can be discarded. In this situation, it would be inconsistent with the spirit of Jainism to discard one,[2] because Jainism seeks to understand reality as it is. Various Jaina thinkers spend a good deal of time and energy arguing for the tenability of both ontological theories. Their strategy is to show that each is coherent and defensible, although they are incompatible, and from this to draw the conclusion that reality is so complex as to be capable of being comprehended in different, incompatible ways.

Now, we could urge on them three other options. We could offer the skeptical alternative that the existence of such incompatible views is a sign of our inability to grasp reality at all. Secondly, we could give the relativistic alternative that we simply construct different schemes, which have no bearing on each other. Finally, we could stand by an absolutist realism and say that the Jaina simply has not searched hard enough to find suitably sophisticated tests with which to settle the dispute between the ontologies. But the Jaina rejects the possibility of skepticism, works on the assumption that relativism is incoherent, and argues that the relevant cases are precisely those that escape even exhaustive analysis. No single "point of view" can present a total or determinate description of reality. This belief in manifoldness is expressed in the doctrines of circumscribed viewpoints and conditional predication.

The doctrine of "circumscribed viewpoints" brings out the epistemic modesty that the Jaina thinks is entailed by the manifoldness of reality. According to Prabhachandra (ninth century CE),

> A circumscribed viewpoint is a subject's particular approach or perspective which cannot repudiate or rule out a conflicting view, and which therefore expresses incomplete grasp of an entity.[3]

Modest though this is, it is not anodyne. A simple and unproblematic move would be to go from saying that reality is manifold to saying that therefore many different theories have to go into describing it. So an entity can be a work of art, daubs of paint, a rectangular canvas with markings, etc. More generally, to describe, say, an object like a human being would be to deploy such "viewpoints" as biology, physics, chemistry, sociology, anthropology, etc., each of which would be circumscribed by its conceptual resources.

If this is the Jaina point, it is anodyne to the point of being trivial. But, of course, this is not so. It simply cannot be so easy to say that there is a way of synthesizing, say, three classical Indian viewpoints of theism, atheism, and monism. These are not views assimilable into one another. These are views that are in conflict about what is identified as a single issue. There is agreement over the question and therefore conflict over the answer. The irreducible nature of this conflict is clearly something the Jainas accept; that, indeed, is their problem: "philosophers contradict each other, none of them is trustworthy."[4] That is to say, there is relativistic incomprehension!

The key phrase in the definition of circumscribed viewpoints given above is that the viewpoint "cannot rule out a conflicting view." So the important sort of viewpoints are not ones that simply lack the resources to comment on the claims of other viewpoints; they are ones that can be in meaningful opposition to others but nevertheless cannot rule them out.

The significant move is from a manifold reality to different, opposed theories used to describe it. This is what is truly circumscribed about viewpoints.

It is irrelevant to our purposes to look at what various Jaina writers say the specific circumscribed views are, for those would be of merely historical interest. For us, they are whatever systems, disciplines, or modes of analysis we find pressing. Now, having stated this doctrine of the irreducible plurality of viewpoints, the Jainas attempt a sort of synthesis. The claim of circumscribed viewpoints is that there can exist different, opposed views about the same entity; further, these views can be entertained together. It is the doctrine embodying this further claim, the doctrine of "conditional predication," which brings down all manner of troubles on the Jainas.

> From a particular point of view, you [Mahavira, the fifth-century BCE founder of Jainism] acknowledge, "it is", and from another point of view you acknowledge, "it is not." So too, "both it is and it is not" as well as "it is inexpressible." All these are asserted with reference to the doctrine of standpoints only, not unconditionally.[5]

Thus writes the fifth-century CE Jaina philosopher Samantabhadra. The particularity of each viewpoint that is opposed to the others is indicated by the use of the Sanskrit term *syāt* ("conditionally" or "under a certain condition").[6]

The idea expressed here becomes the theory of conditions. It is a method in which modes of predication affirm, negate, both affirm and negate, separately or simultaneously, in seven different ways, attributes of a particular object, in given specific contexts, without contradiction (argues Mallishena in the thirteenth century).[7] Famously, this sevenfold doctrine takes the following form:

> For any assertion that $p$ (where $p$ = "the soul is a divine spark"; "abortion is wrong"; "the internet should be unregulated"; "Picasso was the greatest painter ever"; "there are hidden variables in quantum interactions", etc.):
>
> (1) Conditionally, (it is true that) $p$; this is the predicate of *assertion*.
>
> (2) Conditionally, (it is true that) *not-p*; this is the predicate of *denial*.
>
> (3) Conditionally, $p$ and *not-p*; this is the predicate of *successive assertion and denial*.

(4) Conditionally, inexpressibly *p*; this is the predicate of *simultaneous assertion and denial.*

(5) Conditionally, *p* and inexpressibly *p*; (1) and (4).

(6) Conditionally, *not-p* and inexpressibly *p*; (2) and (4).

(7) Conditionally, *p* and *not-p* and inexpressibly *p*; (3) and (4).

We can now see how the doctrine of conditional predication works: it states that given some condition, like "under the use of a particular theory or viewpoint," it is arguable that statements that are "relevantly opposed" can simultaneously be entertained. They are relevant to each other because they are about the same entity, but they are opposed because they use incompatible operators, like assertion and denial. Once it is recognized that incompatible statements are conditioned by the requirements of their respective viewpoints, it is correct to grant that they are true simultaneously. This is where the problem lies. The relevant viewpoints are opposed; that is to say, they cannot be asserted by the same rational subject. To assert them would simply be to state a contradiction: *p and not-p.*[8] How could a doctrine meant to say something about the nature of reality and our claims about it be coherent if it is committed to contradiction?

The Jaina philosophers, as I understand their argument, do not want their doctrine to result in blank contradiction. They are keenly aware of this criticism from their opponents.[9] In fact, they themselves put their opponents' argument trenchantly: the existence and the non-existence of an entity are mutually opposed states; *p* and *not-p* have contradictory semantic values.[10] So it is important for the Jainas to establish the non-contradictory claim of their sevenfold predication, the relevant ones being (3) and (4).

The basic Jaina argument in support of the claim of non-contradiction is that "experience shows that there is no contradiction in reality."[11] How can this be defended meaningfully, in consonance with both the Jaina commitment to conflicting viewpoints and the rational requirement of non-contradiction?

## PROBLEMS AND CHALLENGES

The modern Indian analytic philosopher Bimal Matilal[12] takes seriously the requirement that the points of view from which two opposed statements, *p* and *not-p*, are asserted must in some sense be *in conflict.*[13]

On his interpretation, *p* holds under some condition acceptable to view 1, and *not-p* holds under some condition acceptable to view 2, and these conditions are incompatible. If they are incompatible, they cannot be adhered to simultaneously. There is no contradiction because the statements have been conditionalized differently; but nonetheless, there is non-trivial opposition or disagreement because the two conditions cannot hold simultaneously. Thus, it would not be possible to do a metaphysical analysis of the world simultaneously in terms of persistence (being) *and* of change (becoming); so the world is eternal and it is not eternal (as Mahavira says in the *Bhagavatisutra*, 9.386).

I shall embroider a more mundane example, used by Matilal, to pursue this point. A man has spinal curvature but wishes to join the palace guards. An orthopedist specializing in this condition measures him along the spine when collecting data and finds him six feet tall. But when he goes to see the sergeant-major of the guards, the latter makes him stand on the parade ground and measures him at his shoulder, and finds him less than six feet tall. Now the army man cannot adhere to the condition under which the doctor works and still perform his duty. There is a difference in point of view, and the difference is non-trivial. In that case, the Jaina would say that the man is and is not six feet tall, say that without contradiction, and yet say something interesting about the manifoldness of reality.

This gets us some way toward seeing how the Jaina could be talking of conflicting points of view without running into contradiction. But this is still not a strong enough enunciation of the notion of incompatible viewpoints. This is because there is still some vantage point from which we can resolve the issue so that there is no conflict involved. It would be perfectly consistent for the doctor, were he to be employed to do medical checks by the military, then to pronounce that the man in question was not six feet tall after all. In other words, there is nothing inconsistent about adopting the other condition. There is no conflict after all. If there is no conflict, there are no genuine differences in points of view.

I will give another example to drive home the point. Let there be a view, "it is correct to have government subsidies for farmers in the face of international competition." Then, there is the conflicting view, "it is not correct to ..." The Jaina schema would have us say, "conditionally, it is correct and it is not correct to ..." On the interpretation just given, we would say that there is some hidden meaning in this last statement. The suggestion would be that we ought to conditionalize the first two statements so that they do not conflict; and if they do not conflict, the third statement would not be a contradiction. So, there is some condition P and some condition Q. Condition P is: "there is a vulnerable farming community whose loss of income through the removal of subsidies would threaten the health of the domestic economy." Condition Q is: "the farming community is benefiting at the expense of consumers who have to pay higher prices than they would for imported commodities." Then, obviously, both view 1 – "it is correct to have subsidies" – and view 2 – "it is not correct to have subsidies" – can be made without contradiction, so long as the conditionalizing is explicit. The consequence is that it would be consistent to go from adhering to one condition to adhering to the other on the grounds that the situation has changed. So there is no conflict after all. Yet, what is interesting about this apparent difference of opinion, apart from the earnest but obvious call to look more deeply at common, underlying principles? There is no real challenge involved in claims where imposing conditions removes conflict.

The metaphysical fact is that views that do not conflict but merely give the illusion of conflict do not do much for the idea of an irreducibly plural or manifold reality. A suitably powerful theory (or point of view) can encompass the apparently conflicting claims and would then be a single, sophisticated point of view. In the example given, surely any good economist can develop a model in which different procedures are allowed for depending on the situation. In the more traditional one, surely, a metaphysical realist can encompass the claim that a thing is a pot and is not a cloth, without any difficulty at all. In the end, if the conflict can be resolved by deeper analysis, that analysis must itself be a more powerful theory and therefore a particular or single point of view itself.

In contrast, look at this version of the above example. Again, let there be a view, "it is correct to have government subsidies for farmers in the face of international competition." Then, there is the conflicting claim, "it is not correct to ..." The Jaina schema would have us say, "conditionally, it is correct and it is not correct to ..." But suppose that the former is given by a protectionist trade theorist and the latter by a free-marketeer. The former stands by trade subsidies owing to the need to never depend on foreign sources for vital produce, on the calculation of building long-term competitive advantage even in a currently uncompetitive sector, and what have you. The latter stands by her claim because she believes in letting the markets work, and so on. There is no conditionalizing in either theory.

There is genuine conflict, just as there would have been in the Jaina's time between the Buddhist, who maintained that there was no pot because reality consisted of unconceptualizable point-instants, and the Nyaya philosopher, who asserted that there was a pot because reality consisted of mid-sized objects that existed as presented in conception-loaded experience.

The Jaina seems to be saying that the manifoldness of reality is manifested in just this irreducible plurality – irreducible, that is, to consistency within a larger theory. If that is so, then the Jaina certainly is flirting with contradiction. What could he be doing?[14] I will now look at a suggested solution that takes conflict seriously, but will then argue that it invites a different but still traditional criticism. I will then go back and have a closer look at the Jaina doctrines, reconstruct two underlying principles, and use them to give my own understanding of Jaina philosophy.

The question is: what should we understand the Jaina to be doing when he states that *p and not-p* and a genuine, irreducible conflict is involved? One answer could be that the Jaina is merely attempting to describe or catalogue the various views involved in a debate. So he should be understood as saying, "abortion is wrong, and abortion is acceptable; that is to say, abortion is wrong according to those who stand by the principle that human life is sacred, and the fetus is sacred, whereas abortion is acceptable according to those who think the welfare of the mother justifies abortion before a certain period." The Jaina is merely recording the clash of opinions. The claim that our grasp of reality is multiple is borne out by the different points of view that people have. The Jaina's position simply is that there are contradictory positions. He is not saying, "I assert that *p and not-p*"; he is actually saying, "I assert that *p* is asserted (by someone) and *not-p* is asserted (by someone else)."

This, of course, means that the Jaina himself is not making an assertion whose content is *p and not-p*, after all. Hence, there is no contradiction involved. At the same time, the conflict of different viewpoints is accepted because no attempt is made to assimilate *p* and *not-p* through some wider explanation. But now a new problem emerges: that of assertion or metaphysical commitment. What is the Jaina saying about reality (and, importantly, our grasp of it)? The description of two points of view is not itself a commitment; it does not say what the Jaina believes. As Shankara's original criticism goes, the sevenfold predication must be (of the form of) a "definite assertion"; or else "the resulting claim will not have determinate content" and, "like doubts, lack all epistemic authority."[15] After all, a Jaina teacher is an authority and must "impart knowledge,"[16] but how could he when he makes no definite commitment to what the case is? The Jaina himself recognizes the legitimacy of the requirement that one has to have "the capacity to decide on the determinate nature of entities." The Jaina appends to each conditional statement the word *eva*', which can be translated as "certainly" or "definitely." This performs the assertive function; its work is to assert or define.

Whatever the defence of the Jaina position, the requirement that the Jaina make a commitment – i.e. that he makes a contentful assertion about reality – must be taken seriously. On the present suggestion, this is not the case. A mere description of conflicting positions will not do any more than will an assertion that there is no contradiction.

I will now try to reconstruct the Jaina doctrines in such a way as to meet all our requirements: accept the reality of conflict, avoid contradiction, and make a commitment.

## THE PRINCIPLES OF MULTIPLISM

It must be clear that there is more than a spurious difference between viewpoints; there is real conflict. But this is not all there is to it. The viewpoints are not only in conflict but are circumscribed. We have seen that this cannot be a simple case of partial truth. In what other way could we understand the manner in which conflicting viewpoints are circumscribed? We get a clue from this remark by Siddhasena:

> All the viewpoints are valid in their respective schemes, but they fail if they attempt to refute each other. One who knows the "non-onesidedness" of reality never asserts the unqualified invalidity of a particular view.[17]

The following principle may be extracted from the doctrine of non-onesidedness (*anekāntavāda*):

> *Principle 1* (P1). No particular view 1 that asserts that *p* can from within the rational resources of its own system rule out or refute the claim that *not-p*, made under view 2.

It should, of course, be emphasized that this does not hold of any old claim. Nothing in P1 requires that any and every point of view should be accepted. We are here concerned only with those views that, in some way we cannot determine here, are not amenable to rational resolution.

So this is what the Jaina should be taken as saying. Advaitins cannot, from within their conception of a unified consciousness, rule out the possibility that reality is constituted by such momentariness as the Buddha is said to have experienced. A viewpoint is not a partial grasp of reality in the straightforward sense that it cannot, with its own resources, provide a determinate representation of reality; it is partial in the negative sense that it cannot, with its own resources, determine that *there are no other representations of reality.*

Can we appeal to any further, encompassing reason to try to determine which of view 1 and view 2 is "ultimately" correct? The Jaina cannot countenance this. If there is a further view, then that too could be held to be circumscribed in the way enunciated in P1. There would then be the threat of regress, a traditional objection to the Jaina position. The Jaina accepts that it is not possible to resolve the tension between views 1 and 2. The question of which of them is correct and the other wrong is "unanswerable." All that can be done is to state what holds under view 1 and what under view 2. This is what Mahavira does (in the recording of his words in the *Bhagavatisutras*) in answer to such questions as: What is the nature of the world? What is the nature of the soul? He simply but systematically gives the position under one point of view and then that under its opposing one. There seems, from his method, no further way of reducing the number of available answers. Reality is multiple: the ultimate state is one in which different, incompatible truths co-occur.

Now, one may ask: if one held view 1, one would give a certain answer, and if one held view 2, one would give another answer, but is there some way of deciding which of view 1 and view 2 to hold?

The answer that emerges from the silence is: there is no such way. So, why do people hold one of view 1 and view 2? For no reason as such. That is to say, for no further justifiable reason. They hold their view on non-rational grounds. I think we may reasonably extract another principle, this time derived from the doctrine of circumscribed viewpoints (*nayavada*). This centers on the idea that it is not determinately answerable (i.e. it is not answerable from any final rational viewpoint) as to which is the correct viewpoint to hold:

*Principle 2* (P2). There is no further ground for deciding between view 1 and view 2; they are held on non-rational grounds.

It is important at this point to see in what sense the Jaina takes the grounding of the choice between the views to be inexpressible. Both views are assertible, not because neither is a matter of plain truth, for both are. In other words, the Jainas do not think that there is no final resolution in the choice between viewpoints merely because such choice is only to do with matters of appropriateness or approbation rather than truth. They think that there is no such resolution because the choice between even ultimately truth-giving views is not a rational one.

## HOW TO ASSERT "CONDITIONALLY, *P* AND *NOT-P*"

We can now make an attempt to explain the problematic Jaina statement, "conditionally, *p* and *not-p*." The Jaina enunciates a "meta-ethics of multiplist toleration." Here is the sequence of thoughts that sums it up:

(1) In view 1 (it is true that) *p*; in view 2 (it is true that) *not-p*.

(2) *p* and *not-p* are conditionally assertible in two ways.

    (i) By P1 above (derived from the doctrine of non-onesidedness), even if view 1 is held, it must be assertible that *not-p* in view 2, because view 1 lacks resources internal to itself to rule out *not-p*; and *vice versa* for view 2.

    (ii) By P2 above (derived from the doctrine of circumscribed viewpoints), independently of holding view 1 or view 2, it cannot be decided whether to assert only one of *p* and *not-p*, because, there are no non-rational grounds for holding one of view 1 and view 2.

(3) However, there is conflict between those views that generate assertions of *p* and those that generate assertions of *not-p*. This is because:

    (i) only one view is actually held by anyone; and

    (ii) since only view 1 or view 2 is held, there can be no assertion of both *p* and *not-p* within either view 1 or view 2 alone.

Thus, there is commitment, there is acceptance of conflict, and there is respect for the law of non-contradiction.[18]

What makes this a theory of multiplism, however, is that the Jaina goes from acknowledging the plurality of views to requiring a way of integrating that plurality into a single value, or rather, a meta-value. This meta-value is what may be called Jaina "toleration." Jainas commit themselves to saying that it is correct for each of us, whatever our personal views, to allow for the real possibility of multiple conflicting truths and to approach those with whom we disagree with this overarching value of accepting their hold on truth. In other words, they are committed to changing the attitude of people in conflict, because they are committed to reality being multiple and therefore yielding different, incompatible truths to different, rationally incommensurable viewpoints. The overarching value is not one that adjudicates between the views; rather, it acknowledges them. But that very acknowledgement itself transforms (or calls for the transformation of) the attitudes of those who hold each view. The Jaina takes the fact of conflicting viewpoints, argues to their non-rational grounds without denying their objectivity, and concludes that the rational rejection of incompatibles should not rule out the ethical acceptance of their truthhood. This acceptance may be called "toleration", but only in a way highly specific to Jaina philosophy.

## TOLERATION: THE UNIQUE NATURE OF JAINA ETHICS

The rest of this chapter will be devoted to an exploration of the idea of toleration and the way in which the Jaina arguments make for a special theory of toleration. Toleration I understand here to be the ability to accept, in some way, an irreducibly conflicting view. Toleration is required precisely when there is conflict between different coherent consistent views. The Jaina comes along and says that, conditionally, he asserts both views. He explains this by saying that each view finds itself unable to refute the other on any basis that the other will accept. Further, there is no higher or common basis on which the matter can be decided. Each proponent holds a particular view only for non-rational or pre-rational reasons. Since, the Jaina finds no further reason to prefer one rather than the other view, he is perfectly willing to accept them both. He wants to do this because Jainas think this is what toleration is and it is the celebration of toleration which they take to be a spiritual path. This is what Matilal calls the "path of the inclusive middle."[19]

When the Jaina argues that conditionally *p* and conditionally *not-p*, he's alerting us to the fact that we do not in principle possess the means to rationally discard one of those propositions (given, as usual, that they are in some way relevant and consistent in themselves, and not lunatic statements). He demonstrates the toleration he thinks we ought to possess, by himself asserting the legitimacy of each proposition given the non-rational constraint on the viewpoint from which it is rationally derived.

But this is toleration in a special, very strong sense, for it is vital for the Jaina to be able to hold that the conclusions of both views are assertible, each given a circumscribed viewpoint. So the Jaina takes the way of overcoming conflict (onesidedness) to be an embracing of the conflicting views, suitably conditionalized. Having overcome the charge of contradiction, the Jaina makes a complex commitment to the assertibility of conflicting viewpoints.

This is not what we normally understand as toleration. Toleration is the assertion of one view and a willingness to allow others to assert theirs. But we must now make a distinction between *practical toleration* and *intellectual toleration.* "Practical toleration" is what we normally understand by the word "toleration."

Of the three broad, commonly accepted answers to the question of why we should *practice* toleration, two may be said to be objectivist and one subjectivist. Objectivist answers are based on the notion that the assertions of conflicting viewpoints are matters of fact and truth, whereas the subjectivist answer is based on the notion that these assertions are determined by such intrinsic considerations as appropriateness or the sentiment of approbation.

I will characterize these answers as each having a certain conception of toleration as a value. In order to do this, I must first make an intuitive distinction about *values*: a value is "instrumental" or "provisional" if it is adhered to for the sake of its effectiveness in pursuing ends, the attainment of which would render this value redundant. On the other hand, a value is "basic" or "ultimate" if it is adhered to because so adhering to it is itself an end and not a means to an end.

One objectivist argument for toleration is merely a pragmatic recognition of the nature of belief and the acquisition of viewpoints. People cannot will themselves or be forced to believe views (especially to do with religion), and so it is of no use to try to coerce them to give up their present view and adopt ours. Therefore, if our objective is truly to change the views of those whom we consider mistaken (as opposed to killing them or merely forcing them to conform outwardly to our norms), it is pointless to be intolerant of their views. We simply must put up with their views until we can persuade them through reasoning to come to accept our views.

The other famous objectivist argument is the instrumental one that we simply cannot be sure that our views alone are right. Moreover, even if this were the case, the co-existence of different views simply encourages rational debate, with the hope that ever more coherent views will emerge.

These objectivist arguments use toleration purely as means, not as a value in itself. In the former case, toleration is merely a negative conception of the limits of our ability to deal with a conflicting viewpoint. In the latter, it is a strategy for securing some final correct viewpoint, attainment of which would render toleration redundant. In both accounts, the acceptance of incompatible viewpoints is strictly provisional, a reluctant acknowledgment of the role of these viewpoints.

A more generous attitude toward incompatible viewpoints is found in the subjectivist conception of toleration. Since subjectivism about any particular area involves the idea that there is no determinate fact of the matter which renders certain views right and others wrong, conflict between viewpoints is not always seen as one between truth and falsehood. Incompatible viewpoints might simply be the result of different "sentiments," appropriate subjective states, or whatever. In that case, all we can say about our viewpoint is that it (and maybe it alone) is apt for us rather than that it alone is true. A conflicting viewpoint may be inapt for us (and we may even consider it inapt for the person holding it), but we are not driven to thinking that reality makes that viewpoint wrong. We may be irritated by someone holding a view to which we do not subscribe, but we do not need to think that, in order to be coherent, we must hold that views incompatible with ours are wrong. There is no objective reality against which the views can be checked and found wanting. It is possible to permit, put up with, or tolerate differing views when we are not committed, on pain of inconsistency, to the erroneousness of those views. Toleration is a basic value because it exemplifies a proper approach to viewpoints. Differences between them do not involve truth (and therefore the need to avoid contradiction); toleration is that attitude which recognizes that the constitution of people's subjectivity simply results in different viewpoints.

The worry about this subjectivist conception is that it gains a richer sense of toleration only by weakening the sense of conflict. The conflict between viewpoints is one of what we find appropriate, and it is reasonably clear that different people might find different views appropriate. The inability to assert a viewpoint that differs from mine owes only to my psychological make-up or some such subjective feature; it is not because of the threat of stark contradiction, or the taking of liberties with the requirement of rational consistency.

I do not want to say that these conceptions of toleration are mistaken. I merely point out that objectivist approaches to toleration do not treat it as an ultimate value reflecting the nature of reality but merely as a constraint on the pursuit of truth, whereas subjectivist approaches do treat it as a value reflecting the truth-independent nature of viewpoints but only because they undervalue the rationally irreducible nature of intellectual conflict.

"Intellectual toleration" is not only different; our first thought would be to think it impossible. For consider: what is it to tolerate someone's views? It is to live with something with which you disagree (with which your views are in conflict). But that is only to say that you take your conclusion to be correct and the other person's to be wrong. That is why there is conflict, after all. So, whatever you actually do in terms of putting up with the view with which you disagree, you do not actually accept the possibility of that view being correct. (If you did, then you would not really be in disagreement.) Since it would be inconsistent for you to assert the correctness of your view and at the same time allow for the correctness of another (i.e. opposing) view, you could not make any commitment to its being correct in any circumstances. (You could make a commitment to someone having the right to hold it, even if you hold it to be incorrect, but that is not intellectual toleration *per se*.) There seems to be no such thing as intellectual toleration of an opposed view, because holding one view precisely is to reject an opposing one. Practical toleration is toward the person who holds a view opposed to your own (well-developed and coherent one), not toward the view itself; you have to be committed to its being wrong. To repeat, that is why you put up with it, not agree with or embrace it.

But Jainas do want toleration toward views, not just toward those who hold the views. For them it is not only legitimate for people to hold different views; it is legitimate for there to be different such views. This is because they take reality to be a manifold, irreducibly understandable only in a multiplicity of not necessarily consistent ways.[20]

Now, how might all this translate into practice? What is it to act in this Jaina-tolerant way? The big difference is between those of us who might be persuaded by the Jaina prescription for multiplist toleration and the Jainas themselves.

We are most likely to be persuaded to accept Jaina toleration because we can see no other way of both (1) adhering to non-contradictory views of our own and (2) making sense of and responding to the fact of irreducible intellectual conflict. But we might accept the Jaina concept and still find that acknowledgement of the non-rational ground of our viewpoints does not alter the psychological fact that we do make that choice. Firstly, there is no appeal I can make to the teachings of the Buddhist tradition in order to reject the possibility that I could have been a Christian or to assert that it would be wrong to be a Christian. It is impossible for me to be a Buddhist and a Christian at the same time, but I recognize that I could have been one rather than the other.

If, then, the choice is a non-rational matter, to recognize that it is non-rational may alter my former conviction that it was rational (if I continue to be rational about it, as it were), but since it precisely is a non-rational matter, the rational recognition of its non-rational basis could well have no bearing on my actually making that choice. So, I might well recognize that my being a Buddhist rather than a Christian was a matter of my being born into a certain family, or being educated in a certain way, or my inclination or disposition toward certain teachings and practices rather than others. But precisely for that reason, I find myself carrying on being a Buddhist. In that situation, to remain Jaina-tolerant would be to entertain the possibility that I could have been a Christian and have rationally asserted Christian beliefs and to accept that I do not do so on no extrinsic rational grounds. If I had been otherwise, I might legitimately have been a Christian, but I am not. If I had been a Christian, then I would have asserted Christian beliefs and I could not have been wrong to have done so. But, granted my psychologically given state of being a Buddhist, I cannot escape asserting Buddhist, non-Christian propositions about *nirvana*, etc. I am a Buddhist, but I can see how I could have been a Christian, and I would have a truth-claiming conception of the religious life in either case. The difficulty in having this attitude lies in taking the viewpoint one holds and the viewpoint that one is tolerant toward as both being matters of plain truth.

Now, difficult though this attitude is, it seems psychologically plausible to follow the Jaina's suggestion and hold the assertibility of incompatible views. The position of the Jaina himself is more difficult to anatomise. He adheres to multiplism because he makes a metaphysical commitment to a single reality that contains a multiplicity of incompatible truths. The Jaina does not take himself to be holding any particular viewpoint, such as we might have. He takes the fact of all those viewpoints containing truths to itself be the content of his view. The Jaina's toleration of views is not cultivated as a sensible response to the simultaneous need for coherence and treatment of intellectual conflict as with us. Rather, it flows from the Jaina's metaphysical commitment to an integrated reality of many differing and different truths, which he thinks is indicated by the fact that Mahavira (the *Jina*, the Conquerer) himself deliberately argued, conditionally, for differing and different truths.

For this reason, the Jaina's own position vanishes behind the assertion of toleration. For him the act of toleration obliterates commitment to any one position. The Jaina's personal position just is that of toleration as a principle in itself, not as an attitude held from one position toward another.

What the Jaina hopes to extract from us is an acknowledgment that the position each of us actually holds can contain within it the attitude of multiplist toleration toward other views. Our position does not vanish behind the assertion of toleration but makes space for it. But both the Jaina and we, who accept his prescription for the treatment of intellectual conflict, share multiplism. We acknowledge the fact of irreducible conflict and the principles of the intrinsic limits of rationality and the non-rational grounds of viewpoints (P1 and P2). Consequently, we acknowledge the overarching value of entertaining (in others) a multiplicity of truthful views. This entertainment of multiplicity is what I have called "Jaina toleration."

To be Jaina-tolerant is to be in a state of genuine empathy. It is difficult for us to draw out a more detailed psychological picture of this state of mind from the Jaina ethical literature, with its attention to outward conduct, its endless cataloguing of duties and ritual practice, its often mysterious soteriological claims. But the Jaina has a powerful motivation for his psychologically difficult requirement: to practice a form of intellectual nonviolence. This is to be in that mental state which best expresses a proper orientation toward reality. As the early Jaina commentator Kundakunda (second–third century CE) puts it, to take attitudes of aversion to particular views is to commit acts of intellectual violence toward them (we are, of course, talking of certain relevant views;

the Jaina is certainly prepared to condemn many other views).[21] So to have the conviction that to be a Christian is to hold the Buddhist wrong (however nice one is toward the latter) is, for the Jaina, to commit intellectual violence toward the Buddhist. Any form of onesidedness is intellectual violence, so interpreted, and to practice nonviolence is to "accept" the other person and viewpoint through conditional assertion. Such assertion means that the nonviolent individual does not reject the validity of another viewpoint; he or she does not question the intellectual integrity of the other person.

There is still the elusive notion of acceptance. What sort of mental state should one be in when practicing intellectual nonviolence? To practice toleration, as intellectual nonviolence, one requires a sense of empathy with the person with whose conclusions one has rational disagreement. It seems to me that this sense of empathy consists in having an imaginative location in the sentiments and attitudes of someone whose views are in rational disagreement with yours. By imagining oneself in the intellectual space of the other, one comes to an understanding of what it is to be in that position. Violence occurs through the rejection of the integrity of another; the same holds for intellectual violence. Nonviolence is the acceptance of that integrity, an acceptance brought about through an imaginative self-location in the intellectual space and life of the other.

We have two stages in our acceptance of the Jaina philosophy. By accepting the legitimacy of the Jaina's position (by accepting that it is genuinely a commitment and genuinely non-contradictory), we come to understand what it is to be tolerant and to practice this genuine toleration ourselves. But if we adopt that position ourselves, we become Jainas. It is surely legitimate for the Jaina to give us a method that we can use and cherish in our own lived beliefs, in the hope that we will eventually adopt his own.

NOTES

1. Siddhasena, *Sanmatitarka*, ed. S. Sanghvi and B. Doshi (Ahmedabad: Gujarat Puratattva Mandira Granthavali, 1924), I.11–12.
2. Ibid., III.8–9.
3. Prabhacandra, *Prameyakamalamārtanḍa*, ed. M.K. Shastri (Bombay: Nirnayasagar Press, 1941), p. 676.
4. Samantabhadra, *Āptamīmāṃsā*, ed. G. Jain (Benares: Sanatana Jaina Granthamala, 1914), v. 3.

5. Ibid., v. 14.
6. Following Matilal's interpretation of Samantabhadra's identification of *syāt* with *kadācit* or *kathāñcit*, I shall take the term to mean "under a certain condition" or "conditionally." I shall use "conditional" and "conditionally" as technical terms throughout. B.K. Matilal, *The Central Philosophy of Jainism* (Ahmedabad: L.D. Press, 1981), p. 53.
7. Malliṣeṇa, *Syādvādamañjari*, ed. A.B. Dhruva (Bombay: Bombay University Press, 1933), pp. 142–143.
8. Here, I take (3) to be unproblematic in that, given obvious changes in conditions, it is possible to assert and deny the same proposition; all that is required is that the relevant conditions have changed. So it is the simultaneous assertion and denial which seems to resist any simple dissolution of contradiction.
9. For example, the eighth-century *brahman* philosopher Shankara. See Shankara, *Brahmasūtrabhāṣya*, ed. A.K. Shastri (Bombay: Nirnayasagar Press, 1938), II.2.33, pp. 559ff.
10. Haribhadra, *Anekāntajayapatākā*, ed. H.R. Kapadia (Baroda, India: Baroda Oriental Series, 1940), pp. 11, 44.
11. Prabhacandra, *Prameyakamalamārtaṇḍa*, p. 93.
12. Matilal, *The Central Philosophy of Jainism*, pp. 59–61.
13. See the appendix following the notes for my critique of competing interpretations.
14. The issues discussed here are, of course, applicable to men and women; so that "the Jaina" of the chapter could, in our times, be either. However, the various formulations given are derived from the classical texts, and these, as with the majority of historical texts, East and West, were written by men. So "the Jaina" would actually have been a man, in so far as the philosophical debates were concerned. It is difficult to state precisely where the issue is purely a reconstruction of the historical arguments and where it is a statement of contemporary philosophical strategies. For this reason, the masculine pronoun has been retained.
15. Shankara, *Brahmasūtrabhaṣya*, II.2.33, p. 560.
16. Ibid.
17. Siddhasena, *Sanmatitarka*, I.28.
18. The account can be rounded out with another layer of complex correlation. "By P1 above (derived from the doctrine of non-onesidedness), even if view 1 is held, it must be assertible that not-*p* in view 2, because view 1 lacks resources internal to itself to rule out *not*-p; and *vice versa* for view 2" can be equated with the fourth conditionality, "the predicate of simultaneous assertion and denial" or the view that *p* is inexpressible. "By P2 above (derived from the doctrine of circumscribed viewpoints), independently of holding view 1 or view 2, it cannot be decided whether to

assert only one of *p* and *not-p*, because, there are no non-rational grounds for holding one of view 1 and view 2" can be equated with the third conditionality, "the predicate of successive assertion and denial" or the view that *p* and *not-p*.

19. Matilal, *The Central Philosophy of Jainism*, p. 18.
20. We must be clear that this is not a form of relativism, in which different views have different theories of truth/correctness. If the two views were relative in this way, there would be no conflict. It is precisely because the views identify common entities about which they make assertions that there is conflict. If there is any sort of communication, it must involve a common theory of truth. As a common theory of truth is bound to a common rationality, it follows that there must also be commensuration between the claims of the communicating opponents. The Indian schools of thought are indeed commensurate, as they use a common system for validating knowledge claims. The situation that the Jaina is talking about is one where common conceptions of rationality and truth standards, and thence of meaning, hold.
21. Kundakunda, *Pravacanasāra*, ed. A.N. Upadhyaye (Agas: Rajachandra Jaina Sastramala, 1964), 3.17.

## APPENDIX: TECHNICAL NOTE ON COMPETING INTERPRETATIONS

Modern commentators have usually tried to rescue the Jainas from contradiction. The standard or common interpretation of the Jaina defence is this:

1. They believe in a "complex" reality, whose complexity consists in its being incomprehensible from any one point of view.
2. In consequence, many points of view are taken to be required to comprehend this reality.
3. From this it is supposed to follow that the multiplicity of views includes views that have the appearance of contradiction.

In conclusion, it is held that there is only an appearance of contradiction, since the complexity of reality "admits of opposing predicates from different standpoints" (C. Sharma, *A Critical Survey of Indian Philosophy* [Delhi: Motilal Banarsidass, 1976], p. 52). Sharma specifically defines opposition of predicates as the affirmation and negation of a judgment – which looks clearly to imply contradiction – before denying that this is contradiction.

But this is does not rebut the challenge as it stands. There ought to be no problem with the possibility of multiple points of view; i.e. one could easily grant (1) and (2) without logical qualms. The problem lies in the unmotivated transition from (2) to (3). Multiple views in themselves are logically unproblematic, since they can be held without violating any standard of rationality. We have already commented on that. The usual suggestion

(S.N. Das Gupta, *A History of Indian Philosophy*, vol. 1 [Cambridge: Cambridge University Press, 1922], pp. 179ff; Y.J. Padmarajiah, *The Jaina Theories of Reality and Knowledge*, [Bombay: Jaina Sahitya Vikas Mandal, 1986], p. 153) is that if *x* were a pot, then, the propositions "the pot is (exists)" and "the pot is not (does not exist)" are only *apparently* contradictory: this is simply to assert that a pot *is* a pot ("from the point of view of its own substance"), whereas a pot *is not* cloth or wood ("what is other than potness"; "from the point of view of other substances"); so too, a pot *is*, here and now, but a pot *is not*, in some other time and place (Das Gupta, ibid.).

It is sad that Padmarajiah's exceptionally detailed and patient exposition of Jaina philosophy should be marred by such problematic views. Padmarajiah further confounds the situation by comparing his interpretation of this predicate to the elucidation by the sixth-century CE philosopher of the Hindu Mimamsa school of exegesis, Kumarila Bhatta, of the notion of "existence" (Kumārila Bhaṭṭa, *Slokavārttika*, ed. R.S. Tailanga [Benares: Chawkambha Sanskrit Series, 1898], p. 476). Kumarila is concerned to make a distinction between fictive entities and entities that are absent to cognition (sky-flower as opposed to cloth in the cognition of a pot). So he says of the former that they can never enter into the content of a cognition, even one that leads to a negative judgment, whereas the latter can enter into the content of a cognition when the judgment is a denial. Then, "cloth" enters into the content of the cognition of "pot" when the subject, looking at a pot, denies that it is cloth. In that sense, every existent entity can enter into the content of the cognition of another existent entity even when it (the former entity) is absent (does not exist) at the time of the cognition of the latter existent. That is why the cognition of a pot also can have the content "non-cloth." This is in contrast to fictive entities that do not give content to cognition. This is a quite different issue from the one Padmarajiah is addressing, namely, the simultaneity of complete assertions and denials. The difference should be evident from the following discussion.

This defence, however, is unfair to the Jainas, for it unwittingly implies intellectual dishonesty on their part. All this interpretation does is to make it seem that "*x* is" and "*x* is not" are not, as they seem, well-formed formulae representing propositions predicating existence ("is") and non-existence ("is not") of *x*, but, rather, disguised versions of an incomplete predicative propositional formula, which ought really to be read as two versions of the same partially formed predicative "*x* is ..." (such that "*x* is F" ("this is a pot"), "*x* is *not*-G" ("this is not cloth", etc.). That is to say, the relevant predicates are not "is-ness" and "is-not-ness" at all but some other, hitherto unmentioned "F-ness" ("being-a-pot") and "not-G-ness" ("not-being-cloth"). If this were the case, then, of course, there is no contradiction; but there are no "opposing" predicates either, for obviously "F" ("pot") and "not-G" ("cloth") are not in any sense opposed, but merely two of a list of *x*'s qualifiers. They imply no epistemologically significant "point of view," only a list of qualities. This makes it seem as if the Jainas, while pretending to say something about conflicting points of views, are in reality only suggesting that conflict is an illusion brought about by an incomplete consideration of qualities from one point of view.

Clearly though, the Jainas are trying to say something about *conflicting* views, by the conditional use of *syāt*. But this is not what the examples provided show at all. The point is that in the model provided above "F" and "not-G" can consistently be predicated of *x* from within any *one* school or "point of view" (for example, the Naiyayikas ought to have no difficulty in incorporating the reading of the pot suggested by Das Gupta et al. into their own direct realist ontology). So, the Jainas are rescued from contradiction only at the price of triviality and irrelevance. What is so "inexpressible" about this way of combining *p* and *not-p*? The very motivation behind that term is lost on this interpretation.

Two things have to be done, then, if we are to take the Jaina computation of possible propositional combinations seriously as a technique for resolution of conflict between two different and complete points of view:

1. The interpretation should obviously take "*x* is" and "*x* is not" as two well-formed formulae which can be represented as the complete propositions *p* and *not-p*.
2. *p* and *not-p* must be entertained, respectively, by two different "points of view" (two different ontologies, traditions, schools, paradigms, etc.), and not be assimilable into one "point of view" as in the above examples.

What happens, then, with the standard interpretation is that the charge of contradiction is met only by denying conflict. Without conflict, differences of viewpoints become epistemologically uninteresting and hardly worth the bother. What is so interesting about the assertion that a table is a single entity and is not a single entity, when ordinary language use asserts the former and quantum physics the latter? This interpretation of the Jaina philosophy makes it a small plea for deeper analysis of superficial (often very superficial) differences, but nothing more.

# SELECT BIBLIOGRAPHY

## RELIGION AND ETHICS

Card, C. (ed.) *Feminist Ethics*. Lawrence, University of Kansas Press, 1991

Kekes, J. *The Morality of Pluralism*. Princeton, Princeton University Press, 1993

Kellenberger, J. *Relationship Morality*. University Park, PA, Pennsylvania State University Press, 1995

MacIntyre, A. *After Virtue: A Study in Moral Theory*, 2nd edn. Notre Dame, University of Notre Dame Press, 1984

Phillips, D.Z. (ed.) *Religion and Morality*. London, Macmillan, 1996

Pojman, L.P. *The Moral Life: An Introductory Reader in Ethics and Literature*. Oxford and New York, Oxford University Press, 2000

Runzo, J. *Ethics, Religion, and the Good Society*. Louisville, KY, Westminster/ John Knox, 1992

Stout, J. *Ethics after Babel: The Languages of Morals and Their Discontents*. Boston, Beacon, 1988

## ETHICS AND RELIGION IN THE WEST

Battin, M.P. *Ethics in the Sanctuary: Examining the Practices of Organized Religion*. New Haven and London, Yale University Press, 1990

Bennett, J.C. *Christian Ethics and Social Policy*. New York, C. Scribner's Sons, 1946

Dorff, E.N. and Newman, L.E. (eds) *Contemporary Jewish Ethics and Morality: A Reader*. New York, Oxford, 1995

Gordis, R. *The Dynamics of Judaism: A Study in Jewish Law.* Bloomington, Indiana University Press, 1990

Gustafson, J.M. *Ethics from a Theocentric Perspective. Volume One: Theology and Ethics.* Chicago, University of Chicago Press, 1981

Hick, J. *Evil and the God of Love,* rev. edn. San Francisco, Harper & Row, 1978

Hourani G.F. *Reason and Tradition in Islamic Ethics.* Cambridge, Cambridge University Press, 1985

Mullan, D.G. (ed.) *Religious Pluralism in the West.* Malden, MA and Oxford, Blackwell, 1998

Pannenberg, W. *Ethics.* Philadelphia, Westminster, 1981

Porter, J. *Moral Action and Christian Ethics.* Cambridge, Cambridge University Press, 1995

Rossi, P.J. *Together Toward Hope: A Journey to Moral Theology.* Notre Dame, University of Notre Dame Press, 1983

—— and Soukup, P.A. (eds) *Mass Media and the Moral Imagination.* Kansas City, Sheed & Ward, 1994

Schimmel, S. *The Seven Deadly Sins: Jewish, Christian, and Classical Reflections on Human Nature.* New York, Free Press, 1992

Stowasser B.F. *Women in the Qur'an: Traditions and Interpretation.* New York, Oxford University Press, 1994

Taha, M.M. *The Second Message of Islam,* trans. A.A. An-Na'im. Syracuse, NY, Syracuse University Press, 1987

Westphal, M. (ed.) *Postmodern Philosophy and Christian Thought.* Bloomington, Indiana University Press, 1999

## ETHICS AND RELIGION IN ASIA

Babb, L.A. *Absent Lord: Ascetics and Kings in a Jain Ritual.* Berkeley, University of California Press, 1996

Berthrong, J.H. *Transformations of the Confucian Way.* Boulder, Westview, 1998

Carrithers, M. and Humphrey, C. (eds) *The Assembly of Listeners: Jains in Society.* Cambridge, Cambridge University Press, 1991

Confucius. *The Analects,* trans. D.C. Lau. London, Penguin, 1979

Cort, J. (ed.) *Open Boundaries: Jain Cultures and Communities in India History.* Albany, State University of New York Press, 1998

Dalai Lama. *The Good Heart,* trans. G.T. Jinpa. London, Rider, 1996

Das Gupta, S.N. *A History of Indian Philosophy,* vol. 1. Cambridge, Cambridge University Press, 1922

de Bary, W.T. *The Trouble with Confucianism.* Cambridge, MA, Harvard University Press, 1991

Deutsch, E. (trans.) *The Bhagavad Gita: with Introduction and Critical Essays.* Lanham, MD, New York and London, University Press of America, 1968

Dundas, P. *The Jains.* London, Routledge, 1992

Fingarette, H. *Confucius: The Secular as Sacred*. New York, Harper & Row, 1972

Hanh, T.N. *Cultivating the Mind of Love: The Practice of Looking Deeply in the Mahayana Buddhist Tradition*. Berkeley, Parallax, 1996

—— *The Heart of the Buddha's Teaching: Transforming Suffering into Peace, Joy and Liberation*. London, Rider, 1998

Jaini, P.S. *The Jaina Path of Purification*. Berkeley, University of California Press, 1979

Jensen, L.M. *Manufacturing Confucianism: Chinese Traditions and Universal Civilization*. Durham, NC, Duke University Press, 1997

Keown, D. *The Nature of Buddhist Ethics*. New York, St Martin's Press, 1992

Koller, J.M. and Koller, P. *A Sourcebook in Asian Philosophy*. Upper Saddle River, NJ, Prentice Hall, 1991

Laidlaw, J. *Riches and Renunciation: Religion, Economy, and Society among the Jains*. Oxford, Clarendon Press, 1995

Lao Tzu. *Tao Te Ching*, trans. D.C. Lau. London, Penguin, 1963

Mencius. *Mencius*, trans. D.C. Lau. London, Penguin, 1970

Motilal, B.K. *The Central Philosophy of Jainism*. Ahmedabad, L.D. Press, 1981

—— B.K. (ed.) *Moral Dilemmas in the Mahabharata*. Shimla, Indian Institute of Advanced Study, in association with Motilal Banarsidass, 1989

Padmarajiah, Y.J. *The Jaina Theories of Reality and Knowledge*. Bombay, Jaina Sahitya Vikas Mandal, 1986

Radhakrishnan, S. and Moore, C.A. (eds) *A Sourcebook in Indian Philosophy*. Princeton, Princeton University Press, 1957

Roth, H.D. *Original Tao: Inward Training (Nei-yeh) and the Foundations of Taoist Mysticism*. New York, Columbia University Press, 1999

Rozman, G. (ed.) *Confucian Heritage and Its Modern Adaptation*. Princeton, Princeton University Press, 1991

Saddhatissa, H. *Buddhist Ethics*. London, Allen & Unwin, 1970

Tachibana, S. *The Ethics of Buddhism*. London, Oxford University Press, 1926

Tobias, M. *Life Force: The World of Jainism*. Berkeley, Asian Humanities Press, 1991

## ETHICAL ISSUES ACROSS RELIGIOUS TRADITIONS

Ahmed, L. *Women and Gender in Islam*. New Haven, Yale University Press, 1992

Bainton, R. *Christian Attitudes Toward War and Peace*. Abingdon, Nashville, 1960

Beaudoin, T. *Virtual Faith: The Irreverent Spiritual Quest of Generation X*. San Francisco, Jossey-Bass, 1998

Bernstein, E. (ed.) *Ecology and the Jewish Spirit: Where Nature and the Sacred Meet*. Woodstock, Jewish Lights, 1998

Chapple, C.K. *Nonviolence to Animals, Earth, and Self in Asian Traditions*. Albany, State University of New York Press, 1993

Deutsch, E. (ed.) *Culture and Modernity: East–West Philosophic Perspectives.* Honolulu, University of Hawaii Press, 1991

Dorff, E.N. *Matters of Life and Death: A Jewish Approach to Modern Medical Ethics.* Philadelphia, Jewish Publication Society, 1998

Gilligan, C. *In a Different Voice: Psychological Theory and Women's Development.* Cambridge, MA and London, Harvard University Press, 1982

Kinsley, D. *Ecology and Religion: Ecological Spirituality in Cross-Cultural Perspective.* Englewood Cliffs, NJ, Prentice Hall, 1995

Koehn, D. *Rethinking Feminist Ethics: Care, Trust, and Empathy.* London, Routledge, 1998

LaFleur, W.R. *Liquid Life: Abortion and Buddhism in Japan.* Princeton, Princeton University Press, 1992

Larrabee, M.J. *An Ethic of Care: Feminist and Interdisciplinary Perspectives.* London, Routledge, 1993

Lasserre, J. *War and the Gospel.* Scottdale, Herald, 1962

Li, C. (ed.) *The Sage and the Second Sex: Confucianism, Ethics, and Gender.* Chicago, Open Court, 2000

Nelson, L.E. (ed.) *Purifying the Earthly Body of God: Religion and Ecology in Hindu India.* New York, State University of New York Press, 1998

Noddings, N. *Caring: A Feminine Approach to Ethics and Moral Education.* Berkeley, CA, University of California Press, 1984

Reid, T.R. *Confucius Lives Next Door: What Living in the East Teaches Us about Living in the West.* New York, Random House, 1999

Runzo, J. and Martin, N.M. (eds) *Love, Sex and Gender in the World Religions.* Oxford, Oneworld, 2000

Rutenber, C. *The Dagger and the Cross: An Examination of Christian Pacifism.* Nyack, NY, Fellowship Publications, 1958

Smith-Christopher, D.L. (ed.) *Subverting Hatred: The Challenge of Nonviolence in Religious Traditions.* Boston, Research Center for the 21st Century, 1998

Taylor, C. *Sources of the Self: The Making of the Modern Identity.* Cambridge, Cambridge University Press, 1989

Tucker, M.E. and Grim, J.A. (eds) *Worldviews and Ecology: Religion, Philosophy, and the Environment.* New York, Orbis, 1994

Wood, J.A. *Perspectives on War in the Bible.* Macon, Mercer University Press, 1998

## GLOBALIZING RELIGIOUS ETHICS

Crawford, C. (ed.) *World Religions and Global Ethics.* New York, Paragon House, 1989

Dalai Lama. *Ethics for the New Millennium.* New York, Riverhead, 1999

Esack, F. *Qur'an, Liberation and Pluralism: An Islamic Perspective of Interreligious Solidarity against Oppression.* Oxford, Oneworld, 1997

Hall, D.L. and Ames, R.T. *Thinking from the Han: Self, Truth, and the Transcendence in Chinese and Western Culture*. Albany, State University of New York Press, 1998

Hick, J. *An Interpretation of Religion*. New Haven and London, Yale University Press, 1989

Küng, H. *Global Responsibility: In Search of a New World Ethic*. London, SCM Press, 1991

—— *A Global Ethic for Global Politics and Economics*. London, SCM Press, 1997

Outka, G. and Reeder, Jr, J.P. (eds) *Prospects for a Common Morality*. Princeton, Princeton University Press, 1993

Runzo, J. and Martin, N.M. (eds) *The Meaning of Life in the World Religions*. Oxford, Oneworld, 1999

Shanahan, T. and Wang, R. *Reason and Insight: Western and Eastern Perspectives on the Pursuit of Moral Wisdom*. Belmont, Wadsworth, 1996

Tutu, D. *No Future without Forgiveness*. New York and London, Doubleday, 1999

# INDEX

Page numbers in *italic* refer to plates.